FREE Test Taking Tips Video/DVD Offer

To better serve you, we created videos covering test taking tips that we want to give you for FREE. **These videos cover world-class tips that will help you succeed on your test.**

We just ask that you send us feedback about this product. Please let us know what you thought about it—whether good, bad, or indifferent.

To get your **FREE videos**, you can use the QR code below or email freevideos@studyguideteam.com with "Free Videos" in the subject line and the following information in the body of the email:

   a. The title of your product

   b. Your product rating on a scale of 1-5, with 5 being the highest

   c. Your feedback about the product

If you have any questions or concerns, please don't hesitate to contact us at info@studyguideteam.com.

Thank you!

TExES Social Studies 7-12 232 Study Guide

Exam Prep and Practice Test [3rd Edition]

Lydia Morrison

Copyright © 2024 by TPB Publishing

All rights reserved. No part of this publication may be reproduced, distributed, or transmitted in any form or by any means, including photocopying, recording, or other electronic or mechanical methods, without the prior written permission of the publisher, except in the case of brief quotations embodied in critical reviews and certain other noncommercial uses permitted by copyright law.

Written and edited by TPB Publishing.

TPB Publishing is not associated with or endorsed by any official testing organization. TPB Publishing is a publisher of unofficial educational products. All test and organization names are trademarks of their respective owners. Content in this book is included for utilitarian purposes only and does not constitute an endorsement by TPB Publishing of any particular point of view.

Interested in buying more than 10 copies of our product? Contact us about bulk discounts:
bulkorders@studyguideteam.com

ISBN 13: 9781637751183

Table of Contents

Welcome 1
   FREE Videos/DVD OFFER 1

Quick Overview 2

Test-Taking Strategies 3

Bonus Content & Audiobook 7

Introduction 8

Study Prep Plan for the TExES Social Studies Test 10

World History 14
   Ancient World Civilizations 14
   World History from 600 A.D. to 1450 A.D. 22
   World History from 1450 A.D. to 1750 A.D. 30
   World History from 1750 A.D. to the Present 40
   Practice Quiz 52
   Answer Explanations 53

U.S. History 54
   Exploration and Colonization 54
   Revolutionary Era and the Early Years of the Republic 58
   Westward Expansion, the Civil War, and Reconstruction 64
   The United States as a World Power 69
   Political, Economic, and Social Developments from 1877 to the Present 74
   Practice Quiz 85
   Answer Explanations 86

Texas History 87

Exploration and Colonization 87

Independence, Statehood, Civil War Reconstruction, and Aftermath 90

Texas in the 20th and 21st Centuries 96

Practice Quiz 102

Answer Explanations 103

Geography, Culture, and the Behavioral and Social Sciences 104

Physical Geography Concepts, Natural Processes, and Earth's Physical Features
.... 104

Global and Regional Patterns of Culture and Human Geography 111

Interactions Between Human Groups and the Physical Environment 121

Sociological, Anthropological, and Psychological Concepts and Processes 128

Practice Quiz 136

Answer Explanations 137

Government and Citizenship 138

Democratic Principles and Government in the United States 138

Citizenship and Political Processes in the United States 154

Types of Political Systems 165

Practice Quiz 174

Answer Explanations 175

Economics and Science, Technology, and Society 176

Economic Concepts and Types of Economic Systems 176

Structure and Operation in the U.S. Free Enterprise System 186

Science, Technology, and Society 194

Practice Quiz 206

Answer Explanations 207

Social Studies Foundation, Skills, Research, and Instruction 208

Social Studies Foundations and Skills 208

Sources of Social Studies Information; Interpreting and Communicating Social Studies Information 210

Social Studies Research 218

Social Studies Instruction and Assessment 224

Practice Quiz 232

Answer Explanations 233

Practice Test 234

Answer Explanations 254

Welcome

Dear Reader,

Welcome to your new Test Prep Books study guide! We are pleased that you chose us to help you prepare for your exam. There are many study options to choose from, and we appreciate you choosing us. Studying can be a daunting task, but we have designed a smart, effective study guide to help prepare you for what lies ahead.

Whether you're a parent helping your child learn and grow, a high school student working hard to get into your dream college, or a nursing student studying for a complex exam, we want to help give you the tools you need to succeed. We hope this study guide gives you the skills and the confidence to thrive, and we can't thank you enough for allowing us to be part of your journey.

In an effort to continue to improve our products, we welcome feedback from our customers. We look forward to hearing from you. Suggestions, success stories, and criticisms can all be communicated by emailing us at info@studyguideteam.com.

Sincerely,
Test Prep Books Team

FREE Videos/DVD OFFER

Doing well on your exam requires both knowing the test content and understanding how to use that knowledge to do well on the test. We offer completely FREE test taking tip videos. **These videos cover world-class tips that you can use to succeed on your test.**

To get your **FREE videos**, you can use the QR code below or email freevideos@studyguideteam.com with "Free Videos" in the subject line and the following information in the body of the email:

    a. The title of your product
    b. Your product rating on a scale of 1-5, with 5 being the highest
    c. Your feedback about the product

If you have any questions or concerns, please don't hesitate to contact us at info@studyguideteam.com.

Quick Overview

As you draw closer to taking your exam, effective preparation becomes more and more important. Thankfully, you have this study guide to help you get ready. Use this guide to help keep your studying on track and refer to it often.

This study guide contains several key sections that will help you be successful on your exam. The guide contains tips for what you should do the night before and the day of the test. Also included are test-taking tips. Knowing the right information is not always enough. Many well-prepared test takers struggle with exams. These tips will help equip you to accurately read, assess, and answer test questions.

A large part of the guide is devoted to showing you what content to expect on the exam and to helping you better understand that content. In this guide are practice test questions so that you can see how well you have grasped the content. Then, answer explanations are provided so that you can understand why you missed certain questions.

Don't try to cram the night before you take your exam. This is not a wise strategy for a few reasons. First, your retention of the information will be low. Your time would be better used by reviewing information you already know rather than trying to learn a lot of new information. Second, you will likely become stressed as you try to gain a large amount of knowledge in a short amount of time. Third, you will be depriving yourself of sleep. So be sure to go to bed at a reasonable time the night before. Being well-rested helps you focus and remain calm.

Be sure to eat a substantial breakfast the morning of the exam. If you are taking the exam in the afternoon, be sure to have a good lunch as well. Being hungry is distracting and can make it difficult to focus. You have hopefully spent lots of time preparing for the exam. Don't let an empty stomach get in the way of success!

When travelling to the testing center, leave earlier than needed. That way, you have a buffer in case you experience any delays. This will help you remain calm and will keep you from missing your appointment time at the testing center.

Be sure to pace yourself during the exam. Don't try to rush through the exam. There is no need to risk performing poorly on the exam just so you can leave the testing center early. Allow yourself to use all of the allotted time if needed.

Remain positive while taking the exam even if you feel like you are performing poorly. Thinking about the content you should have mastered will not help you perform better on the exam.

Once the exam is complete, take some time to relax. Even if you feel that you need to take the exam again, you will be well served by some down time before you begin studying again. It's often easier to convince yourself to study if you know that it will come with a reward!

Test-Taking Strategies

1. Predicting the Answer

When you feel confident in your preparation for a multiple-choice test, try predicting the answer before reading the answer choices. This is especially useful on questions that test objective factual knowledge. By predicting the answer before reading the available choices, you eliminate the possibility that you will be distracted or led astray by an incorrect answer choice. You will feel more confident in your selection if you read the question, predict the answer, and then find your prediction among the answer choices. After using this strategy, be sure to still read all of the answer choices carefully and completely. If you feel unprepared, you should not attempt to predict the answers. This would be a waste of time and an opportunity for your mind to wander in the wrong direction.

2. Reading the Whole Question

Too often, test takers scan a multiple-choice question, recognize a few familiar words, and immediately jump to the answer choices. Test authors are aware of this common impatience, and they will sometimes prey upon it. For instance, a test author might subtly turn the question into a negative, or he or she might redirect the focus of the question right at the end. The only way to avoid falling into these traps is to read the entirety of the question carefully before reading the answer choices.

3. Looking for Wrong Answers

Long and complicated multiple-choice questions can be intimidating. One way to simplify a difficult multiple-choice question is to eliminate all of the answer choices that are clearly wrong. In most sets of answers, there will be at least one selection that can be dismissed right away. If the test is administered on paper, the test taker could draw a line through it to indicate that it may be ignored; otherwise, the test taker will have to perform this operation mentally or on scratch paper. In either case, once the obviously incorrect answers have been eliminated, the remaining choices may be considered. Sometimes identifying the clearly wrong answers will give the test taker some information about the correct answer. For instance, if one of the remaining answer choices is a direct opposite of one of the eliminated answer choices, it may well be the correct answer. The opposite of obviously wrong is obviously right! Of course, this is not always the case. Some answers are obviously incorrect simply because they are irrelevant to the question being asked. Still, identifying and eliminating some incorrect answer choices is a good way to simplify a multiple-choice question.

4. Don't Overanalyze

Anxious test takers often overanalyze questions. When you are nervous, your brain will often run wild, causing you to make associations and discover clues that don't actually exist. If you feel that this may be a problem for you, do whatever you can to slow down during the test. Try taking a deep breath or counting to ten. As you read and consider the question, restrict yourself to the particular words used by the author. Avoid thought tangents about what the author *really* meant, or what he or she was *trying* to say. The only things that matter on a multiple-choice test are the words that are actually in the question. You must avoid reading too much into a multiple-choice question, or supposing that the writer meant something other than what he or she wrote.

5. No Need for Panic

It is wise to learn as many strategies as possible before taking a multiple-choice test, but it is likely that you will

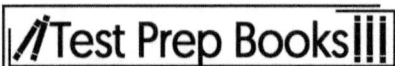

come across a few questions for which you simply don't know the answer. In this situation, avoid panicking. Because most multiple-choice tests include dozens of questions, the relative value of a single wrong answer is small. As much as possible, you should compartmentalize each question on a multiple-choice test. In other words, you should not allow your feelings about one question to affect your success on the others. When you find a question that you either don't understand or don't know how to answer, just take a deep breath and do your best. Read the entire question slowly and carefully. Try rephrasing the question a couple of different ways. Then, read all of the answer choices carefully. After eliminating obviously wrong answers, make a selection and move on to the next question.

6. Confusing Answer Choices

When working on a difficult multiple-choice question, there may be a tendency to focus on the answer choices that are the easiest to understand. Many people, whether consciously or not, gravitate to the answer choices that require the least concentration, knowledge, and memory. This is a mistake. When you come across an answer

choice that is confusing, you should give it extra attention. A question might be confusing because you do not know the subject matter to which it refers. If this is the case, don't eliminate the answer before you have affirmatively settled on another. When you come across an answer choice of this type, set it aside as you look at the remaining choices. If you can confidently assert that one of the other choices is correct, you can leave the confusing answer aside. Otherwise, you will need to take a moment to try to better understand the confusing answer choice. Rephrasing is one way to tease out the sense of a confusing answer choice.

7. Your First Instinct

Many people struggle with multiple-choice tests because they overthink the questions. If you have studied sufficiently for the test, you should be prepared to trust your first instinct once you have carefully and completely read the question and all of the answer choices. There is a great deal of research suggesting that the mind can come to the correct conclusion very quickly once it has obtained all of the relevant information. At times, it may seem to you as if your intuition is working faster even than your reasoning mind. This may in fact be true. The knowledge you obtain while studying may be retrieved from your subconscious before you have a chance to work out the associations that support it. Verify your instinct by working out the reasons that it should be trusted.

8. Key Words

Many test takers struggle with multiple-choice questions because they have poor reading comprehension skills. Quickly reading and understanding a multiple-choice question requires a mixture of skill and experience. To help with this, try jotting down a few key words and phrases on a piece of scrap paper. Doing this concentrates the process of reading and forces the mind to weigh the relative importance of the question's parts. In selecting words and phrases to write down, the test taker thinks about the question more deeply and carefully. This is especially true for multiple-choice questions that are preceded by a long prompt.

Test-Taking Strategies

9. Subtle Negatives

One of the oldest tricks in the multiple-choice test writer's book is to subtly reverse the meaning of a question with a word like *not* or *except*. If you are not paying attention to each word in the question, you can easily be led astray by this trick. For instance, a common question format is, "Which of the following is...?" Obviously, if the question instead is, "Which of the following is not...?," then the answer will be quite different. Even worse, the test makers are aware of the potential for this mistake and will include one answer choice that would be correct if the question were not negated or reversed. A test taker who misses the reversal will find what he or she believes to be a correct answer and will be so confident that he or she will fail to reread the question and discover the original error. The only way to avoid this is to practice a wide variety of multiple-choice questions and to pay close attention to each and every word.

10. Reading Every Answer Choice

It may seem obvious, but you should always read every one of the answer choices! Too many test takers fall into the habit of scanning the question and assuming that they understand the question because they recognize a few key words. From there, they pick the first answer choice that answers the question they believe they have read. Test takers who read all of the answer choices might discover that one of the latter answer choices is actually *more* correct. Moreover, reading all of the answer choices can remind you of facts related to the question that can help you arrive at the correct answer. Sometimes, a misstatement or incorrect detail in one of the latter answer choices will trigger your memory of the subject and will enable you to find the right answer. Failing to read all of the answer choices is like not reading all of the items on a restaurant menu: you might miss out on the perfect choice.

11. Spot the Hedges

One of the keys to success on multiple-choice tests is paying close attention to every word. This is never truer than with words like *almost*, *most*, *some*, and *sometimes*. These words are called "hedges" because they indicate that a statement is not totally true or not true in every place and time. An absolute statement will contain no hedges, but in many subjects, the answers are not always straightforward or absolute. There are always exceptions to the rules

in these subjects. For this reason, you should favor those multiple-choice questions that contain hedging language. The presence of qualifying words indicates that the author is taking special care with his or her words, which is certainly important when composing the right answer. After all, there are many ways to be wrong, but there is only one way to be right! For this reason, it is wise to avoid answers that are absolute when taking a multiple-choice test. An absolute answer is one that says things are either all one way or all another. They often include words like *every*, *always*, *best*, and *never*. If you are taking a multiple-choice test in a subject that doesn't lend itself to absolute answers, be on your guard if you see any of these words.

12. Long Answers

In many subject areas, the answers are not simple. As already mentioned, the right answer often requires hedges. Another common feature of the answers to a complex or subjective question are qualifying clauses, which are groups of words that subtly modify the meaning of the sentence. If the question or answer choice describes a rule to which there are exceptions or the subject matter is complicated, ambiguous, or confusing, the correct answer will require many words in order to be expressed clearly and accurately. In essence, you should not be deterred by answer choices that seem excessively long. Oftentimes, the author of the text will not be able to write the correct answer without offering some qualifications and

modifications. Your job is to read the answer choices thoroughly and completely and to select the one that most accurately and precisely answers the question.

13. Restating to Understand

Sometimes, a question on a multiple-choice test is difficult not because of what it asks but because of how it is written. If this is the case, restate the question or answer choice in different words. This process serves a couple of important purposes. First, it forces you to concentrate on the core of the question. In order to rephrase the question accurately, you have to understand it well. Rephrasing the question will concentrate your mind on the key words and ideas. Second, it will present the information to your mind in a fresh way. This process may trigger your memory and render some useful scrap of information picked up while studying.

14. True Statements

Sometimes an answer choice will be true in itself, but it does not answer the question. This is one of the main reasons why it is essential to read the question carefully and completely before proceeding to the answer choices. Too often, test takers skip ahead to the answer choices and look for true statements. Having found one of these, they are content to select it without reference to the question above. The savvy test taker will always read the entire question before turning to the answer choices. Then, having settled on a correct answer choice, he or she will refer to the original question and ensure that the selected answer is relevant. The mistake of choosing a correct-but-irrelevant answer choice is especially common on questions related to specific pieces of objective knowledge.

15. No Patterns

One of the more dangerous ideas that circulates about multiple-choice tests is that the correct answers tend to fall into patterns. These erroneous ideas range from a belief that B and C are the most common right answers, to the idea that an unprepared test-taker should answer "A-B-A-C-A-D-A-B-A." It cannot be emphasized enough that pattern-seeking of this type is exactly the WRONG way to approach a multiple-choice test. To begin with, it is highly unlikely that the test maker will plot the correct answers according to some predetermined pattern. The questions are scrambled and delivered in a random order. Furthermore, even if the test maker was following a pattern in the assignation of correct answers, there is no reason why the test taker would know which pattern he or she was using. Any attempt to discern a pattern in the answer choices is a waste of time and a distraction from the real work of taking the test. A test taker would be much better served by extra preparation before the test than by reliance on a pattern in the answers.

Bonus Content & Audiobook

We host multiple bonus items online, including the practice test in digital format and the audiobook version of this study guide. Scan the QR code or go to this link to access this content:

testprepbooks.com/bonus/texessocialstudies

The first time you access the tests, you will need to register as a "new user" and verify your email address.

If you have any issues, please email support@testprepbooks.com.

Introduction

Function of the Test

The Texas Examination of Educator Standards (TExES) Social Studies 7-12 (232) test is one of dozens of TExES tests used as part of the certification process for teachers in the state of Texas. Texas law requires every person seeking certification as an educator in Texas to pass comprehensive examinations appropriate to the area in which they wish to teach. The TExES tests have been developed gradually since 2002 as the means by which prospective educators can meet this requirement.

The TExES tests are intended to identify individuals who have the appropriate level of knowledge to teach in Texas public schools. They are governed by the Texas State Board for Educator Certification and the Texas Education Agency. These state agencies have contracted with Educational Testing Service (ETS) to assist in development and deployment of the tests. All TExES tests are based on Texas Essential Knowledge and Skills, the required curriculum for all Texas public school students.

The Social Studies 7-12 (232) test evaluates prospective teachers' skills and preparedness for teaching 7th through 12th grade Social Studies. The test is not used for purposes other than determining whether the test taker qualifies for certification. Understandably, it is almost exclusively taken in Texas, by individuals seeking employment as public educators in Texas. In the 2015-2016 year, the test was taken by 3,000 test takers, of whom 64% passed.

Test Administration

Prospective exam candidates must first get approval to take the test from their Educator Preparation Program (EPP). Once a candidate receives approval from their EPP, he or she can register to take the test through ETS, either online or by phone.

The test is administered by computer at test centers throughout Texas and at selected test centers in states bordering Texas and elsewhere. The test takes five hours, and may be taken in either a morning or afternoon testing session. Candidates taking multiple TExES tests may take different tests in both sessions in one day.

As with all computer-based TExES tests, Texas law requires that a test taker who does not pass the TExES Social Studies 7-12 exam must wait 45 days before retaking the test. A test taker may attempt the test for a maximum of five total administrations (the original plus four retakes).

In accordance with the Americans with Disabilities Act, individuals with documented disabilities can receive testing accommodations. Such individuals must register for their test through ETS and have their desired accommodations approved prior to the testing day.

Test Format

Test takers should arrive at their computer testing center with an admission ticket and appropriate identification. After signing in at the test center, test takers are given the opportunity to secure personal belongings in a locker and then they are assigned a computer. The test consists of 140 scored multiple-choice questions and a variable number of additional multiple-choice questions that are not scored but are used for research purposes for possible inclusion

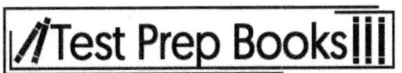

on future tests. Test takers will not be aware of which questions count towards their scores and which are used for evaluation purposes only. The questions cover seven domains of knowledge in the field of Social Studies instruction.

These domains, and the approximate percentage of the test content they comprise, are as follows:

Domain	Approximate Percentage of Test
World History	15%
U.S. History	20%
Texas History	13%
Geography, Culture, and the Behavioral and Social Sciences	13%
Government and Citizenship	13%
Economics and Science, Technology, and Science	13%
Social Studies Foundations, Skills, Research, and Instruction	13%

Scoring

All TExES tests are criterion-referenced, meaning they designed to measure each performance against a reference baseline rather than in relation to other test takers. Raw scores are based on the number of multiple-choice questions answered correctly, with no penalty for guessing incorrectly; therefore, it is prudent for test takers to answer all questions, even if they are unsure of the correct answer. The raw score is then scaled to enable comparison between results on different forms of the test. Scaled scores range from 100 to 300, with a passing score set at 240.

Score reports include both the pass/fail result and the test taker's raw score information broken down by subject matter within the test, for the purpose of aiding preparation for a potential retake attempt. Scores are posted within seven days of the test date to the test taker's account.

Recent/Future Developments

The limit of a maximum five total attempts to pass was instituted effective September 1, 2015. All attempts taken before that date count as one total attempt. No other substantial recent or prospective changes have been announced.

Study Prep Plan for the TExES Social Studies Test

1 **Schedule** - Use one of our study schedules below or come up with one of your own.

2 **Relax** - Test anxiety can hurt even the best students. There are many ways to reduce stress. Find the one that works best for you.

3 **Execute** - Once you have a good plan in place, be sure to stick to it.

One Week Study Schedule

Day 1	World History
Day 2	U.S. History
Day 3	Texas History
Day 4	Government and Citizenship
Day 5	Economics and Science, Technology, and Society
Day 6	Practice Test
Day 7	Take Your Exam!

Two Week Study Schedule

Day 1	World History	Day 8	Government and Citizenship
Day 2	World History from 1450 A.D. to 1750 A.D.	Day 9	Citizenship and Political Processes in the United...
Day 3	U.S. History	Day 10	Economics and Science, Technology, and Society
Day 4	The United States as a World Power	Day 11	Science, Technology, and Society
Day 5	Texas History	Day 12	Social Studies Foundation, Skills...
Day 6	Geography, Culture, and the Behavioral...	Day 13	Practice Test
Day 7	Interactions Between Human Groups...	Day 14	Take Your Exam!

Study Prep Plan for the TExES Social Studies Test | FREE Videos/DVD OFFER

One Month Study Schedule

Day 1	World History	Day 11	Texas History	Day 21	Economics and Science, Technology, and Society
Day 2	World History from 600 A.D. to 1450 A.D.	Day 12	Independence, Statehood, Civil War...	Day 22	Structure and Operation in the U.S. Free...
Day 3	World History from 1450 A.D. to 1750 A.D.	Day 13	Texas in the 20th and 21st Centuries	Day 23	Science, Technology, and Society
Day 4	World History from 1750 A.D. to the...	Day 14	Geography, Culture, and the Behavioral...	Day 24	Social Studies Foundation, Skills...
Day 5	U.S. History	Day 15	Global and Regional Patterns of Culture...	Day 25	Sources of Social Studies Information...
Day 6	Revolutionary Era and the Early Years...	Day 16	Interactions Between Human Groups...	Day 26	Social Studies Research
Day 7	Westward Expansion, the Civil War...	Day 17	Sociological, Anthropological...	Day 27	Social Studies Instruction and Assessment
Day 8	The United States as a World Power	Day 18	Government and Citizenship	Day 28	Practice Test
Day 9	Political, Economic, and Social...	Day 19	Citizenship and Political Processes in...	Day 29	Answer Explanations
Day 10	Significant Events from 1877 to the Present	Day 20	Types of Political Systems	Day 30	Take Your Exam!

Build your own prep plan by visiting:
testprepbooks.com/prep

As you study for your test, we'd like to take the opportunity to remind you that you are capable of great things! With the right tools and dedication, you truly can do anything you set your mind to. The fact that you are holding this book right now shows how committed you are. In case no one has told you lately, you've got this! Our intention behind including this coloring page is to give you the chance to take some time to engage your creative side when you need a little brain-break from studying. As a company, we want to encourage people like you to achieve their dreams by providing good quality study materials for the tests and certifications that improve careers and change lives. As individuals, many of us have taken such tests in our careers, and we know how challenging this process can be. While we can't come alongside you and cheer you on personally, we can offer you the space to recall your purpose, reconnect with your passion, and refresh your brain through an artistic practice. We wish you every success, and happy studying!

World History

Ancient World Civilizations

The study of history from a global perspective is called *world history, global history,* or *transnational history*. Unlike comparative history, world history examines common patterns across nations and cultures on a global scale. A world historian studies how cultures and nations are drawn together and how they are distinct.

The classical civilizations of the world emerged out of the Iron Age, 1200-1000 BCE, with advanced metal tools, written languages, and specialized farming. The characteristics of a civilization include a written language, a geographic state, metal weapons and tools, and the use of a calendar. The prehistoric world developed near fertile river valleys near the Nile River in Egypt, Mesopotamia near ancient Greece, the Indus River in South Asia, and around the Hwang Ho in China. The classical civilizations that emerged out of the ancient world were Greece, Rome, Persia, India, and China.

Development of Early Classical Civilizations

There were a number of powerful civilizations during the classical period. Mesopotamia was home to one of the earliest civilizations between the Euphrates and the Tigris rivers in the Near East. The rivers provided water and vegetation for early humans, but they were surrounded by desert. This led to the beginning of irrigation efforts to expand water and agriculture across the region, which resulted in the area being known as the Fertile Crescent.

The organization necessary to initiate canals and other projects led to the formation of cities and hierarchies, which would have considerable influence on the structure of later civilizations. For instance, the new hierarchies established different classes within the societies, such as kings, priests, artisans, and workers. Over time, these city-states expanded to encompass outside territories, and the city of Akkad became the world's first empire in 2350 B.C. In addition, Mesopotamian scribes developed systemized drawings called pictograms, which were the first system of writing in the world; furthermore, the creation of wedge-shaped cuneiform tablets preserved written records for multiple generations.

Later, Mesopotamian kingdoms made further advancements. For instance, Babylon established a sophisticated mathematical system based on numbers from one to sixty; this not only influenced modern concepts, such as the number of minutes in each hour, but also created the framework for math equations and theories.

Meanwhile, another major civilization began to form around the Nile River in Africa. The Nile's relatively predictable nature allowed farmers to use the river's water and the silt from floods to grow many crops along its banks, which led to further advancements in irrigation. Egyptian rulers mobilized the kingdom's population for incredible construction projects, including the famous pyramids. Egyptians also improved pictographic writing with their more complex system of hieroglyphs, which allowed for more diverse styles of writing. The advancements in writing can be seen through the Egyptians' complex system of religion, with documents such as the *Book of the Dead* outlining not only systems of worship and pantheons of deities but also a deeper, more philosophical concept of the afterlife.

While civilizations in Egypt and Mesopotamia helped to establish class systems and empires, other forms of government emerged in Greece. Despite common ties between different cities, such as the Olympic Games, each settlement, known as a polis, had its own unique culture. Many of the cities were oligarchies, in which a council of distinguished leaders monopolized the government; others were dictatorships ruled by tyrants. Athens was a notable exception by practicing an early form of democracy in which free, landholding men could participate, but it offered more freedom of thought than other systems.

Taking advantage of their proximity to the Mediterranean Sea, Greek cities sent expeditions to establish colonies abroad that developed their own local traditions. In the process, Greek merchants interacted with Phoenician traders, who had developed an alphabetic writing system built on sounds instead of pictures. This diverse network of exchanges made Greece a vibrant center of art, science, and philosophy. For example, the Greek doctor Hippocrates established a system of ethics for doctors called the Hippocratic Oath, which continues to guide the modern medical profession. Complex forms of literature were created, including the epic poem *The Iliad*, and theatrical productions were also developed. Athens in particular sought to spread its vision of democratic freedom throughout the world, which led to the devastating Peloponnesian War between allies of Athens and those of oligarchic Sparta from 431 to 404 B.C.

Alexander the Great helped disseminate Greek culture to new regions, also known as *diffusion*. Alexander was in fact an heir to the throne of Macedon, which was a warrior kingdom to the north of Greece. After finishing his father's work of unifying Greece under Macedonian control, Alexander successfully conquered Mesopotamia, which had been part of the Persian Empire. The spread of Greek institutions throughout the Mediterranean and Near East led to a period of Hellenization, during which various civilizations assimilated Greek culture; this allowed Greek traditions, such as architecture and philosophy, to endure into the present day.

Greek ideas were later assimilated, along with many other concepts, into the Roman Empire. Located west of Greece on the Italian peninsula, Rome greatly expanded its territories and grew to be a powerful empire through the conquering of its neighboring civilizations; by 44 B.C., Rome had conquered much of Western Europe, northern Africa, and the Near East. Romans were very creative, and they adapted new ideas and innovated new technologies to strengthen their power. For instance, Romans built on the engineering knowledge of Greeks to create arched pathways, known as aqueducts, to transport water for long distances and devise advanced plumbing systems.

One of Rome's greatest legacies was its system of government. Early Rome was a republic, a democratic system in which leaders are elected by the people. Although the process still heavily favored wealthy elites, the republican system was a key inspiration for later institutions such as the United States. Octavian Augustus Caesar later made Rome into an empire, and the senate had only a symbolic role in the government. The new imperial system built on the examples of earlier empires to establish a vibrant dynasty that used a sophisticated legal code and a well-trained military to enforce order across vast regions. Even after Rome itself fell to barbarian invaders in fifth century A.D., the eastern half of the empire survived as the Byzantine Empire until 1453 A.D. Furthermore, the Roman Empire's institutions continued to influence and inspire later medieval kingdoms, including the Holy Roman Empire; even rulers in the twentieth century called themselves Kaiser and Tsar, titles which stem from the word caesar.

In addition, the Roman Empire was host to the spread of new religious ideas. In the region of Israel, the religion of Judaism presented a new approach to worship via monotheism, which is the belief in the existence of a single deity. An offshoot of Judaism called Christianity spread across the Roman Empire and gained popularity. While Rome initially suppressed the religion, it later backed Christianity and allowed the religious system to endure as a powerful force in medieval times.

Individuals, Events, and Issues

The earliest hearths of domestication established and dispersed farming practices and breeding techniques that helped small villages in Egypt, Iraq, Pakistan, China, Mexico, Central America, and Peru blossom into complex cultural civilizations. Agriculture likely did not originate in just one of these hearths first, but rather formed independently around the same time. Prior to the First Agricultural Revolution, animals such as horses, pigs, cows, dogs, cats, camels, sheep, and goats roamed wildly in their natural environments. During the Old Stone Age, nomadic hunters would stalk, stampede, and hunt wild creatures for their hides, marrows, and meats.

Archaeological evidence, such as Paleolithic paintings and site-based soil samples, illustrate that Stone Age hunters slaughtered meals by stampeding herds of animals off prehistoric cliffs. These epic, cliff-side bloodbaths allowed nomadic bands of hunters and gatherers to carry out quick, massive kills that clothed and fed packs of thirty or more people for extended periods of time. With the advent of domestication, or the taming of animals, however, humans created even more sustainable food sources, driving herds into human-made grazing enclosures instead of rocky ravines. Within these enclosures, residents tamed, bred, milked, skinned, and butchered animals for a more consistent and sustaining source of food. Gradually, through the processes of animal husbandry and selective breeding, many wild species evolved into domesticated livestock that assisted with the Neolithic Age's higher demand for farm labor.

As feral beasts became extra farmhands via the practices of animal husbandry and selective breeding, several culture hearths around the globe began employing new agricultural techniques that tapped into the potential of animal labor. By around 5500–3500 BCE, Neolithic farmers began using domesticated livestock as a source of farm labor. Livestock became crucial contributors to the new plowing and towing processes that allowed settlements to make the full transition from hunter-gatherer communities to sedentary agricultural societies. Domesticated animals also provided Neolithic farmers with the fertilizer, wool, hides, and leather that assisted with systematic crop production.

Most of the world's earliest hearths of domestication had similar features:

- They were typically located near major sources of water (usually rivers) or on hillsides that attracted natural flow of rainwaters.
- They were typically located in lands with a mild climate that proved favorable for crop growth.
- They all developed similar irrigation systems (canals and ditches) that helped grow surplus crops.
- They all employed animal labor in some capacity to assist with crop production.

Many Neolithic farms also employed new systematic practices such as slash-and-burn farming or terraced farming. The practices helped develop new extensive crops such as wheat and barley. One of the earliest centers of wheat and barley production emerged in an unlikely place: the rolling foothills of the Zagros Mountains, located in the so-called Fertile Crescent of Mesopotamia (modern northeastern Iraq). Today, the Zagros Mountains remain arid and eroded by the unstoppable forces of history; nevertheless, many scholars, including Robert Braidwood, an archaeologist who conducted his world-renowned research in Iraq in the 1950s, believe the Zagros region of Mesopotamia once hosted the world's first hotbed for primitive agriculture. In fact, some scholars believe the village of Jarmo, the target of Braidwood's archaeological dig, laid the foundation for modern life by hosting the world's first domesticated barley and wheat fields some nine thousand years ago.

These early hearths of domestication produced sustainable forms of living that laid the foundations for later classical civilizations such as the Egyptian Empire, the Babylonian Empire, the Incan and Mayan empires in the Americas, and the Macedonian, Greek, and Roman empires of the Mediterranean. These early classical civilizations all suffered similar demises: They became dysfunctional from within and succumbed to outside enemies and attacks. Often these empires were led by charismatic leaders such as Alexander the Great, Julius Cesar, and Montezuma II. These great empires, however, also crumbled in the hands of charismatic leaders.

Major Political, Economic, and Cultural Developments

Ancient Greece
Alexander's father, King Phillip II of Macedon, conquered the Greek city-states, ultimately achieved at the Battle of Chaeronea in 338 BCE, and established the first centralized Greek state in ancient history. Phillip II then set his sights on the Persian Empire and began preparing for an invasion; however, he was assassinated by sources disputed by

contemporary historians. Some speculate they were Persian assassins; others claimed that unhappy leaders of the recently conquered city-states executed the assassination. In any event, Alexander the Great succeeded his father and seized control over their new empire at twenty years old.

In the thirteen years between Alexander's accession to the throne and his own death, he conquered the Persian Empire, which stretched from the Mediterranean to India, fulfilling his father's plans. During this period, education and literacy spread, and new genres of writing were created. The rich cultural interactions between the great ancient civilizations ushered in the Hellenistic period. Architecture was more lavish, and the scientific advancements that began with Aristotle continued throughout the empire. The spread of Greek culture, as well as its interaction with foreign civilizations, had a lasting effect on religion, language, and innovation that endured until Rome conquered Greece and adopted much of the Hellenic culture.

Roman Empire

The formation of Rome is steeped in legend and lore befitting its status as the greatest successor to all previous empires. According to legend, twin brothers Romulus and Remus set out to found a new city but disagreed as to its location. Tensions led to Romulus killing his twin brother and founding a city on the Palatine Hill called Rome. Conquering land from Britain to northern Africa and the Middle East, Rome solidified itself as the greatest empire of the ancient world. At its height, Rome's military conquered and held an unprecedented amount of territory.

Throughout its history, Rome transitioned from a monarchy to a republic and then to an autocratic empire. Historians dispute when Rome was founded, but most agree that it was established somewhere between the tenth and eighth centuries BCE by the Latin tribe of Italy. The Etruscans established control over the region by the late seventh century BCE and were ruled by an aristocratic elite and monarch. Sometime during the latter half of the sixth century BCE, the Latin tribe regained power and established the Roman Republic. Around 509 BCE, a constitution and system of government based on checks and balances and separation of powers was established. The senate functioned as the elected legislative branch, and nobility known as *patricians* controlled it. Consuls functioned as the executive branch, and the senate appointed the consuls for limited terms. The Roman Republic would rise to greatness after first defeating Carthage in the Punic Wars and then the Macedonian and Seleucid empires in the second century BCE. Although still a republic, Rome constituted the premier empire in the Mediterranean, well positioned for expansion.

Persian Empire

Cyrus the Great established the First Persian Empire in 550 BC after stifling the great rebellion of the Medes and subsequently defeating the kingdom of Lydia and the Neo-Babylonian Empire. Initially nomadic shepherds, the Persians steadily consolidated power and created a strong infrastructure and military. At its height, the Persian Empire was the largest in the ancient world and stretched from Eastern Europe to Central and South Asia. His successors, including Darius I, continued to expand the empire until Alexander the Great conquered much of Persia, creating the largest empire until the founding of Rome.

Maurya Empire

The Maurya Empire was the most powerful and influential kingdom in the history of ancient India, ruling from 322 BCE to 185 BCE, and it was one of the largest empires in the word for its time period. The first emperor of Maurya was Chandragupta Maurya, who overthrew the Nanda Dynasty, unified India, and expanded the empire. His success occurred after Alexander the Great's armies withdrew from India, and Chandragupta's armies defeated the satraps and Greek armies that were left behind.

Africa

Between the 1500s and 1800s, over 12 million African slaves were shipped across the globe as free labor for agricultural markets. Slavery had a cultural impact not only on Africa, but also the entire globe, especially the developing colonies and nations of North and South America. The spread of African languages and cultures to the New World (called the African Diaspora) created an entirely new culture in the Americas.

Africa is also responsible for exporting important agricultural and animal domestication techniques, textile creation skills, and other technological advances to the rest of the world in antiquity. North Africans shared shipbuilding techniques with Greek and Roman civilizations, and they became leaders in mathematics and engineering. Ethiopians were the first to cultivate coffee and recognize its energizing properties. The Nile River Valley region is also believed to be one of the first to develop cotton as a textile and agricultural export.

Americas

During the Age of Exploration, indigenous Americans taught European explorers how to cultivate such plants as maize (corn), beans, pumpkins, squash, cacao, beans, vanilla, sweet potatoes, peppers, peanuts, pineapples, sunflowers, gourds, plums, and tobacco. Native American agricultural techniques and harvesting technologies transformed the diets of people around the world. Native Americans also exported domestication techniques for turkeys and certain dog breeds, transforming the trade market for household and farm animals. Additionally, the Native American civilizations advanced studies in mathematics, engineering, and astronomy. In the United States, indigenous culture and mythology still pervades the national psyche even though many Native Americans were slaughtered by the colonial and revolutionary governments of the New World.

Revolution, in and of itself, is also one of the greatest exports of the Americas. The American Revolution, the first of its kind in the New World, became a focal point of later revolutions. Today, many revolutionary forces still look to the American Revolution for inspiration.

Europe

Much of the West's political and philosophical heritage is owed to the Greek and Roman civilizations of European antiquity. The Greeks established democracy, and the Romans established the framework of republicanism. During the Enlightenment, these classical values helped shape the revolutionary sentiments of the Founding Fathers of the United States. Christianity is another essential European export. Europe adopted the religion during Late Antiquity and the Middle Ages. Eventually, Christianity was dispersed throughout the world during the Age of Exploration. During the Enlightenment and Age of Exploration, Europe also became a leader in science, mathematics, and technology, thanks in part to the influences of North Africa, the Middle East, and the Arab world. Europeans became expert shipbuilders and explorers, refining such exploratory tools as the astrolabe and compass.

Middle East

The Middle East has always been a hub of early civilization. Middle Easterners helped develop early mathematical principles (number systems, algebra, geometry) as well as advanced mathematics (trigonometry and calculus). Likewise, Middle Easterners were leaders in engineering and architecture during Late Antiquity and the Middle Ages. Their architectural styles influenced European and American buildings. The Middle East is also the epicenter of monotheistic religion, as the original home of Judaism, Christianity, and Islam.

Asia

Asia was responsible for dispersing gunpowder, silk, fireworks, tea, and spices throughout the world during the Age of Exploration. Following the success of overland travels across the Silk Road in the 1200s and 1300s, Europeans began to develop a fascination with the Far East. This Orientalism drove explorers to find faster sea routes to China and Japan. In many ways, the Far East's grip on the European consciousness is, perhaps, the driving force of the Age of Exploration.

Political Organization, Cultural Characteristics, and Contributions

Ancient Greece

Ancient Greece formed from scattered farming communities between 800 BCE and 500 BCE. In this early era of Greece, the polis, or city-state, held all of the political power locally. City-states were self-ruling and self-sufficient. The idea of a self-governing state had an enduring effect on the government of Greece and would result in the demokratia (rule by the people), which would spread and influence the world. As farming villages grew and marketplaces were built, a government with laws, an organized army, and tax collection took shape.

Each city-state was different from one another, but some unifying traits included a common language, a shared belief system, an agriculturally based economy, and rule by several wealthy citizens instead of rule by a king or queen. However, these few aristocratic rulers, known as *oligarchs*, often owned the best and most land, which created tension as the population grew. As a result, many citizens moved to less populated or newly conquered areas. By 800 BCE, there were over 1500 city-states, each with its own rulers and rules. Greek city-states were concentrated on the coast, resulting in greater contact with other civilizations through trade. City-states' governments and culture continued to diverge as time progressed. For example, in the fifth century BCE, Athens became the first direct democracy in the world, and Athenian citizens would vote directly on legislation. Only adult, male, landowning citizens could vote, but it was a remarkable departure from all contemporary forms of government to provide for direct democracy, especially relative to other city-states' oligarchies. Another world-renowned example is Sparta, which based its entire social system and constitution on military training and ability.

The Greek religion was polytheistic. Every city-state had a temple dedicated to a particular god or goddess; however, the whole of ancient Greece believed that Zeus, residing in Mount Olympus, was the most powerful of the gods. The physical presence of the temple, the rituals and festivals that dotted the Greek year, and the widespread belief in the gods controlling every aspect of human life heavily influenced their agricultural economy, government, and interactions with other ancient civilizations.

The ancient Greeks were known for their citizen-soldiers, known as *hoplites*. No ancient civilization could field a professional military due to economic restraints, such as a lack of a banking system and the need for agricultural laborers, but the hoplites were famous in ancient times for their tactics and skill. Hoplites were armed with spears and large shields, and they would fight in a phalanx formation. The Romans would later adopt many of the Greek military principles. Greek city-states fought numerous wars among each other, the largest being the Peloponnesian War, as well as wars against Persia. Fought between 499 BCE and 449 BCE, the Greco-Persian Wars pitted the Greek city-states against the mighty Persian Empire after the latter invaded.

Although ancient sources are difficult to authenticate, it is certain that the Persian forces vastly outnumbered the Greeks who historically struggled to unite, even against a common enemy. This conflict included the legendary Battle of Thermopylae where three hundred Spartans, led by the Spartan king Leonidas, held off the elite contingent of the Persian army, the Immortals, for two days. After several setbacks and disastrous turns, the Greeks eventually defeated the Persian fleet at the naval Battle of Mycale and forced the Persians out of Europe. Greek unification did not last beyond this victory, and by 404 BCE, Sparta crushed Athens in the Peloponnesian War. Athens would never again attain its status as the leading city-state.

Roman Empire

Although already one of the world's most powerful civilizations, Rome began to strain under political pressure and domestic unrest in the mid-first century BCE. In 48 BCE, Gaius Julius Caesar seized power over the republic, but his assassination in 44 BCE on the Ides of March threw the republic back into turmoil. Caesar's great-nephew turned son adopted by will, Octavian, eventually emerged as the sole leader of Rome, and historians define this point as the beginning of the Roman Empire. Octavian would serve as the first emperor under the name Augustus. His rule would be one of the most peaceful and prosperous in Roman history, often referred to as the *Pax Romana* or *Pax*

Augusta. Although the Roman Empire did not adhere to the republic's democratic principles and separations of powers, the Roman Empire would be the vehicle that enabled Rome to conquer and administer enormous territory.

As Rome became an empire, its influence both in the ancient world and in the modern world began to take shape. Rome's ability to absorb and adapt the cultural achievements of Greece and push them on conquered cultures was a key to their success. Rome was highly influenced by Greek culture, religions, ideas, literature, and politics but kept at its roots the Roman ideals of simplicity, honesty, and loyalty. Rome was able to hold together a government that included multiple races, languages, and cultures in peace through the successful use of these ideas. In addition, Rome applied concepts developed by the Persians in the administration and political organization of its territories. By the time Rome became an empire, the government was highly structured with a complex civil service that addressed and administrated localized affairs.

Rome's decline began well before its eventual fall. There are many aspects to Rome's demise, including social, political, moral, religious, and economic. Each took their toll on the strength of the empire, and by 400 A.D., Rome collapsed under public unrest and religious discord, along with the invasion of the Huns of Mongolia and Germanic tribes. Although ultimately defeated, Rome's legacy extends all the way through to the present day. The Roman Republic's democratic elements and robust civil service would be the model for much of the West, especially the United States. That is to say nothing of the advancements in literature, technology, architecture, urban planning, and hygiene across the empire that influenced every future Western civilization.

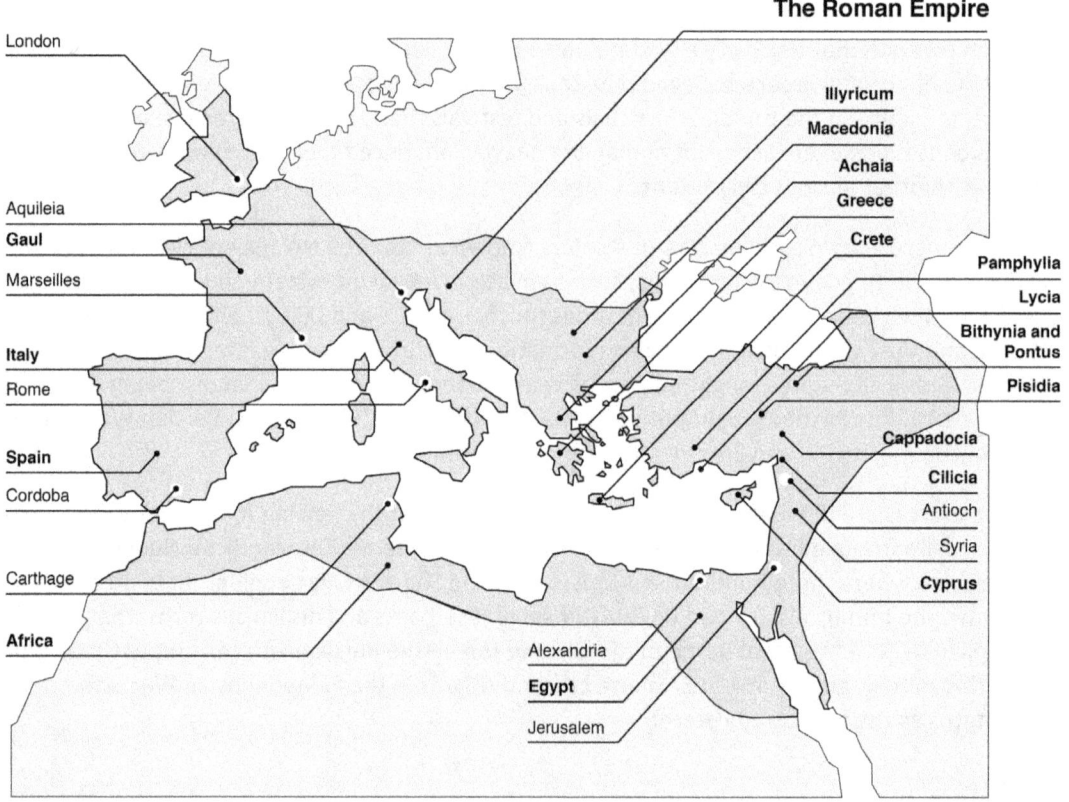

Persian Empire

The Persian Empire consisted of multiple countries, religions, languages, and races governed by a central government. Cyrus the Great was known for his social and political acumen. He was able to navigate the empire's diversity with his carrot or stick approach. Cyrus the Great would offer foreign civilizations some degree of home rule, as long as they paid tribute to Persia and adopted some of its norms, or else the might of the legendary Persian military would crush them. As long as the citizens of Persia paid taxes and were peaceful, they were allowed to keep their own religious customs, local culture, and local economies. It was not until his successors that this political policy began to wane with the onset of multiple rebellions that weakened the centralized government.

The government of Persia delegated power among four governing capitals. Each state had a satrap, or governor. The satrapy government allowed for regional self-governance with a military leader and an official record-keeper that reported to the central government. The empire was also innovative in its road construction and postal systems. By allowing some degree of regional autonomy, Persia was able to rule over an unprecedented territory in ancient history. For example, Babylon even requested to be part of Persia because of its unique policies. The empire's enormity and vast scope influenced world history for centuries. Persian scholars and political philosophers would later influence rulers in the Renaissance and Enlightenment eras.

Maurya Empire

The Maurya Empire established a centralized government to govern its vast territories, and it specialized in tax collection, administration, and the military. It was modeled after the Greek and Persian governments, who, through trade and invasion, had influenced Chandragupta's government layout. Previously, regional chieftains and small armies governed India, which led to continuous skirmishes and wars. Chandragupta cleared out the chieftains and imposed regulated laws and tax reforms. The centralized form of government allowed for a period of peace, scientific advancement, and religious growth.

The centralized government was made up of four provinces organized under one capital. Each emperor had a cabinet of ministers known as a *Mantriparishad,* or Council of Ministers, to help guide him—an idea that is still used in governments across the world. Princes, or Kumaras, likewise oversaw each province, with a council of ministers called the *Mahamatyas*. A civil service was developed to govern many aspects of life and infrastructure, including waterworks, roads, and international trade. The army was expanded into one of the largest in the world at the time. Trade became a major source of revenue as other empires sought spices, food, and cloth from India.

India's three main religions flourished in this period. Hinduism, a blend of multiple beliefs, appeared in the Epic Age and became a central religion. Buddhism appeared as a consequence of the harsh social structure that had left a wide gap in the social and economic freedoms of the people. Chandragupta later accepted Jainism, a religion of total peace and unity with the world. Overall, the Maurya Empire featured a balance of religions that promoted peace as foundational and sought social harmony. The centralized government discouraged the infamous Indian caste system, which organized society by social status and led to discrimination against the lower castes.

Chinese Empire

Between 1000 BCE and 500 A.D., ancient China was unified under three successive dynasties: the Zhou Dynasty, the Qin Dynasty, and the Han Dynasty, in respective chronological order. The Zhou Dynasty was the longest dynasty in Chinese history and began after the fall of the Shang Dynasty. Originally, the Zhou Dynasty had moved away from the Shang Empire, created their own government, and formed alliances with enemies of the Shang. When war eventually broke, the people of Shang, so angered by their own government's foolishness, put up little resistance against the rebellion.

Under the Zhou Dynasty, the kingdom's ruler legitimized their power through the Mandate of Heaven, meaning they believed the rulers of the land were put in place by a higher being that could not be disposed. The Zhou claimed that the Shang Dynasty had forfeited their claim due to their mismanagement of the kingdom. This would be a common theme for dynasty takeovers. A centralized government was established, but the Zhou Dynasty never achieved complete centralized control across the kingdom. The economy was heavily agricultural and organized based on feudalism, an economical system in which a wealthy, landowning class rules the peasant class. These aristocratic rulers retained considerable power and regularly rebelled against the central government.

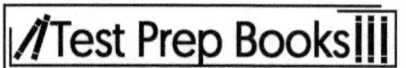

The Qin Dynasty was the first imperial dynasty, originally organized under Emperor Qin Shi Huangdi. The imperial state had a more centralized government, which limited the aristocratic landowners' power, stabilized the economy, and boosted the army. The Qin Dynasty formed a political structure that allowed China to start seriously building projects like the Great Wall of China. Its form of government would be adopted by many dynasties in China's history. The Qin Dynasty was short-lived and ended when Emperor Qin Shi Huangdi died prematurely, and rebel leaders fought for control of the kingdom. Liu Bang of Han defeated Xiang Yu of Chu at the Battle of Gaixia in 202 BCE, establishing the Han Dynasty.

Like the previous imperial dynasty, power was consolidated under a single emperor who dominated the Han Dynasty's centralized government. Under the emperor, a cabinet of ministers and chosen nobility acted as advisors who retained limited power. The Han dynasty was a golden era of Chinese innovation and technology, all driven by the tremendous growth in commerce and trade. To facilitate commerce, the Han Dynasty issued one of the world's earliest currencies under a money economy. Han coinage would remain the dominant currency from its introduction in 119 BCE until the Tang Dynasty in 618 A.D. A uniform currency was an essential part of the legendary Silk Road, which began under the Han Dynasty.

World History from 600 A.D. to 1450 A.D.

World Civilizations from 600 A.D. to 1450 A.D.

Early Middle Ages
The Middle Ages refers to the period from the fifth century to the fifteenth century, beginning with the fall of the Roman Empire and ending with the Renaissance and Age of Exploration. Sharp population decline, intensely localized governance, frequent invasions, famine, and disease defined the early Middle Ages and explain why it is sometimes referred to as the *Dark Ages*. Manorialism and feudalism were the dominant economic systems of the period. Peasants would rent patches of land to farm on enormous manors of aristocrats, while knights and lower nobles would exchange military service with the aristocracy in exchange for control over a manor. In addition, much of the knowledge gained during the Age of Antiquity was lost during this period.

High Middle Ages
During the High Middle Ages, signs of revival began to emerge. Christians began to see the need to live out the fundamental convictions of Christianity and also saw the need for the clergy to exemplify Christ. After several reforms, religious orders developed, such as the Franciscans and Dominicans. The orders protected the knowledge and texts of the church, becoming a strong intellectual body. As a consequence, there was a revival in learning in the monasteries that trickled out to the cathedrals and then to schools.

Around 570 A.D., the Islamic prophet Muhammad was born in Mecca. Muhammad was a trade merchant who, coming into contact with Christian and Jewish traders, blended their religions with his own religious experience in which he believed that Allah was the one true god. He believed that Allah had called him to preach the Islamic religion. At first, he met with little success, as most Arabs believed in many and differing gods. However, in a few years, he was able to unite the nomadic tribes under Islam.

After Muhammad's death, his successors, known as *caliphs*, developed the religion of Islam into a system of government and spread the faith and government control into the Middle East, North Africa, Spain, and southern France. At one point, the Islamic Empire was larger than the Roman Empire. With invasion, Islam spread the Arabic language and embraced Greek science and Indian mathematics. From 900 A.D. to 1100 A.D., Islam experienced a golden age.

In 1066 A.D., William, duke of Normandy, invaded England and defeated the embattled Harold II at the Battle of Hastings in what became known as the Norman Conquest. William replaced many English landholders and clergy with men from Normandy. This helped contribute to significant changes to the politics, language, and culture of England.

In 1095, European Christians launched military strikes against Muslims in the Holy Land, and the entire series of armed religious conflicts is known as the *Crusades*. During the Crusades, Italy's trade flourished because the movement of people facilitated commerce and communication with the Middle East and Africa. In the High Middle Ages, Italy expanded trade into Europe, and merchants across Europe began to settle in areas with good trade routes. Others who had a trade to sell settled in these areas, forming towns and local governments. The development of commerce would be the impetus for the Renaissance.

Developments in Africa, Mesoamerica, Andean South America, Europe, and Asia

Africa

Several African states developed between 1200 and 1450, and many of their empires continued traditional practices, adopted economic and political innovations, and governed diverse populations.

The **Hafsid Dynasty** (1229–1574) established a North African empire in present-day Libya, Tunisia, and Algeria. The Hafsid Dynasty's leaders were Sunni Muslims, and they established a hereditary monarchy that maintained their political power through commercial relationships. North Africa had historically functioned as Europe's gateway to the African caravan trade, and this continued under the Hafsid Dynasty. Likewise, the Hafsid Dynasty developed strong relationships with Ottoman merchants, the Muslim states established in Spain, and African trading powers, especially the Mali Empire. As a result, the Hafsid Dynasty benefited from an innovative and diverse population because the empire's rich trading opportunities attracted Muslim, Christian, and Jewish merchants from all over the world. To foster artistic and economic innovations, the Hafsid Dynasty patronized a wide array of artists and funded large-scale infrastructure projects.

The Hafsid rulers occasionally provoked their trading partners for short-term economic gains. For example, the dynasty legalized piracy against European merchants in the early fifteenth century, and this resulted in Spain and Venice conducting retaliatory strikes against the Hafsid Dynasty. During the early sixteenth century, the Hafsid Dynasty struggled to balance its commercial relationships with Spain and the Ottoman Empire. Eventually, the Ottoman Empire invaded North Africa, captured the capital city of Tunis, and executed the last Hafsid ruler in 1574.

The **Mali Empire** (1235–1650) constituted the largest state in West Africa during this time period. During the early thirteenth century, the Mandinka kingdom established the Mali Empire by seizing control over the traditionally valuable trans-Saharan caravan routes from the rapidly collapsing Ghana Empire. The caravan routes were immensely valuable for the Mali Empire because the government taxed all of the gold, salt, and copper that passed through its territory. In addition, the Mali Empire had three gold mines within its borders, so it was a major source of the gold flowing south on the trans-Saharan caravan routes.

The Mali Empire built a relatively decentralized administrative state to govern its vast territories, particularly in terms of collecting taxes from merchants. A king known as the **mansa** headed the administrative state, but provincial governors held the overwhelming bulk of policy-making powers. In keeping continuity with past practices, local tribes held the power to appoint provincial governors based on customs, which ranged from tribal elections to inheritance. However, the mansa enjoyed the ability to veto or remove disloyal provincial governors. Once appointed, the provincial governors led a local government consisting of county-masters and village-masters. Decentralization allowed the Mali Empire to maintain control over an ethnically and culturally diverse empire. For example, the dozens of tribes within the Mali Empire spoke five different languages and practiced variations of traditional African animist religions as well as Islam. During the late fifteenth century, the Songhai Empire (1464–1594) conquered some of the Mali Empire's wealthiest cities, including Gao, Timbuktu, and Djenné, and became the preeminent power in West Africa.

The **Kingdom of Zimbabwe** (1220–1450) was the largest precolonial South African state in history. A hereditary monarchy ruled the state, but details pertaining to the size and function of the administrative state haven't yet been discovered. That being said, Zimbabwe rulers must have been able to project considerable political power over long distances because the state was able to tax more than 150 neighboring tribes. The Kingdom of Zimbabwe is most commonly associated with its immense and intricate stone structures, some of which have survived into the present day. Archaeologists discovered Asian, Arabic, and West African goods in the ruins of the capital, Great Zimbabwe, demonstrating the empire's extensive commercial ties. During the first half of the fifteenth century, civil war triggered the Kingdom of Zimbabwe's dissolution.

During the latter half of the fourteenth century, the Bakongo tribe conquered territory in Central and West Africa, forming the **Kingdom of Kongo** (1390–1914) in present-day Angola, Gabon, Democratic Republic of the Congo, and Republic of the Congo. The Kongo government was led by a nonhereditary monarch known as the **Mwene Kongo** (King of the Kongo), who served a lifelong term. The King of the Kongo shared control over the central government with a twelve-member Royal Council consisting of four high-level bureaucrats, four matrons with royal blood, and four electors from provinces. The electors appointed the King of the Kongo, although many rulers attempted to choose their own successor with mixed results. This innovative appointment process effectively prevented the creation of an autocracy; however, the Kingdom of Kongo was plagued with crises over the succession of power, many of which spiraled into open rebellions and civil wars. In conjunction with the Royal Council, the King of the Kongo led a centralized bureaucracy charged with collecting taxes, regulating the shell currency, and overseeing the slave trade.

At the local level, the Kingdom of Kongo divided its territory into provinces, and hereditary families led the provincial administrative states somewhat independently from the central government. However, village tribal leaders continued to hold influence within the local governments, especially when it came to day-to-day governance. Following the arrival of Portuguese explorers in the late fifteenth century, the Kingdom of Kongo became a major player in the global slave trade. For several centuries, the Kingdom of Kongo maintained its independence until Portugal abolished the monarchy in 1914 and colonized the empire's former territories.

The **Ajuran Sultanate** (1200–1700) was the most powerful East African state during this period due to its maritime trade and agricultural practices. A world-class navy granted Ajuran merchants uninhibited access to highly lucrative Indian and East Asian markets. Perhaps more impressively, the Ajuran sultanate monopolized water resources through innovative irrigation schemes and the construction of advanced limestone wells. Because the Ajuran sultanate controlled famers' access to water, they enjoyed substantial control over the region's food supply.

The **House of Garen** led the Ajuran Sultanate as a Sunni Muslim hereditary dynasty. As such, the head of the Garen family claimed the title of **Imam**. Although the Imam served as the Ajuran Sultanate's autocratic leader, the powerful central government also included military leaders, viceroys, tax collectors, and chief judges. The government ruled over a predominantly Sunni Muslim population, and the legal system was based on a relatively strict interpretation of Sharia law. Despite its conservative roots, the Ajuran government was a major patron of the arts, architecture, sciences, and academies.

Mesoamerica
During the fifteenth and early sixteenth centuries, the Aztec Empire controlled much of present-day Mexico and Central America. The **Aztec Empire** began as the **Triple Alliance** of three city-states—Tenochtitlan, Texcoco, and Tlacopan—located in present-day Mexico City. **Tenochtitlan** was the Aztec Empire's capital, and it housed the largest population in the pre-Columbian Americans. The Templo Mayor (Great Temple) was constructed in the center of Tenochtitlan, and it featured an enormous stepped pyramid where the Aztecs conducted human sacrifices. Texcoco was the second most populous and powerful city-state, and the city was famous throughout the region for its libraries and education system. Tlacopan was a junior partner within the Triple Alliance, and, as such, it

had a lesser say in policy making and military strategy. Additionally, Tlacopan only received a fifth of the tribute and territory seized by the Aztec Empire.

Following their victory in the Tepanec War during the early fifteenth century, the rulers of the Triple Alliance declared themselves as huetlatoani (emperor). The Triple Alliance then rapidly expanded across Central America, conquering dozens of city-states. Unlike most other empires, the Aztec Empire's government operated as a confederation. The three emperors were the highest officials in the government, and they divided the territory and tribute gained through conquest among their city-states. The Aztec rulers generally granted defeated city-states autonomy, including the right of local nobility to maintain their status, as long as they continued to pay tribute. Rather than an administrative bureaucracy, the Aztec rulers relied on military power and economic coercion to exercise power over their subjects and tributary city-states. Tenochtitlan's ruler also created a council composed of four military generals to serve as strategic advisors, and they held significant decision-making power throughout the entire Aztec Empire.

Given the relatively decentralized nature of the Aztec government, rebellions were commonplace within the tributary city-states. In response, the huetlatoani would generally send military forces to remove and replace the city-state's provincial government. However, the rivalries between city-states represented the Aztec Empire's critical weakness. When the Spanish conquistador Hernan Cortés led an expedition into the Aztec Empire in 1519, he was able to forge alliances with tributary states, and the Aztec Empire collapsed after two years of fighting.

Andean South America

The **Inca Empire** (1438–1533) controlled more territory than any other pre-Columbian civilization. Initially, the Inca Empire began as a city-state known as the Kingdom of Cusco (1197–1438). The city-state's ruler, known as the **Sapa Inca** (the only Inca), held close-to-absolute political power, and the Sapa Inca was selected based on candidates' performance in physical trials, moral evaluations, and spiritual rituals. In exercising their immense power, the Sapa Inca spearheaded the creation of a complex administrative state that collected taxes, provided social assistance, and enforced laws. The Sapa Inca regularly sent officials to test the loyalty, efficiency, and effectiveness of civil servants.

During the early fifteenth century, a Sapa Inca named Pachacuti-Cusi Yupanqui turned the Kingdom of Cusco into the Inca Empire by conquering an enormous stretch of territory along the Andean Mountains. In addition to military conquests, Pachacuti-Cusi Yupanqui used espionage, political intrigue, bribery, extravagant gifts, and military might to acquire territory from rival city-states. By the early sixteenth century, the Inca Empire controlled a vast territory stretching from present-day Peru to Argentina. The Inca Empire governed its territory through a federal system.

The Sapa Inca continued to serve as the absolute ruler of the Inca Empire's central government, but some political power was delegated to four provincial governments. Historians differ as to the size and scope of the Inca Empire's administrative state, but there's a general agreement that its main purpose was tax collection. The central government set the tax rate, and the provincial government was tasked with collecting the tax revenue. Along with taxes, households were responsible for providing mit'a (public service) to the central government. This public service was usually provided through labor on public works projects or military service. The Spanish conquistador Francisco Pizarro exploited a succession crisis over who would become the next Sapa Inca in their conquest of the Inca Empire. The Spaniards executed the sole remaining contender for the title of Sapa Inca in 1533, and the Incas' resistance was fully defeated in 1572.

Europe

From 1200 to 1450, European states were extremely decentralized due to feudalism. In a feudal political system, monarchies granted land rights to nobles (vassals) in exchange for military service and/or tax revenue. As such, the monarchy couldn't enforce laws or otherwise perform most government functions without relying on the local power structures. In contrast, many nobles consolidated power due to their military strength, dominance over the

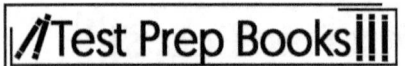

peasant labor force, and control of the food supply. Often, powerful nobles would threaten the monarchy's right to rule, which further incentivized the central government to avoid antagonizing the nobility.

Europe experienced incredible destabilization during this period. The already dysfunctional English and French monarchies fought the **Hundred Years' War** (1337–1453). Frenchmen originally founded the English monarchy, so the English royal family pressed claims to the French throne based on their substantial landholdings in France. France disputed those land rights, claiming the English royal family were the French monarchy's feudal vassals. The prolonged armed conflict was destabilizing, but it ultimately strengthened the French and English monarchies due to the development of professional armies and rise of nationalism. Consequently, by the end of the Hundred Years' War, both the English and French monarchies were able to consolidate political and economic power at the expense of the nobility, which brought an end to the feudal political system.

The Kingdom of Castile and Kingdom of Aragon spent much of this period fighting back against the Muslim states on the Iberian Peninsula. The two Christian kingdoms united in 1474, establishing the state of Spain. Because the Portuguese Crown consolidated political power in the eleventh century, it had a distinct advantage over their European rivals. During the early fifteenth century, Portugal built a world-renowned armada and launched what quickly would become a vast overseas colonial empire. In Central Europe, the Holy Roman Empire struggled to project authority over the territories it claimed in present-day Germany and Italy. The rest of Italy was divided among relatively small city-states, and the papacy constituted the region's most powerful political force. Eastern Europe was destabilized after the Ottomans sacked Constantinople in 1453, which caused the Byzantine Empire to dissolve into three significantly weaker independent states.

The European socioeconomic order revolved around agriculture from 1200 to 1450 due to the prevalence of feudalism. The powerful landed class of feudal nobles typically organized their land under the manorial system. The vast majority of European nobles served as the Lord of the Manor, and their extensive landholdings were known as **fiefs**. Peasants who lived on the fief were allowed to farm the land, but they were obligated to pay the Lord of the Manor taxes either in the form of free labor or percentage of crops. Furthermore, the Lord of the Manor held all political power, and even more importantly, created and oversaw the legal system that applied to the fief. Nobles' legal and economic dominance over the peasants is why they held such power under feudalism. Although trade and urban centers generally increased from 1200 to 1450, Europe was still an overwhelmingly agriculture society due to the number and size of fiefs across the continent.

Islamic States

Numerous Islamic states either developed or expanded between 1200 and 1450. The Delhi Sultanate (1206–1526) conquered most of the Indian subcontinent in the thirteenth century. Following the Abbasid Caliphate's (750–1258) collapse, its rulers established a new state, the Mamluk Sultanate (1261–1517), in present-day Egypt. The Ajuran Sultanate (1200–1700) was one of the most powerful Islamic states in Africa, and it controlled maritime trade on the Indian Ocean for centuries. The **Ottoman Empire** (1299–1922) consolidated power in present-day Turkey and launched a successful invasion of Eastern Europe. With its powerful navy and superior military, the Ottoman Empire controlled Mediterranean trade routes and supported Muslim states, including those established in present-day Spain and Portugal.

Several powerful Islamic states were established between 1200 and 1450. The **Delhi Sultanate** was first established on the northern Indian subcontinent in the early thirteenth century. Following a series of military conquests, the Delhi Sultanate consolidated control over nearly the entire subcontinent. The Delhi Sultanate benefited from trade with Islamic states and Chinese dynasties, particularly in the transfer of critical technological innovations to India. The Delhi Sultanate ultimately collapsed in the aftermath of a Turco-Mongol invasion in the early sixteenth century.

The **Abbasid Caliphate** (750–1258) ruled much of the Middle East and North Africa until the Mongols sacked Baghdad, triggering the government's collapse. The Abbasid Caliphate had been the center of the Muslim world, and following its collapse, the Abbasid rulers relocated to present-day Egypt and formed the **Mamluk Sultanate** (1261–1517). The Mamluk sultans legitimized their rule by declaring themselves the true protector of the Muslim world. Although the Mamluk Sultanate never regained the Abbasid Caliphate's power and prestige, the Mamluk Sultanate constituted one of the most culturally important Islamic states, particularly in its sponsorship of intellectual innovations.

Muslim rule expanded in Afro-Eurasia from 1200 to 1450. Islam spread across Africa along the trans-Saharan caravan network, which connected the Mediterranean, North Africa, West Africa, and East Africa. The Ottoman Empire controlled much of the Mediterranean region throughout this period, and North Africa was mostly under the control of an Islamic state established by the Hafsid Dynasty. Muslim merchants established trading empires in West Africa, and many African states had large Muslim populations, including the Ghana Empire. The Ajuran Sultanate (1200–1700) consolidated economic and political control over East Africa in the thirteenth century, and it dominated maritime trade in the Indian Ocean for several centuries. The Ajuran Sultanate remained the preeminent power in the region until the Portuguese defeated the Ajuran navy in the early sixteenth century.

Europe was decentralized throughout the thirteenth century and most of the fourteenth century. As such, European states feared that the Ottoman Empire would march farther into Europe. The Ottoman Empire's powerful navy also prevented European merchants from traveling the Mediterranean Sea, which partially motivated European monarchs to fund expeditions seeking new trade routes. Furthermore, the Ottoman Empire's navy supported the handful of Islamic states on the Iberian Peninsula (Spain and Portugal). Spain conquered the Muslim Kingdom of Granada in 1492, completing the **Reconquista** that ended Islamic rule on the Iberian Peninsula.

India

The classical age of India came to a sudden end in 535 A.D. when the Huns invaded. Under Hun rule, India held on to its religious and cultural traditions. By the 600s, a Hindu confederation pushed back the Huns, and Harsha, the Hindu king, united the empire once again. At first, his rule was peaceful and humane, but in his later years, oppressive acts caused another overthrow of the empire. This time, it was from the Rajput Indians, descendants of central Asians who had intermarried with Hindus after invading some centuries before.

The Rajput kingdoms were small, regionally ruled areas weakened by disunity. After the spread of Islam in the Middle East, Muslim Turks began to invade India. Beginning in the north, Muslims streamed in and began to convert Hindus to Islam. It took from 712 A.D. to 1236 A.D. for Muslims to control the northern part of India and another hundred years to gain the southern part.

After setting up a new capital in Delhi, the Muslim invaders used sultans, or Muslim authorities, to rule over India. Their government was called the *Delhi Sultanate,* and it was cruel toward those who had not converted to Islam. The sultans remained in power until 1526 A.D. The laws established higher taxes for non-Muslims, which caused many to convert. The strict caste system of Hindu also caused many to convert to the socially equal Muslims. As a result of the invasion and religious conversion, India was divided into Hindus and Muslims, and it remains a dividing point today.

China

The harsh terrain between China and the rest of the world kept it in relative peace and stability for most of Europe's Middle Ages. However, after the Han Dynasty fell, China was in turmoil for nearly four hundred years until a Chinese general, Yang Chien, founded the Sui Dynasty in 581 A.D. It was the Sui Dynasty that rebuilt the foundations of the government and allowed the next two dynasties to flourish with two more golden ages.

Following the collapse of the Sui Dynasty in 618 A.D., the Li family took control of the empire and established the T'ang Dynasty, which lasted for almost two hundred years. Under T'ang, the government moved to a highly centralized, highly regulated form of government run by the empire's scholars. The economy grew with building

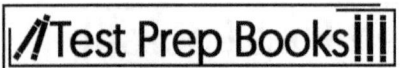

projects that opened new avenues of trade. Canals and ports allowed thousands of foreign merchants to trade in China. The dissemination of ideas and culture, combined with long peaceful stability, allowed the Chinese time to create world-changing inventions, such as gunpowder and block printing. The decline of the T'ang Dynasty began after a series of weak emperors, overtaxation, and persecution led to the deposition of the last T'ang emperor by Chao K'uang-yin.

In 960 A.D., Chao K'uang-yin established the Song Dynasty. Though it would last until 1279 A.D., the Song Dynasty was often fighting off Mongol invaders. The early Khitan invaders were paid off with silver and silk, but the Tungusic people, known as the *Jurchen,* from Manchuria, divided the empire into two—Jurchen's Jin Empire to the north and the Song Empire to the south. Under Song rule, the southern empire flourished, despite the split. Trade increased with the opening of new commercial colonies and ports. As the Chinese began to travel to trade their wares, they introduced new ideas and technology to the world. They also improved sea travel and invented important navigational equipment.

With the empire split, the Jin Dynasty came under attack by Mongols, and after many years of tribute or fighting off, the dynasty gave way under the attacks of Genghis Khan, a brutal but highly effective military commander. In 1215 A.D., Genghis Khan conquered the Jin Dynasty and moved to the West, occupying parts of Russia, Persia, Iraq, and northern India. Genghis Khan's grandson, Kublai Khan, united the empires once again by overthrowing the Song Dynasty in 1279 A.D. and adding the Asian states of Burma, Annam, and Cambodia. He then established the Yuan Dynasty, making Kublai the first foreign ruler in Chinese history.

After the Collapse of the Western Roman Empire

Feudalism
In medieval Europe, feudalism was a legal system that included participation among lords (people who owned the land), vassals (people who were given possession of the land), and fiefs (the land itself). When the lord granted land to the vassal, the vassal would pledge fealty (sworn loyalty) to the lord in return. From 9th century to 15th century A.D., feudalism was a way of managing land in exchange for nobility.

Manorialism
Manorialism was another economic, social, and political system in medieval Europe that lasted well into the 18th century, and gradually died out after that. Manorialism involves lords of a manor receiving payment from their subjects through labor. Serfdom was a characteristic of manorialism, where tenant farmers were given a plot of land to cultivate by the lord of the estate. Manorialism was different from feudalism in that there was no ceremony involved in manorialism to establish a relationship between a lord and a vassal. Instead, manorialism was an economic arrangement that effectively managed the lands of the aristocracy and clergy.

Roman Catholic Church and Eastern Orthodox Church in Medieval Europe

Following the collapse of the Roman Empire into fragmented territories in 476 A.D., the former eastern territory retained its power and regained control over some of Rome's other territories, establishing the Byzantine Empire. Although originally part of the Roman Empire, the Byzantine Empire adopted significantly different policies and cultural practices during and after Rome fell. Under Theodosius I, the Byzantine Empire adopted Christianity as the official religion during the third century. During the sixth century, under the reign of Heraclius, the empire adopted Greek as the official language in its administration and military. The Byzantine Empire protected and advanced the rich culture of art, literature, and philosophy developed by the Romans. The emperor Justinian is by far the most heralded and influential Byzantine ruler. He successfully invaded to reorganize governments and spread law.

Christianity played a special role in the Byzantine Empire, as it was able to take over much of the authority lost by civil and military rulers. Christianity was also able to keep literacy, culture, and philosophy of the ancient world alive.

In addition, the Byzantine Empire's Christian faith would pit it against Muslims in numerous bloody conflicts. By Justinian's time, the church of the east and the west had grown apart. Concerned with growing differences between the two, Justinian sent out missionaries and suppressed heresy and paganism. His attempts failed in the long term and, as a result, the east and west churches split irrevocably into Roman Catholicism and Eastern Orthodox Christianity with the Schism of 1054 A.D.

In 768 A.D., Charlemagne, or Charles the Great, took power and worked to unify an empire under the Roman Catholic Church. By 800 A.D., he was crowned emperor of the Holy Roman Empire. The Holy Roman Empire controlled a complex set of territories in central Europe from the early Middle Ages until it dissolved in 1806. The predominance of Christian thought in Charlemagne's government covered all aspects of government and allowed for a revival in literature and the arts. It also included copying Latin text to preserve knowledge for future generations. This contrasted sharply with the rest of the West, where much of the former Roman territories lived in localized and unorganized communities. The Holy Roman emperors claimed to be the heir to the Roman Empire and clung to the prestige of that claim. Even in the Holy Roman Empire, the West failed to develop the technology and advance the knowledge gained under the Roman Empire. Although the Holy Roman Empire retained the name and wielded substantial power, the actual government was extremely decentralized, like that of other feudal territories with lesser names.

Comparison of Social, Political, Economic, and Religious Aspects of Medieval Europe with Previous Civilizations

As central feudal governments weakened in the High Middle Ages, the church emerged as the most powerful institution in both Western Europe and Byzantium. With the infamous crowning of Charlemagne as the emperor of the Holy Roman Empire in the West, the Catholic Church sought to expand its political role in Europe. The church, once a weakened spiritual institution, became a political machine in Europe. Feudalism still reigned as the dominant social and economic structure, but the church swiftly began to take control of these socioeconomic affairs. While feudalism and the manor/serfdom system created division, the church strove for unification through faith. The Catholic Church provided both physical and spiritual security during these dark times. The church became the center of every community, controlling the daily lives of its participants.

Even the legal system was based on Catholic canon, which unified church and state. During this time, popes wielded as much power as kings. They had the ability to rule the people, deny salvation, and excommunicate members from the community. The church also had the power to execute members who threatened the sanctity of canon law. The local clergy of the Catholic Church demanded as much respect as the feudal knights. The emergence of the church as a social, economic, and political leader set the stage for the wave of Crusades in later centuries. Additionally, it set the stage for the battle between church and state that would carry throughout the Early Modern period. With church and state so closely unified during this period, corruption ran rampant as the Catholic Church asked its followers to pay for their salvation. Diplomatic ties with the Middle East remained tenuous during this time as the Catholic Church declared holy wars on the Muslim Turks.

Political, Religious, and Social Impact of the Crusades and Other Religious Interactions

In 1093, Pope Urban II teamed with the Byzantine emperor Alexius Comnenus to declare a series of holy wars, or Crusades, on the Muslim Turks who were knocking at the door of the Byzantine capital, Constantinople. For two centuries, several waves of Crusades were carried out in the Holy Land, specifically in Jerusalem. The Crusades were not only religious in character, but also economic. On the ground, the Crusades maintained a religious zeal—knights traveled throughout the Mediterranean to fight for their Lord. Behind the scenes, rulers and merchants profited off loans and leases. The Crusades helped make Genoese and Venetian merchants some of the wealthiest in Europe, if not the world. Politically, the Crusades helped unite quarrelsome knights who had been previously warring across Europe. The knights united in a common enemy: Muslims. In terms of a social impact, the Crusades helped further diversify the Holy Land as Jerusalem shifted hands between Western Europe, Byzantium, and the Muslim Turks. By the 1200s, the Crusades had become so common that the sporadic campaigns had too often led to failure. As a result, the power of the pope and the Byzantine Empire began to weaken. The power of feudal nobles also began to weaken.

This helped usher in the end of feudalism in Europe, paving the way to the rise of stronger monarchies and nation-states. As the power of feudal nobles declined, the power of Italian merchants began to increase. This accumulation of wealth eventually paved the way to the trade-driven Age of Exploration in the Early Modern period. Specifically, trade grew between Europe and Asia, spawning an increase in European orientalism. This orientalism encouraged Europeans to find new trade routes to Asia by sea. Additionally, European technology advanced to allow for easier trade and travel. The cultural exchanges between the Muslims and Christians opened the doors to technological advancement in Western Europe. Nevertheless, the bitterness of the Crusades left Christians and Muslims in conflict for centuries to come. The Crusades are still viewed as a historical example of the dangerous roots of Christian hegemony in the Middle East.

World History from 1450 A.D. to 1750 A.D.

While Europe was experiencing a low point in the Middle Ages, with little progress in the arts, technology, or culture, India and China were experiencing multiple golden ages. However, by the 1300s, the tide had shifted. Europe was coming out of its dark age and moving toward a period that would surpass the cultural achievements, wealth, and power that India and China had gained during the Middle Ages. In this emerging Western dominance, the East declined, but it did not remain isolated due to European exploration and colonization.

For Europe, the Middle Ages were a time of feudalism and religious orthodoxy. As the period ended, people began to shift toward the idea of individualism, as they began to seek out political and economic freedom, independence of thought in religious matters, and a desire for greater knowledge. The idea of a renaissance man developed, with Leonardo da Vinci representing the ideal: a person who achieved mastery in many forms or subjects.

World Civilizations from 1450 A.D. to 1750 A.D.

Fall of Constantinople
The fall of Constantinople happened in May 1453 and marked the end of the Roman Empire, a 1500-year imperial state. The Ottoman Empire invaded the capital of the Byzantine Empire following a fifty-three day siege, led by the young Mehmed the Conqueror, sultan of the Ottoman Empire. For some historians, the fall of Constantinople marks the end of the Middle Ages.

Western Religion
The major division between Christianity occurred in the 1500s as a result of the Protestant Reformation. Catholics and Protestants fought several wars to decide what religion would dominate in a particular region. The wars were often for political and economic gain but fought on the basis of religion. In particular, the Thirty Years' War was the bloodiest conflict in world history until the First World War. The Thirty Years' War directly led to the concept of the nation-state, one of the most important developments in modern history. The need for an identifiable nation-state grew out of the need for regions to determine their own religion to prevent future conflict.

During periods of strife and persecution, different denominations of Christianity migrated to the United States, especially during the colonial period. Such groups who sought religious freedom and tolerance included the Quakers, who settled in Pennsylvania; the Dutch Anabaptists and Calvinists, who settled in New York; and the Catholics, who settled in Maryland, among others. The Great Awakening, a religious revival in colonial America during the 1730s and 1740s, contributed to the American Revolution by encouraging people to challenge authority in their pursuit of salvation. Many colonists believed that the war was just in the eyes of God, and so it gave them a moral reason to fight. Ministers, like Jonathan Mayhew, who coined the phrase, "No taxation without representation," preached that the revolution was a religious crusade and that it was the Christian's duty to do battle against tyrants and oppressors.

Martin Luther

Martin Luther, a priest, monk, professor, and composer, was an influential part of the Protestant Reformation. Martin Luther disagreed with the Catholic Church in its then-belief that salvation could be bought instead of bestowed by grace, and nailed his *Ninety-Five Theses* to the wall of a chapel in Wittenberg, Germany in 1517. In addition, Luther also translated the Bible into the German vernacular instead of its usual Latin, allowing the masses to interpret the text on their own. Luther was later excommunicated by the Catholic Church for not renouncing his writings.

The Black Death

Peaking in Europe from 1346 to 1353, the Black Death was a pandemic that is believed to have destroyed nearly half of Europe's total population, an estimated number of 75 to 200 million people. The Black Death was thought to have been carried to Europe by rats on the Silk Road from Central Asia. The symptoms of the plague consisted of buboes (swollen lymph nodes in the armpit or groin) followed by vomiting and fever. The plague made reappearances in Europe until the 19th century, and the world population of 450 million, pre-plague numbers, did not return until the 17th century.

Leonardo da Vinci

Leonardo da Vinci set the ideal for the renaissance man, a person whose genius and talent is depicted in many different areas. He was best known for being a painter, having created the famous works of *Mona Lisa* and *The Last Supper*, but was also known for being an engineer, mathematician, inventor, sculptor, architecture, and scientist, among other things. Leonardo was born to a peasant woman and educated in the studio of Andrea del Verrocchio, a famous Florentine painter. Leonardo is credited with conceptualizing flying machines, the double hull, an adding machine, and concentrated solar power.

Advancements in Technology

Advancements in technology can have positive and negative consequences, but all change the world in some way. Examples of major innovations include the printing press, cotton gin, electricity, gunpowder, and Internet. These discoveries have laid the groundwork for numerous adaptations and new inventions.

Invented by Johannes Gutenberg around 1440, the printing press spread ideas that fueled the Reformation, the American and French revolutions, and the Enlightenment. As a cheaper and quicker way to spread information, the printing press led to an explosion in literacy. Prior to the invention of the printing press, books were handwritten; thus, few copies were available, and the copies that were available were very expensive, so only the elite could read and write. In particular, the explosion of books dramatically altered people's relationship with religion. Before Gutenberg's invention, religious scholars were the only people who could read the Bible, and religious services were the only place where people heard Christianity. After its invention, millions of people could read the Bible for themselves, directly leading to the Reformation, as people arrived at their own interpretations. Similarly, the political order was challenged, as people could more easily communicate and gather news across long distances.

Electrical energy was observed in ancient civilization, but it wasn't until after the spread of information through the printing press that electricity became studied and used. In the 1800s, electrical knowledge was furthered by numerous inventions, such as Alexander Graham Bell's telephone and Thomas Edison's light bulb and phonograph. George Westinghouse's electricity distribution system improved on Edison's direct current with alternating current, which is a much more reliable method of conducting electricity safely across long distances. Electricity completely changed the face of manufacturing and further spurred the Industrial Revolution.

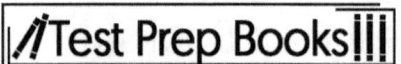

The Chinese invented gunpowder in the ninth century, and the written formula appears in records of the Song dynasty in the eleventh century. Gunpowder spread along the Silk Road, from central Asia to the Middle East to Europe. Gunpowder totally changed the way war was waged, decimating nations and cultures without the technology and making empires for those who had it. Although Europeans did not start using gunpowder until the thirteenth century, gunpowder would provide the means for Europeans to quickly conquer the Americas, including toppling the powerful Incan and Aztec empires. Gunpowder naturally led to the invention of more deadly explosives. War on land, air, and sea became bloodier and more devastating.

Originally created by the United States in the 1960s to connect military networks, the Internet became available for commercial usage in the early 1990s and exponentially increased ever since. The Internet empowers people and nations in various ways. Knowledge is now available at the fingertips of anybody with a working Internet connection. The Internet is the modern-day printing press. Politicians and economists can easily share incredible amounts of technical data and information in an instant. Furthermore, the capital necessary for large-scale investment is more readily available, thanks to improvements in communication technology. Within society, the Internet increases civic engagement by expanding citizens' knowledge of public affairs and broadening political participation. People can now directly communicate with their elected representatives, and those representatives are able to modify their positions based on the will of the people. In addition, watchdog groups are capable of closely monitoring the actions of public officials. More recently, social media networks have further connected people.

Along with these inventions and adaptions, discoveries and improvements in transportation and medicine have dramatically impacted world history. The invention of the steamboat, train, automobile, and airplane allowed people to efficiently travel across long distances. Improvements to transportation would continually increase commerce and communication; however, transportation also served devastating military purposes. During World War II, tanks steamrolled through enemy lines, planes dropped millions of tons of explosives on cities, and submarines sunk unsuspecting ships. Medical improvements, such as penicillin, x-rays, and vaccinations, have saved innumerable lives. People are living longer, healthier lives with a higher standard of living. In 1900, the average life expectancy was thirty-one, and by 2010, the world average was sixty-seven. However, life expectancy is higher in the developed world relative to the developing world where medical advances have not yet fully reached.

Developments in Africa, the Americas, Western and Eastern Europe, Middle East, and Asia

Age of Exploration

The traveling merchants, the Crusades, the conquests of foreign lands, and the writings of ancient Greece expanded the known world of Europeans to include Europe, northern Africa, the Middle East, and Asia. Early explorers such as Marco Polo brought back amazing stories and exotic goods from Asia, while ports in the Middle East and around the Mediterranean spread cultures through trade. However, the very existence of America and Australia was unknown to the ancient and medieval world. Likewise, there was very little knowledge of sub-Saharan Africa until the late Renaissance era.

In an effort to find better trade routes to China, explorers discovered unknown lands that would change the world in dramatic fashion. Over a two-hundred-year period from 1450 to 1650, the great explorers of the age would discover new lands, unknown people, and better trade routes to the silks, spices, precious metals, and other sought-after goods Europe was eager to own.

Portugal and Spain funded the first explorations and, along with Italy, dominated the discovery of new lands and trade routes for the first one hundred years of exploration. In 1488, Portuguese explorer Bartolomeu Dias became the first European to sail around the Cape of Good Hope in South Africa and the first European to sail from the Atlantic Ocean to the Indian Ocean. On a voyage lasting from 1497 to 1499, Vasco da Gama, another Portuguese explorer, followed the route of Dias and became the first European to reach India by sea.

Portuguese explorers' success led to Portugal's dominance over trade with Africa and Asia. In West Africa, the Portuguese traded for slaves, and in east Africa, they captured city-states and opened trading posts. The coastal trading posts were utilized to launch further exploration and trade farther east with China and Japan. During a voyage launched in 1500, Dias went on to reach Brazil after his ship was blown off course to Africa. Brazil would later become Portugal's most lucrative colony due to the sugar plantations farmed by African slaves and indigenous people.

In 1535, Portugal established a commercial port in Macau (southwestern China), but unlike other Portuguese trading posts, the Ming Dynasty forced the Portuguese to pay a substantial rent. After the Portuguese assisted the Ming Dynasty in squashing a piracy threat, they were allowed to create a permanent trading post in 1557. Still, the Ming Dynasty constructed a Barrier Gate to regulate Portuguese access and trade with the rest of its territory. Portuguese merchants purchased valuable Chinese goods, such as silk and porcelain, with gold and silver and then transported the Chinese goods to their trading posts in Nagasaki (Japan) and Malacca (Malaysia).

Chinese goods were especially valuable in Nagasaki due to the Chinese embargo on Japan, which was handed down over issues with Japanese piracy. From Malacca, Portuguese traders sailed to their Indian trading posts where they primarily traded Chinese silk for Indian textiles. Most Portuguese merchants stopped at the trading post located in Goa (southwestern India), which was responsible for managing all Portuguese imports and exports to India, and then sailed back to Portugal around the Cape of Good Hope.

By the 1530s, France, England, the Netherlands, and Scotland were beginning to send explorers on their own expeditions. In 1534, the king of France sent Jacques Cartier to discover a western passage to the Asian markets, and during his voyage in 1534, Cartier became the first European to travel down the Saint Lawrence River and explore Canada, which Cartier named after Iroquois settlements that he encountered. Englishman Francis Drake was the first European to successfully circumnavigate the world, completing the three-year voyage in 1580. Another Englishman, Henry Hudson, was hired by the Dutch East India Company to find a northwest passage to India, and he explored the modern New York metropolitan area in the early seventeenth century. The Dutch would use this knowledge to colonize the area around the Hudson River, including New Amsterdam.

Even more devastating than the loss of their land, contact by Europeans exposed the indigenous people of America to devastating new diseases. Without any type of immunization, mild European diseases decimated the populations of the natives. Often the illness and death of natives made conquering the areas swift, and with it the loss of the culture, traditions, and languages of the native people. However, diseases such as syphilis and cholera were brought back from expeditions, ravaging European countries. The high death toll from disease, coupled with the deaths from native-born slave labor, caused a labor shortage that the Spanish replenished with slaves from their trade deals in West Africa. These slaves were mainly brought to the Caribbean Islands, though they were shipped to other Spanish colonies. The British colonies would later import millions of slaves to the modern-day American South to harvest cotton.

Trading Posts in Africa and Asia

The expansion of the Ottoman Empire reinvigorated interregional trade to an extent not seen since the fall of the Western Roman Empire. The Ottoman Empire began in present-day Turkey, spread into Europe in 1354, and conquered Constantinople in 1453, causing the Byzantine Empire to collapse. By 1683, the Ottomans controlled the Balkans, Greece, Mesopotamia, present-day Syria and Israel, Egypt, and nearly all of the North African coast. As a result, the Ottoman Empire dominated the Mediterranean sea lanes, which were the primary trade routes between Southeastern Europe, North Africa, and West Asia. Like the Roman Empire, the Ottoman administrative state spurred economic growth in the Mediterranean region by connecting ports to overland trade routes, instituting a standardized legal system, establishing an imperial currency, and protecting merchants from piracy.

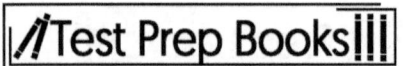

Similar to its role in the Mediterranean region, the Ottoman Empire's consolidation of economic, military, and political power directly led to increased overland trade across Eurasia, including the Silk Road's reemergence as a major trade route. The **Safavid Empire** in present-day Iran also played a critical role in reviving the Silk Road. When the Safavid Empire fought a prolonged military conflict with the Ottoman Empire, they created a new land route that connected China to Europe through Russia. Consequently, interregional trade between East Asia and Europe boomed throughout this period overland as well as through the increasingly prosperous Mediterranean sea lanes.

Interregional maritime trade further increased after Portuguese explorers discovered they could reach the Indian Ocean by sailing around the Cape of Good Hope in 1488. This discovery severely disrupted the Ottoman Empire's monopoly on the Mediterranean sea lanes because it connected Western Europe to East Asia via India. While maritime trade increased throughout the sixteenth and seventeenth centuries, trade was occasionally disrupted by naval wars. Portugal and Spain frequently sparred with the Ottoman Empire in the Mediterranean Sea and Indian Ocean. Similarly, the Safavid Empire fought Portugal to gain control over strategic trade lanes in the Persian Gulf, Gulf of Aden, and Straits of Malacca. With help from the British East India Company, the Safavid Empire was able to fend off the Portuguese. This not only increased English trade with Asia but also opened new economic opportunities for Dutch and French merchants.

India greatly benefited from increased maritime trade based on its geographic position between East Asia and Western Europe. After the **Mughal Empire** consolidated control over the Indian subcontinent, it sought to increase foreign trade. During the late fifteenth century, Emperor Akbar entered into agreements with European trading companies to strengthen economic ties, and as a result, trade steadily increased, particularly in India's textile industry. The Mughal Empire's economy was the largest in the world in the eighteenth century, accounting for an estimated 25% of global economic production.

Increased maritime trade greatly disrupted the trans-Saharan caravan networks. As Portugal explored the West African coast, it built military trading posts. Compared to the danger and expense of crossing the Sahara, these trading posts were very attractive. Saharan trading centers further declined after Morocco invaded and conquered the Songhai Empire, which had dominated West African trade. This conquest destroyed much of the infrastructure that had supported the caravan network. In the aftermath of the Songhai Empire's collapse, Portuguese trading posts filled the political and economic vacuum, delivering unprecedented numbers of African slaves as well as gold to Europe.

New Maritime Empires

European powers raced to establish maritime empires in the Americas to exploit the continents' rich resources. The Portuguese established a new maritime empire in present-day Brazil during the first half of the sixteenth century. Initially, the Portuguese privatized colonization, and the territory was divided into fifteen separate colonies. Portuguese noblemen funded and controlled these colonies, but they failed for a variety of reasons, including agricultural issues, conflicts with Amerindians, and disputes among the noblemen. To save the floundering enterprise, King John III placed Brazil under royal control in 1542. The newly formed central government consolidated its control by conquering the Amerindians and thwarting French attempts at colonizing northern Brazil. In addition, the government converted much of the land into sugarcane plantations, and the intense labor demands led to the importation of African slaves. In the early seventeenth century, the Dutch attempted to seize control over sugarcane production in northwestern Brazil. However, Portuguese forces expelled the Dutch in 1654, leaving Portugal as the uncontested power in Brazil.

The Spanish maritime empire was unprecedented, and it included a substantial amount of territory in the present-day United States, Mexico, Central America, the Caribbean, and South America. In order to construct this empire, Spain had to conquer several advanced Amerindian civilizations. The Spanish conquistador Hernán Cortés launched a campaign against the Aztec Empire in present-day Mexico. Cortés made a strategic alliance with the Tlaxcala city-state, a historic rival of the Aztecs, and the Aztec Empire collapsed in 1521. Another conquistador, Francisco Pizarro, conquered the Inca Empire in 1533. As a result, Spain assumed control over territory in present-day Peru, Bolivia, Argentina, Chile, and Colombia. Other Spanish conquistadors defeated the Muisca Confederation in present-day Colombia as well as numerous Mayan city-states in Central America. Spain divided its massive territories into viceroys, which functioned as provincial administrative states. Along with defending the territories, the viceroys were primarily tasked with mining gold and silver.

The Netherlands relied on the Dutch West India Company to construct its maritime empire. After sponsoring Henry Hudson's voyage to North America, the company established permanent colonies on the Eastern Seaboard of the present-day United States. These colonies were known as **New Netherlands**, and they primarily focused on fur trapping. However, the Dutch had difficulty populating their North American colonies. The most successful colony was New Amsterdam, which was located in present-day New York City. Following their defeat in the Third Anglo-Dutch War, the Dutch ceded New Netherlands to England in 1674. The Dutch also competed with France, England, and Spain in the Caribbean, and they established several successful sugarcane plantations on a series of islands known as the Dutch Antilles.

Colonialism

Although the European explorers never did discover an effective northwest passage to Asia, Europe quickly realized the economic value of their discovery. Mercantilist economic policies viewed the exploitation of colonies and slaves as a positive because it increased the wealth of the home country. Often European nations sought wealth, first through the possibility of finding areas rich in gold, then through agricultural endeavors. The colonies were a way for a country to import goods from their own colonies, becoming more self-sufficient and reducing their reliance on trade with rival powers. As the trade routes became more efficient and the colonies more stable, the transfer of slaves for plantation work in sugar cane and tobacco fields became an ever-increasing source of revenue. To incentivize the creation of permanent colonies, colonists were often given more freedoms than in their home country. Colonial populations also increased as a result of religious persecution throughout Europe.

Spain set up the first colonies in the Caribbean Islands, Florida, California, Mexico, and South America. New Spain, as they called their colonies, was established in the mid-1500s. In 1565, the fort, St. Augustine, was established in modern-day Florida, making it the oldest European settlement in the modern-day United States. Colonies founded by the French, Dutch, and English in the Americas began in the 1600s, including settlements along the eastern coast of North America, eastern Canada, Newfoundland, Great Lakes area, and later along the Mississippi River. In 1624, the Dutch, seeking arable ground, established the New Amsterdam settlement near modern-day Manhattan, which would become an important trading center. The English would capture the New Amsterdam settlement in 1664 and rename it New York City, after the Duke of York.

Sir Walter Raleigh sent an expedition to settle land in the Americas in 1585. The initial attempt to settle Roanoke Island, North Carolina, failed, and the colonists sailed back to England with Sir Francis Drake, who arrived after successfully raiding and pillaging the Spanish colonies in the Caribbean. A second attempt in 1587 also failed. The fate of the lost colony remains disputed as a relief ship, returning to the area in 1591, found no trace of the settlement. England's first permanent settlement was founded in Jamestown, Virginia, in 1607, and subsequently the Virginia Colony was established.

In 1620, the Pilgrims, an English religious group of Anglicans and Separatists, settled in the Cape Cod Bay area of Massachusetts and drew up their own plans for governing their colony. After enduring religious persecution in England, the Mayflower Compact detailed the plan for a colony founded in fair and just laws, offering citizenship to all adult males. Unlike most other colonies, the Plymouth colony did not have a royal charter, so the Mayflower Compact is unique in that it provided one of the first forms of self-government in the colonies. By their eighth year, the Pilgrims had successfully established the Massachusetts Bay Colony, the second of the eventual thirteen British colonies in North America.

The rest of the thirteen colonies formed when royal charters were granted, either to individuals or corporations. The thirteen colonies were allowed limited self-rule. A governor for the colonies was appointed by England, but each colony could rule by its own laws enacted by colonial assemblies. The method in which these men were appointed, and the laws of each colony, differed based on the type of charter each had, if any. In royal colonies, those of Virginia, Massachusetts, New Hampshire, New York, New Jersey, North Carolina, South Carolina, and Georgia, the king of England was the direct authority of the colony and chose the governor, among other things. Proprietary colonies, which included Pennsylvania, Delaware, and Maryland, were under the authority of the owner of the colony, while Rhode Island and Connecticut were self-governing and had no direct authority.

The colonies were divided into sections: New England, Middle Colonies, and Southern Colonies. New England's economy was based on fishing and forest harvesting. The Middle Colonies had arable ground and developed a farming economy with heavy yields in wheat for export. The Southern Colonies, having a warm climate like southern Europe, with rich soil, grew crops such as tobacco, rice, and cotton. By the 1700s, the thirteen colonies were invaluable, making England much wealthier. In early years of colonization, indentured servitude provided much-needed labor. These servants pledged a certain amount of years, usually between five and seven, to pay for their passage and some land and tools to become prosperous citizens once their indentured time was completed. Initially, Africans came as indentured servants. This occurred first in Jamestown in 1619; however, by the late 1600s, slavery within all of the colonies was introduced. The bulk of African slaves were used in the Southern Colonies to work on plantations.

From the 1500s to the 1700s, Spain and Portugal colonized the areas of Mexico, the West Indies, and places in South America. Later, the French and English would gain control of places in the Caribbean Islands and the West Indies. Unlike the thirteen colonies, Spanish rule was authoritarian and centralized, with the government having more power and fewer restrictions. The economies in Mexico, the West Indies, and Latin America were based on mining, plantations, and livestock. Slave labor was in heavy use. In no other place was the Roman Catholic Church more influential abroad than the colonies of the southern Americas. They were second only to the Spanish government, having influence politically and socially. The church owned nearly half of the land, with church officials being part of the wealthy landowning aristocracy.

Founded in 1788, the British colony in Australia was originally a penal colony populated by convicts deported from Britain. Between 1788 and 1868, more than 160,000 British convicts were transported to the Australian penal colony. Criminals were used to settle the area and work the land. If they finished their sentence, they could begin to work for themselves. Many had families that were freed from forced labor. The fertile areas of Australia were used for crop raising and grazing sheep. More and more land was seized from the Aboriginal Australians for agriculture and grazing, pushing the Aboriginals into the less desirable desert region. By the mid-nineteenth century, Australia would be a desirable place for non-convicts due to numerous gold rushes and a booming agricultural industry. Established in 1841, the nearby New Zealand colonists similarly drove out the native Maori tribes and used their land to graze sheep and raise crops. Unlike Australia, New Zealand was never used as a penal colony, though some of its occupants were escaped convicts. Most settlers were former sailors, whalers, or sealers. The exportation of exotic woods, and later the capture and trade of natives into slavery in Australia, were sources of revenue for the colony.

The introduction of new diseases to the Aborigines and the Maoris decimated their numbers. The Maoris' numbers decreased significantly again when, after adopting the English musket as a method of warfare, intertribal wars led to more deadly conflicts. Like Australia, the New Zealand settlers also pushed out the native people, leading to a series of armed conflicts between 1845 and 1872, collectively known as the *New Zealand Wars*. In the end, the settlers prevailed, and the number of Maoris greatly diminished.

Attempts were made to colonize Africa, but disease, resistance, and the difficult terrain caused Europe to limit settlements to trade ports and coastal forts. However, through colonization, indigenous African civilizations were decimated by the slave trade.

European Renaissance and Reformation

The Italian Renaissance

The Renaissance, meaning *rebirth*, began in the fourteenth century in Italy and spread throughout Europe during the fifteenth century. Its philosophy was humanism, or the study of man and his relationship with the world. It was a time when reason and knowledge were highly valued. The Roman Catholic Church kept pace with Europe's focus on mankind and nature, instead of heaven and heavenly beings. Popes sponsored educational enhancements and were, in some instances, as is the case with Pope Pius II, trained as classical scholars. In the early 1500s, Julius II had masters such as Michelangelo create artistic masterpieces that celebrated humans. Indeed, the arts moved toward a more realistic and proportional style with Italian painters such as Leonardo da Vinci, Raphael, and Titian leading the way.

The literary greats of the age were writing in their own vernacular, or language, instead of Latin. This was one of the greatest leaps forward; it not only built their native language, but it also allowed the Italian people to learn and grow in literacy. This and the advances in printing made the written word more accessible and widely dispersed than ever before. The dissemination of knowledge to larger groups of people would change the world, especially as the Renaissance spread to other European nations.

Renaissance in Northern Europe

The ideas in Italy began to spread northward, allowing the arts to flourish in Germany, such as Albrecht Dürer, and in the Netherlands, like Johannes Vermeer and Rembrandt. England began a long history of great literature with Geoffrey Chaucer's *The Canterbury Tales* and Edmund Spenser's *The Faerie Queene*. The highest literary achievements of the Renaissance came from two English playwrights, Christopher Marlowe and his better-known contemporary, William Shakespeare. But the Renaissance did not stray far from religious themes; instead, they humanized them, as is the case of Italian works of art. It was also an early changing point in Christianity, as theologians like Meister Eckhart, Thomas à Kempis, and Sir Thomas More began to use humanism to question the need for priestly intervention, favoring instead direct worship of God.

The invention of movable type by Johannes Gutenberg in 1439 started a revolution in printing that saw the expansion of books go from approximately 100,000 laboriously hand-copied books in Europe to over 9 million by 1500. The literacy rate in Europe improved vastly, as did the printing of religious writings. News could now travel to distant places, allowing for unprecedented communication both locally and globally. Movable type would be one of the major inventions of the Renaissance, heavily influencing the Reformation and Enlightenment.

The Reformation

In 1517, Martin Luther, a German monk and professor of theology, nailed his famous *Ninety-Five Theses,* or *Disputation on the Power of Indulgences,* to the door of the cathedral in Wittenberg, Germany. Pope Leo X demanded Luther to rescind, but Luther stood his ground, which launched the Protestant Reformation. There were serious problems in the Catholic Church, including clergy accepting simony, or the sale of church offices; pluralism, or having multiple offices; and the violation of vows. In addition, the worldly behavior of the church leaders and the biblical ignorance of the lower clergy prompted Luther to ignite a fire that could not be swept away or cleared up. The Roman Catholic Church could not weather this call for reform like it had done before. This was instead a call to cast off the Catholic faith for Protestantism. Many church denominations were formed under Protestantism, the first being Lutheranism, which gained strength in Germany and Switzerland.

Shortly after, the Roman Catholic Church issued a Counter Reformation in an attempt to quell the spread of Protestantism by addressing some of the complaints. In its initial stages, the Counter Reformation had little effect, and many Germans adopted Lutheranism as its officially recognized religion. By 1555, the Catholic Church recognized Lutheranism under the Peace of Augsburg, which allowed rulers to decide on which religion their kingdom would follow. In Germany there was peace, but civil wars broke out in France and the Netherlands. The Spanish-ruled Netherlands' struggle was as political as it was social, with other countries joining the fight against Catholic Spain.

In the 1600s, the peace in Germany faded as the country allied itself with either the Protestant Union or the Catholic League. The Thirty Years' War broke out in 1618 and became one of the most destructive wars in European history. It was a war of political and religious hostility that would involve Germany, Denmark, France, Austria, Spain, and Sweden, to some degree. Though it ended in 1648 with the Peace of Westphalia, France and Spain would wage war until 1659. The Treaty of Westphalia emphasized national self-determination, which directly led to the development of the nation-state. For the first time in human history, local people controlled the right to build a nation-state with the accompanying legitimacy to control their region. The new states, most of which were carved out of the Holy Roman Empire, were allowed to determine their religion, including Catholicism, Lutheranism, and Calvinism.

The Enlightenment

In the Enlightenment, also known as the *Age of Reason,* that followed the Renaissance, Europe began to move toward a view that men were capable of improving the world, including themselves, through rational thinking. The Enlightenment placed a heavy emphasis on individualism and rationalism. During the Renaissance, scholars looked at the Middle Ages as a lost period and considered their own time as modern and new. The Enlightenment, building on the foundations of humanism, began a prolific era of literature, philosophy, and invention.

By the 1700s, Europe had entered the High Enlightenment Age, where events started to take place as a result of the rational thought promoted by the first half of the age. The idea that everything in the universe could be reasoned and cataloged became a theme that set Diderot to work at the first encyclopedia and inspired Thomas Paine and Thomas Jefferson during the initial political unrest in the American colonies.

In the later years of the Enlightenment, the ideal vision that society could be reborn through reason was tested in the French Revolution of 1789. Instead of becoming a leader in rational thinking and orderly government, the revolution turned into the Reign of Terror that saw the mass execution of French citizens and opened the way for the rise of Napoleon.

European Expansion

Columbian Exchange

European exploration in North America dates back to around 1000 AD when Scandinavian Vikings, led by Leif Eriksson, first made their way to Greenland and then journeyed on to modern-day Newfoundland. They settled briefly in an area now known as L'Anse Meadows. However, clashes with the Native American people living nearby caused them to return to Greenland a few years later. The first permanent settlements in North America began after Italian sailor Christopher Columbus landed in the Caribbean in 1492. This was a significant breakthrough since most Europeans did not know that this huge landmass even existed. It initiated a period of discovery, conquest, and colonization of the Americas by the Europeans. Often referred to as the *Columbian Exchange*, this period allowed people who had been cut off from each other for 15,000 years to share knowledge, ideas, culture, food, plants and animals, technology, and religion; this led to significant changes and enhancements for both regions.

Atlantic Slave Trade

Slavery is believed to be as old as civilization itself, likely beginning during the First Agricultural Revolution nearly ten thousand years ago. The enslavement of human beings was integral to such early civilizations as Egypt, China, the Mayan Empire, Greece, and Rome. Nevertheless, race did not become the primary driving force behind human captivity and forced labor until the so-called Age of Exploration. Previously, slaves were held captive as prisoners of war. In the case of Egypt, the Jews were enslaved because of their ethnic origins and religious beliefs, but not their race. Race is a construct that did not develop fully until the Early Modern period of world history. Once the Europeans made contact with the New World, they developed a new system of slavery in the Atlantic World that categorized black and indigenous persons as naturally inferior.

The Transatlantic Slave Trade was built upon the foundations of the need for cheap labor. Slavery in the Americas became a hereditary phenomenon during the peak centuries of the Transatlantic Slave Trade. This slave trade was also economic in origin: The sugar and tobacco plantations of the Americas demanded an excess of cheap or free labor. Initially, European Americans looked to Native Americans as their enslaved labor supply. Quickly, however, millions of Native Americans died because of the spread of unfamiliar diseases. By the 18th century, the slave trade industry grew because of the higher labor demands. This slave trade lasted from the 1400s well into the late nineteenth century.

Impact of Political, Economic, and Cultural Imperialism on Both Colonizers and the Colonized

Expansion of the Ottoman Empire

The Ottoman Empire came into existence in the early 1300s as the Byzantine Empire's grasp on the Middle East and Balkans slowly dwindled. Anatolian Turks—a group of militaristic nomads—began to settle in the region formerly known as Christian Byzantium. These Turks believed they were ghazis, or warriors for Islam. They began raiding Christian territories in hopes of forcing these so-called infidels into submitting to their strict Islamic codes. The most successful ghazi at this time was named Osman I. Osman I became known as Othman by westerners, and he eventually adopted the name, calling his followers Ottomans. At first, the Ottomans acted kindly to the people they conquered, protecting them with Turkish armies.

The dramatic expansion of the Ottoman Empire, however, did not occur until nearly 150 years after its founding. Under the leadership of such powerful conquerors as Mehmet II, the Ottoman Empire expanded rapidly in the late 1400s and 1500s. Mehmet II is famous for conquering the Christian capital of Constantinople and renaming it Istanbul in 1453. In the century that followed, the Ottoman Empire was led by three more powerful sultans who expanded the empire into North Africa, Mesopotamia, the Middle East, the Balkans, Egypt, and eastern Europe. From the late 1500s until the end of World War I, the Ottoman Empire entered a period of slow decline. Internal corruption and external conflicts brought the empire to its knees. At the end of World War I, the Ottoman Empire was finally dissolved with the creation of Turkey.

Conquest of the Aztec

Hernàn Cortés was the first great Spanish explorer and conquistador, and he conquered present-day Mexico, defeating the mighty Aztec Empire. Within two years of his landing in 1519, most of the vast Aztec Empire fell under Spanish rule. Gold and silver were the prizes for the Spanish in Mexico, as they robbed the Aztecs of much of their precious metals. Francisco Pizarro explored modern-day Peru and conquered the Incan Empire in 1533, making it the second of the two most powerful ancient civilizations in the history of the Americas to fall under Spanish rule. Spain sent thousands of new settlers to America to mine precious metals and start plantations and ranches.

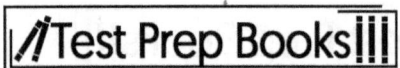

World History from 1750 A.D. to the Present

World Civilizations from 1750 A.D. to the Present

Prohibition and The Great Depression

Prohibition (the 18th Amendment to the US Constitution) was passed in 1919 and prohibited the production and sale of alcoholic beverages. This amendment fueled corruption since people made, sold, and transported liquor illegally. The 21st Amendment repealed it in 1933. Women had been campaigning for the right to vote since the 1840s, and these suffragettes used the outbreak of World War I to leverage their fight, stating they would help support the war if they were granted the right to vote. The 19th Amendment, which guaranteed women the right to vote in federal elections, was finally passed by Congress in 1919 and ratified the following year. On October 29, 1929 (referred to as Black Tuesday) the stock market crashed, marking the beginning of the Great Depression that lasted through the 1930s. President Franklin Delano Roosevelt's solution was the *New Deal*—a variety of new programs and laws to provide government funding to help rebuild America's economy.

Holocaust

Aside from the incredible casualties resulting from intense fighting and bombings of cities, World War II is marked by the worst war crimes in human history. Germany conducted a systematic genocide of six million Jewish people during the Holocaust, sending two-thirds of Europe's Jewish population to be executed in death camps. Millions of non-Jews were also exterminated during the Holocaust, including Slavs, Poles, Romani, people of color, Communists, homosexuals, and disabled people, among others. It is estimated that anywhere between six and eleven million people were executed in the Holocaust.

Decolonization

The start of decolonization in India occurred after World War I, with the Government of India Act of 1919. While the war was raging, Britain promised India more self-rule if they supported the war effort. However, the act did not grant freedom in taxation, foreign policy, or justice and only went as far as allowing local matters to be addressed by native-born citizens. For the Indian National Congress, India's largest political party, this fell short of what they had expected. In the 1920s, Mahatma Gandhi, leader of the Indian National Congress, protested using civil disobedience. In August 1947, England granted independence to India and split the British Indian Empire into India and Pakistan.

Political Revolutions and Movements of the Eighteenth Through the Twentieth Centuries

American Revolution

The American Revolution occurred as a result of changing values in the Thirteen Colonies that broke from their traditional relationship with England. Early on in the colonization of North America, the colonial social structure tried to mirror the stratified order of Great Britain. In England, the landed elites were seen as intellectually and morally superior to the common man, which led to a paternalistic relationship. This style of governance was similarly applied to the colonial system; government was left to the property-owning upper class, and the colonies as a whole could be seen as a child dutifully serving Mother England.

However, the colonies' distance from England meant that actual, hereditary aristocrats from Britain only formed a small percentage of the overall population and did not even fill all the positions of power. By the mid-eighteenth century, much of the American upper class consisted of local families who acquired status through business rather than lineage. Despite this, representatives from Britain were appointed to govern the colonies. As a result, a rift began to form between the colonists and British officials.

Uncertain about whether they should remain loyal to Britain, representatives from twelve colonies formed the First Continental Congress in 1774 to discuss what they should do next. When Patriot militiamen at Lexington and Concord fought British soldiers in April 1775, the Revolutionary War began. While the rebel forces worked to present the struggle as a united, patriotic effort, the colonies remained divided throughout the war. Thousands of colonists, known as Loyalists or Tories, supported Britain. Even the revolutionaries proved to be significantly fragmented, and many militias only served in their home states. The Continental Congress was also divided over whether to reconcile with Britain or push for full separation. These issues hindered the ability of the revolutionary armies to resist the British, who had superior training and resources at their disposal.

Even so, the Continental Army, under General George Washington, gradually built up a force that utilized Prussian military training and backwoods guerrilla tactics to make up for their limited resources. Although the British forces continued to win significant battles, the Continental Army gradually reduced Britain's will to fight as the years passed. Furthermore, Americans appealed to the rivalry that other European nations had with the British Empire. The support was initially limited to indirect assistance, but aid gradually increased. After the American victory at the Battle of Saratoga in 1777, France and other nations began to actively support the American cause by providing much-needed troops and equipment.

In 1781, the primary British army under General Cornwallis was defeated by an American and French coalition at Yorktown, Virginia, which paved the way for peace negotiations. The Treaty of Paris in 1783 ended the war, recognized the former colonies' independence from Great Britain, and gave America control over territory between the Appalachian Mountains and Mississippi River. However, the state of the new nation was still uncertain. The new nation's government initially stemmed from the state-based structure of the Continental Congress and was incorporated into the Articles of Confederation in 1777.

French Revolution

Unlike the United States' revolution against a ruler across the ocean, the French Revolution was an internal fight. In 1789, tension between the lower class (peasants) and middle class (bourgeois) and the extravagant wealthy upper class of France came to a head. The Old Regime, headed by the monarchy, was overthrown, and the Third Estate, made up of the bourgeois class, seized power. The American Revolution, overtaxation, years of bad harvests, drastic income inequality, and the Enlightenment influenced the French Revolution. In August 1789, the National Constituent Assembly, a democratic assembly formed during the French Revolution, passed the Declaration of the Rights of Man and of the Citizen, which defined the natural right of men to be free and equal under the law. Unlike the American Revolution, however, the French Revolution led to the brutal murders of French aristocrats and other political leaders and the French government was eventually overthrown by Napoleon Bonaparte in 1799, effectively ending the French Revolution. Napoleon declared himself emperor of France in 1804 and then attempted to conquer Europe.

Napoleon

France radically changed the government from a monarchy to a democracy with provisions for civil rights, religious freedoms, and decriminalization of various morality crimes, like same-sex relationships. Two political powers emerged: liberal republicans called *Girondists* and radical revolutionaries, known as Jacobins. Conflict between the parties resulted in the Reign of Terror—a period of mass executions—and eventually the rise of Napoleon who set up a nationalist military dictatorship. During the revolution, Napoleon Bonaparte consolidated power after becoming famous for his heroism during the revolutionary wars against Britain, Austria, and other monarchies that sought to retain their right of royal rule. However, by 1804, Napoleon declared himself emperor and remilitarized France, and he conquered most of Europe in a series of global conflicts collectively known as the Napoleonic Wars, starting in 1803 and continuing until Napoleon's defeat at the Battle of Waterloo in 1815.

After the chaos sparked by the French Revolution that fanned across Europe during the revolutionary wars, European powers met at the Congress of Vienna in November 1814 to June 1815 to rebalance power and restore old boundaries. The Congress of Vienna carved out new territories, changing the map of Europe. France lost all of its conquered territories, while Prussia, Austria, and Russia expanded their own. With the restoration of a balance of power, Europe enjoyed nearly fifty years of peace.

Latin American Wars of Independence

Fueled by the successful American and French Revolutions and the writings of the Enlightenment, a spirit of revolution swept across the Americas. The French colony in Haiti was the first major revolution occurring in 1791. The Haitian Revolution was the largest slave uprising since the Roman Empire, and it holds a unique place in history because it is the only slave uprising to establish a slave-free nation ruled by nonwhites and former slaves. In 1804, the Haitians achieved independence from France and became the first independent nation in Latin America.

When Napoleon conquered Spain in 1808, Latin American colonies refused to recognize his elder brother, Joseph Bonaparte, as the new Spanish monarch and advocated for their own independence. Known as the Latin American Wars of Independence, Venezuela, Colombia, Ecuador, Argentina, Uruguay, Paraguay, Chile, Peru, and Bolivia all achieved independence between 1810 and 1830. In 1824, Mexico declared itself a republic when, after several attempts by the lower classes of Mexico to revolt against Spain, the wealthier classes joined and launched a final and successful revolt. When Napoleon overtook Portugal in 1807, King John VI fled to Brazil and set up court. John VI returned to Portugal in 1821 and left his son Pedro behind to rule Brazil. In 1822 Pedro launched a revolution against Portugal that saw him crowned emperor of Brazil.

By the mid-1800s, the revolutions of Latin America ceased and only a few areas remained under European rule. The U.S. President James Monroe issued the Monroe Doctrine (1823), which stated that the Americas could no longer be colonized. It was an attempt to stop European nations, especially Spain, from colonizing areas, or attempting to recapture areas, they had previously colonized. England's navy contributed to the success of the doctrine, as they were eager to increase trade with the Americas and establish an alliance with the United States.

Simon Bolivar

Simon Bolivar was a wealthy Venezuelan creole who helped inaugurate a chain of revolutions in South America in the early nineteenth century. Declaring independence from Spain in 1811, Simon Bolivar and his fellow revolutionaries entered a brutal war with its former Mother Country. At first, Bolivar and his army suffered a series of devastating defeats at the hands of the Spanish army in Venezuela. In August 1819, after years of a back-and-forth struggle for independence, Bolivar, who had previously been forced into exile, marched across the Andes Mountains with two thousand men to face the Spanish army in modern-day Colombia. This daring tactic proved to be fruitful—Bolivar surprised the Spanish army in Bogota, inaugurating a decisive victory. In 1821, in just two years after this infamous sneak attack, Simon Bolivar and his revolutionaries officially won their independence. However, the independence of Venezuela was not enough for the famous creole rebel—Bolivar continued marching south into Ecuador, meeting up with fellow revolutionary Jose de San Martin. The meeting of these two revolutionaries catalyzed yet another string of hard-fought independences in South America.

Russian Revolution

The first shots of the Russian Revolution occurred on January 22, 1905, as a result of a growing discontent among workers and their families. The Russian masses rose up against the government in response to the rapid industrialization of the nation, which paved the way to the unchecked economic exploitation of Russian citizens. Anger over socioeconomic inequalities encouraged workers to push back against the oppressive rule of Russian czars such as Nicholas II. These agitated workers not only protested against the government, but also against the traditions of the Russian Orthodox Church. On January 22, 1905, hundreds of thousands of workers and peasants stormed the czar's Winter Palace in St. Petersburg, demanding better working conditions and an elected national legislature. At this time, czar Nicolas II of Russia was not in his palace. However, his generals ordered soldiers to fire on the angry mob of 200,000-plus people. Nearly one thousand unarmed citizens were killed as a result. This day, known as Bloody Sunday, provoked a wave of strikes and violence that eventually encouraged Nicholas II to establish some political reform, including the creation of the Duma, Russia's first parliament.

Nonetheless, the Duma remained essentially powerless, as the czar dissolved it in less than ten weeks. This angered the people even more, setting the stage for the March Revolution of 1917, which witnessed the creation of a provisional Soviet government. The March Revolution succeeded in forcing Nicholas II to abdicate his throne, but it failed to create a strong central government. The weakened provisional Soviet government eventually toppled as a result of the Bolshevik Revolution in the fall of 1917. The Bolshevik Revolution was led by Vladimir Lenin, who eventually quelled a civil war and carried out Marxist political reforms that were integral in establishing the USSR.

Political, Economic, and Cultural Expansion

British Empire
The British Empire stretched across the world, and at one point had over 450 million people under its rule. With the loss of its American colonies, England began to focus on other areas of the world. In the mid-1700s, India was the first target of British imperialism. Opposition to the ruling Mughal Empire allowed the British army an inroad at the Battle of Plassey in 1757, where General Robert Clive and his army overtook Bengal in northeast India. Next, the British forced the Mughal emperor to give all tax-collecting rights to England. In 1784, Parliament passed the East India Company Act, also known as Pitt's India Act, which brought the East India Company's rule in India under control of the British government. Railway systems to expedite the shipment of goods to Great Britain were built, and a new government called the British Raj was established. Indians were educated to work in the government and, at first, used their education to promote reform in India. Many of these civil service workers would take on the mantle of nationalism and advocate for India's independence. Great Britain further expanded its empire into areas of Africa and solidified its rule in Australia, capitalizing on exports from Australia and Canada. It also had what is seen as an informal empire in China and other nations due to its ability to dominate trade and influence economic policy.

Japanese Imperialism
Imperialism was also seen in Japan, a country that moved from a primitive and feudal system to a strong empire quickly and overtook Taiwan, Korea, many islands in the Pacific Ocean, and parts of China. It was not until the end of World War II that Japan was forced to surrender control of its accumulated empire. Germany, Russia, and the Ottoman Empire also gained land through imperialism during the years before World War I, most of which was lost by the end of the Great War.

Industrial Revolution

Economic Revolution
During the Renaissance, commercial trade was revived and caused a revolution in the European marketplace and economy. The division of labor, urbanization, and population growth led to a more advanced market economy. Europeans were buying what they had historically made for themselves and were working in a particular trade, which transformed the economy and increased commercial productivity. By 1760, the Industrial Revolution began in England and revolutionized commerce when mechanized textile manufacturing, steam power, and iron making became the norm.

Europe mainly traded among itself, as India and China were not interested in Europe's exports, seeing them as primitive. Europe, however, desired the spices, silk, and tea only available from the East. China especially demanded coin money for exchanges, which at first made it difficult and expensive to purchase such items. The need for a monetary system was evident. During the sixteenth century, European countries would adopt mercantilism as their economic policy, which promoted governmental regulation of the country's economy for the purposes of increasing national wealth. Mercantilist policies developed national currencies, monetary reserves, and positive trade balances to ensure that imports exceeded exports. The Commercial Revolution transformed Europe from a humble trading system into a sophisticated market economy with banking, stocks, and government protection to promote trade. The revolution of trade coincided with exploration and colonization, which brought slave labor into the market, further increasing productivity.

Industrial Revolution

While Europe was in the midst of colonization and revolutions, they experienced an industrial revolution that would impact the social and economic fabric of life. Starting in the 1760s, with humble origins in England's textile economy, it lasted until the 1820s and changed the way people worked and lived. The revolution brought new scientific developments and improvements to agriculture and textile manufacturing. It was also a time of great invention in steam- and water-powered engines, machines, tools, chemicals, transportation, factories, lighting, glass, cement, medicines, and many more. Additional information concerning the Industrial Revolution and the Second Industrial Revolution are included in the section called The Major Economic Transformations that Have Affected World Societies.

In some ways, it improved people's standard of living, but in many ways, it made life harder. Falling prices on goods made nutrition levels improve and allowed people more buying power. Medicines and better transportation also improved the quality of life for many. However, crowded living quarters in the booming urban centers were often appalling, as were the diseases brought on by working in factory conditions. The use of child labor eventually brought about reform, and labor unions had an effect on working conditions, but it took many years for either of these problems to be properly addressed.

Totalitarianism in the Twentieth Century

Totalitarianism is a political ideology where the state controls all aspects of public and private life. It is an extreme version of authoritarianism, which is only concerned with the state consolidating political power and retaining dominance over the political system. In contrast, totalitarianism utilizes extensive propaganda, surveillance, and state-controlled mass media to dictate all aspects of life within the country. Totalitarianism often involves a single political party led by a dictator, oppression of political opponents, state monopoly over weapons and communication, centralized political direction and economic control, and the use of terror, such as a secret police. Fascism is a form of totalitarianism that became popular in Europe after World War I. Fascists advocated for an all-powerful government led by a strong dictator that would be prepared for total war and the mass mobilization of resources for the benefit of the state. Fascism is often tied with nationalism.

Adolf Hitler's Nazi Party is the most infamous example of a fascist totalitarian government. Italy was also considered a fascist regime in the years between 1922 and 1943, with Benito Mussolini as the head of government. Italy allied with Nazi Germany in World War II. The Union of Soviet Socialist Republics had emerged through the Bolshevik Revolution in 1917 in Russia and militantly supported Communism—a socialist system of government that called for the overthrow of capitalism. Although the Soviet Union formed an alliance with the United States during World War II, relations chilled, and the Cold War began in 1947. Although no true war was declared between the two nations, both the Union of Soviet Socialist Republics and the United States engaged in indirect conflict by supporting and overthrowing foreign governments.

World War I and World War II

First World War

The onset of World War I began with the precarious balance of power and the geographic divisions written by the Napoleonic Wars' Vienna Congress.

Austria-Hungary's large empire was diverse in culture and included various peoples of several nationalities, languages, and beliefs. However, minorities in their lands in the Balkans grew tired of foreign control. This was especially true in Bosnia, which was all but under control by the nationalistic secret military society, the Black Hand. This nationalistic sentiment grew until, in 1914, Gavrilo Princip, a Serb patriot and member of the Black Hand, assassinated Archduke Franz Ferdinand, heir presumptive to the throne of Austria-Hungary. In response, Emperor Franz Joseph I of Austria-Hungary declared war on the kingdom of Serbia, officially launching the First World War.

Europe had tied itself into a tangled web of alliances and mutual protection pacts. Germany and Austria-Hungary were allies. Russia promised protection to France and Serbia, and England maintained a tacit support to its past allies throughout the mainland. Each of the Allies soon mobilized to support each other. Germany had already planned for declarations of war, however, and was nervous about fighting a two-border war against both France and Russia, so it developed the Schlieffen Plan—a strategy to quickly demolish French resistance before turning around to fight Russia on the Eastern Front. However, this plan relied on the neutrality of England; after Germany invaded Belgium to attack France, England's declaration of war ensured that a long war would be inevitable.

The Great War lasted from 1914 to 1918 and was the deadliest war in European history until World War II, with approximately 16 million combatants and civilians dying in the conflict. The carnage was largely a result of technological innovation outpacing military tactics. World War I was the first military conflict to deploy millions of soldiers and the first war to involve telephones, tanks, aircrafts, chemical weapons, and heavy artillery. These twentieth-century technological innovations were deployed alongside outdated military tactics, particularly trench warfare. As a result, hundreds of thousands of troops would die during battles without achieving any meaningful strategic gains. Countries were devastated by the loss of the male population and struggled to cope with a depleted workforce, and widows and orphans struggled to regain any degree of normalcy.

Due to the high death tolls, the Allies' need of financial support, and the anger associated with the war, the Treaty of Versailles harshly punished Germany, who the Allies blamed for the war. The Allies coerced Germany into signing the treaty that was a death sentence to their country's economy. It contained a guilt clause, which, unlike the Congress of Vienna's terms for the similarly belligerent France, made oppressive demands on Germany. The treaty took German lands, enforced a heavy reparations debt that was impossible to pay, and stripped Germany of its colonies. After suffering enormous losses during the war itself, the Treaty of Versailles ensured that no national recovery would be possible.

In the aftermath, Russia, Italy, and Germany turned to totalitarian governments, and colonies of Europe started to have nationalistic, anticolonial movements. The Russian Revolution of 1917 led to a civil war in which the Bolsheviks, or Communists, took control under the guidance of Communist revolutionary Vladimir Lenin and established the Soviet Union. The Communist government turned into a dictatorship when Stalin emerged as leader in 1924. Stalin ruled with an iron fist and executed all of his political opponents, including the Bolsheviks. Dissatisfaction with the treaty in Italy led to the rise of fascist leader Benito Mussolini. Germany suffered through several small revolutions, splintering political parties, and class division; this, combined with wartime debt and hyperinflation—a result of the Treaty of Versailles—caused many to become desperate, especially during the throes of the Great Depression. Adolf Hitler, a popular leader in the National Socialist German Workers' Party (Nazi Party), organized street violence against Communists. In the 1932 parliamentary elections, the Nazis emerged as the largest party in the *Reichstag* (German Parliament), but the Nazis did not have enough votes to name Hitler as chancellor. The street violence against Communists and Jews continued unabated, and on January 30, 1933, political pressure led to President von Hindenburg naming Adolf Hitler the chancellor of Germany. Hitler immediately expelled Communists, the second most popular political party, from the *Reichstag*, and coerced the *Reichstag* to pass the Enabling Act of 1933, effectively creating a dictatorship.

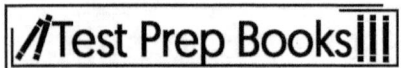

Second World War

Nazi Germany had risen to power through the 1920s and 1930s, with Hitler's belief that Germany would only recover its honor if it had a resounding military victory over Europe. Nazi ideology adhered to an extreme nationalism advocating for the superiority of the German people and the necessity of expanding their lands into an empire. Jews, Communists, and other nonconformists were banned from political and social participation.

In 1936, German troops violated the Treaty of Versailles by moving outside Germany's borders, with a remilitarization of the Rhineland. The Rome-Berlin Axis, an alliance between Germany and Italy, was forged in the same year. Germany was the only European power to support Italy's invasion and annexation of Ethiopia, and in exchange, Italy supported Germany's annexation of Austria. In 1936, a civil war broke out in Spain between Spanish nationalist rebels and the government of the Spanish Republic. Mussolini and Hitler supported the Spanish nationalist general Francisco Franco and used the Spanish Civil War as a testing ground for their new alliance. The Allies did not respond to these actions, and when Germany demanded the return of the Sudetenland, a territory in Czechoslovakia, France and Great Britain agreed in hopes of an appeasement despite the protests of the Czech government. Hitler then moved into more areas farther afield, which prompted the Soviet Union to sign a nonaggression pact with Germany. On September 1, 1939, Germany invaded Poland, and on September 3, 1939, France and Great Britain declared war on Germany, jumpstarting the deadliest conflict in world history.

Although less discussed than the Holocaust, the Japanese military committed similar war crimes across Asia, executing between three and ten million Chinese and Koreans, among others, between 1937 and 1945. In one event, the Rape of Nanking, Japanese soldiers captured Nanking and brutally murdered 300,000 civilians. An additional twenty thousand women, children, and elderly were raped during the massacre. Japanese newspapers closely covered a contest between two Japanese officers to see who could kill more people with a sword during the Rape of Nanking. Stalin also committed heinous war crimes during World War II, with estimates ranging from four to ten million deaths as a result of executions and sentences to the Gulag. The United States has also faced criticism for its decision to drop two nuclear bombs on the Japanese cities of Hiroshima and Nagasaki, killing more than 129,000 civilians, leveling both cities, and ending the war. The American government justified the use of nuclear weapons as the only way to avoid a ground invasion of Japan that would have cost more Japanese and American lives than the bombs.

Towns and cities had been leveled, civilian and soldier death tolls were crippling to economies, and countries struggled well into the 1950s to recover economically. It became a breeding ground for Communism, and in China, the end of the war meant a reprisal of the civil war between Mao Zedong's Communists and nationalists that had been interrupted by world war. Another result of the war was a changed map of the world, as countries were divided or newly formed, and the end of most of Britain's colonialism occurred as a result of the empire's economic and military losses. Following the war, Great Britain, France, Portugal, Belgium, Italy, the Netherlands, and Japan had either granted freedom to colonies or lost areas during the war. Many African and Middle Eastern countries would be granted their independence; however, the newly formed countries' borders were drawn according to those of the former colonies, creating ethnic and religious tensions that still exist today.

In an effort to stop a world war from occurring again, the Allies created the United Nations to be a safeguard and upholder of peace. This proved especially important, yet difficult, as the world was divided between a capitalist Western bloc and a Communist Eastern bloc. Germany was divided between the United States and Soviet Union to maintain peace and to better control the reconstruction of Germany; occupation zones were established, with East Germany occupied by the Soviet Union and West Germany occupied by Great Britain, France, and the United States.

World History | World History from 1750 A.D. to the Present

Spread and Fall of Communism and the Post-Cold War World

Cold War

Within two years of World War II, the world was involved in a different kind of war—a Cold War—that pitted capitalism and Communism against each other. World War II left Europe on the brink of collapse, leaving the United States and Soviet Union as the world's undisputed remaining superpowers. The United States and its Allies embarked on a campaign of containment in an attempt to keep Communism from spreading to other countries.

In the 1940s, U.S. president Harry S. Truman, in an effort to contain Communism, offered U.S. military and economic support to any nation threatened by Communist takeover, whether from external or internal forces. This became known as the Truman Doctrine (1947). In 1949, the United States, Canada, and ten European nations developed an alliance known as the North Atlantic Treaty Organization (NATO) based on the principles of the Truman Doctrine and preventing the spread of Communism. When West Germany was invited into NATO in 1955, the Soviet Union responded with a similar alliance known as the Warsaw Pact. The Warsaw Pact and NATO were vehicles for the United States and Soviet Union to flex their military might. In addition to conventional arms, the two superpowers competed in a nuclear arms race throughout the Cold War. The nuclear arms race resulted in a policy of deterrence known as mutual assured destruction (MAD) – the concept that, if one superpower detonated its nuclear missiles, the other would do the same and both would be destroyed. There were several close calls during the Cold War due to mixed signals, misunderstandings, or provocation—the most notorious being the Cuban Missile Crisis (October 1962) when the Soviet Union placed nuclear missiles in Cuba, ninety miles away from Florida.

The United States fought a series of proxy wars against the Soviet Union to prevent the spread of Communism. The Korean War, 1950 – 1953, was an attempt by Communist North Korea to take over nominally democratic, anti-Communist South Korea. Korea was part of the Japanese Empire until the end of World War II, when the Soviet Union and the United States divided it along the 38th Parallel into a northern zone, administered by the Soviets, and a southern zone, administered by the United States. North and South Korea became sovereign states during the Cold War, and each government claimed to be the only true government of Korea. After North Korea invaded South Korea in 1950, China and the Soviet Union joined together to support North Korea while the United Nations, particularly the United States, supported South Korea until an armistice was signed in 1953. The armistice established the Korean Demilitarized Zone (DMZ) that once again divided Korea into a Communist North and a democratic South, although it now deviates from the 38th Parallel. The 38th Parallel was an important demarcation during the war itself, as America was reluctant to pursue the North Koreans across the parallel and risk escalating the proxy war into a conventional one against the Soviets.

The Vietnam War, 1955 – 1975, was another proxy war pitting the United States against Communism. North Vietnam, supported by China and the Soviet Union, fought against South Vietnam, supported by the United States, South Korea, and other nations dedicated to preventing the spread of Communism. The North Vietnam military directed and supported the Viet Cong guerilla fighters, officially known as the National Liberation front of South Vietnam, who were a communist political organization in South Vietnam determined to overthrow the South Vietnamese government and unify Vietnam. Although the United States was the superior conventional military force, the American military struggled mightily against the guerilla tactics of the Viet Cong. As intense opposition to the war mounted in the United States, the United States withdrew (1973) and the North Vietnamese captured Saigon in April 1975. The war encompassed the Laotian Civil War and the Cambodian Civil war and ended with Vietnam, Laos, and Cambodia all falling to Communism. The Soviet Union similarly struggled against guerilla forces backed by the United States during the Soviet-Afghan War, which lasted from 1979 to 1989. The United States provided military and financial support to the Afghans during the conflict, many of whom would later found al-Qaeda or join the Taliban to fight the United States, including Osama bin Laden.

Protests and new leaders gave some economic freedom and recovery to these European nations after WWII, but East Germany was excluded. In 1961, a wall was built to separate East and West Germany in an attempt to keep

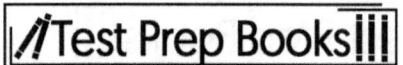

people from fleeing the Soviet-controlled East. However, in 1985, Mikhail Gorbachev became the Soviet leader and began to change politics in the Soviet Union, with *glasnost*—a policy of government transparency and openness—and *perestroika,* a government reform. He allowed the Eastern European satellite countries more economic freedom and limited self-government. The Soviet economy could not keep up with the United States, especially when President Reagan increased American military spending. Pushed to the brink of economic collapse, the Soviet Union could no longer maintain control over their satellites and Allies, who were increasingly agitated for complete autonomy. On November 9, 1989, the Soviet Union ordered the Berlin Wall to be knocked down, an important step toward thawing the Cold War. On December 26, 1991, the Soviet Union officially collapsed and broke up into fifteen distinct countries.

Post-Cold War World
The collapse of the Soviet Union left the United States as the sole world superpower. In addition, Communism no longer represented a viable political ideology, cementing the market economy as the leading economic system, which is later discussed in greater detail. In the mid-1990s, the Internet emerged as a driving force in globalization, connecting people across the world and providing instantaneous access to vast stores of information. Globalization further presented itself in the form of supranational governance. In 1992, the European Union was established for the purpose of creating a common market for goods and capital. Other supranational political entities would lead the way toward the creation of a globalized economy.

Founded in 1995, the World Trade Organization is a supranational organization composed of 164 member states, and it establishes regulations, norms, and dispute resolution to govern trade agreements between countries. Trade agreements between two entities are referred to as bilateral agreements, and any larger type of agreement is classified as multilateral. The entity entering into the trade agreement can be either a single nation-state or a trade bloc—an informal group of countries who negotiate as a single entity. The most common type of trade agreement is free trade, which offers preferential treatment through the elimination of trade restrictions, like tariffs and quotas. Trade agreements force countries to rely on the economic health of their trade partners, which naturally leads to interdependence. Examples of trade agreements include the North America Free Trade Agreement and Association of Southeast Asian Nations.

Trade agreements form the basis of a globalized economy as countries seek to maximize the economic principle of economies of scale, which defines how countries can function most efficiently within markets and vis-à-vis competitors. It encourages countries to specialize in what they do best and devote the bulk of their resources to maximizing that specialty. In theory, increasing production will make the output more efficient and cost effective. Incentivizing countries to boost their production and pursue their competitive advantage inherently leads to greater economic interdependence and globalization; trading countries are necessarily dependent on their partners to meet some need. For example, in the North America Free Trade Agreement, the United States provides technology and white-collar skills, while Mexico primarily focuses on manufacturing.

Despite the trend toward supranational political and economic entities, nationalism has reemerged as a powerful force in the post-Cold War Era. Nationalism is best understood as people seeking independence for some collective reason, like geographical proximity or cultural similarities. In addition, nationalism is primarily expressed via its opposition to external influences. Just as nationalism served as a rallying cry for colonial people fighting to gain their independence, nationalism has come back into vogue as the means for people to advocate for greater local control.

The Yugoslav Wars of 1991 to 2001 and eventual collapse of Yugoslavia illustrate how ethnic nationalism exists as a powerful countervailing force to globalization trends. The former Socialist Federal Republic of Yugoslavia contained several republics that consisted of distinct ethnic groups, including Bosnia and Herzegovina, Croatia, Macedonia, Serbia, and Slovenia. Additionally, Serbia was further divided between Kosovo and Vojvodina. After the death of Yugoslavia's founding authoritarian ruler, Josip Broz Tito, the country eventually collapsed under separatist nationalist movements. Following a series of bloody wars and war crimes, collectively known as the Yugoslav Wars, seven newly independent states emerged out of Yugoslavia—Bosnia and Herzegovina, Croatia, Kosovo, Macedonia, Montenegro, Serbia, and Slovenia.

Religious fundamentalism has increased dramatically in the post-Cold War Era. Specifically, the globalized economy has directly resulted in cultural clashes between the West and Islamic fundamentalism. The most infamous modern terrorist attack occurred on September 11, 2001, when terrorists associated with al-Qaeda hijacked four commercial airliners and flew two into the World Trade Center and one into the U.S. Pentagon (one crashed in a field). The 9/11 attack initially led to the United States' invasion of Afghanistan and later contributed to the decision to invade Iraq.

Additionally, the Arab Spring created a spirit of unrest in many Middle Eastern countries with a history of authoritarian rule. Following the Americans' withdrawal from Iraq and uprisings in neighboring Syria, the religious extremists declared an Islamic State in the region, known as the Islamic State of Iraq and Levant, ensuring the proliferation of Islamic fundamentalism and terrorism for the foreseeable future.

Nationalism is also on the rise in Western democracies as people grapple with the consequences of a globalized economy and greater involvement of supranational political entities beyond their control. In June 2016, the United Kingdom held a referendum on the country's membership in the European Union, and British citizens voted to withdraw, which is commonly referred to as the Brexit (British exit). Nationalism greatly influenced British citizens' reluctance to cede any degree of sovereignty, pay taxes, or follow regulations from the European Union.

Significant Individuals of the Nineteenth and Twentieth Centuries

Charles Darwin
Charles Darwin is known as the Father of Evolution, and was a naturalist and geologist. Darwin collected samples and made extensive observations in his Voyage of the Beagle from 1831 to 1836. His most famous spot was the Galápagos Islands, where he discovered varying species of finches from island to island. His theory of natural selection proposed that organisms best suited to their surrounding environment were most likely to survive.

Mao Zedong
In China, Mao Zedong, the chairman of the Communist Party and leader of the People's Republic of China, attempted to quickly transform China into a Communist state through an ineffective and devastating economic program known as the *Great Leap Forward,* which abolished private ownership of property and featured collective communes. The Great Leap Forward caused a humanitarian disaster, resulting in tens of millions of deaths, due to inefficient economic planning under a poorly devised Communist system.

Mohandas Gandhi
Mohandas Gandhi became the leader of the Indian independence movement following the passage of the Rowlatt Act, which allowed the British colonial government to jail Indian protesters without a trial by jury. Returning World War I veterans and human rights advocates in India violently rejected the Rowlatt Act as a stumbling block to Indian self-government and a threat to Indian rights. In an act of defiance against the colonial British government in the spring of 1919, ten thousand Hindu and Muslim protesters flocked to Amristar, the capital city of the Punjab province in India. During this protest, British troops killed over four hundred Indians and injured over one thousand protesters. This controversial moment in history paved the way for Gandhi to emerge as the respected leader of Indian resistance. Unlike other revolutionaries at that time in history, Gandhi urged his followers to employ nonviolent noncooperation tactics against the British government. The former lawyer called upon the nonviolent principles of world religions to instill in his followers the principle of satyagraha (truth force). In the Western world, Gandhi's principle of satyagraha has become colloquially known as passive resistance or civil disobedience.

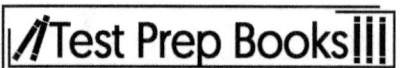

In the 1920s and 1930s, Gandhi launched a passive resistance campaign that combined peaceful marches with economic boycotts. These nonviolent means of resistance eventually led to the passage of the Government of India Act by the British Parliament in 1935, which offered Indians limited democratic elections and local self-government. This act, however, was not respected by the British government during World War II when it deployed Indian troops without the consent of local government officials. During this time, Gandhi pressed the Indian people to find peace during these controversial times. Nevertheless, in the postwar years, by 1947, Indians were becoming increasingly violent, not only with British officials, but also with each other. Muslims and Hindus grew increasingly at odds with one another in the postwar years. Despite all his passive efforts, Gandhi's hope for a united, independent India was only half realized: On July 16, 1947, the British government partitioned the Indian subcontinent into two countries, Pakistan and India. In 1948, Mohandas Gandhi's life was taken by a Hindu extremist who disliked his attempts to achieve equal treatment for both Muslims and Hindus. Gandhi's nonviolent ethos has, nevertheless, continued to reverberate through history, namely in the work of such civil rights advocates as Martin Luther King Jr. and Nelson Mandela.

Adolf Hitler

Adolf Hitler was an Austrian-born soldier who was awarded the Iron Cross on two occasions for his service in the German army during World War I. Following the end of the war, Hitler joined a small, right-wing political group that threatened to overturn the Treaty of Versailles, which placed sanctions on the postwar German military, government, and economy. Hitler also joined the group in vowing to destroy global Communism. As the group expanded, it became known as the National Socialist German Workers' Party, often abbreviated as Nazis. Nazism became the German brand of fascism, promising to protect the middle and lower-middle classes from postwar sanctions and the global overreach of Communism. Like Benito Mussolini, the Fascist leader of Italy, Adolf Hitler had the ability to command and manipulate a crowd with his fiery speeches. His public-speaking skills eventually led to his assumption of the position as chosen *der Führer*—or leader —of the Nazis. A failed attempt to seize power in Munich in 1923 landed Hitler and many of his fellow Nazis in prison. While in prison, Hitler wrote his famous book *Mein Kampf* (*My Struggle*). This book served as the blueprint for Nazism, labeling Jews, Slavs, gypsies, and other groups as subhuman and calling for the eugenic creation of the Aryan race. By 1933, Hitler and his book *Mein Kampf* had gained so much popular support that he became chancellor of Germany, paving the way to World War II, the Holocaust, and the eventual fall of Nazism in Germany.

Nelson Mandela

Born to a royal family of the Xhosa-speaking South African Thembu tribe in 1918, Nelson Mandela became one of the premier civil rights activists in world history. In the 1940s, Mandela joined the African National Congress party, joining fellow black leaders in South Africa in their fight against the white minority's oppressive regime. This regime had its roots in colonial practices that legitimized the oppression and marginalization of black and interracial South Africans. The white minority leadership created an apartheid system of social segregation. Mandela joined other revolutionaries in protests and armed conflicts, leading to his eventual imprisonment. Following his release from prison in 1990, Nelson Mandela continued his civil rights battle in the racially divided South Africa. He eventually helped end apartheid in South Africa, becoming the first black president in 1994. As president, he formed a multiethnic government, using his position of power to fight racial prejudice throughout the globe. He died in 2013 at the age of ninety-five.

Mother Teresa

Born Agnes Gonxha Bojaxhiu, Mother Teresa (1910–1997) became one of the most beloved religious figures and missionaries in the twentieth century. Recipient of the Nobel Peace Prize in 1979, Mother Teresa dedicated her life to helping the poor, the elderly, the sick, and the disabled in South Asia and the rest of the world. After joining the sisterhood in Ireland, she left the convent for missionary work in Calcutta, India. In 1948, she established the Order of the Missionaries of Charity in Calcutta. This organization established schools, refugee camps, hospitals, churches, and convents throughout the world. Clad in her iconic plain white sari with a blue border, Mother Teresa became famous for helping the downtrodden of the Third World. Millions lamented her death in 1997, knowing that they lost one of the most dedicated missionaries in modern history. Her work is as iconic as other social justice warriors such as Dr. Martin Luther King Jr. and Mohandas Gandhi.

Practice Quiz

1. Which of the following statements accurately describes the European Union?
    a. It was formed in 1945 after World War II.
    b. It was founded as a result of the Paris Peace Conference that ended the first World War.
    c. It aims to ensure free movement of people, goods, services, and capital within the internal market.
    d. It was founded to avoid repeating the Great War.

2. By the end of the Reformation period, women had obtained what right in most Protestant communities?
    a. The right to vote in elections
    b. The right to buy and sell land
    c. The right to divorce and remarry
    d. The right to serve in the military

3. Which of the following nations saw their standing during the nineteenth century fall as other powers were rising?
    a. Ottoman Empire
    b. England
    c. Germany
    d. Russia

4. Governments deployed large-scale propaganda for the FIRST time during which one of the following military conflicts?
    a. Russo-Turkish War
    b. First Sino-Japanese War
    c. Spanish Civil War
    d. World War I

5. Which of the following was a long-term consequence of explorers looking for a northwest passage?
    a. European powers gained a faster route to the Pacific Ocean.
    b. European powers abandoned international trade networks.
    c. European powers forged alliances with Amerindian empires.
    d. European powers colonized the Americas.

See answers on the next page.

Answer Explanations

1. C: The European Union aims to ensure free movement of people, goods, services, and capital within the internal market. The United Nations was formed in 1945 after World War II, making Choice A incorrect. The League of Nations was founded as a result of the Paris Peace Conference that ended the first World War and was also founded to avoid repetition of the first World War, making Choices B and D incorrect.

2. C: By the end of the Reformation, women had a larger role in society. Still, the right to vote in most elections was not given, Choice A. Land was also still owned by men, Choice B, with most women barred from owning any. Military service was also still restricted, with women expected to be homebound, Choice D. However, Protestant communities did finally grant women the right to divorce and remarry.

3. A: Throughout the nineteenth century, most European nations grew through trade and expansion. Germany saw unification and expansion as their trade power grew. England saw the largest growth, becoming the dominant European power by the end of the nineteenth century. Russia also grew, expanding through military might and trading alliances in the region. The Ottoman Empire, however, once a proud nation, saw war and trade deficits end their reign as a major European power.

4. D: Governments first deployed large-scale propaganda during World War I. Propaganda was a critical part of the governments' total war strategy, which called for the mobilization of every possible resource for the war effort. In order to fight this unprecedented global conflict, governments had to convince the public to sacrifice their food, goods, and lives to the war effort like never before. Thus, Choice D is the correct answer. Propaganda was used in the Russo-Turkish War (1877–1878) and First Sino-Japanese War (1894–1895), but it was not widespread and orchestrated by the government. During World War I, nearly every government created official propaganda departments for the first time in history. So, Choices A and B are incorrect. Choice C is the second best answer choice. The Spanish, German, and Soviet governments all published a significant amount of propaganda. However, World War I (1914–1918) occurred several decades before the Spanish Civil War (1936–1939). Therefore, Choice C is incorrect.

5. D: European explorers never found the Northwest Passage, but the search uncovered the Americas' economic potential. European colonization started almost immediately after Columbus reached the Caribbean, and it spread across both continents as explorers continued to search for the elusive route to Asia. Although Ferdinand Magellan found a passage to Asia through the southern Atlantic, it was much slower than sailing around the Cape of Good Hope. So, Choice A is incorrect. The search for a Northwest Passage exponentially increased international trade, so Choice B is incorrect. European powers occasionally made strategic short-term alliances with individual Amerindian tribes, but alliances weren't a long-term consequence of European exploration in the Americas. As such, Choice C is incorrect.

U.S. History

Exploration and Colonization

European Exploration and Colonization of North America

When examining how Europeans explored what would become the United States of America, one must first examine why Europeans came to explore the New World as a whole. In the fifteenth century, tensions increased between the Eastern and Mediterranean nations of Europe and the expanding Ottoman Empire to the east. As war and piracy spread across the Mediterranean, the once-prosperous trade routes across Asia's Silk Road began to decline, and nations across Europe began to explore alternative routes for trade.

Italian explorer Christopher Columbus proposed a westward route. Contrary to popular lore, the main challenge that Columbus faced in finding backers was not proving that the world was round. In fact, much of Europe's educated elite knew that the world was round; the real issue was that they rightly believed that a westward route to Asia, even assuming a lack of obstacles, would be too long to be practical. Nevertheless, Columbus set sail in 1492 after obtaining support from Spain and arrived in the West Indies three months later.

Spain launched further expeditions to the new continents and established *New Spain*. The colony consisted not only of Central America and Mexico, but also the American Southwest and Florida. France claimed much of what would become Canada, along with the Mississippi River region and the Midwest. In addition, the Dutch established colonies that covered New Jersey, New York, and Connecticut. Each nation managed its colonies differently, and thus influenced how they would assimilate into the United States. For instance, Spain strove to establish a system of Christian missions throughout its territory, while France focused on trading networks and had limited infrastructure in regions such as the Midwest.

Even in cases of limited colonial growth, the land of America was hardly vacant, because a diverse array of Native American nations and groups were already present. Throughout much of colonial history, European settlers commonly misperceived native peoples as a singular, static entity. In reality, Native Americans had a variety of traditions depending on their history and environment. Additionally, their culture continued to change through the course of interactions with European settlers; for instance, tribes, such as the Cheyenne and Comanche, used horses, which were introduced by white settlers, to become powerful warrior nations. However, a few generalizations can be made: many, but not all, tribes were matrilineal, which gave women a fair degree of power, and land was commonly seen as belonging to everyone. These differences, particularly European settlers' continual focus on land ownership, contributed to increasing prejudice and violence.

Colonial Society and Interactions Among Europeans, Africans, and American Indians

Native Americans played an important role in the early history of Britain's North American colonies. Squanto was an Algonquian Indian who helped English settlers in Massachusetts survive by teaching them how to plant native crops. Some Native American tribes were friendly towards the colonists and traded with them.

However, Native Americans and Europeans often came into conflict, frequently over land disputes. The Native Americans and Europeans had very different concepts of land use and ownership. Native Americans did not understand the concept of landownership or sale. When they entered into agreements with the colonists, Native Americans thought they were allowing the settlers to farm the land temporarily, rather than retain it in perpetuity. On the other hand, colonists were frustrated when Native Americans continued to hunt and fish on lands they had sold. These, and other disagreements, eventually led to bloody conflicts that gradually weakened Native American tribes.

U.S. History | Exploration and Colonization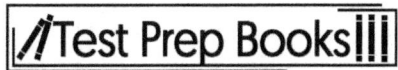

Native Americans were also vulnerable to diseases to which the Europeans had developed immunity. These diseases included bubonic plague, cholera, chicken pox, pneumonic plague, influenza, measles, scarlet fever, typhus, smallpox, and tuberculosis. These diseases killed millions of Native Americans and were sometimes used as a biological weapon. Historians estimate that as much as 80% of the Native American population died through disease and warfare.

The southern colonies, including Virginia, Maryland, the Carolinas, and Georgia, were also organized by county. The southern economy focused on labor-intensive crops such as tobacco and rice, and as a result, landowners relied on indentured servants and African slaves. Slaves were present in most colonies, but were more common in the south.

Thirteen Colonies

News of his success sparked a number of other expeditions and the British, French, Dutch, Spanish, and Portuguese all eventually laid claim to lands in the New World. Columbus himself made three more voyages to the Americas. The French and Dutch focused mostly on the lucrative fur trade in North America. The Spanish and Portuguese sought gold in Central and South America but also tried to convert Native Americans to Christianity. British settlers also sought economic opportunity and created the first British colony at Jamestown, Virginia, in 1607. However, the Puritans who landed at Plymouth Rock in 1620 left for the New World in order to establish their ideal religious community.

Connecticut, New Hampshire, Massachusetts, and Rhode Island were considered the New England colonies. The settlements in New England were based around an economy focused on fishing and lumber. These colonies maintained puritanical and Congregationalist religious beliefs. While English Puritans mostly settled in New England, a wide variety of colonists settled in the mid-Atlantic region. English, Scottish, Dutch, and Swedish settlers came to Delaware, New York, New Jersey, and Pennsylvania. As a result, the mid-Atlantic colonies were more religiously diverse and tolerant than the settlements in New England. Agriculture was the foundation of the economy in mid-Atlantic colonies. This meant that settlements were more dispersed. Government and administration were based on counties instead of towns.

Political power was distributed differently among the colonies. Some colonies, such as New York and Virginia, were royal colonies ruled directly by the king. Pennsylvania was a proprietary colony—the king allowed William Penn to appoint officials and govern the colony as he saw fit. Corporate colonies, such as Rhode Island and Connecticut, were administered by a group of investors. But, by the early 1700s, the king had revoked the charters of most proprietary and corporate colonies and assumed direct control himself.

Foundations of Representative Government in the United States

Virginia House of Burgesses
The Virginia House of Burgesses, which convened for the first time in 1619, became the first elected assembly ever established in the English colonies. The House of Burgesses only elected white landowners. Moreover, the Virginia Company and the Virginia governor reserved the right to nullify any policy passed by the House. Although the House of Burgesses was, therefore, far from democratic in character, it still established a precedent for assembly-style government within the English colonies in North America and later the independent United States of America.

Mayflower Compact
On November 21, 1620, before landing on the coast of present-day Massachusetts, forty-one male Puritans drafted and signed a document that became known as the Mayflower Compact. The Mayflower Compact represents one of the first attempts at self-government in the English colonies of North America. These Separatist Puritans—sometimes referred to as pilgrims—wanted to establish their own basic laws and social rules. They believed these laws should be devised by the colonists themselves rather than the English Crown (though the compact did honor

the colony's relationship with the king). The founding principles of the Mayflower Compact referenced basic Christian values such as justice and covenantal agreements with neighbors and God. The document also highlights notions of equality, which became even more prevalent during the heart of the Enlightenment in the 1700s. These foundational values served as a source of information for later representative government documents such as colonial charters, the Declaration of Independence, state constitutions, the Articles of Confederation, and the US Constitution.

Iroquois Confederacy

Although not a primary shaper of the Articles of Confederation or US Constitution, the governmental structure of the Iroquois Confederacy did influence some of the political principles of the Founding Fathers. The Iroquois Confederacy, much like the U.S. government, was federal in nature. The Iroquois Confederacy comprised five or six Native American tribes that worked together to resolve diplomatic issues with an overarching government. Much like the states within the Union, the tribes within the Confederacy maintained local self-government while addressing issues of common importance at a federal level. Some historians even believe the Iroquois system of government employed basic tenets of representational democracy. Other historians believe it acted more like the United Nations than the United States of America. Nevertheless, the Iroquois Confederacy should not be downplayed as a foundational contributor to the democratic-republican values of the Early Republic—the Iroquois Confederacy, much like the Mayflower Compact and the Plymouth Colony, served as a historical example of a unique governing body the Founding Fathers could draw inspiration from.

Fundamental Orders of Connecticut

The Fundamental Orders of Connecticut, written by Thomas Hooker in 1639, established basic principles of democratic rule in the English colonies, paving the way to the democratic character of future government documents in the United States of America. The Fundamental Orders of Connecticut expanded the right to vote in Connecticut by offering suffrage to men who did not belong to the church. Hooker's gradual expansion of voting rights preceded later democratic milestones such as the constitutional extension of voting rights to working-class men (the Age of Jacksonian Democracy), black men (post–Civil War), and women's suffrage (1920s). Early documents such as state constitutions, the Articles of Confederation, and the US Constitution employed Hooker's methods by extending voting rights to all secular, landowning men.

Development of Colonial Society

Situated on the Atlantic Coast, the Thirteen Colonies that would become the United States of America constituted only a small portion of North America. Even those colonies had significant differences that stemmed from their different origins. For instance, the Virginia colony under John Smith in 1607 started with male bachelors seeking gold, whereas families of Puritans settled Massachusetts. As a result, the Thirteen Colonies—Virginia, Massachusetts, Connecticut, Maryland, New York, New Jersey, Pennsylvania, Delaware, Rhode Island, New Hampshire, Georgia, North Carolina, and South Carolina—had different structures and customs that would each influence the United States.

Colonies in the Americas had difficulty attracting a free labor supply due to the cost, danger, and lack of infrastructure. The voyage across the Atlantic Ocean was unaffordable to nearly everyone who wasn't a societal elite, and life in the Americas wasn't necessarily desirable. For example, several British settlements failed due to the lack of food and/or conflicts with Amerindians. Given the limited size of their populations, colonies didn't have the necessary infrastructure, such as secure food supplies and long-term housing, to support families. As such, colonial economies in the Americas depended on coerced labor systems, such as indentured servitude, forced servitude of Amerindians, and African slavery.

U.S. History | Exploration and Colonization

Slavery in the Americas was driven by the expansion of plantations, which became the dominant economic model due to their profitability. Plantations mass-produced raw goods that were exported to Europe and turned into finished products.

Plantations quickly became the dominant economic model in the Americas due to their profitability. Rather than diversifying crops, plantations focused solely on cash crops, such as tobacco and sugarcane. Cash crops fetched a higher market price because their supply was limited outside of the production in the Americas. Plantations were also profitable because they were centers of mass production, benefiting from the economic principle known as **economies of scale**. In other words, as the plantation grew in size, the cost of producing cash crops decreased. As such, plantations required a tremendous amount of labor to meet the demands of mass production. While indentured servants and Amerindians worked on plantations, the demand was mostly met through the importation of African slaves.

From 1525 to 1866, the transatlantic slave trade transported nearly 12.5 million Africans across the Middle Passage between Africa and the Americas, and approximately 10.7 million Africans arrived at their destination. On most plantations, African slaves vastly outnumbered Europeans. In order to maintain control and maximize productivity, plantation owners empowered overseers to exact harsh punishments on slaves. Often, overseers forced slaves to carry out the punishment on each other to undermine the threat of collective action. Most colonial governments also passed strict slave codes to prevent slaves from attaining literacy and legal rights, which would have destroyed the plantation economic system.

The mass transfer of Africans and Europeans to the Americas created an unprecedented mixing of cultures and people that led to spatial exchange, the spread of idea and cultural traits between two different cultures. Early European colonists benefited enormously from contact with Amerindians, the indigenous people of the Americas. For example, if not for Amerindians' agricultural assistance, the Jamestown settlement likely would have collapsed almost immediately, like England's earlier settlement attempts at Roanoke. Amerindian culture placed heavy emphasis on the natural world, and Europeans settling frontier areas, especially French and British fur traders, adopted some of this lifestyle. Amerindian culture also changed through the adoption of horses and guns. Horses facilitated more nomadic lifestyles, and when combined with guns, hunting practices became far more efficient.

Britain continued to hold onto its other colonies, such as Canada and the West Indies, which reflects the continued power of multiple nations across North America, even as the United States began to expand across the continent. Many Americans advocated expansion regardless of the land's current inhabitants, but the results were often mixed. Still, events both abroad and within North America contributed to the growth of the United States. For instance, the rising tumult in France during the French Revolution and the rise of Napoleon led France to sell the Louisiana Purchase, a large chunk of land consisting not only of Louisiana but also much of the Midwest, to the United States in 1803. Meanwhile, as Spanish power declined, Mexico claimed independence in 1821, but the new nation became increasingly vulnerable to foreign pressure. In the Mexican-American War from 1846 to 1848, Mexico surrendered territory to the United States that eventually became California, Nevada, Utah, and New Mexico, as well as parts of Arizona, Colorado, and Wyoming.

Even as the United States sought new inland territory, American interests were also expanding overseas via trade. As early as 1784, the ship *Empress of China* traveled to China to establish trading connections. American interests had international dimensions throughout the nation's history. For instance, during the presidency of Andrew Jackson, the ship *Potomac* was dispatched to the Pacific island of Sumatra in 1832 to avenge the deaths of American sailors. This incident exemplifies how U.S. foreign trade connected with imperial expansion.

This combination of continental and seaward growth adds a deeper layer to American development because it was not purely focused on western expansion. For example, take the 1849 Gold Rush; a large number of Americans and other immigrants traveled to California by ship and settled western territories before more eastern areas, such as

Nevada and Idaho. Therefore, the United States' early history of colonization and expansion is a complex network of diverse cultures.

Revolutionary Era and the Early Years of the Republic

U.S. Society During the Revolutionary Era and Early Years of the Republic

The French colonies in Canada also threatened the British settlements. France and Britain had been enemies for centuries. Religious differences reinforced their hostility; the British were Protestant, and the French were mostly Catholic. Far fewer colonists settled in New France, but they often clashed with the British, especially over the lucrative fur trade. Both the British and French sought to dominate the trade in beaver pelts, which were used to make hats in Europe. The British and French fought a series of colonial wars between 1689 and 1748 that failed to resolve the struggle for dominance in North America.

Eventually, the contest culminated in the French and Indian War (which was part of the Seven Years' War), which ended in 1763. The French initially enjoyed the upper hand because they were able to persuade more Native American tribes to support them. The Native Americans felt the French were less likely to encroach on their territory than the land-hungry British. The Native Americans launched devastating raids along the British colonial frontier. However, the British eventually emerged victorious after they blockaded the French colonies in Canada. This prevented the French from bringing in reinforcements or from resupplying their Native American allies with gunpowder and ammunition. Native American raids subsided and eventually the French surrendered almost all of their colonial possessions in North America. Some historians consider this war the first global conflict because battles were also fought in Europe, Asia, and Africa.

The French defeat radically altered the balance of power in North America. Previously, Native Americans had been able to play the French and British against each other, but now they were without many of their French allies. In addition, the French and Indian War also set the stage for the American Revolution. Although victorious, the British monarchy spent an enormous amount of money and the war doubled the national debt. In order to pay off the debts, King George III began imposing taxes upon the North American colonies, which eventually led to revolution.

The Molasses Act in 1731 was another outgrowth of mercantilism. This law imposed a higher tax on the molasses that colonists purchased from the Dutch, French, or Spanish colonies. The tax was unpopular with the colonists and British imperial officials eventually decided not to enforce the tax. The Molasses Act had threatened to disrupt the pattern of triangular trade that had emerged in the Atlantic world. First, ships from Britain's North American colonies carried rum to Africa where it was traded for slaves and gold. Then, the ships took the slaves to French and Spanish colonies in the Caribbean and exchanged them for sugar or molasses. In the last part of the triangular trade system, merchants sailed back to North America where the sugar and molasses was used to make rum, and the cycle could start over again.

In addition to economic connections, many other bonds also bridged the Atlantic Ocean. Most colonists shared a common language, common religion, and common culture. However, as the colonies grew in population, they began to develop local institutions and a separate sense of identity. For example, it became common for ministers to receive their education at seminaries in North America rather than Britain. Newspapers began to focus on printing more local news as well. Perhaps most importantly, the colonies began to exercise more control over their own political affairs. The British government retained control over international issues, such as war and trade, but the colonists controlled their own domestic affairs. Colonies began to form their own political assemblies and elect landowners who represented local districts. In addition, communications between the colonies and Britain were very slow because it took months for a ship to cross the Atlantic and return with a response.

U.S. History | Revolutionary Era and the Early Years of the Republic

American Revolution

Competition among several imperial powers in eastern areas of North America led to conflicts that would later bring about the independence of the United States. The French and Indian War from 1754 to 1763, which was a subsidiary war of the Seven Years' War, ended with Great Britain claiming France's Canadian territories as well as the Ohio Valley. The war was costly for all the powers involved, which led to increased taxes on the Thirteen Colonies. In addition, the new lands to the west of the colonies attracted new settlers, and they came into conflict with Native Americans and British troops that were trying to maintain the boundaries laid out by treaties between Great Britain and the Native American tribes. These growing tensions with Great Britain, as well as other issues, eventually led to the American Revolution, which ended with Britain relinquishing its control of the colonies.

A number of political acts by the British monarchy also led to more discontent among the colonies. After the French and Indian War ended in 1763, the king declared that the colonists could not settle west of the Appalachian Mountains. This was known as the Proclamation of 1763. Many colonists were frustrated because they had expected this territory would be open for expansion after the French had been defeated.

Additionally, taxes were imposed in an effort to help reduce the debt Britain amassed during the French and Indian War. In 1764, Parliament passed the Sugar Act, which reduced the tax on molasses but also provided for greater enforcement powers. Some colonists protested by organizing boycotts on British goods. One year later, in 1765, Parliament passed the Quartering Act, which required colonists to provide housing and food to British troops. This law was also very unpopular and led to protests in the North American colonies.

The Stamp Act of 1765 required the colonists to pay a tax on legal documents, newspapers, magazines, and other printed materials. Colonial assemblies protested the tax and petitioned the British government in order to have it repealed. Merchants also organized boycotts and established correspondence committees in order to share information. Eventually, Parliament repealed the Stamp Act but simultaneously reaffirmed the Crown's right to tax the colonies.

In 1767, Parliament introduced the Townshend Acts, which imposed a tax on goods the colonies imported from Britain, such as tea, lead, paint, glass, and paper. The colonies protested again, and British imperial officials were assaulted in some cases. The British government sent additional troops to North America to restore order. The arrival of troops in Boston only led to more tension that eventually culminated in the Boston Massacre in 1770, where five colonists were killed and eight were wounded. Except for the duty on tea, all of the Townshend Act taxes were repealed after the Boston Massacre.

Parliament passed the Tea Act in 1773 and, although it actually reduced the price of tea, it was another unpopular piece of legislation. The Tea Act made the British East India Company the sole legal seller of tea in the colonies in North America and allowed the Company to ship its products directly to the colonies without stopping in England and paying import taxes, effectively cutting out colonial merchants and stirring more Anglo-American anger and resentment. This resulted in the Boston Tea Party in 1773, an incident in which colonial tea merchants disguised themselves as Indians before storming several British ships that were anchored in Boston harbor. Once aboard, the disguised colonists dumped more than 300 chests of tea into the water.

Because the British government was unable to identify the perpetrators, Parliament passed a series of laws that punished the entire colony of Massachusetts. These acts were known as the Coercive or Intolerable Acts. The first law closed the port of Boston until the tea had been paid for (an estimated $1.7 million in today's currency). The second act curtailed the authority of Massachusetts' colonial government. Instead of being elected by colonists, most government officials were now appointed by the king. In addition, the act restricted town meetings, the basic form of government in Massachusetts, and limited most villages to one meeting per year. This act angered colonists throughout the thirteen colonies because they feared their rights could be stripped away as well. A third act allowed

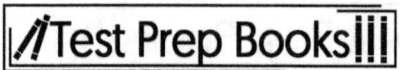

for British soldiers to be tried in Britain if they were accused of a crime. The fourth act once again required colonists to provide food and shelter to British soldiers.

Colonists responded by forming the First Continental Congress in 1774, and all the colonies except for Georgia sent delegates. The delegates sought a compromise with the British government instead of launching an armed revolt. The First Continental Congress sent a petition to King George III affirming their loyalty but demanding the repeal of the Intolerable Acts. The delegates organized a boycott of imports from and exports to Britain until their demands were met.

The colonists began to form militias and gather weapons and ammunition. The first battle of the revolution began at Lexington and Concord in April 1775 when British troops tried to seize a supply of gunpowder and were confronted by about eighty Minutemen. A brief skirmish left eight colonists dead and ten wounded. Colonial reinforcements poured in and harassed the British force as they retreated to Boston. Although the battle did not result in many casualties, it marked the beginning of war.

A month later, the Second Continental Congress convened in Philadelphia. The delegates formed an army and appointed George Washington as commander in chief. Delegates were still reluctant to repudiate their allegiance to King George III and did not do so until they issued the Declaration of Independence on July 4, 1776. The Declaration drew on the ideas of the Enlightenment and declared that the colonists had the right to life, liberty, and the pursuit of happiness. The Declaration stated that the colonists had to break away from Britain because King George III had violated their rights.

After the Battle of Lexington and Concord, British troops retreated to Boston and the colonial militias laid siege to the city. Colonists built fortifications on Bunker Hill outside the city and British troops attacked the position in June 1775. The colonists inflicted heavy casualties on the British and killed a number of officers. However, the defenders ran out of ammunition and British troops captured Bunker Hill on the third assault. Although it was a defeat for the colonists, the Battle of Bunker Hill demonstrated that they could stand and fight against the disciplined and professional British army.

The British army initially had the upper hand and defeated colonial forces in a number of engagements. The Americans did not achieve a victory until the Battle of Trenton in December 1776. Washington famously crossed the Delaware River on Christmas Day and launched a surprise attack against Hessian mercenaries. They captured more than 1,000 soldiers and suffered minimal casualties. The victory at Trenton bolstered American morale and showed that they could defeat professional European soldiers.

The Battle of Saratoga in New York in the fall of 1777 was an important turning point in the American War for Independence. American troops surrounded and captured more than 6,000 British soldiers. This victory convinced the French king to support the revolutionaries by sending troops, money, weapons, and ships to the American continent. French officers who fought alongside the Patriots brought back many ideas with them that eventually sparked a revolution in France in 1789.

Revolutionary Era

Navigation Acts

Since 1651, the British crown had tried to control trade within its empire, which eventually led to tension and discontent in the North American colonies. That year, the monarchy introduced the Navigation Acts, which prevented the North American colonies from trading directly with other European powers—all goods had to be shipped to Britain first. This was an attempt to keep wealth within the British Empire and to prevent other empires from profiting from their colonies. This was an example of mercantilism—an economic policy that formed the foundation of Britain's empire. Mercantilism called for government regulation in the form of tariffs, a tax on imports from other countries. This raised prices on foreign goods and encouraged British imperial subjects to purchase goods made in Britain or the colonies. This reduced imports and maximized exports, thus enriching the British Empire.

Lexington and Concord

The battles at Concord and Lexington, considered to be the beginning of the Revolutionary War, may seem to be instantaneous eruptions of violence during the American Revolution, but they stemmed from a variety of factors. The most obvious influences behind those two battles were the assortment of taxes and policies imposed on the Thirteen Colonies following the French and Indian War from 1754 to 1763. Taxation without direct representation, combined with the deployment of British soldiers to enforce these policies, greatly increased American resistance. Earlier events, such as the Boston Massacre and the Boston Tea Party, similarly stemmed from conflicts between British soldiers and local colonists over perceived tyranny and rebelliousness. Therefore, the start of the American Revolution progressed from preceding developments.

Winter at Valley Forge

In December of 1777, George Washington and the Continental Army made their winter camp at Valley Forge. The army was lacking in general provisions and ill-equipped to face the winter weather. In spite of these conditions, the winter was a significant time for the Continental Army. The army remained largely intact and was able to improve their battle tactics and maneuvers due to the arrival of Baron von Steuben and Marquis de Lafayette. Both of these foreign military men joined the Continental Army at this time and were instrumental in training the continental soldiers.

Treaty of Paris of 1783

French support was very important in the last major battle of the revolution at Yorktown, Virginia, in 1781. American troops laid siege to General Cornwallis's British forces at Yorktown. The French fleet defeated a British naval squadron sent to relieve Cornwallis. French and American troops began attacking the British fortifications in Yorktown; a sustained artillery bombardment by American guns eventually forced Cornwallis to surrender. This ended the Revolutionary War, and in 1783 the British signed the Treaty of Paris. Britain recognized the United States as an independent country and set the Mississippi River as the nation's western border. However, British troops continued to occupy several forts in the Great Lakes region.

In addition, tens of thousands of colonists who remained loyal to the British Empire fled the United States after the war. They were known as loyalists and many thousands had joined militias and fought against the patriots. Some loyalists fled to Canada or Britain, but many remained in the United States. Many Native American tribes had sided with the British as well in an attempt to curb western expansion. No Native American leaders signed the Treaty of Paris and they refused to give up their territories, which led to further conflict as the new American nation began to expand westward.

Foundations of Representative Government in the United States

America's first system of government was actually laid out in the Articles of Confederation, and not the Constitution. The Articles of Confederation were ratified during the Revolutionary War and went into effect in 1781. The Articles of Confederation created a relatively weak central government and allowed individual states to retain most of the power. Under this system, the national government did not have a president or judiciary. Each state had only one vote in the Confederation Congress and most major decisions required unanimous approval by all thirteen states. Despite this requirement, the Confederation Congress did pass some important legislation, including the Northwest Ordinance, which organized the land west of Appalachian Mountains. The territories eventually became the states of Ohio, Indiana, Michigan, Illinois, Wisconsin, and Minnesota. However, Congress did not have the power to tax and could only request money from the states without any way to enforce its demands. A Revolutionary War veteran named Daniel Shays led an armed insurrection in western Massachusetts in 1787. Although Shay's Rebellion was defeated, it drew attention to the weaknesses of the Articles of Confederation.

The Constitutional Convention met in Philadelphia in May 1787 after the new country was rocked by economic troubles and Shays' Rebellion, an uprising in Massachusetts due to the debt crisis from the Revolutionary War, with the goal of creating a stronger federal government. However, delegates disagreed over how to structure the new system. The Virginia Plan was one proposal that included a bicameral legislature where states were awarded representation based on their population size. This would benefit more populous states at the expense of smaller states. The other main proposal was the New Jersey Plan, which retained many elements of the Articles of Confederation including a unicameral legislature with one vote per state. This plan would put states on an equal footing regardless of population.

Eventually, delegates agreed to support the Connecticut Compromise (also known as the Great Compromise), which incorporated elements from both the Virginia and New Jersey Plans and embodied federalism. Under the new Constitution, Congress would be a bicameral body. In the House of Representatives, states would be allocated seats based on population, but in the Senate each state would have two votes. The Constitution also included a president and judiciary that would each serve to check the power of other branches of government. In addition, Congress had the power to tax and had more enforcement powers.

Slavery was another contentious issue during the Constitutional Convention. Slavery was more common in the Southern states and less common in the North. The Southern states wanted slaves to be counted when calculating representation in Congress but not when it came to assessing taxes. Northern states wanted the opposite and eventually the two sides agreed to the Three-Fifths Compromise where slaves were counted as three-fifths of a person for the purposes of both taxation and representation. The Constitution also included a provision that allowed slave owners to recover slaves who had escaped and permitted the international slave trade to continue until 1808.

Once the Constitution had been drafted, nine of the thirteen states had to ratify it for it to take effect. Vigorous debate erupted over whether or not the Constitution should be approved. Two different political factions emerged. The Federalists supported the Constitution because they felt a stronger central government was necessary in order to promote economic growth and improve national security. Several leading federalists, including Alexander Hamilton, John Jay, and James Madison, published a series of articles collectively called the Federalist Papers urging voters to support the Constitution. However, the Anti-Federalists, including Thomas Jefferson and Patrick Henry, felt that the Constitution took too much power away from the states and gave it to the national government. They also thought there weren't enough protections for individual rights and lobbied for the addition of a Bill of Rights that guaranteed basic liberties. Ultimately, the Constitution was ratified in 1788 and the Bill of Rights was approved a year later.

The Electoral College unanimously elected George Washington as the nation's first president in 1789. Despite this appearance of unity, deep political divisions led to the formation of the nation's first party system. Washington supported the Federalist ideology and appointed several Federalists to his cabinet, including Alexander Hamilton as secretary of the treasury. The Anti-Federalist faction evolved into the Democratic-Republican Party and favored stronger state governments instead of a powerful federal government. As settlers moved into the new Northwest Territories, Washington helped pacify Indians who opposed further expansion. He also successfully put down a rebellion in western Pennsylvania by farmers opposed to a federal tax on whiskey.

Washington declined to seek a third term and another Federalist, John Adams, became our second president. Adams signed the Alien and Sedition Acts, which made it a criminal offense to criticize the government, and allowed the president to deport aliens suspected of treason. Adams and the Federalists argued that the laws were necessary in order to improve security as Europe became embroiled in a war against the new French republic. Jefferson and the Democratic-Republicans said the laws restricted free speech. Jefferson made the acts an important topic in 1800 when he successfully ran for president.

Jefferson's victory marked a turning point in the political system because the Democratic-Republicans gained more power while the Federalists went into decline. He repealed the Alien and Sedition Acts when he was elected. The Federalists were further weakened when Hamilton was killed in a duel in 1804.

Jefferson accomplished several significant achievements during his presidency, and one of the most important was the Louisiana Purchase in 1803. For $15 million, Jefferson bought French territory west of the Mississippi River that doubled the size of the United States. He then appointed Meriwether Lewis and William Clark to lead an expedition to explore the vast new territory and study its geography, vegetation, and plant life. Clark also brought his African-American slave, York, on the journey. York helped hunt and even saved Clark's life during a flood. The expedition was also aided by Sacagawea, a Shoshone woman who acted as a guide and interpreter. The explorers established relations with Native American tribes and set the stage for further western expansion in the 1800s.

American Political System and Political Parties

The Founding Fathers of the United States opposed the divisiveness they associated with political parties, and President George Washington railed against the evil of political parties in his Farewell Address. However, the ratification of the Constitution led to the creation of the first two American political parties, the Federalists and the anti-Federalist Democratic-Republican Party. When Andrew Jackson became the seventh president of the United States as a Democrat, his opposition organized under the Whig Party. The Whigs asserted Congress' supremacy over the president and primarily focused on economic concerns like a national bank and infrastructure projects.

A number of different issues divided the Federalists and the Democratic-Republicans, including the French Revolution, which began in 1789. Initially, many Americans supported the French effort to replace their monarchy and create a republican government. However, the French Revolution quickly became more violent, as thousands of suspected opponents of the revolution were executed during the Reign of Terror. The Federalists, including Washington, were horrified by the violence, while Jefferson and the Democratic-Republicans thought the United States should help its former ally. Washington ensured that the country remain officially neutral.

Early Years of the Republic and the Age of Jackson

Following the fervor of the American Revolution, political leaders from across the newly founded United States joined together to discuss the governmental frameworks of the new nation. In many cases, these political leaders did not come to a consensus; they debated basic principles regarding the role of the federal, state, and local governments. Additionally, they debated what economic programs, tariffs and taxes, court systems, and foreign policies to employ. When the Second Continental Congress met in 1775, it drafted a governing document that became known as the Articles of Confederation. The Articles of Confederation mandated the creation of a Congress that would possess limited federal powers. The Articles of Confederation provided states with more power than the federal government—each state had its own militia, dissolving any remnants of a national revolutionary army. In its weakened state, the new federal government faced great threats from its former colonial enforcer, Great Britain. British soldiers posted in Canada threatened the safety and security of the United States of America.

The British also tried to squeeze the United States economically by enforcing high tariffs on the new nation. The British closed off markets in the West Indies, which negatively affected the domestic economy of the United States of America. Under the Articles of Confederation, the United States could not regulate interstate economy; moreover, the excessive printing of bank notes during the Revolution led to years of postwar inflation. The loss of trade, the increase in tariffs, and the minimal commercial regulations eventually thrust the United States into a depression. This depression led to social division, paving the way to heavy farming debts, rising domestic taxes, and the ensuing Shays' Rebellion. Although the rebellion failed, it had a lasting effect on the political conscience of the country. Many political leaders inaugurated a call for change that culminated in the ratification of the current US Constitution.

After months of debate and compromise, the Constitution was created at the Constitutional Convention of 1787. Delaware became the first state to ratify the Constitution in December 1787, and Rhode Island was the last state to ratify the Constitution in 1790. In the years that followed the ratification of the Constitution, debates continued to wage on about the role of the federal government and economy in American life. Perhaps the most famous of these debates was the one between Thomas Jefferson and Alexander Hamilton. Jefferson opposed the creation of a national bank, and Hamilton supported its creation. Eventually, Hamilton's view took precedence with the creation of the first national bank in 1791. During the Age of Jackson, following the election of 1824, the expansion of the American frontier bolstered sectional differences, paving the way to debates over Indian removal and slavery/abolition. The era of Jackson also witnessed the democratization of voting in America with the extension of voting rights to working-class white men who did not own land.

Indian Removal

The Cherokee, Chickasaw, Choctaw, Creek, and Seminole tribes of the Southeastern United States were known as the Five Civilized Tribes because they had developed a written language and many members had become Christians. Nevertheless, Andrew Jackson signed the Indian Removal Act of 1830, which gave him the power to continue buying land from various tribes. The Cherokee filed a lawsuit to protect their territory and won their arguments before the Supreme Court. However, President Andrew Jackson ignored the ruling and eventually used troops to force many tribes off their land and sent them west to Oklahoma during the 1830s. This was known as the Trail of Tears because thousands of Native Americans died from starvation, exposure, and disease along the way.

Westward Expansion, the Civil War, and Reconstruction

Westward Expansion

Constant immigration meant that land prices in the eastern United States rose and people sought new economic opportunities on the frontier where land was cheaper. The United States government tried purchasing land from Native Americans, but most refused to relinquish their territories. Native Americans continued to defend their land until the Shawnee chief Tecumseh, who had formed a confederacy of Native American tribes to establish a self-governing Indian nation and oppose U.S. expansion into the Northwest Territory, was defeated and killed in the War of 1812. This defeat helped secure the Northwest Territory, and more settlers began pouring in. After the Louisiana Purchase, Lewis and Clark paved the way for expansion into the Great Plains and further west.

Several important laws also stimulated western expansion during the second half of the 19th century. Congress passed the Homestead Act in 1862, which allowed citizens to claim 160 acres for only $1.25 per acre. The settler also had to live on the land for five years and make improvements. That same year, Congress also passed the Pacific Railroad Act, which supported the construction of a transcontinental railroad. The United States government provided land and financial support to railroad companies and the first transcontinental link was established in 1869. This facilitated trade and communication between the eastern and western United States.

As Americans poured westward, conflict again broke out between settlers and Native Americans. The discovery of gold in the Black Hills of South Dakota caused prospectors to flood into the area although the U.S. government had recognized the territory as belonging to the Sioux. General George Armstrong Custer brought in troops to try and take possession of the Black Hills. This led to disaster when Custer and more than 250 soldiers died at the Battle of Little Bighorn in 1876 fighting against Crazy Horse, who initially led the Lakota Sioux and Cheyenne forces.

The U.S. government continued its efforts to control Native American tribes. The Dawes Act of 1887 encouraged Native Americans to settle on reservations and become farmers in exchange for U.S. citizenship. Chief Joseph was a leader of the Nez Perce tribe who refused to live on a reservation and tried to flee to Canada. However, the U.S. captured Chief Joseph and his tribe and forced them onto a reservation. Reformers also required Native Americans to send their children to boarding schools where they had to speak English and dress like Caucasians instead of maintaining their traditional culture. The schools were often crowded, and students were also subjected to physical and sexual abuse.

In 1890, the Lakota Indians tried to preserve their traditional beliefs by performing a special ceremony called a Ghost Dance. U.S. government officials felt threatened and sent soldiers to try and disarm the Lakota. This led to the Massacre at Wounded Knee in 1890 where at least 150 Lakota, including many women and children, were slaughtered. It was the last major conflict between Native Americans and U.S. forces.

Manifest Destiny

The concept of Manifest Destiny emerged during the 1800s and introduced the idea that God wanted Americans to civilize and control the entire North American continent. This led to conflict when the province of Texas declared its independence from Mexico and asked to be annexed by the United States. President James K. Polk tried to buy Texas, but when Mexico refused, he sent troops into the disputed territory. Mexican troops responded by attacking an American unit, which led to the Mexican-American War (1846 – 1848). by attacking an American unit, which led to war in 1846.

Manifest Destiny also sparked a desire to expand American influence into Central and South America. Adventurers launched several unsuccessful attempts to invade Nicaragua and Cuba.

Territorial Acquisitions

The United States purchased Alaska from Russia in 1867 for $7.2 million. At the time, the purchase was unpopular with the public, but seal hunting became very profitable and gold was discovered in 1896. Alaska became a state in 1959.

In 1893, American businessmen launched an armed coup, overthrew the queen of Hawaii, and asked Congress to annex Hawaii. The businessmen owned sugar plantations and feared the queen's attempts to enact reform would threaten their political influence. Hawaii became a U.S. territory in 1898 and a state in 1959.

A new phase of American territorial expansion occurred as a result of the Spanish-American War in 1898. New ideas arose in the late 19th century that helped justify further expansion. Some intellectuals applied Charles Darwin's idea of natural selection, often summarized as survival of the fittest, to the human race and called this new concept Social Darwinism. They used this idea to justify stronger groups of people colonizing and exploiting weaker groups. In addition, imperialists also used the idea of the White Man's Burden to justify further expansion. They claimed that Caucasians were obligated to civilize and govern groups thought to be less advanced.

These ideas were used to justify America's new status as a colonial power as a result of the Spanish-American War. Although Spain had once been a powerful empire, it had been in decline. The United States went to war against Spain in 1898 when the American battleship USS Maine exploded in Havana Harbor and killed more than 250 sailors. The U.S. Navy defeated the Spanish fleet in several engagements and then the Army followed up with a victory at San Juan Hill, which included the famous charge by Teddy Roosevelt and the Rough Riders.

The war lasted less than four months and made the United States a world power. The U.S. also acquired several Spanish colonies including Puerto Rico, Guam, and the Philippines. Guam became an important refueling station for American naval forces in the Pacific and remains a U.S. territory today, along with Puerto Rico. While the Treaty of

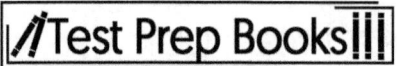

Paris ended the war with Spain in 1898, the First Philippine Republic objected to the terms of the treaty. The Philippine-American War, which the Filipino people considered to be a continuation of their war for independence against Spain, lasted for three years, with individual groups in the Philippines continuing to fight until 1913. While the U.S. eventually won the war, hundreds of thousands of Filipino civilians died, largely as a result of famine and disease. There were also reports of atrocities committed on both sides. The Philippines would remain an American territory until 1946.

United States-Mexican War

The Mexican-American War (1846 – 1848) began over a border dispute. The Republic of Texas declared its independence from Mexico in 1836 and applied to join the United States. However, in a desire to avoid war with Mexico, the administration of President Martin van Buren decided not to annex Texas. Two administrations later, President John Tyler, with the support of President-Elect James K. Polk, was able to pass a bill to annex Texas right before he left office in 1845, which Polk then signed. The Texas and Mexican governments disagreed on where the Texas border ended. Polk sent in the U.S. Army under Zachary Taylor to occupy the disputed territory. After a failed attempt to purchase the disputed territory from Mexico, the United States declared war on Mexico in 1846. The American troops won several battles although the Mexican army usually outnumbered them. The Mexican troops were poorly armed and trained, and the Americans made use of their highly skilled artillery force. The Americans eventually captured Mexico City in 1847 and forced the Mexican government to sign the Treaty of Guadalupe-Hidalgo in 1848. The treaty recognized American control over Texas and also ceded territory that would become the states of California, Utah, Colorado, Arizona, New Mexico, and Nevada in exchange for $15 million. Tens of thousands of prospectors flooded into California when gold was discovered in 1849. The prospectors often encroached on Native American lands, which led to further conflict. In 1854, the United States also acquired additional territories in what would become Arizona and New Mexico as part of the Gadsden Purchase, which was part of the Treaty of Mesilla between Mexico and the United States. The acquisition of so much new territory sparked a debate over whether the land would be open or closed to slavery.

Sectionalism and the Civil War

In the early 1800s, political and economic differences between the North and South became more apparent. Politically, a small but vocal group of abolitionists emerged in the North who demanded a complete end to slavery throughout the United States. William Lloyd Garrison edited the abolitionist newspaper *The Liberator* and vehemently denounced the brutality of slavery. His criticism was so vicious that the legislature of Georgia offered a $5,000 bounty to anyone who could capture Garrison and deliver him to state authorities. Other activists participated in the Underground Railroad—a network that helped fugitive slaves escape to the Northern United States or Canada.

Economic differences emerged as the North began to industrialize, especially in the textile industry where factories increased productivity. However, the Southern economy remained largely agricultural and focused on labor-intensive crops such as tobacco and cotton. This meant that slavery remained an essential part of the Southern economy. In addition, the North built more roads, railroads, and canals, while the Southern transportation system lagged behind. The Northern economy was also based on cash, while many Southerners still bartered for goods and services. This led to growing sectional tension between the North and South as their economies began to diverge.

These economic differences led to political tension as well, especially over the debate about the expansion of slavery. This debate became more important as the United States expanded westward into the Louisiana Purchase and acquired more land after the Mexican-American War. Most Northerners were not abolitionists. However, many opposed the expansion of slavery into the western territories because it would limit their economic opportunities. If a territory was open to slavery, it would be more attractive to wealthy slave owners who could afford to buy up the best land. In addition, the presence of slave labor would make it hard for independent farmers, artisans, and craftsman to make a living because they would have to compete against slaves who did not earn any wages. For their part, Southerners felt it was essential to continue expanding in order to strengthen the southern economy and ensure that the Southern way of life survived. As intensive farming depleted the soil of nutrients, Southern slave owners sought more fertile land in the west.

Both the North and South also feared losing political power as more states were admitted to the nation. For example, neither side wanted to lose influence in the United States senate if the careful balance of free and slave state representation was disrupted. Several compromises were negotiated in Congress, but they only temporarily quieted the debate. The first such effort, called the Missouri Compromise, was passed in 1820, and it maintained political parity in the U.S. Senate by admitting Missouri as a slave state and Maine as a free state. The Missouri Compromise banned slavery in the portion of the Louisiana Purchase that was north of the 36°30' parallel and permitted slavery in the portion south of that line as well as Missouri.

However, the slavery debate erupted again after the acquisition of new territory during the Mexican-American War. The Compromise of 1850 admitted California as a free state and ended the slave trade in Washington, D.C., but not slavery itself, in order to please Northern politicians. In return, Southern politicians were able to pass a stronger fugitive slave law and demanded that New Mexico and Utah be allowed to vote on whether or not slavery would be permitted in their state constitutions. This introduced the idea of popular sovereignty where the residents of each new territory, and not the federal government, could decide whether or not states entering the union would become a slave state or a free state. This essentially negated the Missouri Compromise of 1820. The enhanced fugitive slave law also angered many Northerners because it empowered federal marshals to deputize anyone, even residents of a free state, and force them to help recapture escaped slaves. Anyone who refused would be subject to a $1,000 fine (equivalent to more than $28,000 in 2015).

The debate over slavery erupted again only a few years later when the territories of Kansas and Nebraska were created by the Kansas-Nebraska Act in 1854. The application of popular sovereignty meant that pro- and anti-slavery settlers flooded into these two territories to ensure that their faction would have a majority when it came time to vote on the state constitution. Tension between pro- and anti-slavery forces in Kansas led to an armed conflict known as Bleeding Kansas.

John Brown was a militant abolitionist who fought in Bleeding Kansas and murdered five pro-slavery settlers there in 1856 in response to a pro-slavery attack on Lawrence, Kansas, that resulted in widespread looting and destruction. He returned to the eastern United States and attacked the federal arsenal at Harper's Ferry, Virginia, in 1859. He hoped to seize the weapons there and launch a slave rebellion, but federal troops killed or captured most of Brown's accomplices and Brown himself was executed. The attack terrified Southerners and reflected the increasing hostility between North and South.

The sectional differences that emerged in the last several decades culminated in the presidential election of 1860. Abraham Lincoln led the new Republican Party, which opposed slavery on moral and economic grounds. The question of how best to expand slavery into new territories split the Democratic Party into two different factions that each nominated a presidential candidate. A fourth candidate also ran on a platform of preserving the union by trying to ignore the slavery controversy.

Lincoln found little support outside of the North but managed to win the White House since the Democratic Party was divided. Southern states felt threatened by Lincoln's anti-slavery stance and feared he would abolish slavery throughout the country. South Carolina was the first Southern state to secede from the Union and ten more eventually followed. By February 1861, they had formed the new nation of the Confederate States of America, electing Jefferson Davis as their president in November of that year.

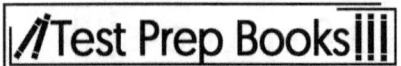

Lincoln declared that the Union could not be dissolved and swore to defend federal installations. The Civil War began when Confederate troops fired on Fort Sumter in Charleston in 1861.

Civil War

The First Battle of Bull Run (also known as the First Battle of Manassas) in 1861 was the first major infantry engagement of the Civil War. Both the Northern and Southern troops were inexperienced and, although they had equal numbers, the Confederates emerged victorious. Many had thought the war would be short, but it continued for another four years.

The Union navy imposed a blockade on the Confederacy and captured the port of New Orleans in 1862. The Union navy was much stronger than the Confederate fleet and prevented the Southern states from selling cotton to foreign countries or buying weapons.

In 1862, Union forces thwarted a Confederate invasion of Maryland at the Battle of Antietam. This engagement was the single bloodiest day of the war and more than 23,000 men on both sides were killed or wounded. Union troops forced the Confederates to retreat, and that gave Lincoln the political capital he needed to issue the Emancipation Proclamation in 1863. This declaration did not abolish slavery, but it did free slaves in Southern territory. It also allowed African Americans to join the Union Army and Navy and about 200,000 did so. The 54th Massachusetts Infantry was a famous unit of African American soldiers who led an assault on Fort Wagner in South Carolina in 1863. Although the attack failed, the 54th Massachusetts demonstrated African American troops fighting bravely under fire.

The Siege of Vicksburg in 1863 was a major Union victory because the Union gained control of the Mississippi River and cut the Confederacy in half. This made it difficult the Confederacy to move troops around and communicate with their forces. General Ulysses S. Grant commanded the Northern forces in the siege and eventually became the Union army's top general.

The Battle of Gettysburg in 1863 marked the turning point of the Civil War. Robert E. Lee led Confederate troops into Pennsylvania, but in three days of heavy fighting, the Union army forced them to retreat. The victory bolstered Northern morale and weakened Southern resolve. Never again would Confederate forces threaten Northern territory.

In 1864, Union general William T. Sherman captured Atlanta, Georgia, and then marched more than 200 miles to Savannah. Along the way, he destroyed anything that could support the Southern war effort, such as railroads and cotton mills. At this point, the Southern economy was beginning to collapse. The North had more manpower than the South and could afford to sustain more casualties. The North also had more industrial capacity to produce weapons and supplies and more railroads to transport men and equipment.

Eventually, Robert E. Lee surrendered to Ulysses S. Grant at Appomattox, Virginia, on April 9, 1865. Five days later, John Wilkes Booth assassinated Lincoln in Washington, D.C. Vice President Andrew Johnson, a Democrat, succeeded him and soon came into conflict with Republicans in Congress about how to reintegrate Southern states into the nation. This process was known as Reconstruction and lasted from 1865 to 1877.

Reconstruction

Johnson opposed equal rights for African Americans and pardoned many Confederate leaders. However, many Congressional Republicans wanted to harshly punish Southerners for their attempts to secede from the Union. They were known as Radical Republicans because they also wanted to give former slaves equal rights.

Johnson vetoed bills that were designed to protect the rights of freed slaves, but Congress overrode his vetoes. This led to increasing conflict between Johnson and Congress, which eventually caused Radical Republicans to impeach him. Although Johnson was acquitted in 1868, he had very little power, and Radical Republicans took control of the Reconstruction process.

Republicans passed three important constitutional amendments as part of the Reconstruction process. The Thirteenth Amendment was ratified in 1865, and it abolished slavery throughout the country. The Fourteenth Amendment was ratified in 1868 and gave equal rights to all citizens. The Fifteenth Amendment was ratified in 1870 and specifically granted all men the right to vote regardless of race.

Southerners resisted these demands and passed laws that prohibited freed slaves from owning weapons or testifying against whites. They also formed militias and vigilante groups, such as the Ku Klux Klan, in order to intimidate African Americans who tried to vote. Congress sent federal troops into Southern states in order to enforce the law and prevent vigilante violence.

Reconstruction officially ended with the Compromise of 1877. After the intensely disputed election of 1876, the Democrats offered to let the Republicans have the White House if they agreed to end Reconstruction. After the Republicans agreed, federal troops were withdrawn and African Americans in the South were subjected to discrimination until the Civil Rights movement of the 1960s. Scholars often consider the Reconstruction era the beginning of Jim Crow and a transition into a new form of institutionalized racism.

The United States as a World Power

Emergence of the United States as a World Power Between 1898 and 1920

The Panic of 1893 was a worldwide economic depression that devastated the American economy. Businesses went bankrupt, banks collapsed, and unemployment rose to approximately 17%. The economy began to recover by 1897, and the beginning of World War I boosted the U.S. economy as European nations bought American goods.

The development of imperialism began in the mid-nineteenth century and lasted until the twentieth century, with much of the imperialized world gaining freedom after World Wars I and II. The spread of imperialism that was to follow the revolutions of the eighteenth and nineteenth centuries can be traced, in part, to the idea of nationalism. Some countries believed they were doing a good, and even a moral, thing by conquering and colonizing new territory to spread their culture, traditions, religion, and government. However, a darker side of nationalism—the feeling of superiority and right—caused the takeover of areas and the enforcement of foreign rules and laws. The United States was initially against imperialism after having been a colony itself and even solidified these ideas in the Monroe Doctrine; however, by the late nineteenth and early twentieth centuries, the United States defeated Spain in the Spanish-American War and annexed Hawaii, Guam, and the Philippines.

The United States gained prestige and international status after the Spanish-American War of 1898, because the United States defeated Spain and acquired several colonies. American participation in World War I made the United States an economic and financial leader as well. The United States loaned money to Britain and France and supplied weapons and equipment that helped the Triple Entente achieve victory. The United States and USSR emerged from World War II as the only surviving superpowers because so much of the rest of the world had been devastated. This system was described as bipolar because there were two centers of power.

The United States was the leader of the free world during the Cold War and formed military and economic alliances with other nations. With the collapse of the USSR in 1991, the United States was the only surviving world power. This era was a unipolar system because there were no other major powers that could rival the United States.

National and International Conflicts Between World War I and World War II

World War I began in 1914 with the assassination of Franz Ferdinand, the heir apparent of the Austro-Hungarian Empire. A network of secret alliances meant that most European nations were quickly drawn into the conflict, although President Woodrow Wilson initially tried to keep the United States neutral. The United States, as far back as the colonial days, had practiced political isolationism which had been suggested by early American figures such as Thomas Paine and George Washington. The war involved two major European alliances: the Triple Entente of the United Kingdom, France, and Russia and the Central Powers which included Germany and Austria-Hungary. The British implemented a naval blockade that was very successful, and the Germans retaliated by launching submarine attacks. German submarines attacked any ship carrying supplies to the Triple Entente, including the passenger ship RMS Lusitania in 1915. About 1,200 people died, including more than 100 Americans. The Germans temporarily halted their unrestricted submarine campaign but eventually resumed the attacks in 1917. In addition, in 1917, Germany asked Mexico to attack the United States in a communiqué known as the Zimmerman telegram. These events led the United States to join the Triple Entente in 1917, although significant numbers of American troops did not arrive in Europe until 1918. American reinforcement helped the British and French, who had been fighting continuously since 1914, launch a final offensive that defeated Germany in 1918. American forces suffered about 320,000 casualties. World War I also led to significant changes on the home front as women took on new responsibilities and thousands of African Americans migrated north in search of work. World War I also led to a communist revolution that transformed Russia into the U.S.S.R. in 1922.

After Germany was defeated in 1918, Wilson made a proposal known as the Fourteen Points and argued that the best way to resolve the conflict was by promoting free trade and democracy. For instance, Wilson wanted nations to respect the right to navigate in international waters and create a League of Nations that would resolve future disputes. Some of his suggestions, such as the League of Nations, were adopted, but many were not. In 1919, Germany was forced to sign the Treaty of Versailles, which imposed harsh economic penalties and restricted the German military. Ultimately, the Treaty of Versailles created resentment in Germany that led to World War II. America emerged as an important player in world affairs after World War I because the American economy had supplied the Triple Entente with arms and equipment and American soldiers helped to achieve victory.

How National and International Conflicts from World War II to the Present

In the period between the world wars, fascism became popular in many European countries that were ravaged by the Great Depression. Fascism is a political ideology that advocates for a dictatorship in order to provide stability and unity. Adolf Hitler emerged as a prominent fascist leader in Germany and eventually brought the Nazi party to power in 1933. Germany, Italy, and Japan formed an alliance called the Axis and began to threaten other countries. The League of Nations could not diffuse the conflict. World War II broke out when Germany invaded Poland in 1939. Hitler quickly conquered most of Europe with a strategy known as "blitzkrieg," or lightning war. By June of 1940 Great Britain was the only Western European nation still independent from Germany. Germany relentlessly attacked Britain, including bombing raids known as the Blitz from September 1940 to May 1941, in preparation for an invasion, and attacked the U.S.S.R. in 1941. The United States sent military equipment and weapons to Britain and the U.S.S.R. but did not formally join the war until the Japanese attacked Pearl Harbor on December 7, 1941. Again, women played an important role on the home front by working in factories to build guns, tanks, planes, and ships. African Americans, Native Americans, and Japanese Americans also contributed by fighting on the front lines.

American forces first landed in North Africa where they, along with British and French troops, defeated German and Italian forces in 1942. In 1943, Allied forces invaded Italy, and Soviet troops began to push the German army back out of the USSR. Allied troops landed in France in 1944 and the Soviets began to advance on Germany as well. By May 1945, Hitler had committed suicide and Germany had been defeated.

This also brought about an end to the Holocaust. The Holocaust was a genocide committed by Hitler's Nazi Germany and collaborators that resulted in the deaths of more than 6 million Jews and 5 million Romans, gypsies, Afro-Europeans, disabled citizens, and homosexuals. A network of facilities in Germany and its territories were used to house victims for slave labor and mass murder, among other heinous crimes. The Nuremberg trials were part of the aftermath of the Holocaust, which served to prosecute important members of Nazi Germany leadership.

In the Pacific theater, American naval forces defeated the Japanese fleet in several key engagements, including the battle of Midway in 1942. American troops began recapturing territory in the Pacific as well and eventually pushed the Japanese back to their home islands in 1945. The Japanese refused to surrender until American planes dropped atomic bombs on the cities of Nagasaki and Hiroshima in August 1945.

Because World War II devastated most of Europe, the United States and the USSR emerged as the only superpowers when it ended. However, the erstwhile allies were suspicious of each other, which led to the Cold War.

Significant Individuals Who Shaped U.S. Foreign Policy from 1898 to the Present

Alfred Thayer Mahan

Alfred Thayer Mahan was a U.S. naval officer and historian who became famous after publishing a book titled *The Influence of Sea Power Upon History, 1600–1783* (1890). Mahan is famous for extending America's Manifest Destiny beyond its coasts and into the seas. Mahan believed that the future of world dominance and democratic hegemony rested upon the creation of a strong navy. He thus encouraged the United States to carry out its imperial dreams on the high seas, paving the way for the aggressive expansionist initiatives of the U.S. government in the late 1800s.

Theodore Roosevelt

President Theodore Roosevelt, who led the nation between 1901 and 1909, is famous for a series of modernization and conservation projects. Additionally, Roosevelt is famous for adding the Roosevelt Corollary (1904) to the Monroe Doctrine. The Corollary stated that the U.S. would take on the role of an international police power to resolve disputes between European and Latin American countries, rather than allowing Europeans to intervene themselves. The Roosevelt Corollary, backed by an impressive U.S. Navy, allowed the United States to have unchecked power in Latin America for decades after the Roosevelt administration. One result of the U.S. interest in Latin America was Roosevelt enthusiastically offering the Panamanian governor $10 million per year to build and operate the Panama Canal. Operating under U.S. leadership between 1914 and 1999, the Panama Canal remained a last symbol of Roosevelt's diplomatic legacy in Latin America. The canal is a beacon of the United States strong-armed diplomatic influence in Latin America during the years of the Roosevelt Corollary. During Roosevelt's presidency, the United States occupied many Latin American countries for self-serving reasons. Nevertheless, not all of Roosevelt's policies were as self-serving—the rough-and-tumble president is also responsible for establishing the National Park System in the United States and setting aside hundreds of thousands of acres of land for conservation.

Woodrow Wilson

President Woodrow Wilson declared war on Germany on April 2, 1917. American troops helped defeat the German army in September 1918. Fighting ended in November of that year after Germany signed a peace agreement. President Woodrow Wilson's plan for peace was the League of Nations, which was adopted as part of the Treaty of Versailles in 1919, but then rejected by the U.S. Senate.

Franklin D. Roosevelt

Democratic candidate Franklin D. Roosevelt was elected president in 1932 on his promise to help the economy recover by increasing government spending. After taking office in 1933, Roosevelt introduced a barrage of proposals, called the New Deal, that he hoped would boost employment, stimulate demand, and increase government regulation. Some elements of the New Deal were temporary, such as the Civilian Conservation Corps, which put young men to work improving parks between 1933 and 1942. Other New Deal programs endure to this day, such as the Social Security Administration, which has provided pensions to retirees, temporary payments to unemployed workers, and benefits to handicapped individuals since 1935. In addition, the Securities and Exchange Commission was created in 1934 and continues to regulate stock markets and investment companies. The Wagner Act of 1935 was also an important part of the New Deal because it guaranteed the right of workers to unionize and go on strike. The 21st Amendment was ratified in 1933 and repealed Prohibition, which had been hard to enforce and was unpopular. Roosevelt also hoped it would create jobs and stimulate spending. The New Deal helped reduce unemployment, but the economy did not completely recover until America entered World War II and production increased in order to support the war efforts.

Henry Kissinger

Henry Kissinger is a Jewish refugee who fled Hitler's Nazi Germany in 1938. Kissinger rose to prominence as a foreign diplomat and political scientist for the United States of America. He is best known for his tenure as a secretary of state and national security advisor during the Nixon and Ford administrations. Between 1969 and 1977, Kissinger gained notoriety as a Cold Warrior who supported *Realpolitik* and *détente* approaches to Cold War diplomacy with the Soviet Union. He is renowned as the secretary of state who assisted President Richard Nixon in opening relations with China. He won a Nobel Peace Prize in 1973 for orchestrating a cease-fire in Vietnam. Opinions regarding his work as secretary of state are often divided. Some point to his practical approach to the Cold War; others condemn him for his support of controversial CIA missions in foreign nations.

Significant Events that Shaped U.S. Foreign Policy from 1898 to the Present

Marshall Plan

After World War II, the United States offered European countries the Marshall Plan—a grant of American subsidies to help Europe and Japan recover economically. The largest recipients were England, France, and West Germany. Aside from sincere humanitarian desires, the Marshall Plan also served the interests of the United States by ensuring that Europe's citizens did not resort to Communism out of desperation. In turn, the Soviet Union developed their own plan, the Molotov Plan, to help their Communist Allies' recovery.

NATO

NATO (North Atlantic Treaty Organization) is an organization of states from North America and Europe, led by the United States. This organization was formed after the end of World War II to counter the Soviet Union and Warsaw Pact's efforts to spread Communism across the world.

Berlin Airlift

Following the Second World War, France, Great Britain, and the United States began occupying Berlin, Germany, in hopes of rebuilding Europe and providing stability to the region. The USSR also encroached on the territory, specifically West Germany, hoping to weaken the former Nazi stronghold and strengthen their western military front. In 1948, the former Allies—France, Great Britain, and the United States—tried to withdraw their forces from Berlin, allowing their three occupation zones to unite. The USSR responded to the West's withdrawal by holding the western side of Berlin hostage. Much like Germany at large, the capital city of Berlin was previously divided into four sections following the war. In a strategic attempt to declare dominance over the former Nazi capital, the USSR's military blockaded the highways, waterways, and railways leading into West Berlin. The leader of the USSR—Joseph Stalin—believed the blockade would intimidate the former allies. Stalin's blockade forced many West Berliners into starvation. To prevent starvation, the American and British air forces flew over the blockade on a regular basis, dropping supplies to West Berlin. In a little over a year, the allied air forces made 277,000 flights over West Berlin. This strategy—known as the Berlin Airlift—eventually forced Stalin and the USSR to lift the blockade in May 1948.

McCarthyism

Wisconsin senator Joseph McCarthy led the charge in a series of investigations and trials that sought to uncover communist agents and propagandists in the U.S. government, Hollywood, and other public institutions. Anti-communist sentiment rose sharply in the U.S. after World War II as the Soviet Union began expanding its influence throughout Europe and establishing Communist governments in territory it acquired during the war. The Soviet development of a nuclear bomb and the rise of Communism in China, both in 1949, and the invasion of South Korea by Communist North Korea in 1950 exacerbated the fears of U.S. citizens regarding Communism itself, and especially the concern of espionage in the United States. McCarthy was elected to the Senate in 1946, and in 1950, became famous when he claimed there were over 200 communists infiltrating the State Department. These claims led to a series of investigations and public hearings which reached their peak in 1954 with thirty-six days of televised hearings. Despite claims to the contrary, the Soviet messages intercepted and decoded by the Venona Project (1943 – 1980) proved that there were hundreds of Americans passing information to the Russians. However, McCarthy often put forward wild and unsubstantiated claims, which he then backed to the hilt. In 1954 he was censored by the Senate and by 1957 the Second Red Scare was largely over. McCarthyism is now a term that has become synonymous with Cold War fears and any type of public defamation or indiscriminate allegations.

Korean War

When Communist North Korea invaded South Korea in June 1950, the U.N. sent a group of troops led by the U.S. to help South Korea. This action led to a three-year conflict that ended in a cease-fire in 1953. Although war was never officially declared and neither side won, the fighting showcased President Truman's hard stance against Communism.

Vietnam War

In 1954, rebels seized control of Vietnam from France. The country was split into two regimes with the northern part under Communist leadership. As the threat of communism continued to loom, the U.S. sent advisors and weapons to South Vietnam beginning in 1955. The U.S. got more directly involved in the 1960s during the presidency of Lyndon B. Johnson, who sent troops in great numbers to help South Vietnam win the fight. Many Americans opposed the war, which caused anti-war protests and unrest. A cease-fire was signed in 1973, and the last U.S. forces pulled out in 1975.

Cuban Missile Crisis

The Cuban Missile Crisis in 1962 was sparked by the failed invasion of Cuba by the U.S. a year earlier. After the invasion, the Soviets placed nuclear missiles aimed at the U.S. in Cuba. However, when U.S. spy planes spotted them, President John F. Kennedy demanded the dismantling and removal of the missile sites, and as a concession agreed to go forward with the planned removal of U.S. missile sites in Turkey. A year later on November 22, 1963, President Kennedy was assassinated in Dallas by Lee Harvey Oswald.

Sputnik I

The Cold War prompted the *space race* between the U.S. and Soviets, each attempting to outdo the other with different space exploration milestones. In 1957, the Russians launched *Sputnik*, the first satellite, into space. This prompted President Eisenhower to establish the National Aeronautics and Space Administration (NASA) in 1958. Although the Soviets were also the first nation to send a human into space in 1961, the U.S. quickly caught up. President Kennedy vowed to land an American on the Moon by 1969—a feat that was accomplished by astronaut Neil Armstrong on July 20, 1969.

Gulf War

In 1990, Iraqi dictator Saddam Hussein invaded Kuwait in order to take possession of the tiny country's huge oil fields. A few months later, U.S. President George H.W. Bush launched Operation Desert Storm with a coalition of

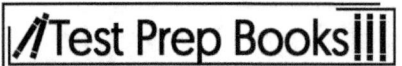

several Middle Eastern and European countries. This Gulf War started with air bombings and ended in a five-day ground war that drove Hussein out.

Major Foreign Policy Issues Currently Facing the United States

For over twenty years after the terrorist attacks on the World Trade Center in New York City, the United States was entangled in the politics of the Middle East, and to this day the United States is still working to find ways to cope with the ongoing threat of global terrorism. The events of September 11, 2011—often referred to as *9/11*—galvanized the United States of America into a self-declared war on terrorism. These events have challenged and changed many relationships between the United States and the world. Some scholars, for instance, saw the war on terrorism as the final blow to old Cold War politics. However, recent military events in Eastern Europe, Syria, and the broader Middle East indicate that the Cold War may be heating up again on the geopolitical stage.

U.S. economy remains the largest in the world, making it a strong contender to continue its role as Leader of the Free World. Although U.S. economic hegemony has declined, relatively, in an era of globalization and North American Free Trade Agreement (NAFTA), the United States is poised to remain an economic player in the coming decades.

Political, Economic, and Social Developments from 1877 to the Present

United States from 1877 to the Present

The post-World War II era led to a number of social, economic, and technological changes in the United States. The counter-culture phenomenon was one of the most powerful social movements in the latter half of the twentieth century in the U.S. The counter-culture movement challenged social norms and rejected traditional authority figures. The movement began in the 1950s with the beatniks, a group of non-conformist writers and artists who were dissatisfied with society. The beatniks sought inspiration in African and Asian cultures and many eschewed materialism.

Political Developments

President Franklin D. Roosevelt created the New Deal in order to stimulate the economy and improve government regulation. The New Deal also marked an important shift in American politics because the Democratic Party began to favor government intervention while Republicans opposed it. This was a reversal of the parties' previous platforms. The Democratic Party relied on a coalition of labor unions, Catholics, African Americans, and other minorities. The Republican Party included conservatives, evangelicals, and business leaders.

The Great Society was another major government program that the Democratic Party supported. President Lyndon B. Johnson sought to end poverty and improve education. For example, he raised the minimum wage and created programs to provide poor Americans with job training. The Great Society also implemented a number of Civil Rights laws that will be discussed in greater detail later.

The presidential election of 1980 was another watershed moment. Republican nominee Ronald Reagan carried forty-three states, and the Republicans won a majority in the U.S. Senate after twenty-eight years of Democratic control. Reagan presented an optimistic message and broadcast a television advertisement that proclaimed, "It's morning again in America." He promised to restore America's military power, cut government regulations, and reduce taxes. Reagan enjoyed the support of resurgent conservative Christian evangelicals, who wanted to restore morality to American society. They were particularly concerned about issues such as abortion. The Moral Majority, founded by Baptist minister Jerry Falwell in 1979, was one key group that helped Reagan win the election. This coalition helped realign party loyalties as more liberal Republicans and conservative Democrats shifted their allegiance to support Reagan's platform.

Economic Developments

America emerged as one of the most powerful economies in the world after 1945. The US economy, especially manufacturing, was very prosperous during the 1950s and 1960s. The economy successfully switched from wartime production, and consumer demand was very high. During the Great Depression, few families had disposable income. Although most workers earned good wages during World War II, they had little to spend it on because most goods were rationed. Once production of consumer goods resumed, families used their savings to buy cars, household appliances, and televisions. This was good for the economy, and unemployment remained below 5% for most of the 1950s and 1960s. However, during the latter part of the 20th century, the manufacturing base in the North and Midwest began to crumble and the area became known as the Rust Belt. Manufacturing jobs began to move from the North and Midwest to states in the South and West, known as the Sun Belt, where land was cheap, and wages were low.

The world economy also became increasingly interconnected during the post-World War II era. This accelerated the process of globalization, which is the integration of ideas and products from different cultures. This benefitted the United States economically because businesses, such as McDonald's and Coca-Cola, found many consumers around the world who were eager to consume American goods. However, the process works both ways, and many aspects of foreign culture, such as Japanese cartoons and animation, have become very popular in the United States. Many critics also point out that globalization has hurt the American economy in recent decades because manufacturing jobs have gone overseas to countries in South America and Asia where wages are low.

Social Developments

Counter-Culture Movement

The counterculture movement became popular during the 1960s as millions of children from the Baby Boomer generation entered into adulthood. Many of these young adults were disaffected and unhappy with the social norms of their parents' generation. In general, they rejected ideas such as segregation, support for the Vietnam war, traditional sexual mores, and traditional gender roles for women. The counterculture movement also included widespread experimentation with drugs. Many members of the counterculture movement inherited the beatnik's interest in African and Asian cultures, and many, often called hippies, adopted alternative lifestyles. One of the key elements of the movement was an emphasis on experimentation, artistry, and self-expression. As a result, the counterculture movement produced many musicians and avant-garde artists.

The counter-culture movement was also closely connected to other protest movements during the 1960s, including the Civil Rights movement, which will be discussed later. Many members of the counter-culture movement during the 1960s also opposed the war in Vietnam. The Baby Boomers could be conscripted to fight in Vietnam whether they wanted to or not. In 1965, young men began burning their draft cards, which was a criminal offense, in protest. Massive demonstrations against the war occurred around the country, especially on college campuses, but many other people also refused to support the war effort, including clergymen and even some veterans who had fought in Vietnam. The counterculture movement had a lasting impact on the social and cultural history of the United States.

Race, Gender, and Ethnicity

Race, gender, and ethnicity have been important themes in American history from the colonial era to the present. Individuals from different races, ethnicities, and genders have had very different experiences throughout the same historical events or eras. It is important to distinguish between race and ethnicity: race refers to a group of people with common ancestry, while ethnicity refers to cultural background, such as language and tradition.

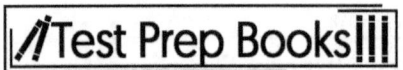

Race played an important part in colonial America because both Caucasians and Africans occupied positions of servitude. White immigrants who could not purchase passage to the New World sometimes agreed to become indentured servants. Their employers paid for their passage across the Atlantic, and in exchange, the indentured servant agreed to work without wages for at least five years. However, African slaves were rarely able to free themselves. The strong connection between slavery and race meant that all blacks, whether free or enslaved, were viewed as inferior. After the American Revolution, most free blacks, even those living in northern states, were denied the right to vote. Although the Civil Rights Movement in the 1960s made great gains, many activists claim more must be done in order to overcome the legacy of racial inequality in America.

Japanese Americans experienced discrimination during and after World War II, specifically with the implementation of Japanese internment camps in America. This forced 110,000 to 120,000 Japanese Americans into camps, 62% of which were United States citizens.

Discrimination against certain ethnicities is also prominent throughout American history as well. For example, many Americans resented the arrival of German and Irish immigrants during the 1800s because they spoke a different language or practiced different religions. Hispanics were also subject to discrimination, and in 1943, a number of Hispanic youths were attacked during the Zoot Suit Riots.

Gender differences in the United States have also been impossible to ignore. For example, until the 1840s, most married women in the United States were unable to enter into contracts, own property, or retain their own wages. Women were unable to vote until the 19th Amendment was ratified in 1920. The Women's Rights Movement in the U.S. ranged from 1848 to 1920. This movement called for a woman's right to vote, the right to bodily autonomy, freedom from sexual violence, the right to hold public office, the right to work, the right to fair wages and equal pay, and the right to own property and obtain an education. Women continue to demand change during the twenty-first century for reasons such as the gender wage gap, better resources for women's health, female reproductive rights, and protection of basic human rights, such as bringing greater awareness to rape culture, violence against women, and protection against female sex trafficking.

Technological Changes

Several technological changes have had a significant impact on the U.S. economy as well. The Cold War led to advances in nuclear power and aerospace engineering. The development of computers, in particular, has helped accelerate the transition to a post-industrial economy where information technology and other services have replaced traditional manufacturing jobs. The first computers were used to break coded messages during World War II and had very limited computing power. The invention of transistor technology in 1947 made computers cheaper, smaller, and more reliable. The invention of integrated circuits in the 1960s and 1970s increased computing power and gave birth to the first personal computers. The Internet was created in 1969, but widespread use in business and academia did not begin until the 1980s. These developments have made it much easier to share information and have increased economic opportunities. But, the increasing use of robots, especially in the manufacturing industry, have also made the economy more efficient while also causing layoffs.

Third Party Movements

Populism

Populism advocates for incorporating advances in technology, social organization, science, and economics into the government to benefit society. It is fueled by the idea that social goals should be achieved by the actions of the people, and not the dominant elites. The term *populism* became popular in the 1890s by farmers and labor unions in reaction to the Gilded Age, and returned in the 1950s. Some populist political parties in the U.S. include Greenback Party, Progressive Party of 1912, Progressive Party of 1924, and the Share Our Wealth movement by Huey Long.

Progressive Era Reforms

The social inequalities and economic abuses of the Gilded Age did not go unnoticed, and in the 1890s many reformers began to demand change. This period was called the Progressive Era and included activists in both the Democratic and Republican parties. The Progressives wanted to use scientific methods and government regulation to improve society. For example, they advocated the use of direct democracy procedures such as the ballot initiative (citizens changing a law directly rather than through their legislatures), the referendum (a direct vote on a law passed by Congress), and recall (voters removing public officials from office) to make government more responsive to its citizens. Progressives also argued that it was necessary to break up large monopolies (known as trust busting) in order to promote equal economic competition. In 1911, Rockefeller's Standard Oil was split up into thirty-four different companies in order to promote competition, and the Federal Trade Commission was established in 1914 in order to prevent other monopolies from forming. Many Progressives also supported several constitutional amendments that were ratified in early 20th century, including the Seventeenth Amendment, which established the direct election of U.S. Senators in 1913 (previously state legislatures had elected senators). They also favored the prohibition of alcohol that went into effect with the Eighteenth Amendment in 1919. Progressives also advocated for women's rights and backed the Nineteenth Amendment, which gave women the right to vote in 1920.

New Deal

In 1933, President Franklin D. Roosevelt introduced the New Deal, which was a series of executive orders and laws passed by Congress in response to the Great Depression. The programs focused on relief, recovery, and reform, and were enacted until 1938. The second New Deal from 1935-1938 promoted the Social Security Act, labor unions, and aided tenant farmers and migrant workers who were struggling from the economic devastation of the Great Depression.

Susan B. Anthony

Susan B. Anthony was a woman's rights activist who was committed to social equality during the women's suffrage movement. She advocated for women's rights as well as the abolition of slavery. Anthony is widely known for her involvement in the National American Woman Suffrage Association, as well as her conviction and subsequent fine for voting in her hometown of Rochester, New York in 1872.

W.E.B. Du Bois

Du Bois was one of the co-founders of National Association for the Advancement of Colored People (NAACP) and was a sociologist, civil rights activist, Pan-Africanist, author, and historian. Du Bois was the first African American to earn a Ph.D. from Harvard University in 1895. W.E.B. DuBois wrote several prolific works, including *The Souls of Black Folk*, and *Black Reconstruction in America*, a text that challenged the notion that the failures of the Reconstruction Eras were the faults of African Americans.

George Wallace

Running on a third-party platform, George Wallace entered the 1968 presidential election as an Independent who was a founder and card-carrying member of the far-right American Independent Party (AIP). Under the leadership of George Wallace, who was a former governor of Alabama, the AIP promulgated a segregationist political platform that called for the reinstatement of Jim Crow and an unraveling of civil rights progress across the United States. As a southern neo-Dixiecrat, Wallace lamented the social and political advances of the civil rights movement in the mid-1960s. Even years earlier, as an Alabama governor, he promised his voters that he stood for "segregation now, segregation tomorrow, [and] segregation forever." During his 1968 election against Richard M. Nixon and Hubert H. Humphrey, Wallace acquired a record five states as a third-party candidate: Georgia, Mississippi, Alabama, Louisiana, and Arkansas. The state of third-party politics has remained weakened since the 1968 election, and no other platform has ever gained as many electoral votes as Wallace's AIP.

Industrialization in the United States

After the end of the Civil War, America experienced a period of intense industrialization, immigration, and urbanization, and all three trends were interrelated. The process of industrialization had begun before the Civil War but expanded into more sectors of the economy in the later part of the century. This era is often called the Second Industrial Revolution and included growth in the chemical, petroleum, iron, steel, and telecommunications industries.

The writer Mark Twain called the late 19th century the Gilded Age because the era was also one of extreme social inequality. Some corporations expanded and began to control entire industries. For example, by 1890, the Standard Oil Company produced 88% of all the refined oil in the nation. This made a few individuals, such as Standard Oil owner John D. Rockefeller, extremely wealthy. On the other hand, many workers earned low wages and began to form labor unions, such as the American Federation of Labor in 1886, to demand better working conditions and higher pay. Strikes were one of the most common ways workers could express their dissatisfaction, and the Pullman Strike of 1894 was one of the largest such incidents in the nineteenth century. Workers went on strike after the Pullman Company, which manufactured railroad cars, cut wages by about 25%. More than 125,000 workers around the country walked off the job and attacked workers hired to replace them. Federal troops were sent in to end the strike, and more than eighty workers were killed or wounded during confrontations. The strike was unsuccessful, but Congress passed a law making Labor Day a federal holiday in order to placate union members.

Immigration also played an important part in the economic and social changes that occurred during the late 19th century. Immigration patterns changed during this time and immigrants from Southern and Eastern Europe, such as Italy and Poland, began to surpass the number of arrivals from Northern and Western Europe. The immigrants sought economic opportunity in the United States because wages for unskilled workers were higher than in their home countries. Some Americans resented the influx of immigrants because they spoke different languages and many practiced Catholicism. As a result, in 1924 Congress passed the Immigration Act of 1924, which included the Asian Exclusion Act and the National Origins Act, that prohibited immigration from Asian and significantly restricted immigration from Southern and Eastern Europe.

Increased urbanization was the last factor that contributed to the rapid changes of the Gilded Age. Factories were located near cities in order to draw upon a large pool of potential employees. Immigrants flooded into cities in search of work, and new arrivals often settled in the same neighborhoods where their compatriots lived. Between 1860 and 1890, the urbanization rate increased from about 20% to 35%. Cities struggled to keep up with growing populations, and services such as sanitation and water often lagged behind demand. Immigrants often lived in crowded conditions that facilitated the spread of diseases.

Significant Individuals from 1877 to the Present

Jane Addams
Jane Addams is known as one of the most prominent reformers of the Progressive Era. She was a pioneer in Social Work and advocated for the health of mothers, the needs of children, world peace, and public health. She was also an activist, author, and leader in the women's suffrage movement. In 1931, she became the first American woman to be awarded the Nobel Peace Prize.

Henry Ford
Henry Ford is famous for the development of the assembly line technique, which gave rise to mass production. Known best as an American industrialist, he founded the Ford Motor Company in 1903.

Franklin D. Roosevelt

FDR was the 32nd President of the United States, elected in 1933. He is widely known for his New Deal policy, which was a program of relief for the Great Depression. He also obtained approval for the declaration of War on Japan and on Germany, effectively entering the U.S. into World War II. FDR was also known for his efforts at conservation of the environment, and created 140 national wildlife refuges. He also expanded and funded National Park and National Forest systems.

Martin Luther King Jr.

Martin Luther King, Jr. was a Civil Rights leader and activist as well as a Baptist minister. King argued for nonviolent resistance during the Civil Rights movement, for which he won the Nobel Peace Prize in 1964. King was assassinated on April 4, 1968, in Memphis, Tennessee.

King gave his speech *I Have a Dream* as part of the 1963 March on Washington. Drawing on Lincoln's past speech at Gettysburg, Dr. King argued that America's journey to true equality was not over. His references to biblical passages gave the speech a spiritual tone, but he also mentioned specific locations across the nation to emphasize that local struggles were tied with national consequences. By emphasizing his optimism, King's speech reflects not only civil rights activism but also the American dream of freedom and progress.

Cesar Chavez

Cesar Chavez was a labor union activist who organized transient Hispanic agricultural workers in an effort to obtain better working conditions in the 1960s and 1970s. He co-founded the National Farm Workers Association. Chavez became a historical icon after his death and is famous for popularizing the slogan "Sí, se puede," or "Yes, it can be done."

Betty Friedan

Betty Friedan was an American feminist and writer in the second wave of feminism in the 1960s who was elected the first president of the Nation Organization for Women (NOW). Her book, *The Feminine Mystique,* is widely regarded as the spark that began this second wave. Friedan aimed to empower women to be in an equal partnership with men. She also led the Women's Strike for Equality in 1970, which advocated for equal opportunities for women in jobs and education.

Malcolm X

An African American human rights activist and Muslim minister named Malcolm X advocated for the rights of African Americans and against nonviolence. He became a member of the Nation of Islam, and through that platform promoted the separation of black and white Americans and black supremacy (although he eventually left the Nation of Islam and founded Muslim Mosque, Inc., and the Organization of Afro-American Unity). Malcolm X rejected the Civil Rights movement for its emphasis on integration as well as passive resistance. Malcolm X is known to his admirers as a courageous and important figure in African American history.

Significant Events from 1877 to the Present

In the late 1800s and early 1900s, the forces of urbanization and industrialization combined to create rampant urban plight across the metropolitan centers of the United States. During this era, many progressive political leaders and groups rose to power, opening the door to urban-based reforms in labor, health care, education, women's rights, and temperance. These reforms coalesced in what is now referred to by historians as the Progressive Era.

Antitrust legislation appeared in the late 1800s and early 1900s in response to the unchecked creation of trusts—"legal arrangements in which one board of trustees controls a variety of companies"—and monopolies—"sole vertical and horizontal control of a field business." As a result of these trusts and monopolies, many U.S. citizens had to pay more for railroad transportation, oil and gas, and loans. In the late 1800s and early 1900s, many progressive legislators looked to "bust" these trusts and monopolies. The Sherman Act of 1890, the Clayton Act of 1914, and the Federal Trade Commission Act of 1914 are all examples of "trust-busting" legislation. Using the Sherman Act of 1890, President Theodore Roosevelt dissolved forty-four monopolies and became known as the trust-buster.

The late 1800s and early 1900s also witnessed increased restrictions in immigration. Passed by President Chester A. Arthur, the Chinese Exclusion Act of 1882 inaugurated a decade-long moratorium on Chinese labor immigration. Likewise, the Johnson-Reed Immigration Act of 1924 placed semi-permanent limitations on the number of immigrants who could enter the United States per year. The act established quotas based on national origin, limiting immigration from the Asia-Pacific Triangle. The act also placed quotas on European, African, and Middle Eastern immigration.

Ratification of the 19th Amendment

With the ratification of the 19th Amendment in 1920, women obtained the right to vote. This achievement was partly due to women's contributions on the home front during World War I. Women served as Army nurses and worked in factories to help produce weapons, ammunition, and equipment. As more women entered the workforce, they became more financially independent and began to socialize without being supervised by a chaperone, as was the norm during the 19th century. Overall, women during this period, known as *New Women*, took on a more active role in public life, pursued higher education in greater numbers, and sought more sexual freedom. During the 1920s, women, known as *flappers*, began to flaunt social conventions by wearing short skirts, bobbing hair, smoking cigarettes, and driving automobiles. Nevertheless, a "glass ceiling" still remains in place decades after women's suffrage in regards to a gender wage gap.

Great Depression

Stock market speculation increased during the 1920s, and investors borrowed money in order to purchase shares. This did not cause any concern as long as the stock market went up, but it led to disaster when stock prices fell sharply in October 1929 and investors were unable to repay their loans. The stock market crash may have triggered the Great Depression, but it did not cause it. The Great Depression spread around the globe as nations stopped trading with each other. In the United States, families lost their savings when banks failed because there was no federal insurance. The economy went into a downward spiral because as more people lost their jobs, they had little money to spend, which led to further layoffs and more economic contraction. Unemployment peaked at 25% between 1932 and 1933.

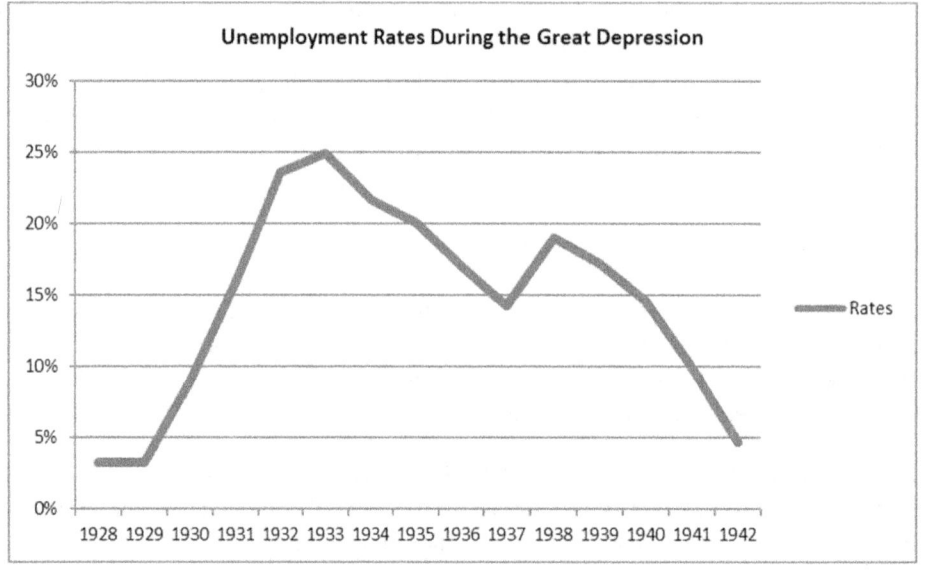

U.S. History | Political, Economic, and Social Developments from 1877 to the Present

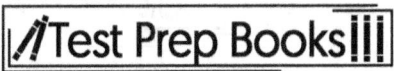

Civil Rights Act of 1964

When the Supreme Court ruled that school segregation was illegal in 1954 in the revolutionary case *Brown vs. the Board of Education*, the Civil Rights Movement was set in motion. This movement continued throughout the 1950s and 1960s and included dozens of nonviolent protests such as the Montgomery bus boycott in Alabama. The boycott was organized after Rosa Parks was arrested because she refused to give up her seat on the bus to a white man. The Southern Christian Leadership Conference (SCLC) was soon formed as a way to bring African Americans together to help fight segregation in a peaceful way. The Reverend Dr. Martin Luther King, Jr. was its first president. Dr. King and his supporters kept up the fight throughout the 1960s, staging sit-ins at segregated lunch counters, Freedom Rides on segregated buses, and marches and protests in segregated cities, such as Birmingham, Alabama. The demonstrations often ended in violence and police brutality, which served to aid the movement and led to the passage of the Civil Rights Act in 1964.

Globalization

The twentieth century marked increasing globalization. The process had already been under way in the nineteenth century as technological improvements and imperial expansions connected different parts of the world, but the late twentieth century brought globalization to a new level. Trade became international, and local customs from different lands also gained prominence worldwide. Cultural exchanges occur on a frequent basis, and many people have begun to ponder the consequences of such rapid exchanges. One example of globalization was the 1993 establishment of the European Union—an economic and political alliance between several European nations.

Terrorism

Islamic fundamentalism often resorts to terrorism to fight against their conventionally more powerful enemies. The most infamous modern terrorist attack occurred on September 11, 2001, when terrorists associated with al-Qaeda hijacked four commercial airliners and flew the planes into the World Trade Center and Pentagon. The 9/11 attack initially led to the United States' invasion of Afghanistan and later contributed to the decision to invade Iraq. These wars heightened the interaction between the Western and Arab worlds, and fundamentalism has increased ever since. Jihadists and religious extremists have flooded the region to defend Islam against what they perceive as the invading West. Additionally, the Arab Spring created a spirit of unrest in many Middle Eastern countries with a history of authoritarian rule. Following the Americans' withdrawal from Iraq and uprisings in neighboring Syria, the religious extremists declared an Islamic State in the region, known as the Islamic State of Iraq and Levant, ensuring the proliferation of Islamic fundamentalism and terrorism for the foreseeable future.

Civil Rights Movements

Although the Declaration of Independence declared "all men are created equal," blacks, women, and other minorities struggled for more than a century to make this dream a reality. Slavery was not abolished until the Thirteenth Amendment to the US Constitution was ratified in 1865. The Fourteenth Amendment, ratified in 1868, granted African Americans citizenship, and the Fifteenth Amendment, ratified in 1870, explicitly granted them the right to vote. However, Jim Crow laws in the South prevented blacks from exercising their rights and, when that failed, Southern whites often relied on violence and intimidation to oppress African Americans. For example, many Southern states required voters to pass literacy tests and used them to prevent blacks from casting a ballot. Whites were either exempt from the test or were held to much lower standards. Blacks who protested their oppression could be assaulted and even killed with impunity. The 1896 Supreme Court decision Plessy v. Ferguson upheld segregation, ruling that segregation laws did not violate the US Constitution as long as equal facilities were available for each race. This led to the separate but equal doctrine; however, in reality, black facilities were almost always inferior to those provided for whites.

The emergence of the Civil Rights Movement after World War II finally destroyed the Jim Crow system. In the 1954 decision *Brown vs. Board of Education*, the Supreme Court reversed the "separate but equal" doctrine and declared

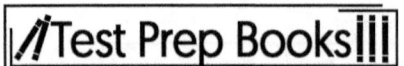

that separate schools were inherently unequal because they stigmatized African American students. In 1957, President Dwight D. Eisenhower used federal troops to force the high school in Little Rock, Arkansas, to integrate and accept nine black students. This encouraged civil rights activists to demand additional reforms. In 1955, Rosa Parks refused to give up her seat on a bus in Montgomery, Alabama, which led to a boycott. Martin Luther King Jr. led the bus boycott and became a national leader in the Civil Rights Movement. In 1960, four students in Greensboro, North Carolina, launched a peaceful sit-in at a segregated lunch counter, which sparked similar protests around the country. White activists from the North went south to help blacks register to vote, and in 1964 three activists were murdered in Mississippi. That same year, King led 250,000 protesters in a march on Washington D.C. where he delivered his famous, *I Have a Dream* Speech.

Although King advocated for peaceful protests, many other civil rights activists disagreed with him. For example, Malcolm X believed that blacks should use violence to defend themselves. Furthermore, King worked with white activists while Malcom X rejected any cooperation. Malcolm X was assassinated in 1965, and, despite his reputation as a non-violent leader, King was also gunned down in 1968.

Under mounting pressure, Congress passed several important pieces of legislation. The 1964 Civil Rights Act banned discrimination based on race, color, religion, sex, or national origin. The Voting Rights Act of 1965 prohibited the use of poll taxes or literacy tests to prohibit voting. The Civil Rights Act of 1968 banned housing discrimination. In 1967, Carl Stokes became the first black mayor of a major American city, Cleveland. That same year, Thurgood Marshall became the first African American to serve on the Supreme Court. President Gerald Ford declared February to be black history month. In 1989, Colin Powell became the first black chairman of the Joint Chiefs of Staff. Despite these reforms, activists claim institutional racism is still a problem in the 21st century. The Civil Rights movement inspired women, Latinos, and other groups to make similar demands for equal rights.

Women

In 1776, Abigail Adams urged her husband, founding father John Adams, to advocate for women's rights, but it would take more than a century before women could vote. In 1848, activists organized a convention in Seneca Falls, New York, to organize the women's suffrage movement, and their efforts slowly gained momentum. The ratification of the 19th Amendment in 1920 finally gave women the right to vote.

Although women had achieved political equality, they continued to demand reform throughout the twentieth century. In the early 1900s, Margaret Sanger provided women with information about birth control, which was illegal at the time. Women entered the industrial workforce in large numbers during World War II, but when the war ended, they were fired so that veterans would have jobs when they came home. Many women were frustrated when told they had to return to their domestic lives. Simone de Beauvoir, a French writer, published her book *The Second Sex* after World War II, and an English translation was published in 1953. It highlighted the unequal treatment of women throughout history and sparked a feminist movement in the United States. In 1963, Betty Friedan published a book, called *The Feminine Mystique*, that revealed how frustrated many suburban wives were with the social norms that kept them at home. During the 1960s, women participated in the sexual revolution and exerted more control over their own sexuality. In 1972, Congress passed Title IX, which prohibited sexual discrimination in education and expanded women's sports programs. In the 1970s, women's rights activists also pushed for greater access to birth control, and in 1973 the Supreme Court issued the controversial decision *Roe vs. Wade* which removed many barriers to abortion services. Women also demanded greater protection from domestic abuse and greater access to divorce.

During the 20th century, many American women made notable achievements, including Amelia Earhart, who was the first woman to cross the Atlantic in an airplane in 1928. In 1981, Sandra Day O'Connor became the first woman to serve on the Supreme Court. In 1983, Sally Ride became the first female astronaut. In 1984, Geraldine Ferraro became the first woman to run for vice-president, although she was unsuccessful. However, many activists continue to demand reform in the 21st century. For example, women only account for 20% of the U.S. Senate and House of

Representatives. Furthermore, women earn approximately 82% of what men in similar jobs are paid. In 1980, President Jimmy Carter declared March to be Women's History Month.

Hispanics

After World War II, many Hispanics also began to demand greater equality. In 1949, veterans protested a refusal by a Texas town to bury a Mexican American soldier, who died during World War II, in the local cemetery, because only whites could be buried there. Activists called themselves Chicanos, a term that previously was used as a pejorative to describe Mexican Americans. Cesar Chavez was a labor union activist who organized transient Hispanic agricultural workers in an effort to obtain better working conditions in the 1960s and 1970s. Activists encouraged a sense of pride in Chicano identity, especially in arts and literature. In 1968, President Lyndon B. Johnson declared National Hispanic Heritage Month would run from mid-September to mid-October.

In 1959, biochemist Severo Ochoa became the first Hispanic to win a Nobel Prize. Franklin Chang-Diaz became the first Hispanic astronaut in 1986, and he flew a total of seven space shuttle missions. In 1990, Oscar Hijuelos became the first Hispanic American to win the Pulitzer Prize. Sonja Sotomayor became the first Hispanic to serve on the Supreme Court in 2009.

Native Americans

Native Americans suffered centuries of oppression at the hands of European colonists, and later American settlers as they pushed further west. Native Americans resisted attempts to encroach on their lands but were pushed onto smaller and smaller reservations. The Massacre at Wounded Knee in 1890 was the last major conflict between Native Americans and U.S. forces. However, American officials continued to try and force Native Americans to assimilate into white culture.

In 1968, a group of Native Americans formed the American Indian Movement in order to combat racism and demand greater independence. Between 1969 and 1971, a group of Native American activists occupied the federal prison on Alcatraz Island near San Francisco, although it had been closed since 1963. The activists offered to buy back the island for $9.40 in order to draw attention to how the federal government had forced tribes to sell their lands at low prices. Other activists disrupted Thanksgiving Day ceremonies aboard a replica of the Mayflower in Boston in 1970. In 1971, Native American activists also occupied Mount Rushmore, which is located on ground the Native Americans consider sacred. Violence broke out between activists and law enforcement officials in 1973 when Native Americans occupied the town of Wounded Knee, sight of the famous massacre.

In 1970, President Richard Nixon granted Native American tribes more autonomy. In 1978, Congress passed the American Indian Religious Freedom Act, which guaranteed Native Americans' rights to practice their religious ceremonies and visit sacred sites. In 1990, President George H.W. Bush declared November Native American History Month. In 1969, Navarre Scott Momaday became the first Native American to win a Pulitzer Prize for his book, *House Made of Dawn*. In 2014, Diane Humetewa, a member of the Hopi tribe, became the first Native American woman to serve as a federal judge. However, many Native American communities still suffer from high rates of unemployment, alcoholism, and domestic abuse.

Asian Americans

Asian Americans also faced discrimination throughout American history and in 1882, Congress passed a law banning all Chinese immigrants. During World War II, more than 100,000 Japanese Americans were interned in concentration camps. In 1982, two American autoworkers beat Vincent Chin to death with a baseball bat because his assailants blamed him for the loss of jobs in the automotive manufacturing industry.

In the 1960s, activists demanded that the term *Asian American* replace the word *oriental*, because it carried a stigma. Asian Americans also promoted a sense of pride in their cultural identity and successfully pushed for the

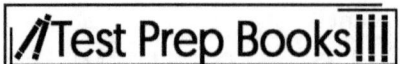

creation of ethnic studies programs. Ellison Onizuka became the first Asian American astronaut in 1985, although he perished in the space shuttle Challenger disaster. In 1990, President George H.W. Bush declared May Asian Pacific American Heritage Month and Sheryl WuDunn became the first Asian American to win a Pulitzer Prize that same year.

Practice Quiz

1. Which of the following was NOT a problem presented by the Articles of Confederation?
    a. Infighting between branches of government
    b. The inability to implement and collect taxes to pay off debt
    c. Slow responses from the government toward rebellions
    d. Ineffective raising of armies for wartime

2. Which of the following was NOT an issue contributing to the American Revolution?
    a. Increased taxes on the colonies
    b. Britain's defeat in the French and Indian War
    c. The stationing of British soldiers in colonists' homes
    d. Changes in class relations

3. In 1850, the ten most populous cities in the United States, in order from most populous to least, were New York, NY; Baltimore, MD; Boston, MA; Philadelphia, PA; New Orleans, LA; Cincinnati, OH; Brooklyn, NY; St. Louis, MO; Spring Garden, PA; and Albany, NY. How many of these cities are located in a state that was one of the original thirteen colonies?
    a. 6
    b. 7
    c. 8
    d. 9

4. What was a consequence of the industrialization that followed the Civil War?
    a. Decreased immigration
    b. Increased urbanization
    c. Decreased socioeconomic inequality
    d. Increased rights for workers

5. What was a concern that George Washington warned of in his Farewell Address?
    a. The danger of political parties
    b. To be prepared to intervene in Europe's affairs
    c. The abolition of slavery
    d. To protect states' rights through sectionalism

See answers on the next page.

Answer Explanations

1. A: Despite all of the issues of the Articles of Confederation, infighting among the governmental branches was not one of them. This was mainly because there weren't many branches of government, but also because the federal government didn't meet very often. Problems with debt, slow military response, and an army were all problems of the Confederation that prompted the change to a more steadfast and central solution.

2. B: Britain was not defeated in the French and Indian War, and, in fact, disputes with the colonies over the new territories it won contributed to the growing tensions. All other options were key motivations behind the Revolutionary War.

3. B: The original thirteen colonies were Virginia, New York, Massachusetts, Maryland, Rhode Island, Connecticut, New Hampshire, Delaware, North Carolina, South Carolina, New Jersey, Pennsylvania, and Georgia. Thus, all but three cities on the list (New Orleans, Cincinnati, St. Louis) are in states that were one of the original thirteen colonies, so the correct answer is Choice *B*, 7.

4. B: Industrialization directly caused an increase in urbanization. Factories were located near cities to draw upon a large pool of potential employees. Between 1860 and 1890, the urbanization rate increased from about 20% to 35%. The other three choices are factually incorrect. Choice *A* is incorrect because immigration increased during industrialization, as immigrants flooded into America to search for work. Choice *C* is incorrect because socioeconomic problems plagued the period due to social ills caused by rapid urbanization. Choice *D* is incorrect because labor unrest was common as unions advocated for workers' rights and organized national strikes.

5. A: George Washington was concerned that sectionalism could destroy the United States, and he warned against it. He also advised that Americans avoid getting involved in European affairs. He did not make abolition a theme in his Farewell Address.

Texas History

Exploration and Colonization

American Indian Groups in Texas

Texas was home to Paleoindians during the prehistoric period. In fact, people have lived in Texas for over 12,000 years. Anthropologists and archaeologists working in Texas have discovered artifacts of the Clovis culture that developed in North America some 11,000-12,000 years ago. During the First Agricultural Revolution, many hunter-gatherers of nomadic Paleoindian groups began to settle permanently or semi-permanently in Texas. These earliest Native American groups included the Karankawas, the Coahuiltecans, the Caddos, the Witchitas, the Atakapas, the Jumanos, the Tonkawas, and the Apaches. Additionally, many Native Americans resettled in Texas during the era of Indian Removal and Manifest Destiny. These included the Comanches and Kiowas.

Puebloans were one of the first American Indian tribes to settle in Texas. Agricultural innovations facilitated the Puebloans' ability to develop relatively large communities, and the Puebloans constructed complex multi-story and multi-purpose buildings. With their relatively large population and tight-knit community, the Puebloans became the first American Indian group to drive Europeans out of their lands for an extended period of time, which they did in 1680.

Several American Indian tribes established dominance in the Texas Plains region during this period. The Nations were an alliance of autonomous groups consisting of kinship bands, and they quickly adopted European horses and leveraged this advantage to hunt bison herds and consolidate control over strategic waterways during the late seventeenth and eighteenth centuries. The Comanche emerged as the most powerful Texas Plains tribe during the late eighteenth century, scoring decisive victories over the Puebloans, the Apache, and Spanish colonists.

American Indian tribes in southeastern Texas had more permanent settlements than existed on the Plains. These tribes typically adopted a mix of hunter-gatherer and agriculture-based economic systems. Permanent settlements facilitated more complex architectural structures, such as the Caddo Nation's temple mounds in southeastern Texas. During the late eighteenth century, the Alabama migrated to this region, allied with the Coushatta, and created some of the largest settlements in Texas.

American Indian tribes in the Texas Gulf Coast benefited from the area's rich fishing opportunities. The Atakapa organized kinship bands similar to the Apache, and they primarily lived off shellfish, fish, maize cultivation, and hunting. The Karankawa practiced a similarly semi-nomadic lifestyle, and their enduring societal and civic institutions allowed them to repel attacks from Spanish, French, and English colonizers throughout the eighteenth century.

History of Texas During Spanish Colonial Period

In the 1500s, Spanish conquistadors and French settlers began exploring the Gulf Coast region. In 1519, Spanish explorer Alonso Alvarez de Pineda became one of the first conquistadors to probe the Texas coast. There is no evidence that he reached the Texas mainland, but his expedition increased Spanish interest in Texas. Spanish explorer Panfilo de Narvaez's expedition became the first to explore the Texas mainland, albeit accidentally. During this expedition, Narvaez's ships wrecked, and explorer Alvar Nunez Cabeza de Vaca was taken in by Karankawa Indians. This first contact, which occurred in 1528, encouraged Cabeza de Vaca to continue his travels, even after he was captured and placed in captivity by Coahuiltecan Indians. Between 1528 and 1536, Cabeza de Vaca and a band of other shipwrecked survivors wandered across Texas and modern-day Mexico. Eventually they reached Mexico City in 1536 with the help of Spanish soldiers they encountered on their journey.

European Exploration and Colonization of Texas

Cabeza de Vaca later published an account of his expedition, which caught the attention of Spanish viceroys and explorers. This led conquistador Francisco Vasquez de Coronado to embark on a journey with a force of over 1,300 men in 1540 in search of gold. While Coronado never found gold, he and his men did become some of the first Europeans to see the Grand Canyon and travel through modern-day West Texas. By the 1600s, after years of expeditions, the Spanish colonial government began establishing missions along the frontiers of modern-day Mexico, New Mexico, California, and Texas. Some settlements sprouted up along the Rio Grande in South Texas. French explorer Robert de La Salle led several expeditions in East Texas in the 1680s. Control over East Texas shifted hands from the Spanish and French on multiple occasions in the late 1600s and early 1700s until Spain took possession due to the missionary efforts of men like Father Francisco Hidalgo, a Franciscan priest who established missions in East Texas for the Spanish crown. Throughout the 1700s, Spain continued to establish missions, presidios, and ranches throughout Texas. Life in Spanish Texas during this era was marked by extreme isolation, loose government control, and border skirmishes. The Spanish crown had a hard time controlling the region based on its remoteness and a lack of manpower.

Significant Individuals, Events, and Issues in Early Texas History

Numerous individuals, events, and issues influenced Texas history between the Spanish Colonial Era and Mexican National Era.

Alonso Álvarez de Pineda was a Spanish conquistador, explorer, and cartographer. Following his exploration of the Florida Keys and the Mississippi River, Álvarez de Pineda headed west and entered Corpus Christi Bay. While it is unclear whether he ever set foot in present-day Texas, he was the first European to create a map of Texas and the Gulf Coast region of the present-day United States.

Álvar Núñez Cabeza de Vaca worked as a lead explorer, trader, and missionary in the Narváez expedition (1527–1536), which explored the present-day American Southwest and Texas Gulf Coast. Cabeza de Vaca is best known for his study of indigenous tribes. Unlike the vast majority of his contemporaries, Cabeza de Vaca greatly respected American Indian culture, and his groundbreaking book, *The Account and Commentaries* (1542), provided Europeans with their first account of tribes living in the Texas Gulf Coast.

José de Escandón rose in the ranks of the Spanish military due to his skill at conquering American Indian tribes during the early eighteenth century. Escandón famously pioneered the strategy of forming alliances with friendly tribes and mercilessly attacking enemy tribes, and he is credited with defending Spanish territory from European rivals and subduing numerous American Indian rebellions across New Spain. In addition, Escandón played a leading role in establishing and governing the colony of Nuevo Santander, which stretched from the present-day Mexican state of Veracruz into present-day Texas.

Fray Damián Massanet served as a Franciscan missionary in New Spain. Massanet established the first missionary college, the College of Santa Cruz, in 1683 in present-day Querétaro, Mexico. Several years later, Massanet received orders to create the Mission San Francisco de los Tejas in eastern Texas, but he argued with Spanish colonial leaders over how to best defend the mission. Approximately three years after its establishment in 1690, Massanet burned down and abandoned the failing mission, and he left eastern Texas to return to the College of Santa Cruz.

Francisco Hidalgo served as a Franciscan missionary in present-day northern Mexico during the late seventeenth and early eighteenth centuries. Following the failure of the Mission San Francisco de los Tejas, Hidalgo continued to press Spanish authorities to fund and defend his missionary work in present-day eastern Texas. Frustrated by their refusals, Hidalgo approached the French governor of Louisiana to acquire assistance for his missionary work, which convinced Spain to fully colonize Texas to create a buffer zone between New Spain and the French colonies.

Consequently, Hidalgo led several Franciscan missionaries in Spanish-controlled areas in present-day eastern Texas and San Antonio.

Moses Austin was an American pioneer and businessmen. The Spanish Crown provided Austin with a land grant to create a colony in Spanish Texas in 1820, but he died before the settlement was completed. Austin's son, Stephen F. Austin, took control over the grant and established an Anglo-American settlement known as the Old Three Hundred in 1822.

Impact of Major Geographic Features of Texas

Aside from its immense size, Texas has unparalleled geographical, ecological, and climatic diversity. In order to gain a better understanding of this vast and variable geographical area, geographers have classified Texas into ten climatic regions, fourteen soil regions, and eleven ecological regions. This incredible variety is a product of Texas's far-ranging geographic landforms, including plains, valleys, mountains, deserts, and forests. Texas also has 367 miles of coastline along the Gulf of Mexico and dozens of estuaries where saltwater combines with freshwater to create dynamic ecological zones, such as Corpus Christi Bay, Galveston Bay, and Sabine Lake. Additionally, several major freshwater systems flow through Texas, including the Rio Grande, Red River, Brazos River, Pecos River, Canadian River, and Colorado River. Human societies have adopted a variety of land-use practices to alter Texas's geographical features and ecological systems for their benefit.

American Indians were the first group to settle in Texas, and they benefited greatly from Texas's rich bounty of natural resources, which they leveraged through land-use practices based on the local conditions. American Indians practiced irrigation along major waterways prior to the arrival of Europeans in the early 16th century, especially along the Rio Grande. Irrigation was essential for watering crops and preventing floods from destroying harvests; however, this land-use practice altered the landscape by diverting waterways' natural course. American Indians' land-use practices also altered southeastern Texas as tribes built permanent settlements out of stone and adobe, and these settlements resulted in the introduction of some waste products into pristine wilderness areas. Additionally, some American Indian tribes relied on slash-and-burn agriculture to systematically transform woodlands into arable land. The growth of American Indian tribes transformed the natural ecosystems through hunting, fishing, and gathering vegetation. Given the interrelatedness and complexity of ecosystems, even the most sustainable practices inherently had a cascading impact up and down the food chain. For example, in the northern Plains, the success American Indians enjoyed hunting bison and deer altered the migratory pattern of wolves and other predators.

European colonizers initially struggled to adapt to Texas's unique geography, but they forged friendships with American Indians to learn how to live off the land. For example, Spain constructed most of its early settlements around waterways where they adopted American Indian irrigation practices to grow maize. Rather than stone and adobe, Europeans generally preferred to construct buildings from timber, which involved cutting down stretches of forest. While the American Indians exploited natural resources, they generally viewed themselves as a part of the natural environment. In contrast, European settlers considered nature to be something that could be exploited for monetary gain regardless of the consequences. In addition, European colonizers' struggle to survive in a foreign land meant they were far more concerned with short-term viability than long-term conservatorship. Thus, Europeans were less likely to consider sustainability when hunting, fishing, fur trapping, clearing land, and irrigating fields. Their deleterious environmental and ecological impact was magnified as more Europeans and Americans migrated to eastern Texas, particularly after the Industrial Revolution spread from Great Britain to the rest of Europe and the Americas during the nineteenth century.

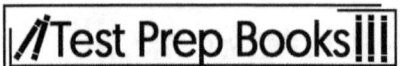

The Mexican National Period

Following Mexican independence from Spain in September 1821, Texas became part of the new Republic of Mexico. Young Tejano ranchers, now generations removed from their grandparents' settlement in the region, became the new lifeblood of Texas under Mexican national rule. During this era, Texas became a key frontier for both Mexico and the United States. The Mexican government created plans to colonize the region while many Anglo-Americans also founded frontier homes on Mexican land. Catalyzed by the free labor of slaves, farming and ranching became the economic cornerstones of the regions. Gradually, Texans established a unique cultural identity that resisted the loose control of the Mexican Republic.

Eventually, Mexican and Texan identities became so distinct that the Texans decided to rebel against the centralist Mexican government. The ensuing Texas Revolution, which took place in 1835 and 1836, allowed Texas to declare independence from Mexico. A flood of United States volunteers assisted in helping Texans to found the Republic of Texas, which officially received its independence via the Consultation of 1836. The Republic of Texas was a short-lived nation because its people quickly accepted annexation by the United States of America in 1845.

The Republic of Texas declared its independence from Mexico in 1836 and applied for entry into the United States in the same year; this request was denied. However, right before he left office in March 1845, President John Tyler initiated an annexation bill, which President James K. Polk officially signed in December 1845. The Republic of Texas officially revoked its sovereignty, lawfully agreeing to become the 28th state of the Union, in February 1846. The Mexican-American War (1846 – 1848), in many ways, was a direct response to President Polk's annexation of Texas. The war ended in the Treaty of Guadalupe-Hidalgo, which resulted in the Mexican Cession of half of its territory, nearly doubled the size of the United States, and officially brought parts of what would become Texas, New Mexico, Arizona, and California within the territory of the United States. One social impact of U.S. annexation and the Mexican-American War was increased political tensions over the role of slavery in new territories.

Independence, Statehood, Civil War Reconstruction, and Aftermath

Mexico Becoming an Independent Nation

When Mexico won independence from Spain in 1821, Texas—which used to be a frontier region in the Spanish colony—became part of the Mexican Republic. Few Mexican residents occupied this frontier region prior to independence, so there were not that many permanent settlements in Texas during the early Mexican Republic. The Mexican government understood that the climate and large amount of available space in Texas made it an ideal region for colonization and a budding ranching industry. Thus, the Mexican government encouraged people to migrate to Texas. Many of the immigrants who relocated to Texas were actually Anglo-Americans. These Anglo-American frontiersmen helped Mexico ward off attacks from the Native Americans. Moreover, they strengthened the local economy through ranching, farming, and paying taxes. The Mexican government created an *empresario* system to attract even more immigrants. *Empresarios* were land agents who helped settlers acquire land in Texas. Among these *empresarios* was future Texas revolutionary Stephen F. Austin. Austin persuaded Anglo-American settlers to move to the northern frontier of Mexico in exchange for large land acquisitions. These immigration policies laid the groundwork for the Texas Revolution. Many of the Anglo-American settlers ignored Mexican laws; others arrived illegally and maintained allegiances to the United States of America. The Mexican government tried to end immigration by passing the anti-immigration Law of April 6, 1830. Although the law did little to control illegal immigration, it did successfully instill discontent and distrust in the Anglo-American settlers of Texas. This discontent and distrust eventually led Texas to its independence.

Texas Revolution

By 1833, Anglo-American immigrants and their Tejano counterparts had begun to embody a growing sense of separateness along Mexico's frontier region in Texas. These settlers were grounded in revolutionary republican principles and became very independent minded when it came to their relationship with the federal government in Mexico City. These settlers disregarded many Mexican laws and capitalized on the fact that the federal government maintained little control over their territory. Prominent leaders in the region, such as David Burnet, called for the residents of Texas to separate from the Mexican Republic. Since the Mexican government hardly ever defended these frontiersmen, they were used to creating their own militias and defending themselves. Tejanos such as Juan Seguin and Ambrosio Rodriguez joined in the resistance, noting that the Law of April 6, 1830, not only threatened the liberty of Anglo-Americans in the region, but also the liberty of Tejanos.

The Fredonian Rebellion (1826–1827) began over land disputes. Haden Edwards, a land speculator, instigated conflicts to displace Spanish-speaking settlers in eastern Texas in 1825. When Mexican authorities intervened, Edwards' Anglo-American supporters seized Nacogdoches and founded the Republic of Fredonia on December 21, 1826. The Mexican military immediately squashed the revolt, and Edwards fled to the United States. Believing the United States had supported the revolt, the Mexican government passed laws to restrict immigration and regulate Anglo-American settlements. The settlers' defiant response to these laws marked the beginning of widespread popular support for independence.

As tensions increased, the Mexican government and military tried to assert greater control over the region. In September and October of 1835, the Mexican military arrived at the settlement of Gonzales to reclaim a cannon that was issued by the federal government. The ensuing skirmish between Mexicans and Texans over a government-issued cannon paved the way for the Texas Revolution. The Texans antagonized the Mexican military with the defiant slogan "Come and take it!" And as the Mexican army did, indeed, try to take it on October 2, 1835, Texas citizens fought back under the leadership of John Henry Moore. Shots were fired that day, making the Texas Revolution a violent reality.

The surrender at Goliad resulted in the mass execution of Texan prisoners, and these events served as a powerful rallying cry for independence. General José de Urrea's forces easily overran and outmaneuvered Colonel James Fannin's retreating forces at the Battle of Coleto on March 19–20, 1836. Fannin's lack of military experience heavily contributed to the Texans' surrender at Goliad, and he was the last man executed during the ensuing massacre. General Urrea argued for humane treatment of the prisoners, but President Santa Anna overruled him.

William B. Travis played a leading role in the Anahuac Disturbances of 1832 and 1835, during which his armed militias challenged Mexico's claims of sovereignty over Texas. Travis later served as a lieutenant colonel during the Texas Revolution, and he was the commander of the Texas regulars at the Battle of the Alamo (1836). Travis died on the last day of fighting at the Alamo, but he was outlived by his famous *Victory or Death* letter from the Alamo, which garnered sympathy and support from the United States.

Antonio López de Santa Anna served as the lead general and president of Mexico during the Texas Revolution. Santa Anna deeply resented American settlers' refusal to pay taxes and follow Mexican laws, including continual violations of Mexico's anti-slavery laws. In 1835, Santa Anna responded by repealing the Mexican Constitution of 1824, which triggered the Texas Revolution. However, after his defeat at the Battle of San Jacinto (April 21, 1836), Santa Anna recognized Texas's independence to save his own life.

Following the events of Gonzales and the infamous Battle at the Alamo, fifty-nine Texan delegates gathered at Washington-on-the-Brazos for an assembly that would be remembered as the Convention of 1836. At this convention, on March 2, 1836, the fifty-nine delegates officially declared independence from the Mexican Republic.

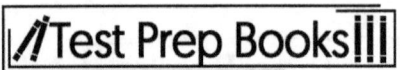

The Republic of Texas was born, but was not fully conceived until the final shots were fired at the Battle of San Jacinto on April 21, 1836. The Texans won this battle, bringing about an official end to the Texas Revolution.

George Childress was a lawyer and politician from Nashville before he became a fundraiser and recruiter for Texas's independence. Shortly after illegally migrating to Texas, Childress was elected as a delegate to the Convention of 1836, and he spearheaded the drafting of the Texas Declaration of Independence, which the delegates signed on March 3, 1836.

Republic of Texas and Early Texas Statehood

The Republic of Texas only lasted a short ten years, from 1836 to 1846. However, these short years were rich with a unique history and culture. The Treaties of Valesco—which were signed on May 14, 1836—officially ended Texas's war with Mexico, at least in the eyes of the United States and Texas. Nevertheless, the Mexican government refused to initially recognize the terms of the treaties, stating that President Santa Anna was no longer an official representative of the federal government as a prisoner of war. Tensions, therefore, continued with Mexico, although the war remained behind both nations for nearly a decade. David G. Burnet—the interim president of the Republic of Texas—eventually stepped down as the nation's leader following the ratification of the Constitution of 1836 and the election of 1836. The constitutional committee elected Sam Houston as the first president and Mirabeau B. Lamar as the first vice president. The committee also debated U.S. annexation, with many delegates expressing a desire to make Texas a part of the United States of America.

During this time of tension and change there were many individuals, events, and issues that both challenged and enriched the Republic of Texas and helped lead to its eventual statehood.

Lorenzo de Zavala oversaw the drafting of Mexico's inaugural constitution in 1824, and he worked for the new Mexican government in a variety of capacities. After President Santa Anna repealed Mexico's Constitution of 1824 to establish a militarized dictatorship, Zavala fled to Texas and advocated for its independence. Zavala later participated in the Texas constitutional convention, designed the official flag, and served as the first vice president of Texas.

Joshua Houston was a slave, skilled artisan, and politician. Sam Houston's wife owned Joshua, and Sam Houston depended on Joshua's skills and labor to build his family mansion at Raven Hill. Shortly before Sam Houston's death, he freed his slaves, including Joshua. Once free, Joshua set up a blacksmith shop and served as an alderman and county commissioner.

Mary Maverick was one of the first female settlers to migrate to the Republic of Texas, and her son was the first Anglo-American child to be born and raised in San Antonio. Maverick later worked to preserve the history of the Republic of Texas, and she published a memoir in 1895 that provided unique insight into daily life during this era.

The Córdova Rebellion (1838) was a failed uprising against the Republic of Texas. Simmering with anger over the Texas Revolution, the Mexican government worked with Vicente Córdova to recruit Hispanic supporters and Cherokee allies. However, local militia members uncovered this plot, and Texas Rangers led the militia to a decisive victory, effectively ending the uprising before it began. Upon discovering the Cherokees' participation, President of the Republic of Texas Mirabeau B. Lamar violently expelled the Cherokees from Texas.

The Council House Fight (1840) began with delegations from the Republic of Texas and the Comanche meeting at a peace conference in San Antonio to discuss a prisoner exchange. The Comanche didn't bring the requested number of captives, and the Texans responded by attempting to hold the Comanche chiefs hostage. When the Comanche sought to escape, the Texans opened fire and killed thirty-five members of the peace delegation. In retaliation, the Comanche tortured thirteen prisoners to death and launched raids on nearby villages.

Texas History | Independence, Statehood, Civil War Reconstruction, and Aftermath

The Santa Fe Expedition (1841) involved a plan to covertly purchase the valuable Santa Fe Trail in New Mexico, which would have allowed Texas to control trade between the United States and Mexico. This plan proved overly ambitious. The Santa Fe Expedition was a debacle from the outset, and the Mexican Army intercepted and arrested the survivors.

For ten years Texas remained its own independent nation. Following the revolution, the Republic of Texas faced new challenges under the leadership of its first and only presidents: Sam Houston, Mirabeau B. Lamar, and Anson Jones. Economically, the Republic of Texas struggled post-independence. The war had accrued a large amount of debt. Texas was threatened on its borders by the expansionist policies of the U.S. government, Native American skirmishes, and the bitter sentiment of the Mexican government. The Republic of Texas opened its borders to thousands of immigrants from the United States and Mexico, which diversified its demographics. By December 29, 1845, this diversified body of Texas citizens decided that it was time for Texas to become the twenty-eighth state of the United States of America. Annexation presented new challenges, including a U.S. war with Mexico. The earliest years of statehood were therefore tied to war and transition, as the Republic of Texas evolved into the Lone Star State. During these early years of statehood, thousands of Americans flocked to the fertile soil and mild climates of the twenty-eighth state of the Union.

Civil War and Reconstruction in Texas

By 1860, cotton had become the leading crop in the Lone Star State. Texas helped cotton become king in the American South, shipping hundreds of thousands of cotton bales out of crucial gulf ports such as Houston and Galveston. From Houston and Galveston, the cotton bales set sail to the industrial northeast or Europe. Texas helped make cotton the white gold of America, but not without cost. The cotton industry was built on the backs of enslaved African Americans. These African Americans helped whites and Tejanos in Texas amass great fortunes on their vast Southern plantations. As the debate over slavery and abolition waged on in the late 1850s and early 1860s, most Texans concluded that slavery was a necessary and essential component to the booming Texas economy. These Texans saw abolition as a direct threat to their personal prosperity.

Jack Coffee Hays is widely credited with turning the Texas Rangers into an elite military division, and the regiments of Rangers achieved national acclaim for their fighting prowess during the Mexican-American War (1846–1848). After the outbreak of the American Civil War (1861–1865), Hays turned down commands in both the United States and the Confederacy to focus on public service and real estate development in California.

John Bell Hood volunteered his services to Texas at the beginning of the American Civil War. While many Southerners enlisted out of a desire to protect their family or show loyalty to their state, Hood was a self-avowed white supremacist who viewed slavery as highly beneficial to African-Americans. Hood served in Robert E. Lee's famed Army of Northern Virginia, and, after losing an arm at the Battle of Gettysburg (1863) and a leg at the Battle of Chickamauga (1863), he became the youngest general in the Civil War.

John Magruder served as the Confederate military administrator of Arizona, Arkansas, New Mexico, and Texas. Magruder devised the audacious Confederate strategy that broke the naval blockade of Galveston, and he managed to fend off successive Union assaults in eastern Texas. After the Confederacy surrendered, Magruder fled to Mexico and launched an ill-advised scheme to establish Confederate colonies, which flopped when Napoleon III abandoned the Emperor of Mexico, Maximilian I.

Following the election of Abraham Lincoln in 1860, the citizens and politicians of Texas voted to secede from the Union. Residents in Texas were overwhelmingly in support of Texas joining the Confederate States of America. The governor at that time—Sam Houston—openly lamented this decision. After he refused to take an oath of loyalty to the Confederate States of America, Texans removed him from office. Growing divisions over states' rights and slavery placed Texas right at the heart of the imminent American Civil War. During the Civil War, Texans participated in such key coastal battles as the Battle of Galveston and the Battle of Sabine Pass. These battles along the Gulf Coast placed Texas at the heart of the Confederacy's cotton diplomacy, which used cotton shipments and boycotts to seduce the British as allies. Although this diplomacy essentially failed, Texas continued to use its cottonclads (ironclads used for cotton shipments) in naval battles. Texas maintained ties with the Confederacy all the way to the war's close in 1863, and some Texans declared their ties to the Confederacy well into the era of Reconstruction.

The Battle of Palmito Ranch occurred on May 12–13, 1865. This battle is highly unusual for two reasons. First, it occurred more than a month after Robert Lee surrendered at Appomattox Court House, and two days after the Confederacy officially dissolved. Second, it is unknown why the Union broke the ceasefire that had brought peace to southern Texas for months. In any event, the Confederacy won this postwar battle while suffering minimal casualties.

Effects of Reconstruction on Texas

Following the war, many Texans rebelled against Reconstructionist policies by joining such white-supremacist terrorist groups as the Ku Klux Klan (KKK). During postwar Reconstruction, the power of the KKK seeped into the governmental structures of Texas, forcing many politicians, such as Senators Matthew Gaines and George T. Ruby, to fight back against the crimes committed by KKK members and politicians. Prior to the Civil War, Democrats dominated Texas politics, but during the era of Reconstruction, radical Republicans held the most power in the Texas legislature. This temporary control, however, ended following the heated election of 1873. This election allowed Democrats, under the leadership of Governor Richard Coke, a former Confederate soldier, to regain Texas politics by a landslide. This election witnessed a dramatic sociocultural shift toward a staunchly segregationist Texas in the Jim Crow South. Economically speaking, this antiblack sentiment placed freed African Americans back into exploitative labor situations. Slavery gave way to tenant farming and sharecropping in the cotton fields of Texas. The tenant farming and sharecropping systems of agriculture placed many freed African Americans into substantial debt to large landowners. Essentially, although they were free, they became paid slaves.

Expansion of Settlement Along the Frontier in Texas

Throughout the 1860s, many Native American groups along the frontiers of Texas took advantage of the absence of frontiersmen during the Civil War. The outbreak of the American Civil War offered an opportunity for many Plains Indians groups to reestablish their foothold in northern, central, and western Texas. Comanche groups raided settlements around the Fredericksburg region of Hill Country during this time. Once frontiersmen returned from battles in the Civil War, they often returned to violent fights with Native American groups. During this time, many former Union soldiers were also stationed in Texas to carry out Reconstructionist policies and protect the frontier. Between the 1860s and 1880s, several wars between the U.S. Army and Native Americans erupted across the landscape of Texas. The 1860s to 1880s witnessed several wars, battles, and raids such as the Elm Creek Raid (1864), the Salt Creek Raid (1971), the Mackenzie's Raids (1871), the Red River War (1874), the Battle of Adobe Walls (1874), and the Battle of Palo Duro Canyon (1874).

Quanah Parker was the son of a Comanche chief and led a powerful Comanche band during the Red River War (1874-1875). The United States launched this conflict to forcibly remove American Indian bands from the southern Plains of the Texas Panhandle and relocate them further north to the Indian Territory, which was in present-day Oklahoma. Due to the mobility and transience of American Indian tribes, the Red River War mostly involved small-scale raids and skirmishes. Parker's Comanche band was the last American Indian group to resist relocation, but Parker ultimately surrendered in 1875 due to the simultaneous challenge of constant warfare and dwindling food supplies as Americans intentionally annihilated bison herds. While living in the Indian Territories, Parker gained wealth as a rancher, led the Native American Church movement, and served as the southwestern American Indian tribes' top diplomat to the United States.

Texas History | Independence, Statehood, Civil War Reconstruction, and Aftermath

Today the Texas Rangers is a law enforcement agency, but Stephen F. Austin established the group in 1823 for the explicit purpose of protecting Anglo-American settlers from hostile groups. Thus, the Rangers functioned more like a paramilitary organization, and the Rangers fought in the Texas Revolution (1835–1836), the Mexican-American War (1846–1848), and the American Civil War (1861–1865). In addition, the Rangers constantly battled American Indians during a series of conflicts collectively known as the Texas-Indian Wars (1820–1875). President of the Republic of Texas Mirabeau Bonaparte Lamar viewed American Indians as an existential threat to Texas, and he tasked the Rangers with exterminating the American Indians. During the latter half of the nineteenth century, the Rangers increasingly focused on law enforcement as the United States Army took a larger role in displacing and corralling American Indians to clear land for white settlers.

Buffalo Soldiers were all-black units of the United States Army, and they were formed in the aftermath of the American Civil War. Historians debate the etymology of Buffalo Soldiers, but American Indians inarguably coined the name. Buffalo Soldiers were first stationed in Texas during the Reconstruction era (1863–1877), and they fought in the Texas-Indian Wars. Aside from warfare, Buffalo Soldiers completed a wide variety of tasks to support settlements on the frontier, such as transporting supplies, protecting caravans, escorting mail carriers, and building critical infrastructure. Despite their valuable contributions to the expansion and development of the frontier, Buffalo Soldiers were regularly discriminated against and attacked in Texas.

This era also saw the creation of many treaties and peace policies that forced thousands of Native Americans onto reservations in the West. The expansionist efforts of settlers and troops in Texas assisted with the widespread slaughter of the buffalo. This slaughter angered Native American groups who depended on the buffalo for survival.

Economic and Technological Developments in Texas in the Period 1821 to 1900

The advent of steam power and steamboats in the early 1800s marked the beginning of a transportation revolution in Texas and the broader North American continent. These steam-powered ships were used not only to transport cotton across the rivers and along the coasts of Texas, but they were also used during the battles of the Civil War. Ironclads and cottonclads assisted the Confederate navy in its war with the Union. Steam, however, marked only the beginning of Texas's transportation revolution. The railroad boom, on the other hand, sent Texas and the United States of America chugging at Godspeed toward modernity. The railroad boom in Texas took place between 1870 and 1900. In the beginning, only around five hundred miles of tracks were laid. By the turn of the century, there were nearly ten thousand railroad tracks across the state. Locomotives brought travelers and settlers across the state.

With the advent of electricity and electrical power plants in the 1880s, Texas also saw its fair share of electrified streetcars across the main streets of the Lone Star State. New technologies brought new industries to Texas, including an increasingly technological Texas agricultural industry. Commercial farming—a product of technological advancement—slowly became the economic backbone of the state. Mills, mines, meatpacking plants, and factories also sprouted up in Texas during the broader Industrial Revolution of the nineteenth century. But by the late 1800s, it became clear that Texas had found its new gold: oil. The budding automobile and gasoline industries of the late 1800s and early 1900s made Texas into the petroleum capital of the United States of America. Oil became big business in Texas, drawing thousands of workers and their families to the Lone Star State.

Geographic Features of Texas

The varied geographic landscapes of Texas state have impacted migration, settlement patterns, and economic development in different ways. Moreover, these varied landscapes have led to different methods for altering the natural environment. The plains in parts of west, central, and north Texas have lent themselves to agriculture and ranching throughout history. These plains have historically hosted the production of cotton, wheat, and sorghum. Additionally, they have become ranching and meatpacking centers. Ranches and farms in Texas are usually divided

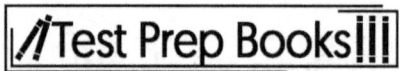

into large tracts of land, and at times, this can lead to land disputes. The rolling hills and valleys of Hill Country have made Texas a center for vineyards and wine making. Hill Country also produces peaches and pecans depending on the season. East Texas maintains more of a Gulf Coast climate, making it perfect for rice fields and oil refineries. Texas oil production has littered the Gulf Coast with large, mechanical refineries and plants. Cities like Dallas, Austin, San Antonio, and Houston maintain their own unique relationships with the land, setting aside large plots for urban infrastructure. These cities, which are currently experiencing a period of rapid growth, have ravaged the land for the sake of roadways, river walks, and railroads.

Cultural Developments in Texas in the Period 1821 to 1900

Between 1821 and 1900, Texas shifted its national identity on several occasions: It went from being a region in the Mexican Republic to its own Republic of Texas to part of the United States of America to part of the Confederate States of America and back to being part of the Union. It witnessed the collateral postwar years following the Mexican Revolution, the heart of the Texas Revolution and Mexican-American War, and the reverberations of the Civil War and the Spanish-American War. During this time, Texas's identity shifted with its national allegiances and its conflicts. Texas became a unified yet conflicted state. Its boundaries were formed and re-formed, and its identity was constantly in flux. Yet there remained a cultural strain through all these years of revolution and conflict: The Lone Star State became a symbol of American perseverance and diversity.

Texas remains one of the most diverse states due to these historical foundations. Mexican and Southern culture still reign supreme. In these years, Texas also transitioned from being an agricultural state to an industrial hub. The discovery of oil in Texas made it one of the wealthiest industrializing beacons at the turn of the century. These cultural developments created a stubborn sense of independence in the state psyche, but they also tied Texas closer to the broader American Dream. Texas became the center of heated debates over war and peace, colonization and liberation, abolition and slavery, national progress and moral regression, state rights and federal rights, local control and federal power, and industrialization and deindustrialization. These cultural fibers made Texas into a cross-cultural and intercultural tapestry of the American psyche.

Texas in the 20th and 21st Centuries

Reform Movements in Texas in the Late Nineteenth and Twentieth Centuries

The Progressive movement in Texas was led by such reform-minded legislators as Alexander W. Terrell, the sponsor of the forward-looking Terrell Election Law of 1905. This law attacked election fraud and established primary elections to choose state, district, and county officials. The law of 1905 preceded such democratic federal voting changes as the Seventeenth Amendment (1913), which allowed for the direct election of U.S. senators by the American people. Progressives in Texas and beyond looked to also reform labor, education, urban planning, health care, women's rights/suffrage, and rampant alcoholism. The culminating reform of the Progressive movement was the passage of the Eighteenth and Nineteenth Amendments, which respectively instituted prohibition and mandated women's suffrage. These progressive reforms, however, also had their limits: The era witnessed a rise in poll taxes and interracial violence as many African Americans were either illegally, financially, or extralegally banned from the polls.

The failures of these reforms paved the way to the Long Civil Rights Movement that gained steam in the 1920s and reached its pinnacle in the 1960s. In Texas and beyond, the civil rights movement manifested itself most noticeably in the desegregation of public space and public schooling. The civil rights movement expanded to include rights in other communities such as the American Indian community, the Hispanic community, and the LGBTQ community. The civil rights fervor of the early to mid-1960s eventually led to race riots in the late 1960s, exposing the world to the necessity of even more reforms.

Jane McCallum advocated for women's suffrage and Prohibition during the late eighteenth and early nineteenth centuries. To spread awareness about women's rights, McCallum wrote columns in local Texas newspapers, and she led the Austin Women Suffrage Association and Texas Suffrage Association. After the passage of the 19th Amendment, she worked as a political fundraiser and served as the Secretary of State of Texas between 1927 and 1933.

Lulu Belle Madison White was a civil rights activist in the 1940s and 1950s. White's work primarily focused on expanding the educational, political, and professional opportunities of African Americans. She played a critical role in ending white-only Democratic primaries while serving as the president and executive secretary of the National Association for the Advancement of Colored People (NAACP) chapter in Houston.

Manuel C. Gonzales was a civil rights activist, and he helped found the League of United Latin American Citizens (LULAC) in 1929. LULAC worked to prohibit ethnic discrimination and advocate for the rights of Latinos. Gonzales also helped found a legal-aid organization for Mexicans, wrote the founding documents for the Mexican Chamber of Commerce, and worked as a diplomat to Mexico and Guatemala.

Oveta Culp Hobby was a women's rights advocate, a colonel in the United States Army, and wife of the 27th Governor of Texas, William P. Hobby. During World War II (1939–1945), Hobby headed the newly created Women's Army Corps, improved standards for women in the military, and extended G.I. Bill benefits to women. Hobby later worked as an advisor to the Eisenhower administration, and she served as the first United States Secretary of Health, Education, and Welfare.

James Hogg was a lawyer, progressive politician, and the first native-born Texas governor (1891–1895). Hogg won the governorship on the basis of his progressive policies, including public regulation of the railroads, restrictions on out-of-state land ownership, and antitrust initiatives. Additionally, Hogg secured more funding for public schools and state universities, and he advocated for an anti-lynching bill to prevent the extrajudicial killing of African Americans.

Hector Garcia was a World War II veteran, doctor, and civil rights activist. Garcia founded the American G.I. Forum, and it established forty chapters in Texas to help Mexican-American veterans file claims to receive G.I. Bill benefits. The American G.I. Forum also served as a powerful lobbying group, and it campaigned against poll taxes, discrimination against migrant laborers, and the segregation of schools in southern Texas.

Impact of World War I, the Great Depression, World War II, and the Cold War on Texas

During World War I, Texas slowly urbanized as the Lone Star State's economy expanded to meet the needs of the United States' blossoming military-industrial complex. Throughout the Great War, Texans supplied U.S. forces with the oil, lumber, minerals, and agricultural products they needed to sustain military battles across the Atlantic Ocean. Wartime production inaugurated an economic boom that encouraged thousands of Texas farmers to borrow more land and equipment to create larger commercial farms. Texas transformed from a rural state to a largely urban state throughout the twentieth century.

The growing military-industrial complex encouraged many Texans to assume new jobs in factories, plants, and offices across the state. The booming oil and commercial farming industries brought hundreds of thousands of migrants and immigrants to Texas soil. These economic excesses paved the way to the economic busts and social unrests of the Great Depression. The postwar 1920s witnessed continued growth followed by a stark economic decline brought about by the stock market crash in 1929. The 1930s in Texas, like much of the United States, was marked by industry crises, rampant unemployment, and agricultural devastation brought on by the Dust Bowl. Some New Deal programs helped stave off hunger, unemployment, and economic devastation in Texas, but in reality, it

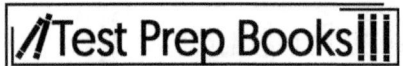

was the wartime economy of the Second World War that brought Texas and the rest of the country out of the Depression.

Texas's budding aerospace industry thrived during World War II. The military-industrial complex in Texas expanded even more rapidly during World War II than it did during World War I. Texas also urbanized more rapidly in the years following the Second World War. The ensuing Cold War with the Soviet Union made Texas one of the country's postwar military-industrial juggernauts. The defense industry and the National Aeronautics and Space Administration (NASA) in Houston placed Texas at the epicenter of a global Space Race. High-tech industries flocked to Texas between 1950 and 1980, contributing to urban growth in the broader Sunbelt region of the South. Texas played a critical role in placing the first man on the Moon and contributed to the scientific advances and technologies necessary to continue exploring space throughout the Cold War.

Major Events in Texas in the Latter Half of the Twentieth and Early Twenty-First Centuries

Following the boom and bust of the oil industry in the 1970s and 1980s, Texas and other states scrambled to diversify their economies. This diversification was built on the backs of the Richards, Bush, and Perry gubernatorial administrations.

Kay Bailey Hutchison served as a member of the Texas House of Representatives (1973–1976), Treasurer of Texas (1991–1993), and United States Senator (1993–2013). Hutchison is a conservative Republican who has most vocally supported single-sex education, prohibitions on same-sex marriage, fiscal conservatism, gun ownership, and the oil and gas industry.

In 1967, Barbara Jordan became the first African American to serve in the Texas Senate since the end of Reconstruction, and she was elected to the United States House of Representatives in 1973. Jordan supported the economic development of low-income communities, expanded the Voting Rights Act of 1965 to protect Hispanic voters, and worked to drastically reduce immigration and refugee relocation to the United States.

Eddie Bernice Johnson is a liberal Democratic politician who served in the Texas state legislature for a decade. Johnson was first elected to the United States House of Representatives in 1993, and most recently won reelection in 2018. Johnson has supported greater investments in public housing, healthcare, STEM education, and economic development programs for low-income communities.

Henry B. Gonzalez represented Texas in the United House of Representatives (1961–1999) as a liberal Democrat. Gonzalez championed the Civil Rights Act of 1964, Voting Rights Act of 1965, and Civil Rights Act of 1968. Following President John F. Kennedy's assassination in Dallas on November 22, 1963, Gonzalez challenged the official account.

Lyndon B. Johnson represented Texas in the United States Congress for more than two decades, and after President Kennedy's assassination, he served as President of the United States (1963– 1969). While escalating the Vietnam War (1955–1975), President Johnson passed numerous civil rights bills as well as his War on Poverty, which dramatically expanded the social safety net.

James Farmer was a prominent leader of the Civil Rights Movement (1954–1968). Farmer promoted nonviolent protests to challenge segregation, and in 1942, he cofounded the Congress of Racial Equality (CORE). While serving as the national director of CORE, Farmer organized the Freedom Rides of 1961 and March on Washington in 1963.

George Walker Bush served as the Governor of Texas (1995–2000) and President of the United States (2001–2008). During his governorship, Bush spearheaded the largest tax cut in Texas history, emphasized educational testing, and championed Christian organizations. Bush pursued a similar domestic policy program as president, and he responded to the September 11th attacks by launching the highly controversial War on Terror.

Craig Anthony Washington served in the Texas legislature for nearly two decades and United States House of Representatives (1989–1995). Washington opposed the controversial Omnibus Crime Bill (1994), defended the use of racial quotas in employment, and voted against several projects that would have created jobs in his Houston district, including expanding the Lyndon B. Johnson Space Center.

Texas, like much of the Sunbelt South, struggled to cope with the deindustrialized changes brought about by the passage of the North American Free Trade Agreement (NAFTA) in 1994. Unlike the Rust Belt North, however, Texas experienced a slight economic boom in the decades following the decline of industry. Cities like Dallas, Austin, and San Antonio became centers for a dramatic growth in telecommunications, computers, and high-tech manufacturing. NAFTA also catalyzed trade between these cities and Mexico to the South. During this time, Texas developed one of the United States' leading medical technology industries. Tourism and retail trade also became a cornerstone in the region, thanks to the influx of immigrants and visitors. As the economy diversified, so did the populace—thousands of immigrants and migrants flocked to the urban hubs of Texas to find new jobs in the booming economy.

Alteration of the Natural Environment from 1900 to the Present

The processes of industrialization, urbanization, and suburbanization throughout the early to mid-twentieth century inevitably affected the natural landscapes and environments of the Lone Star State. The rapid urban growth of Texas cities in the earliest years of the twentieth century made it difficult for city governments to provide the necessary services to construct sewers and collect garbage. Some Texas cities grew at such a rapid rate that they were unable to provide basic infrastructure such as a sustainable water supply. Public health became a concern as poor infrastructure and pollution led to high rates of death from disease. Eventually, reforms and infrastructural changes helped alleviate Texas of these public health concerns, but continued population expansion over the last century has often come at the cost of the environment. To sustain the blossoming populations of Texas cities, many dams had to be built. These dams have helped supply thousands of residents with water, but often at the expense of local ecosystems. Plenty of plants and animals have had their natural habitats destroyed by the ever-growing force of Texas urbanization.

At first, urbanization in Texas was sustained by the forces of industrialization. Specifically, Texas cities have been able to grow, thanks to advances in industrial technologies. Electricity—which first came to Texas via the construction of an electric power plant in Galveston in the early 1880s—revolutionized the way Texans communicated, traveled, and manufactured goods. By the early 1920s, Texas became the leader in electric streetcar transit systems for states located west of the Mississippi River. These streetcars established Texas's first major suburbs. Electricity also lit up the budding skyscraper systems in cities such as Waco and Dallas.

The explosion of the petroleum and gasoline industry in Texas helped catalyze automobile manufacturing in the early 1900s. The discovery of Spindletop, an oil field located near Beaumont, revolutionized the American oil and gas industry in 1901. Drilling operations at Spindletop triggered the largest gusher in world history, and the sheer amount of oil produced at Spindletop led to the establishment of both Gulf Oil and Texaco. In the aftermath of the Spindletop discovery, Texas experienced an oil boom, and the United States assumed the status of a leading oil producer.

Eventually, rails gave way to paved roadways, as cities abandoned streetcars for Henry Ford's mass-produced Model T. As Texas became one of the oil capitals of the world throughout the twentieth century, it paved the way to the creation of suburbs and superhighways. These developments coincided with growth of the commercial agriculture industry in Texas. Electricity, oil, and gasoline fueled large-scale commercial farms that shipped produce, dairy, poultry, and meats from remote rural locations to thriving urban and suburban centers of development. The creation of suburbs and superhighways cut across the once-pristine prairies and hills of Texas, destroying the natural environment.

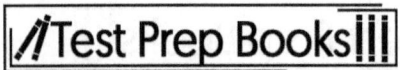

Suburbanization refers to the expansion of low-density communities—suburbs—in cities' outlying areas. The suburban population in Texas has skyrocketed since the end of World War II, primarily due to white Americans leaving urban areas (a phenomenon called *white flight*), the retirement of baby boomers, and domestic migration related to economic opportunities and lower taxes. While suburbanization has stimulated significant economic growth in Texas, it has also led to increased pollution due to increased highway construction and automobile ownership.

Cotton production initially declined after the abolition of slavery; however, Texas's Jim Crow laws allowed sharecropping to replace slavery as the primary means of exploiting African Americans and securing a source of cheap labor for cotton production. Following the Great Migration (1916–1940) of African Americans to northern cities, Texas farmers increasingly turned to mechanized means of planting, harvesting, and baling cotton, which has allowed Texas to maintain its position as the leading producer of cotton in the United States.

Citrus production increased in Texas during the twentieth century as farmers more fully realized the potential of the Rio Grande Valley. Innovations in irrigation, pesticides, and fertilizer enhanced the large-scale production of numerous citrus crops, such as grapefruits, oranges, tangerines, and lemons. Production further increased in the mid-twentieth century due to advances in refrigerated containers.

Texas is currently a global leader in beef and dairy production, boasting nearly twice as many cattle as the next highest state. During the twentieth century, barbed wire and electric fences allowed ranches to dramatically increase the size of their herds, and refrigeration facilitated transportation of products over longer distances. Furthermore, artificial insemination and antibiotics reduced costs, supported larger herds, and increased production per cow.

Eventually, manufacturing, commercial farming, and the oil industry packed their bags for foreign soil in the 1970s to 1990s, contributing to rampant deindustrialization. Texas, benefitting from the rise of the Sunbelt economy, was not delivered a direct blow by deindustrialization, but still felt the reverberations from America's Rust Belt. The result was a decrease in jobs and an increase in abandoned manufacturing sectors. Today, across Texas and most of the United States, one can still witness the aftermath of deindustrialization—dilapidated factories and farms pepper the natural American landscape with decaying scenes of the past.

Computer Technology, Transportation, and Medical Research in Texas

Thanks to its dedication to high-tech improvements in computer technology, transportation, and medical research, Texas experienced a slight economic boom in the decades following the decline of the oil industry. Cities like Houston, Dallas-Fort Worth, Austin, and San Antonio blossomed into southwestern hubs for the tech industries. The Dallas-Fort Worth metroplex, for instance, became one of the leading centers for the nation's growth in telecommunications, computers, and high-tech manufacturing. Hosting over five hundred tech companies, the Dallas-Fort Worth metroplex became a leader in telecommunications, employing nearly seventy thousand people in tech alone. Recently, Austin has also become a magnet for the tech industry. This has shifted the social demographics of the region, bringing in more young professionals, immigrants, and migrants. Medical research, in particular, has boomed alongside the tech industry, as places like Dallas, Austin, and Houston have become leaders in medical technology and health care.

Transportation has continued to evolve through the late twentieth and early twenty-first centuries in Texas. The continued market dominance of cars fueled suburbanization as well as the development of sprawling networks of highways. Widespread car ownership and extensive investment in roads have somewhat frustrated the development of mass transit options in Texas compared to other large states, but this has changed in recent decades. Most notably, Dallas Area Rapid Transit (DART) is the longest and sixth most ridden light rail system in the United States.

Over the latter half of the twentieth century, Texas emerged as a global leader in aerospace engineering, manufacturing, and research. Two of the busiest airport hubs in the world—Dallas/Fort Worth International Airport and George Bush Intercontinental Airport—are in Texas. Additionally, the Lyndon B. Johnson Space Center in Houston has contributed to every NASA spaceflight since 1965, including the Apollo 11 Moon landing.

Practice Quiz

1. Which of the following was a missionary who took part in the Narváez expedition?
    a. Alonso Álvarez de Pineda
    b. Francisco Hidalgo
    c. Álvar Núñez Cabeza de Vaca
    d. José de Escandón

2. What mass execution of Texas prisoners contributed to the Texas Revolution?
    a. Surrender at Goliad
    b. Fredonian Rebellion
    c. Battle of the Alamo
    d. Battle of Coleto

3. Why is the Battle of Palmito Ranch considered unusual?
    a. It was the last battle of the Texas Revolution.
    b. It was part of the Cordova Rebellion.
    c. It took place during the time Texas was an independent nation.
    d. It occurred after the end of the Civil War.

4. How did Oveta Culp Hobby contribute to reform movements in Texas?
    a. She promoted women's suffrage and Prohibition.
    b. She improved standards for women in the military.
    c. She expanded opportunities for African Americans.
    d. She supported the economic development of low-income communities.

5. In which Texas city did the discovery of oil revolutionize the American oil and gas industry?
    a. Galveston
    b. Austin
    c. Houston
    d. Beaumont

See answers on the next page.

Answer Explanations

1. C: Álvar Núñez Cabeza de Vaca was a missionary and explorer who participated in the Narváez expedition. Choice *A*, Alonso Álvarez de Pineda, was an explorer and cartographer who created one of the first maps of Texas. Choice *B*, Francisco Hidalgo, led several Franciscan missionaries in parts of Texas. Choice *D*, José de Escandón, was a member of the Spanish military who conquered many American Indian tribes in Texas.

2. A: The surrender at Goliad, which resulted in the mass execution of Texan prisoners following the Battle of Coleto, served as a powerful rallying cry for Texas independence. Choices *B*, *C*, and *D* are other events that contributed to the Texas Revolution.

3. D: The Battle of Palmito Ranch occurred after Robert Lee surrendered at Appomattox Court House and the Confederacy was dissolved. It is considered the last battle of the Civil War even thought it was fought after the war was technically over.

4. B: Oveta Culp Hobby contributed to reform movements in Texas by improving standards for women in the military. Jane McCallum promoted women's suffrage and Prohibition, Choice *A*. Lulu Belle Madison White expanded opportunities for African Americans, Choice *C*. Barbara Jordan supported the economic development of low-income communities, Choice *D*.

5. D: The Spindletop oil gusher was located near Beaumont, Texas and helped create an oil boom in Texas. This in turn helped the United States become a leading oil producer.

Geography, Culture, and the Behavioral and Social Sciences

Physical Geography Concepts, Natural Processes, and Earth's Physical Features

Physical Region

<u>Soils and River Systems</u>
The Earth's surface, like many other things in the broader universe, does not remain the same for long; in fact, it changes daily. The Earth's surface is subject to a variety of physical processes that continue to shape its appearance. Water, wind, temperature, or sunlight play a role in continually altering the Earth's surface.

Erosion involves the movement of soil from one place to another and can be caused by a variety of stimuli including ice, snow, water, wind, and ocean waves. Wind erosion occurs in generally flat, dry areas with loose topsoil. Over time, the persistent winds can dislodge significant amounts of soil into the air, reshaping the land and wreaking havoc on those who depend on agriculture for their livelihoods. Water can also cause erosion. For example, erosion caused by the Colorado River helped to form the Grand Canyon. Over time, the river moved millions of tons of soil, cutting a huge gorge in the Earth along the way. In water erosion, material carried by the water is referred to as sediment. With time, some sediment can collect at the mouths of rivers, forming deltas, which become small islands of fertile soil. This process of detaching loose soils and transporting them to a different location where they remain for an extended period of time is referred to as **deposition**, which is the end result of the erosion process.

In contrast to erosion, weathering does not involve the movement of any outside stimuli. Instead, the surface of the Earth is broken down physically or chemically. Physical weathering involves the effects of atmospheric conditions such as water, ice, heat, or pressure. For example, when ice forms in the cracks of large rocks or pavement, it can break down or split open the material. Chemical weathering generally occurs in warmer climates and involves organic material that breaks down rocks, minerals, or soil. Scientists believe this process led to the creation of fossil fuels such as oil, coal, and natural gas.

<u>Climate</u>
Weather is the condition of the Earth's atmosphere at a particular time. Climate is different; instead of focusing on one particular day, climate is the relative pattern of weather in a place for an extended period of time. For example, the city of Atlanta, Georgia generally has a humid subtropical climate; however, it also occasionally experiences snowstorms in the winter months. Over time, geographers, meteorologists, and other Earth scientists have determined these patterns that are indicative to north Georgia. Almost all parts of the world have predictable climate patterns, which are influenced by the surrounding geography.

The Central Coast of California is an example of a place with a predictable climate pattern. Santa Barbara, California, one of the region's larger cities, has almost the same temperature for most of the year, with only minimal fluctuation during the winter months. The temperatures there, which average between 75° and 65° Fahrenheit regardless of the time of year, are influenced by a variety of different climatological factors including elevation, location relative to the mountains and ocean, and ocean currents.

Other factors affecting climate include elevation, prevailing winds, vegetation, and latitudinal position on the globe.

Physical Processes

Earth is a complex system of the atmosphere (air), hydrosphere (water), as well as continental land (land). All work together to support the biosphere (life).

The atmosphere is divided into several layers: the troposphere, stratosphere, mesosphere, and thermosphere. The troposphere is at the bottom and is about seven and a half miles thick. Above the troposphere is the 30-mile-thick stratosphere. Above the stratosphere is the mesosphere, a 20-mile layer, followed by the thermosphere, which is more than 300 miles thick.

The troposphere is closest to Earth and has the greatest pressure due to the pull of gravity on its gas particles as well as pressure from the layers above. 78% of the atmosphere is made of nitrogen. Surprisingly, the oxygen that we breathe only makes up 21% of the gases, and the carbon dioxide critical to insulating Earth makes up less than 1% of the atmosphere. There are other trace gases present in the atmosphere, including water vapor.

Although the stratosphere has minimal wind activity, it is critical for supporting the biosphere because it contains the ozone layer, which absorbs the sun's damaging ultra-violet rays and protects living organisms. Due to its low level of air movement, airplanes travel in the stratosphere. The mesosphere contains few gas particles, and the gas levels are so insignificant in the thermosphere that it is considered space.

Visible light is colors reflecting off particles. If all colors reflect, we see white; if no colors reflect, we see black. This means a colored object is reflecting only that color—a red ball reflects red light and absorbs other colors.

Because the thermosphere has so few particles to reflect light rays (photons), it appears black. The troposphere appears blue in the day, and various shades of yellow and orange at sunset due to the angle of the sun hitting particles that refract, or bend, the light. In certain instances, the entire visible spectrum can be seen in the form of rainbows. Rainbows occur when sunlight passes through water droplets and is refracted in many different directions by the water particles.

The hydrosphere, or water-containing portion of the Earth's surface, plays a major role in supporting the biosphere. In the picture below, a single water molecule (molecular formula H_2O) looks like a mouse head. The small ears of the mouse are the two hydrogen atoms connected to the larger oxygen atom in the middle.

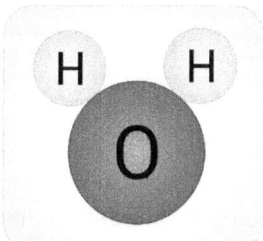

Each hydrogen atom has one proton (positively charged, like the plus end of a magnet) in its nucleus (center), while oxygen has eight protons in its center. Hydrogen also has only one electron (negatively charged, like the minus end of a magnet) orbiting around the nucleus. Because hydrogen has only one proton, its electron is pulled more toward the oxygen nucleus (more powerful magnet). This makes hydrogen exist without an electron most of the time, so it is positively charged. On the other hand, oxygen often has two extra electrons (one from each hydrogen), so it is negatively charged. These bonds between the oxygen and hydrogen are called covalent bonds.

This charged situation is what makes water such a versatile substance; it also causes different molecules of water to interact with each other.

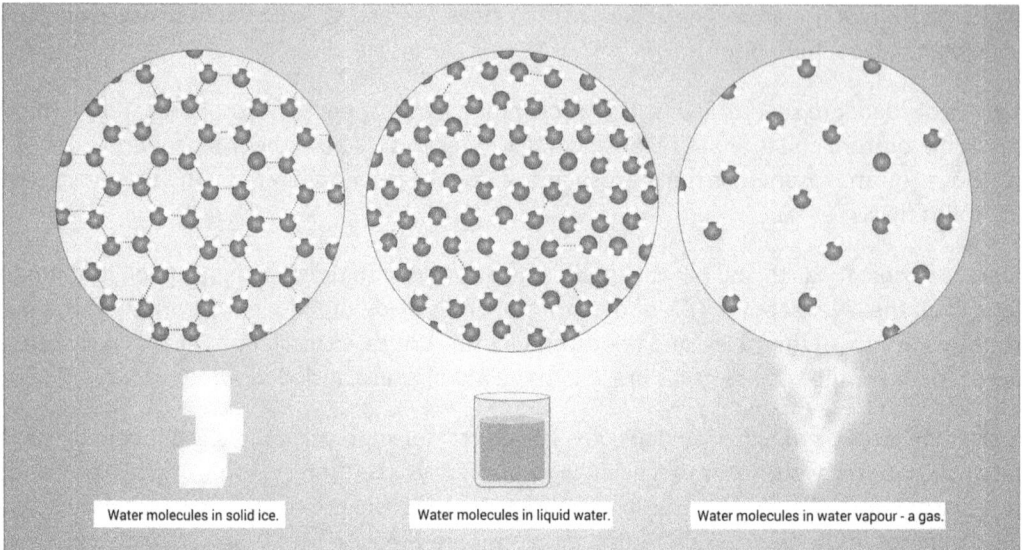

| Water molecules in solid ice. | Water molecules in liquid water. | Water molecules in water vapour - a gas. |

In a solid form (ice), water lines up in a crystal structure because the positive hydrogen atoms prefer to be next to the negative oxygen atoms that belong to other water molecules. These attractions are represented by the blue lines in the molecular picture of ice above. As heat is added and the ice melts, the water molecules have more kinetic energy and move faster; therefore, they are unable to perfectly arrange in the lattice structure of ice and turn into liquid. If enough heat is added, the water molecules will have so much kinetic energy they vaporize into gas. At this point, there are no bonds holding the water together because the molecules aren't close enough.

Notice how ice in its intricate arrangement has more space between the particles than liquid water, which shows that the ice is less dense than water. This contradicts the scientific fact that solids are denser than liquids. In water's case only, the solid will float due to a lower density! This is significant for the hydrosphere, because if temperatures drop to lower than freezing, frozen water will float to the surface of lakes or oceans and insulate the water underneath so that life can continue in liquid water. If ice was not less dense than liquid water, bodies of water would freeze from the bottom up and aquatic ecosystems would be trapped in a block of ice.

The hydrosphere has two components: seawater and freshwater (less than 5% of the hydrosphere). Water covers more than 70% of the Earth's surface.

The final piece of the biosphere is the lithosphere, the rocky portion of earth. Geology is the study of solid earth. Earth's surface is composed of elemental chunks called minerals, which are simply crystallized groups of bonded atoms. Minerals that have the same composition but different arrangements are called polymorphs, like graphite and diamonds. All minerals contain physical properties such as luster (shine), color, hardness, density, and boiling point. Their chemical properties, or how they react with other compounds, are also different. Minerals combine to form the rocks that make up Earth.

Earth has distinct layers—a thin, solid outer surface, a dense, solid core, and the majority of its matter between them. It is kind of like an egg: the thin crust is the shell, the inner core is the yolk, and the mantle and outer core that compose the space in between are like the egg white.

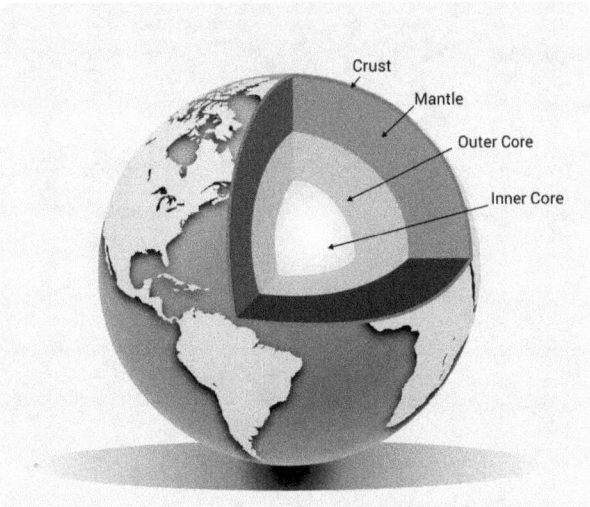

The outer crust of Earth consists of igneous or sedimentary rocks over metamorphic rocks (dense compacted rock underneath). The crust, combined with the upper portion of the mantle, forms the lithosphere, which is broken into several different plates, like puzzle pieces.

Earth-Sun Relationships

Other major lines of latitude and longitude exist to divide the world into regions relative to the direct rays of the sun. These lines correspond with the Earth's tilt, and are responsible for the seasons. For example, the northern hemisphere is tilted toward the sun from June 22 to September 23, which creates the summer season in that part of the world. Conversely, the southern hemisphere is tilted away from the direct rays of the sun and experiences winter during those same months.

The area between the **Tropic of Cancer** and the **Tropic of Capricorn** (called the tropics) has more direct exposure to the sun, tends to be warmer year-round, and experiences fewer variations in seasonal temperatures. Most of the Earth's population lives in the area between the Tropic of Cancer and the Arctic Circle (66.5 degrees north), which is one of the middle latitudes. In the Southern Hemisphere, the middle latitudes exist between the Tropic of Capricorn and the Antarctic Circle (66.5 degrees south). In both of these places, indirect rays of the sun strike the Earth. Therefore, seasons are more pronounced, and milder temperatures generally prevail. The final region, known as the high latitudes, is found north of the Arctic Circle and south of the Antarctic Circle. These regions generally tend to be cold all year, and experience nearly twenty-four hours of sunlight during their respective summer solstice and twenty-four hours of darkness during the winter solstice.

Seasons in the Southern Hemispheres are opposite of those in the Northern Hemisphere due to the position of the Earth as it rotates around the sun. An **equinox** occurs when the sun's rays are directly over the Equator, and day and night are of almost equal length throughout the world. Equinoxes occur twice a year; the autumnal equinox occurs around September 22nd, while the spring equinox occurs around March 20th. Since the Northern and Southern hemispheres experience opposite seasons, the season names vary based on location (i.e. when the Northern Hemisphere is experiencing summer, the Southern Hemisphere is in winter).

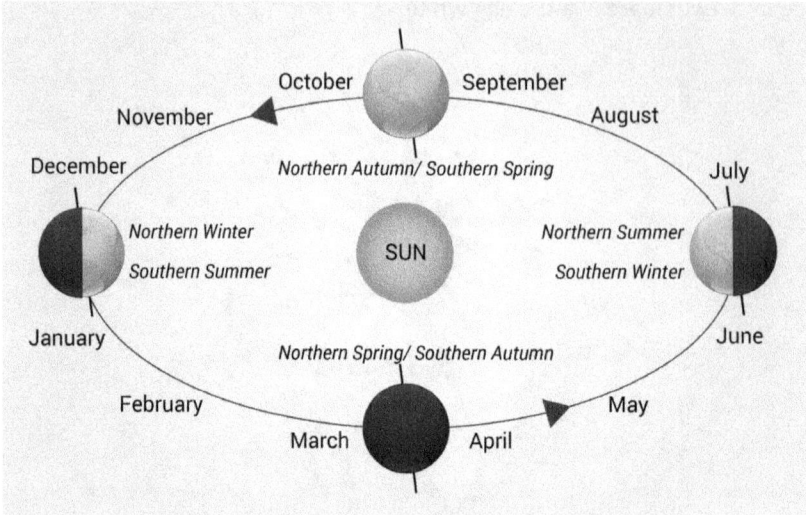

Climate, Vegetation, Soil, and Geology

Climate inevitably affects the vegetation, soil, and geology/geomorphology of particular regions around the globe. In terms of vegetation, the world can be divided into four major biomes: forest, savannah, grassland, and desert. These biomes produce different types of land vegetation. In a forest biome, trees form a continuous canopy. In a savannah biome, trees are with various grasses. In a grassland biome, the entire environment is covered in grass. In a desert biome, there is little to no land vegetation. Vegetation is both a product of the soil and a contributor to the soil. Erosion of the soil, for instance, can be minimized through planting crops and conserving the environment. The earth's geology/geomorphology is also fundamentally tied to vegetation and the soil. Different elevations and climates, for instance, produce different vegetation and soil. Likewise, the nutrients present in vegetation and the soil may affect the geological components of the earth.

Climate zones are created by the Earth's tilt as it travels around the Sun. These zones are delineated by the equator and four other special latitudinal lines: the Tropic of Cancer or Northern Tropic at 23.5° North; the Tropic of Capricorn or Southern Tropic at 23.5° South; the Arctic Circle at 66.5° North; and the Antarctic Circle at 66.5° South. The areas between these lines of latitude represent different climate zones. Tropical climates are hot and wet, like rainforests, and tend to have abundant plant and animal life, while polar climates are cold and usually have little plant and animal life. Temperate zones can vary and experience the four seasons.

Major Landforms, Climates, and Ecosystems

Earth is an incredibly large place filled with a variety of land and water ecosystems. Marine ecosystems cover over 75% of the Earth's surface and contain over 95% of the Earth's water. Marine ecosystems can be broken down into two primary subgroups: freshwater ecosystems, which only encompass around 2% of the earth's surface; and ocean ecosystems, which make up over 70%. Terrestrial ecosystems vary based on latitudinal distance from the equator, elevation, and proximity to mountains or bodies of water. For example, in the high latitudinal regions north of the Arctic Circle and south of the Antarctic Circle, frozen tundra dominates. Tundra, which is characterized by low temperatures, short growing seasons, and minimal vegetation, is only found in regions that are far away from the direct rays of the sun.

In contrast, deserts can be found throughout the globe and are created by different ecological factors. For example, the world's largest desert, the Sahara, is almost entirely within the tropics; however, other deserts like the Gobi in China, the Mojave in the United States, and the Atacama in Chile, are close to mountain ranges such as the Himalayas, the Sierra Nevada, and the Andes, respectively. In the United States, temperate deciduous forests dominate the southeastern region. The midwestern states such as Nebraska, Kansas, and the Dakotas, are primarily grasslands. The states of the Rocky Mountains can have decidedly different climates relative to elevation. Denver, Colorado, will often see snowfalls well into April or May due to colder temperatures, whereas cities in the eastern part of the state, with much lower elevations, may see their last significant snowfall in March.

The tropics generally experience warmer temperatures due to their position on the Earth in relation to the sun. However, like most of the world, the tropics also experience a variety of climatological regions. In Brazil, Southeast Asia, Central America, and even Northern Australia, tropical rainforests are common. These forests, which are known for abundant vegetation, daily rainfall, and a wide variety of animal life, are essential to the health of the world's ecosystems. For example, the Amazon Rain Forest's billions of trees produce substantial amounts of oxygen and absorb an equivalent amount of carbon dioxide—the substance that many climatologists assert is causing climate change or global warming. Unlike temperate deciduous forests whose trees lose their leaves during the fall and winter months, tropical rain forests are always lush, green, and warm. In fact, some rainforests are so dense with vegetation that a few indigenous tribes have managed to exist within them without being influenced by any sort of modern technology, virtually maintaining their ancient way of life in the modern era.

The world's largest land ecosystem, the taiga, is found primarily in high latitudinal areas, which receive very little direct sunlight. These forests are generally made up of coniferous trees, which do not lose their leaves at any point during the year as deciduous trees do. Taigas are cold-climate regions that make up almost 30% of the world's land area. These forests dominate the northern regions of Canada, Scandinavia, and Russia, and provide the vast majority of the world's lumber.

Climates are influenced by five major factors: elevation, latitude, proximity to mountains, ocean currents, and wind patterns. For example, the cold currents off the coast of California provide the West Coast of the United States with pleasant year-round temperatures. Conversely, Western Europe, which is at the nearly the same latitude as most of Canada, is influenced by the warm waters of the Gulf Stream, an ocean current that acts as a conveyor belt, moving warm tropical waters to the icy north. In fact, the Gulf Stream's influence is so profound that it even keeps Iceland—an island nation in the far North Atlantic—relatively warm.

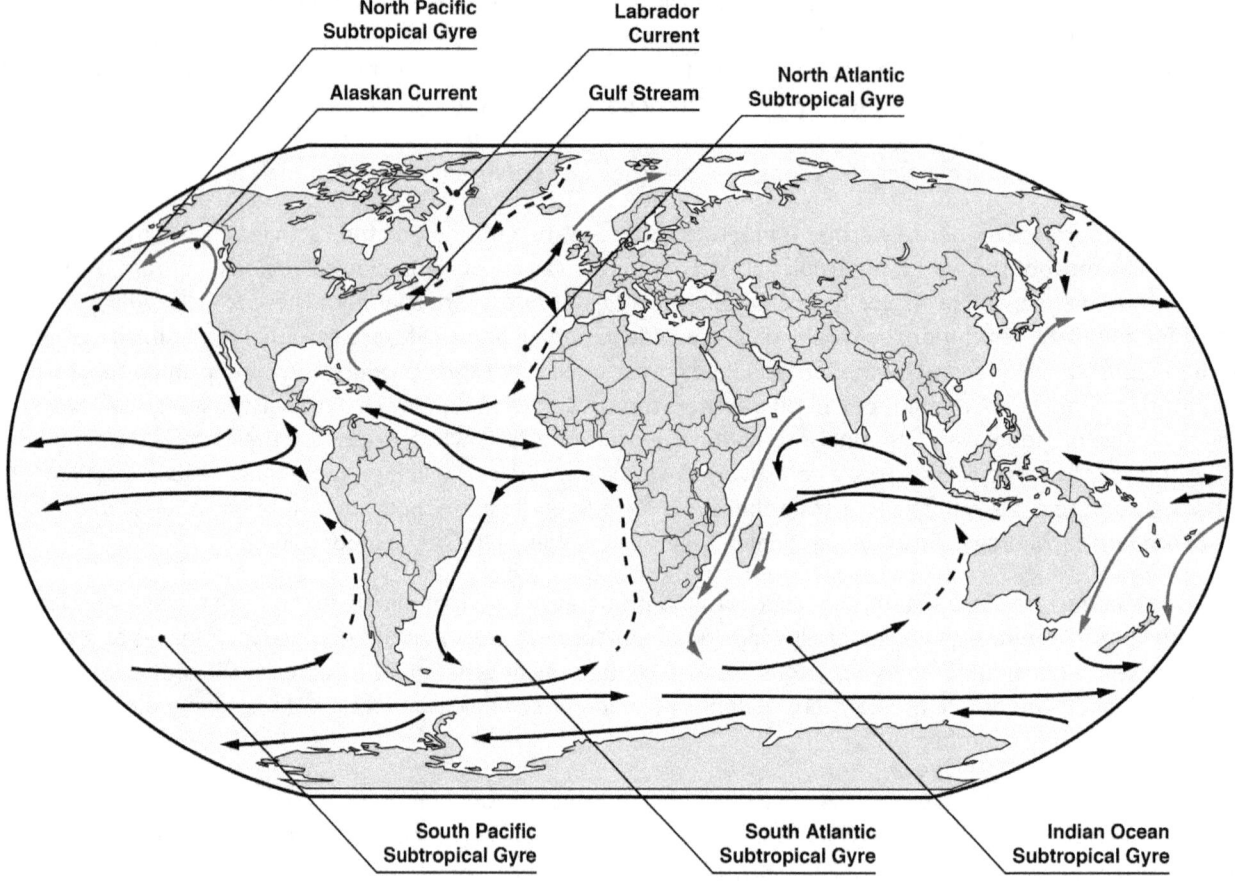

There are seven or eight major plates in the lithosphere and several minor plates. These tectonic plates explain the changing topography, or shape, of earth.

There are three types of boundaries between plates: divergent, convergent, and transform. All boundaries can be sites of volcanic activity. A divergent boundary occurs when plates separate. Lava fills in the space the plates create and hardens into rock, which creates oceanic crust. In a convergent boundary, if one of the plates is in the ocean, that plate is denser due to the weight of water. The dense ocean plate will slip under the land plate, causing a subduction zone where the plate moves underneath. Where plates converge on land, the continental crusts are both lighter with a similar density, and as a result they will buckle together and create mountains.

In transform boundaries, adjacent plates sliding past each other create friction and pressure that destroy the edges of the boundary and cause earthquakes. Transform boundaries don't produce magma, as they involve lateral movement.

Just as plates pushing together cause mountains, canyons are deep trenches caused by plates moving apart. Weather and erosion from rivers and precipitation run-off also create canyons. Deltas form when rivers dump their sediments and water into oceans. They are triangular flat stretches of land that are kind of like a triangular spatula; the handle represents the river, and the triangle represents the mouth of a delta.

Sand dunes are another landform caused by wind or waves in combination with the absence of plants to hold sand in place. These are found in sandy areas like the desert or the ocean.

Global and Regional Patterns of Culture and Human Geography

Cultural Region

Regions

Geographers divide the world into regions in order to more fully understand differences inherent with the world, its people, and its environment. Lines of latitude such as the Equator, the Tropics, and the Arctic and Antarctic Circles already divide the Earth into solar regions relative to the amount of either direct or indirect sunlight that they receive. Although not the same throughout, the middle latitudes generally have a milder climate than areas found within the tropics. Furthermore, tropical locations are usually warmer than places in the middle latitudes, but that is not always the case. For example, the lowest place in the United States—Death Valley, California—is also home to the nation's highest-ever recorded temperature. Likewise, the Andes Mountains in Peru and Ecuador, although found near the Equator, are also home to heavy snow, low temperatures, and dry conditions, due to their elevation.

Formal regions are spatially defined areas that have overarching similarities or some level of homogeneity or uniformity. Although not exactly alike, a formal region generally has at least one characteristic that is consistent throughout the entire area. For example, the United States could be classified as one massive formal region because English is the primary language spoken in all fifty states. Even more specifically, the United States is a linguistic region—a place where everyone generally speaks the same language.

Functional regions are areas that also have similar characteristics but do not have clear boundaries. Large cities and their metropolitan areas form functional regions, as people from outside the official city limit must travel into the city regularly for work, entertainment, restaurants, etc. Other determining factors of a functional region could be a sports team, a school district, or a shopping center. For example, New York City has two professional baseball, basketball, and football teams. As a result, its citizens may have affinities for different teams even though they live in the same city. Conversely, a citizen in rural Idaho may cheer for the Seattle Seahawks, even though they live over 500 miles from Seattle.

Linguistics

Linguistics, or the study of language, groups certain languages together according to their commonalities. For example, the Romance languages—French, Spanish, Italian, Romanian, and Portuguese—all share language traits from Latin. These languages, also known as vernaculars, or more commonly spoken dialects, evolved over centuries of physical isolation on the European continent. The Spanish form of Latin emerged into today's Spanish language. Similarly, the Bantu people of Africa travelled extensively and spread their language, now called Swahili, which became the first Pan-African language. Since thousands of languages exist, it is important to have a widespread means of communication that can interconnect people from different parts of the world. One way to do this is through a lingua franca, or a common language used for business, diplomacy, and other cross-national relationships. English is a primary lingua franca around the world, but there are many others in use as well.

Religion

Religion has played a tremendous role in creating the world's cultures. Devout Christians crossed the Atlantic in hopes of finding religious freedom in New England, Muslim missionaries and traders travelled to the Spice Islands of the East Indies to teach about the Koran, and Buddhist monks traversed the Himalayan Mountains into Tibet to spread their faith. In some countries, religion helps to shape legal systems. These nations, termed theocracies, have no separation of church and state and are more common in Islamic nations such as Saudi Arabia, Iran, and Qatar. In contrast, even though religion has played a tremendous role in the history of the United States, its government remains secular, or nonreligious, due to the influence of European Enlightenment philosophy at the time of its inception. Like ethnicity and language, religion is a primary way that individuals and people groups self-identify. As a result, religious influences can shape a region's laws, architecture, literature, and music. For example, when the Ottoman Turks, who are Muslim, conquered Constantinople, which was once the home of the Eastern Orthodox Christian Church, they replaced Christian places of worship with mosques. Additionally, they replaced different forms of Roman architecture with those influenced by Arabic traditions.

Economics

Economic activity also has a spatial component. Nations with few natural resources generally tend to import what they need from nations willing to export raw materials to them. Furthermore, areas that are home to certain raw materials generally tend to alter their environment in order to maintain production of those materials. In the San Joaquin Valley of California, an area known for extreme heat and desert-like conditions, local residents have engineered elaborate drip irrigation systems to adequately water lemon, lime, olive, and orange trees, utilizing the warm temperatures to constantly produce citrus fruits. Additionally, other nations with abundant petroleum reserves build elaborate infrastructures in order to pump, house, refine, and transport their materials to nations who require gasoline, diesel, or natural gas. Essentially, inhabitants of different spatial regions on Earth create jobs, infrastructure, and transportation systems to ensure the continued flow of goods, raw materials, and resources out of their location so long as financial resources keep flowing into the area.

Political System

The terms nation and state are often used interchangeably, but in political theory, they are two very distinct concepts. Nation refers to a people's cultural identity, while state refers to a territory's political organization and government.

Unlike states, there are no definitive requirements to be a nation; the nation just needs to include a group that is bound together by some shared defining characteristics such as the following:

- Language
- Culture and traditions
- Beliefs and religion
- Homeland
- Ethnicity
- History
- Mythology

The term state is commonly used to reference a nation-state, especially in regard to their government. There are four requirements for a political entity to be recognized as a state:

- Territory: a clearly defined geographic area with distinct borders
- Population: citizens and noncitizens living within the borders of the territory with some degree of permanence
- Legitimacy: legal authority to rule that is recognized by the citizens of the state and by other states
- Sovereignty: a political entity's right and power to self-govern without interference from external forces

Nation-state is the term used to describe a political entity with both a clearly defined nation and state. In a nation-state, the majority population of the state is a nation that identifies the territory as their homeland and shares a common history and culture. It is also possible to have several nations in the same nation-state. For example, there are Canadians in Canada and nations of Aboriginal peoples. The presence of multiple nations raises issues related to sovereignty.

Example of a nation: Sikhs in India

Example of a state: Vatican City

Example of a nation-state: Germany

Innovation and Diffusion

Technological innovation in the earliest hearths of domestication, allowed the regions to become centers for trade, government, art, science, language acquisition, writing systems, and specialized economic activities. Additionally, these agricultural hearths became epicenters for economic inequality and social stratification, as increases in the wealth of certain farmers and merchants inevitably led to financial strata in each hearth.

As the varying cultures residing in each of the earliest hearths of domestication developed and evolved via spontaneous ideological adaptations, inventive technological advancements, and self-perpetuating cycles of population growth, elaborate continental trading systems emerged. A larger process of cultural diffusion allowed disparate ideas, traditions, and practices to be outwardly spread and exchanged between groups. This transfer of culture and knowledge impacted the daily interactions of previously isolated groups, thrusting them into a new, broader world of complex, multilateral social exchange.

Major World Regions

East Asia is the easternmost region of Asia, and it includes the countries of China, Japan, Mongolia, North Korea, South Korea, and Taiwan. Hong Kong and Macau are also in East Asia. The climate of East Asia is relatively temperate and predictable because of the East Asian monsoon flow, which produces cold, dry winters and extremely rainy summers. As the oldest and largest country in East Asia, China has a disproportionate impact on East Asian culture, particularly in terms of philosophy, language, and religion. Aside from Japan, East Asian countries continue to follow some aspects of the traditional Chinese calendar and celebrate the Lunar New Year.

Sub-Saharan Africa refers to the region of Africa that is south of the Sahara, encompassing forty-six out of the fifty-four countries in Africa. Sub-Saharan Africa has some of the most diverse climate zones in the world, ranging from tropical rainforests in Central Africa to hot deserts in the Horn of Africa. The culture of sub-Saharan Africa is similarly diverse, with more than 1,000 languages spoken in the region. Traditional African belief systems and traditions have remained intact in sub-Saharan Africa, and cultural practices often vary from village to village. Sub-Saharan African countries also have a shared history with European colonization, which is why Christianity is the most popular regional religion. Colonization and imperialism left a brutal legacy in the region, heavily contributing to its endemic poverty and sectarian conflicts.

Latin America refers to a region in North and South America that was colonized by Spain, France, and Portugal. The precise definition of Latin America varies, but the most common grouping includes Mexico, the Caribbean, Central America, and South America. The climate and geography of Latin America differs by region, and examples of this climatic diversity include Caribbean tropics, Brazilian and Colombian rainforests, the hot deserts of Mexico, and the cold deserts of Argentina. European colonization had a lasting impact on contemporary Latin American culture. The region is overwhelmingly Catholic, nearly all countries predominantly speak the Romance language of their colonizers, and most countries have a syncretic culture that blends European, African, and indigenous traditions.

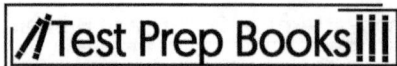

Europe is in the western half of the Eurasian continental area with its western edge bordering Atlantic Ocean to the west, its southern edge bordering North Africa to the south, and its southeastern edge bordering Turkey. Russia and Turkey are transcontinental countries with European territory, and their inclusion in Europe is a matter of perspective. Western Europe has a mild oceanic climate, Southern Europe has a Mediterranean climate, Northern Europe (Scandinavia) has a cold climate, and Eastern Europe has a temperate continental climate. European culture is heavily influenced by the Roman Empire, and Europeans overwhelmingly practice Christianity.

Southwest Asia comprises the bulk of the Middle East, and it consists of countries in Mesopotamia and the Arabian Peninsula. Southwest Asia's climate is generally hot and arid with the notable exception of the Tigris and Euphrates watersheds in Mesopotamia, which forms part of the Fertile Crescent. Additionally, Southwest Asia has a significant amount of coastal areas due to its borders with the Mediterranean Sea, Red Sea, Persian Gulf, and Caspian Sea. Southwest Asian culture is closely tied to Islam, and the five most spoken languages are Arabic, Hebrew, Kurdish, Persian (Farsi), and Turkish. Southwest Asian culture is generally more traditionally patriarchal than other regions, and sectarian violence is widespread due to the region's colonial borders, religious conflicts, and resource disputes.

North Africa refers to the northernmost region of Africa, and its eastern region is commonly included as part of the Middle East. Aside from the northern coast's Mediterranean climate and Nile River Valley, the rest of North Africa has a hot and arid desert climate. North Africa has strong ethnic, cultural, and linguistic ties to Southwest Asia, which date back to the Muslim conquest of the region between 600 and 1000 C.E. Coptic Christians are the largest minority group, with significant populations in Algeria, Egypt, Morocco, and Tunisia. In addition, nomadic tribe-based societies continue to operate in the Western Sahara.

The United States has numerous regions. The Atlantic seaboard and the West Coast are commonly grouped together due to their similarities, including extensive coastlines, concentration of wealth, high population density, and metropolitan culture. The Northeast and Pacific Northwest have some of the densest forests in the United States. The Upper Midwest has extreme variations between its summer and winter temperatures, while the Lower Midwest is part of the Great Plains, which lies between the Mississippi River and Rocky Mountains. The South has a subtropical climate, and it has the most conservative and traditional culture in the United States by a significant margin. The Southwest is home to vast hot deserts, and, given its shared history and proximity to Mexico, Hispanic Americans strongly influence Southwestern culture.

Texas is in the Northern Hemisphere, the northern half of the Earth between the equator and the North Pole. Texas is located on the North American continent, a landmass in the Western Hemisphere that encompasses half of the Earth to the west of the prime meridian. Texas is part of the United States of America, and it's usually considered part of the Southwestern or Sunbelt regions. Texas is bordered by the states of Louisiana to the east, Oklahoma to the north, Arkansas to the northeast, and New Mexico to the west. Texas is also bordered by Mexico to the south and the Gulf of Mexico to the southeast. The Gulf of Mexico is a large body of saltwater that serves as a major port for international trade, making Texas a leader in the American shipping industry. The state of Texas, from Port Arthur (coastal east) to El Paso (mountainous west), spans nearly 773 miles.

How the Components of Culture Affect the Way People Live

Humans both adapt themselves to their environment and adapt their environment to suit their needs. Humans create social systems with the goal of providing people with access to what they need to live more productive, fulfilling, and meaningful lives. Sometimes, humans create destructive systems, but generally speaking, humans tend to leverage their environments to make their lives easier. For example, in warmer climates, people tend to wear lighter clothing such as shorts, linen shirts, and hats. In the excessively sun-drenched nations of the Middle East, both men and women wear flowing white clothing complete with both a head and neck covering in order to prevent the blistering effects of exposure to the sun. Likewise, the native Inuit peoples of northern Canada and Alaska use the thick furs from the animals they kill to insulate their bodies against the bitter cold.

Humans must also manipulate their environments to ensure that they have sufficient access to food and water. In locations where water is not readily available, humans have had to invent ways to redirect water for drinking or agriculture. For example, the city of Los Angeles, America's second most populous city, did not have adequate freshwater resources to sustain its population. However, city and state officials realized that abundant water resources existed approximately three hundred miles to the east. Rather than relocating some of its population to areas with more abundant water resources, the State of California undertook one of the largest construction projects in the history of the world, the Los Angeles Aqueduct, which is a massive water transportation system that connects water-rich areas with the thirsty citizens of Los Angeles.

Farming is another way in which humans use the environment for their advantage. The very first permanent British Colony in North America, Jamestown, VA, was characterized by a hot and humid climate with fertile soil. Consequently, its inhabitants engaged in agriculture for both food and profit. Twelve years after Jamestown's founding in 1607, it was producing millions of dollars of tobacco each year. In order to sustain this booming industry, millions of African slaves and indentured servants from Europe were imported to provide labor. Conversely, poor soil in the New England colonies did not allow for widespread cash crop production, and the settlers there generally only grew enough food for themselves on small subsistence farms. Due in part to this environmental difference, slavery failed to take a strong foothold in these states, thus creating distinct cultures within the same country.

Systems of education have a powerful impact on people's way of life as well as regional characteristics. Most countries require universal attendance in primary school; however, there is tremendous variety in secondary school and higher education.

Advanced industrial countries in North America, Europe, East Asia, and Australia commonly use standardized test results to sort secondary school students into special education, vocational, general education, and rigorous academic programs. This stratification shapes the socioeconomic roles students will later adopt in capitalist economies. Furthermore, students' professional and social trajectories are differentiated based on their participation in higher education systems.

Countries with emerging economies, such as China and India, place a premium on education due to the close relationship between education and economic development. As a result, many families tailor daily life around educational achievement, mirroring or exceeding the focus on it in advanced industrial countries. Many students in emerging economies also seek higher education opportunities in advanced industrial countries.

Less developed regions in Africa, Latin America, and the Middle East generally have weak secondary education programs and limited higher education opportunities. Additionally, female students tend to receive fewer educational opportunities, which reinforces traditional gender norms. Overall, the lack of universal education systems undermines development.

World Populations and Globalization

Two primary realms exist within the study of geography. The first, **physical geography**, essentially correlates with the land, water, and foliage of the Earth. The second, **human geography**, is the study of the Earth's people and how they interact with their environment. Several geographical factors impact the human condition, such as access to natural resources. For example, human populations tend to be higher around more reliable sources of fresh water. The metropolitan area of New York City, which has abundant freshwater resources, is home to over 18 million people. Australia, on the other hand, an entire country and continent, has much less accessibility to fresh water and houses only 7 million more people. Although water is not the only factor in this disparity, it certainly plays a role in population density—the total number of people in a particular place divided by the total land area, usually in square miles or square kilometers. Australia's population density is about 7 people per square mile, while the most densely populated nation on Earth, Bangladesh, is home to 2,889 people per square mile.

Population density can have a devastating impact on both the physical environment/ecosystem and the humans who live within the environment/ecosystem of a particular place. For example, Delhi, one of India's most populated cities, is home to nearly five million gasoline-powered vehicles. Each day, those vehicles emit an enormous amount of carbon monoxide into the atmosphere, which directly affects the Delhi citizens' quality of life. In fact, the smog and pollution problems have gotten so severe that many drivers cannot see fifty feet in front of them. Additionally, densely populated areas within third-world nations, or developing nations, struggle significantly in their quest to balance the demands of the modern economy with their nation's lack of infrastructure. For example, nearly as many automobiles operate every day in major American cities like New York and Los Angeles as they do in Delhi, but they create significantly less pollution due to cleaner burning engines, better fuels, and governmental emission regulations.

One of the most significant demographic trends in world history is the increase in populations, which began to increase exponentially in the twentieth century. Before the 1800s, it took thousands of years to reach 1 billion people in the world. However, by 1999, the world population had increased to more than 6 billion people. As of 2016, the world population is 7.4 billion, and it is estimated that the population will increase to more than 11 billion by 2100. This is largely a result of a lower child mortality rate and higher life expectancy due to scientific progress. The effects of having a larger population are most visible in Africa and Asia, especially in India and China. Although larger populations provide for a larger workforce, they also put strain on the economy because more young people require employment.

Migration is governed by two primary causes: push factors that cause someone to leave an area, and pull factors that lure someone to a particular place. These two factors often work in concert with one another. For example, the United States of America has experienced significant internal migration from the industrial states in the Northeast (such as New York, New Jersey, Connecticut) to the Southern and Western states. This massive migration, which continues into the present-day, is due to high rents in the northeast, dreadfully cold winters, and lack of adequate retirement housing, all of which are push factors. These push factors lead to migration to the Sunbelt, a term geographers use to describe states with warm climates and less intense winters.

International migration also takes place between countries, continents, and other regions. The United States has long been the world's leading nation in regard to immigration, the process by which people permanently relocate to a new nation. Conversely, developing nations that suffer from high levels of poverty, pollution, warfare, and other violence all have significant push factors, which cause people to leave and move elsewhere. This process, known as emigration, is when people in a particular area leave in order to seek a better life in a different—usually better— location.

Immigration has changed the demographics of countries and can have positive and negative effects. Migration and immigration have occurred due to famine, warfare, and lack of economic prospects. Immigration can aid countries struggling to maintain a workforce, and it can also bring in needed medical professionals, scientists, and others with special training. However, immigration also puts strain on developed economies to support migrants who arrive without the necessary education and training to thrive in the advanced economies. Until recently, immigrants were encouraged, or in some cases, forced to assimilate and take on the customs and culture of their new country. For example, in the United States, legislation was passed to force German immigrants to learn English. More recently, developed countries have struggled to assimilate new arrivals to their countries, such as the recent surge of refugees into Europe. Unfortunately, the failure to adequately assimilate immigrants has created greater inequality and prevalence of radical behavior.

Geography

Due to improvements in transportation and communication, the world has become figuratively smaller. For example, university students now compete directly with others all over the world to obtain the skills that employers desire. Additionally, many corporations in developed nations have begun to outsource labor to nations with high levels of educational achievement but lower wage expectations. **Globalization**, the process of opening the marketplace to all nations throughout the world, has only just started to take hold in the modern economy. As industrial sites shift to the developing world, more opportunities become available for those nation's citizens as well. However, due to the massive amounts of pollution produced by factories, the process of globalization also has had significant ecological impacts. The most widely known impact, climate change, which most climatologists assert is caused by an increase of carbon dioxide in the atmosphere, remains a serious problem that has posed challenges for developing nations, who need industries in order to raise their standard of living, and developed nations, whose citizens use a tremendous amount of fossil fuels to run their cars, heat their homes, and maintain their ways of life.

Cultural Patterns and Characteristics in Various Regions

Although it is a significant factor, population density is not the only source of strain on a place's resources. Historical forces such as civil war, religious conflict, genocide, and government corruption can also profoundly alter the lives of a nation's citizens. For example, the war-torn nation of Somalia has not had a functioning government for nearly three decades. As a result, the nation's citizens have virtually no access to hospital care, vaccinations, or proper facilities for childbirth. Due to these and other factors, the nation's infant mortality rate, or the total number of child deaths per 1,000 live births, stands at 98.39/1000. When compared to Iceland's 1.82/1000, it's quite evident that Somalia struggles to provide basic services in the realm of childbirth and there is a dire need for humanitarian assistance.

Literacy rates, like infant mortality rates, are also excellent indicators of the relative level of development in a particular place. Many developing nations have both economic and social factors that hinder their ability to educate their own citizens. Due to radical religious factions within some nations like Afghanistan and Pakistan, girls are often denied the ability to attend school, which further reduces the nation's overall literacy rate. For example, girls in Afghanistan have a 24.2% literacy rate, one of the lowest rates of any record-keeping nation on Earth. Although literacy rates are useful in determining a nation's development level, high literacy rates do exist within developing nations. For example, Suriname, which has a significantly lower GDP (Gross Domestic Product) than Afghanistan, enjoys a 94% literacy rate among both sexes. Utilizing this and other data, geographers can form questions and conduct further research about such phenomena. Demographic data, such as population density, the infant mortality rate, and the literacy rate all provide insight into the characteristics of a particular place and help geographers better understand the spatial world.

The demographic transition model is a concept that explains the pattern of population change by examining two key statistics of a country: birth rate and death rate. This model suggests that as a country becomes more developed, the birth and death rates move through a predictable cycle.

History and Significance of Major Religious and Philosophical Traditions

Modern world religions include Christianity, Islam, Hinduism, Buddhism, Taoism, Shinto, Sikhism, and Judaism. Christianity, Islam, and Judaism are Abrahamic religions because they all trace their origin to, or recognize the importance of, the tribal patriarch Abraham. Hinduism, Buddhism, and Sikhism are often referred to as *Dharmic* faiths because they originated in the Indian subcontinent. Taoism is one of the most popular religions practiced in China, and Shinto is the largest religion in Japan. From ancient times through modernity, religion has played an important role in world history.

Despite their considerable similarities in religious beliefs, the conflict between Christianity and Islam is one of the most fraught relationships in world history. Between 1095 CE and 1291 CE, Christians and Muslims fought a series of

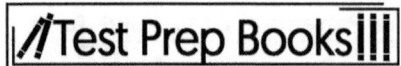

wars commonly referred to as the Crusades. In 1095 CE, Pope Urban II launched the First Crusade at the request of the Byzantine emperor to fight the Turks. The First Crusade ended with Christian forces massacring Muslim and Jewish inhabitants of Jerusalem. History would repeat itself from the twelfth century through the fourteenth century, as Christians fought Muslims from Jerusalem to the Rhineland to the Iberian Peninsula. Despite the rampant pillaging and bloodthirsty killing, the West gained immensely from their contact with Islamic civilizations, which were far more advanced. Christians rediscovered forgotten Greek and Roman texts in Muslim libraries and adopted advances in science, hygiene, and urban development. However, the Crusades' ultimate legacy would be to sow distrust and hostility between the world's two most popular religions. Hostility would only grow after the defeat and partition of the Ottoman Empire after World War I. Christian nations, such as France and England, colonized and occupied the Middle East until after World War II. The hostility between Christianity and Islam is particularly heightened in modern times due to the rise of Islamic fundamentalism.

Throughout most of world history, the Jewish people have faced anti-Semitism, but nothing compares to the Holocaust, the worst genocide in human history. Adolf Hitler's Nazi Party systematically executed 6 million European Jews, more than two-thirds of the European Jewish population. Following World War II, Great Britain withdrew from Palestine, and the United Nations passed a mandate to create a Jewish state in the region. On May 14, 1948, David Ben-Gurion declared the establishment of the State of Israel. The creation of a Jewish state is one of the most important events in modern history due to the ensuing conflict between Israel and the Muslim world. In fact, one day after Israel declared independence, the Arab League invaded the fledgling Jewish state and launched the 1948 Arab-Israeli War. Israel would again fight and defeat Arab countries in the Six-Day War and the 1973 Arab-Israeli War. A close ally to the United States, Israel plays an integral role in the West's foreign policy.

Religion has a long history of influencing the ruling dynasties until the Chinese Communist Revolution. Confucianism, Buddhism, and Taoism, collectively referred to as the three teachings, contributed to many golden ages of Chinese culture. In fact, Chinese emperors justified their right to rule based on the Mandate of Heaven, declaring that the gods had hand selected the emperor to rule. The legendary scholar Confucius developed a set of philosophy based on humanism and rationalism. Confucianism heavily influenced the Sui dynasty's imperial examination system, which established an efficient meritocracy within the civil service. During the Han dynasty, Taoism and Buddhism emerged as popular religions and added a spiritual element to Chinese religious practice. This spiritual melting pot would last until Mao Zedong's Communist forces overthrew the government. Communism is unique in its opposition to religious practice. As was the case in the Soviet Union, Mao Zedong would outlaw religious practice and oppress all spiritual movements.

Hinduism is arguably the oldest religion actively practiced in the world, and it currently has the third most religious followers in the world after Christianity and Islam, respectively. Hinduism developed as a syncretic fusion of ancient Vedic spiritualism, Brahmanism, and Indian cultural traditions. In contrast to most other religions, Hinduism doesn't recognize a common founder, and many practitioners believe Hinduism is eternal, with a founding that predates human history. Modern-day Hinduism reflects its syncretic evolution through the incorporation of cosmology, mythology, philosophy, ritualism, and spiritualism.

Major aspects of Hinduism include traditional ethics and duties (dharma), four eternal objectives of human life (puruṣārthas), the relationship between actions, intent, and consequences (karma), cycles of death and rebirth (saṃsāra), and liberation (moksha) from the cycles of death and rebirth. The cycles of life and death are related to the Indian caste system, though there's debate over whether the caste system is an explicit part of Hinduism or a socially constructed system loosely based on Hinduism. In practice, Hindus participate in a wide variety of religious practices, including worship (puja), meditation (dhyana), mantras (japa), and monasticism (sannyasa).

Philosophical traditions have played an influential role in societies since at least the sixth century B.C.E. The Classical Greek philosopher Socrates (470–399 B.C.E.) is widely considered to be the father of Western philosophy, but regional philosophical traditions in East Asia, the Middle East, India, and indigenous societies all predated Socrates.

Geography

In general, philosophical traditions provide frameworks for organizing and analyzing knowledge related to logic, reason, language, the natural world, spiritualism, and/or human experiences. Most philosophical traditions involve some form of discussions, questioning of authorities, and argumentation. Philosophical traditions have influenced the development of numerous fields, including economics, mathematics, politics, and science. Two of the most influential Western philosophical traditions are realism and idealism.

Realism is a philosophical tradition based on the belief that objective reality exists independent of human observation and humanity's conceptual schemes of understanding reality. Realism dates back to the Middle Ages (400–1500) when European philosophers discovered, analyzed, and adapted ancient Greek philosophical texts. Realism's contemporary impact cannot be overstated because it forms the basis of how most people lead their daily lives regardless of whether they're aware of realism as a philosophical tradition. Additionally, realism laid the foundation for modern science and mathematics, such as the scientific method, the philosophy of mathematics, and quantum mechanics in physics.

Idealism is a philosophical tradition dating back to the ancient world, particularly as developed by Hindu, Buddhist, and Greek philosophers. However, idealism mostly lay dormant until the German philosopher Immanuel Kant (1724–1804) founded the school of transcendental idealism, which argued that the human mind shapes and alters experiences with space, time, and the causation of events. While Kant stipulated that some things in reality exist independently of human experiences, traditional idealists argue that nothing exists in the material world outside of human perception. Idealism faced relatively heavy criticism in the twentieth century, but its core tenets have remained influential in modern philosophical traditions.

Importance of Place for Populations

Place

While absolute and relative location identify where something is, the concept of place identifies the distinguishing physical and human characteristics of specific locations. People use **toponyms**, names of locations, to define and further orient themselves with their sense of place. Toponyms may be derived from geographical features, important historical figures in the area, or even wildlife commonly found there. For example, many cities in the state of Texas are named in honor of military leaders who fought in the Texas Revolution (such as Houston and Austin), while Mississippi and Alabama got their toponyms from Native American words.

Historically, Mecca, Jerusalem, Cuzco, the Ganges River, and the Shrine of Guadalupe have all represented sacred places of pilgrimage or worship. All religious groups are influenced in some way by the physical environment around them—they sanctify significant persons, events, and calendar days by elevating the spaces/objects around them to a holy position. Two kinds of elements from the physical environment can be sanctified by religious groups: distinctive physical environments (mountains, rivers, forests, stones, etc.) and significant objects (shrines, temples, churches, etc.). In Islam, Mecca remains the holiest city for Muslims. Mecca is the birthplace of the prophet Mohammed. Mecca also contains one of the most sacred shrines of the major world religions—the Ka'bah. Believed to have been built by Ishmael, Abraham's biblical son, the Ka'bah has become the final destination of Muslims who take annual pilgrimages, known as a *hajj*. Likewise, Jerusalem remains one of the holiest cities in the Judeo-Christian tradition because it is the site of the First and Second Temples of Jewish antiquity. Jerusalem was also a site of early Christian proselytism. Even Muslims see Jerusalem as a holy city, making it the epicenter of many historical religious wars such as the Crusades. Cuzco was a sacred location for the ancient Incan civilization, and it still holds a spiritual value in modern-day Peru. The Ganges River is the holiest river in India; it is the focal point of Hindu purification. Millions of Hindus flock to the Ganges riverbanks each year to bathe in its holy waters. Lastly, the Shrine of Guadalupe is a Roman Catholic holy site located near Mexico City that commemorates a historical vision of the Blessed Mother, Mary. The Marian commemoration site is dedicated to the Blessed Mother's protection of the American continent.

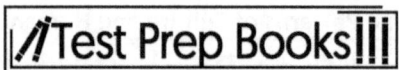

Religion in the United States

Religion has also been an important, albeit divisive, theme in American history since the colonial period. The British colonies in North America attracted settlers from many different religions, including Catholics in Maryland, Quakers in Pennsylvania, Puritans in New England, and Anglicans in Virginia. This led to conflict and tension. For example, Puritans in New England expelled dissenters and even executed four Quakers between 1659 and 1661.

In the 1730s and 1740s, a religious revival known as the First Great Awakening swept through the British colonies in North America. This movement emphasized a more personal connection to Christ, and some Protestant preachers, such as Jonathan Edwards, began to present their sermons in a more passionate and emotional style. This fire and brimstone form of religious dissemination became the cornerstone of the First Great Awakening. These passionate sermons—and the emotions that they stirred—caused divisions within Protestant congregations. Those who supported the Great Awakening were known as New Lights while those who opposed it were called Old Lights. The Baptists and Methodists became more popular during the revival because they embraced this new style of preaching.

The Second Great Awakening occurred in the early 1800s and urged Protestants to work not only for their own salvation but for the salvation of others as well. This helped fuel a social reform movement that promoted the abolition of slavery, temperance, and prison reform. The question of slavery caused schisms in the Baptist and Methodist churches during the 1840s. The Second Great Awakening, much like the First Great Awakening, inaugurated the creation of several New Religious Movements (NRMs) in the United States, especially in the southern states.

A third revival occurred in the late 1800s that emphasized temperance. The religious right emerged after World War II and began to play an important part in American politics, especially during the election of President Ronald Reagan in 1980.

Although Catholics were a minority during the colonial period of American history, Catholicism had become the largest religious denomination in the United States by the mid nineteenth century. Many colonial governments had actually banned Catholicism, but the American Revolution brought more toleration. However, anti-Catholic sentiment renewed in the 1800s as immigrants from Ireland and Germany, many of whom were Catholic, arrived in ever-increasing numbers. The arrival of Italian immigrants in the late 1800s and early 1900s also increased Protestant-Catholic tension in America. Many Americans feared that Catholic immigrants would be more loyal to Pope than they would be to the Constitution. This led to the creation of the Know Nothing movement, which sought to limit immigration and precipitated violence against Catholics. Anti-Catholic sentiment remained an issue until the presidential election of 1960 when John F. Kennedy, a Catholic, won the Democratic nomination. Kennedy helped allay fears by promising to respect the separation of church and state. Since then, anti-Catholicism has largely disappeared.

Small numbers of Jews immigrated to the U.S. during the colonial period, but large numbers of Jews from Eastern Europe began to arrive in the late 19th and early 20th centuries. Jews contributed to the American economy in many different ways but drew criticism from anti-Semites because of their prominence in the financial industry. The Anti-Defamation League was founded in 1913 to combat anti-Semitic sentiments. In the 1920s, the resurgent Ku Klux Klan revived anti-Semitism. The Anti-Defamation League sponsored events after World War II to commemorate the Holocaust and repudiate Holocaust deniers. Anti-Semitism has declined, but the Anti-Defamation League reported that more than 900 anti-Semitic incidents occurred across the country in 2014.

Muslim immigration in the 1800s remained modest. The first mosque was not constructed in the United States until the 20th century. In the latter part of the 20th century, more Muslims, especially from Pakistan, began arriving in the United States. In the wake of the 9/11 attacks, Islamophobic incidents increased, and Muslims were victims of harassment, intimidation, and assaults. The United States' current battle with ISIS in the Middle East, North Africa, and Europe has also increased Islamophobia.

Arts in the United States and World Areas

It's also important to study different time periods of art and architecture. In the Classical period, Greek artists focused on physical beauty and the human form, paying particular attention to Olympian gods and their idealized proportions in their works. The Medieval period that occurred in Europe from 500 to 1400 CE saw a flourish of Romanesque style art that shifted the emphasis from portraying realism to conveying a message, particularly symbolic Christian ideals. Students should also learn about the history of art in other countries such as China, with its jade, pottery, bronze, porcelain, and calligraphy. Educators should focus on how various influences over time affected the predominant artwork each period. For example, Buddhism in the early first century BCE increased calligraphy on silks, the Song dynasty created landscape paintings that were popular, and the Ming and Qing dynasties developed color painting and printing with an evolution towards individualism. As China became increasingly influenced by Western society in the nineteenth and early twentieth centuries, social realism predominated. In addition to covering other Asian nations, educators should expose students to traditional African art, which generally demonstrates moral values, focuses on human subjects, and seeks to please the viewer. Educators can also introduce art from the American Indians such as woodcarving, weaving, stitchery, and beading. Art in American Indian populations varies widely from tribe to tribe but tends to beautify everyday objects and create items of spiritual significance. Students should be exposed to music and theater from other cultures and observe the costumes, movements, instruments, and themes in performing arts from places like the Caribbean islands, Japan, Mexico, Australia, Africa, Italy, and Russia.

Throughout U.S. history, art has been created by individuals to communicate a social message. For example, the Harlem Renaissance used music, poetry, literature, and various iconography to depict the doings and sufferings of early 20th century African Americans. During WWII, the images of Rosie the Riveter were used to enlist women to support the war effort in industry. During the Cold War, the U.S. and the USSR utilized art/propaganda to win over adherents. Political commentary and satire have also been used throughout U.S. history, from Mark Twain to Stephen Colbert.

It can be argued that the primary functions of art are personal, social, and physical. When art is used personally, it can have a host of functions. An artist can create art for personal enjoyment, the refinement of a skill, aesthetic reasons, religious reasons, therapeutic reasons, political reasons, sensual reasons, and beyond. No matter an artist's intent, an artist's finished piece can be interpreted in a variety of ways—ways that the artist may not have intended.

Interactions Between Human Groups and the Physical Environment

The Physical Environment in Cultural and Technological Contexts

As civilizations blossomed globally in river valleys, disparate cultures such as the Israelites, Babylonians, and Egyptians entered into long-term, unofficial social contracts, forcing populations into a constant cultural dialogue with the processes of acculturation, assimilation, and ethnic genocide. In many ways, these complex, multilateral patterns of cultural diffusion marked the beginnings of the long process of globalization that has affected humanity's exchange of goods and ideas for centuries. Moreover, these cultural and technological changes inevitably had *natural* and/or *ecological* ramifications—as humanity shifted from nomadic to domesticated life, the earth was forever impacted by the transformative processes of domestication. At times, these processes have had a positive impact on global ecology and physical geography; in most cases, they have ravaged the land for the sake of human existence.

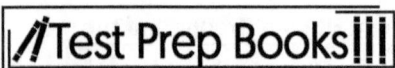

Geography, Culture, and the Behavioral and Social Sciences

The microcosmic processes of war, trade, migration, drought, famine, personal contact, and mass communication catalyzed this larger process of cultural diffusion, forcing each civilization into a sort of cultural symbiosis with the other. Each burgeoning city-state relied on other city-states for obtaining new objects, ideas, and customs. The transformation from village to city-state—and the accompanying cultural diffusions that followed—spanned several generations, making it difficult for scholars to pinpoint the origins of many specific agricultural-based practices. The cultural diffusion spawned by the First Agricultural Revolution created a web of interrelated objects, ideas, and practices that multilaterally affected the social institutions and geographic dispositions of many of the world's first civilizations.

The diffusion and exchange of new tools (hoes, sickles, plow sticks) and new farming practices (slash-and-burn farming, terrace farming, animal husbandry) impacted not only the original hearts of domestication in the Fertile Crescent, but also the budding agricultural civilizations that came into contact with these hearths. The First Agricultural Revolution, which began in communities like Jarmo and Catal Huyuk, thus marked a dramatic change in the ways in which communities interacted with their neighbors. As small neighboring villages altered into elaborate collections of regional city-states, each budding civilization connected with its neighboring civilizations via the superstructural process of cultural diffusion. At times, cultural diffusion was a conscious process; in most cases, it was an unconscious aggregate of proximal interactions.

Interdependence of People, Places, and Environments

Natural hazards also affect human societies. In tropical and subtropical climates, hurricanes and typhoons that form over warm water can have devastating effects. Additionally, tornadoes, which are powerful cyclonic windstorms, are responsible for widespread destruction in many parts of the world. Earthquakes, caused by shifting plates along faults deep below the Earth's surface, also bring widespread devastation, particularly in nations with poor infrastructure. For example, San Francisco, which experiences earthquakes regularly due to its position near the San Andreas Fault, saw relatively little destruction and death as a result of a major earthquake in 1989. However, in 2010, an earthquake of similar magnitude reportedly killed over 200,000 people in the Western Hemisphere's poorest nation, Haiti. Although a variety of factors may be responsible for the disparity, modern engineering methods and better building materials most likely helped to minimize destruction in San Francisco. Other natural hazards, such as tsunamis, mudslides, avalanches, forest fires, dust storms, flooding, volcanic eruptions, and blizzards, also affect human societies throughout the world.

Processes of Settlement Development Over Time

From a geographer's point of view, the most important aspect of any geographic network is its connectivity attributes. Connectivity makes contact and interaction possible through communication and transportation. Connectivity also dictates the availability of resources, or accessibility. Accessibility is the opportunity to take advantage of certain resources from a given point or location. Although distance is only one aspect of accessibility, it is, perhaps, the most important aspect. Connectivity and the availability of resources throughout history have often been dictated by transportation routes. From the Nile River to the Silk Road to the Eisenhower Interstate System, human geographic settlement patterns have often depended on transportation routes. These transportation routes—especially in an increasingly technological and globalized world—have been crucial for cultural diffusion and human settlement. The oceanic transportation routes of the Age of Exploration, for instance, were crucial in developing a Triangle Trade System that forced cultures into economic, cultural, and social change.

Demography, the study of human populations, investigates a variety of factors related to the human experience. First, economic factors play a significant role in the movement of people, as do climate, natural disasters, or internal unrest. A recent example of this phenomenon is found in the millions of Syrian immigrants who have moved as far away as possible from the danger in their war-torn homeland. As previously mentioned, people tend to live near reliable sources of food and water and away from extreme temperatures. Furthermore, the vast majority of people live in the Northern Hemisphere because more land lies in that part of the Earth. In keeping with these factors, human populations tend to be greater where human necessities are easily accessible, or at least more readily available. In other words, such areas have a greater chance of having a higher population density than places without such characteristics.

Demographic patterns on earth are not always stagnant. In contrast, people move and will continue to move as both push and pull factors fluctuate along with the flow of time. While thousands of Europeans fled their homelands in the 1940s due to the impact of the Second World War, the opposite is true today as thousands of migrants arrive on European shores each month due to conflicts in the Levant and difficult economic conditions in Northern Africa. Furthermore, people tend to migrate to places with a greater economic benefit for themselves and their families. As a result, developed nations such as the United States, Germany, Canada, and Australia have a net gain of migrants, while developing nations such as Somalia, Zambia, and Cambodia generally tend to see thousands of their citizens seek better lives elsewhere.

Religion and religious conflict also play a role in determining the composition and location of human populations. For example, the Nation of Israel won its independence in 1948 and has since attracted thousands of Jewish people from all over the world. Additionally, the United States has long been a popular destination due to its promise of religious freedom inherent within its own Constitution. In contrast, nations like Saudi Arabia and Iran do not typically tolerate different religions, resulting in a decidedly uniform religious—and oftentimes ethnic—composition. Other factors such as economic opportunity, social unrest, and cost of living also play a vital role in demographic composition.

Physical and Human Geographic Factors

Dust Bowl

One need not look further than the United States' Dust Bowl example in the 1930s to envision the detrimental effects human development and agricultural overproduction can have on the soils of nutrient-rich regions. Crops such as wheat and barley tend to deplete the soil of its nutrients. In the late 1920s and 1930s, agricultural overproduction in the Heartland of the United States of America depleted the soil to the point that it was arid. The arid nature of the soil created a so-called Dust Bowl, a series of devastating dust storms that destroyed rural agricultural communities and forced families to migrate. Many families died as a result of the ecological impact of the Dust Bowl; they died from the starvation and disease that stemmed from poor environmental conditions. The Dust Bowl not only affected the health of human beings in the Heartland, but it also completely transformed the political, social, cultural, technological, and economic character of the entire region. For decades, families uprooted themselves from the region over fear that history would repeat itself and once again they would be forced into economic tatters.

Panama Canal

The building of the Panama Canal revolutionized global travel and trade and is largely considered one of the greatest feats in modern engineering. The construction of the 51-mile canal was mired in geopolitical controversy even before the first ditch was dug by the United States of America. The French had previously tried to build a canal through Central America, but failed. The United States went as far as to assist Panamanians in fighting for independence from Colombia to make the impressive construction project a reality. In 1903, President Theodore Roosevelt deployed the U.S. Navy to assist the Panamanian province in its revolution against Colombia. Economics also drove the geographic development of the Panama Canal—Roosevelt promised to pay Panama $10 million per year to build the canal and maintain ownership over it.

The United States of America benefitted heavily from the canal once it was completed. The United States controlled the tollgate, making money off the thousands of ships that used the Panama Canal to expedite travel between the

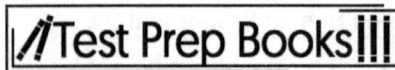

Atlantic and Pacific Oceans. At its peak, the Panama Canal brought in $340 million each year for the U.S. government. The building and operation of the canal, however, did not come without its own costs. Many Americans and Panamanians lost their lives building and operating the canal, thanks to floods, heat, and disease-carrying mosquitoes. Many workers lost their lives to yellow fever and malaria. The canal became a cross-cultural phenomenon, as over seventy nations utilized its waterways each year. The construction of the Panama Canal, however, did strain relationships between the United States and Latin America. The United States controlled the waterways of the canal until December 31, 1999. On this date, the U.S. government handed over the canal to the Panamanians. Nonetheless, many Latin American countries still lament the U.S. exploitative involvement in the creation of Panama and its world-famous canal. Over the years, technological advances in dam construction, lockbuilding, and shipbuilding adapted to fit the needs of the unique structures of the Panama Canal. Thus, the Panama Canal was not only an agent of change in politics and economics, but also in maritime technological advances and human engineering.

Suez Canal

The construction of the Suez Canal, much like the construction of the Panama Canal, was marred in political and economic controversy. Egyptians began building the Suez Canal under the modernization efforts of Isma'il Pasha, who is often referred to by Egyptian historians as Ismail the Magnificent. Isma'il Pasha was the grandson of former Ottomon leader Mohammed Ali Pasha. Much like his grandfather, Isma'il wanted to modernize Egypt for the growing global economy. He decided to build a canal that cut through the Isthmus of Suez and connected the Red Sea and the Mediterranean Sea. Isma'il tapped into French money and labor to make the public works project a success. In 1969, the Suez Canal opened with a grand international celebration. The project, however, proved to be extremely expensive. Egypt accrued $450 million in debt to fund canal construction; they consequently owed European bankers, making them financially indebted to colonial governments such as the British Empire. Noticing an opportunity to take advantage of the poor financial choices of the Egyptians, the British government assumed control over the canal in 1882 as they began to occupy Egypt. The Suez Canal expedited travel between Europe, the Middle East, and South Asia, but it remained the focal point of anti-colonial protest and geopolitical conflict well into the twentieth century.

Neolithic Agricultural Revolution

Since the genesis of farming as a means of food production, agriculture has been essential to human existence. Humans no longer had to forage and hunt for food, and more consistent food supplies allowed societies to stabilize and grow. In modern times, farming has changed drastically in order to keep up with the increasing world population.

Until the twentieth century, the vast majority of people on Earth engaged in subsistence farming, the practice of growing only enough food to feed oneself and one's family. Inventions such as the steel plow, the mechanical reaper, and the seed drill allowed farmers to produce more crops on the same amount of land. As food became cheaper and easier to obtain, populations grew, but fewer people farmed. After the advent of mechanized farming in developed nations, small farms became less common, and many were either abandoned or absorbed by massive commercial farms producing staple crops and cash crops.

In recent years, agricultural practices have undergone further changes in order to keep up with the rapidly growing population. Due in part to the Green Revolution, which introduced the widespread use of fertilizers to produce massive amounts of crops, farming techniques and practices continue to evolve. For example, genetically modified organisms, or GMOs, are plants or animals whose genetic makeup has been modified using different strands of DNA in hopes of producing more resilient strains of staple crops, livestock, and other foodstuffs. This process, which is a form of biotechnology, attempts to solve the world's food production problems through the use of genetic engineering. Although these crops are abundant and resistant to pests, drought, or frost, they are also the subject of intense scrutiny. For example, the international food company, Monsanto, has faced an incredible amount of criticism regarding its use of GMOs. Many activists assert that such artificial food production processes are inherently problematic and that the resulting food products are dangerous to human health. Despite the controversy, GMOs and biotechnologies continue to change the agricultural landscape and the world's food supply.

Agribusinesses exist throughout the world and produce food for human consumption as well as farming equipment, fertilizers, agrichemicals, and breeding and slaughtering services for livestock. These companies are generally headquartered near the product they produce, like the cereal manufacturer General Mills in the Midwestern United States located near its supply of wheat and corn—the primary ingredients in its cereals.

Population Growth and Modernization

Population growth and modernization, sparked by the technological transformations of the Industrial Revolution, catalyzed the growth of urban centers. Mechanical inventions, medical advances, and agricultural transformations helped human beings live longer and reproduce more. As a result, more infrastructure was built to maintain growing civilizations in industrialized countries. Modernity became synonymous with pollution, animal extinction, and ecological devastation. The advent of locomotive and automobile transportations allowed for greater human connections, but they often came at the expense of the earth. Railroads and roadways swiftly carved up the landscape of burgeoning countries such as the United States and Russia/USSR in the late 1800s and early 1900s.

Fossil fuels began to dominate, leading to the devastation of mountainous regions such as Appalachia. An increased need for timber, ore, and stone also tore up the ground in the name of extravagant buildings and skyscrapers. Modernity ravaged the physical environment of most industrial countries, powering the way to urban decay and suburban sprawl. By the 1950s to 1980s, many industrial nations had their fair share of environmental catastrophes. With the advent of the nuclear age, these environmental issues became even more evident across the globe. The dropping of the atomic bombs on Hiroshima and Nagasaki made the remnants of these former Japanese hubs look like the apocalypse. Nuclear meltdowns in places like Chernobyl, Russia, and Three Mile Island, Pennsylvania, poisoned the surrounding earth and air. Population growth and modernization also led to the construction of large agribusinesses and meatpacking plants that laid waste to the environment much like an Upton Sinclair novel.

Management of Key Natural Resources

Renewable resources are self-replenishing, such as solar, wind, water, and geothermal energy. Nonrenewable resources, also known as fossil fuels, such as oil, natural gas, and coal, take much longer to replenish but are generally abundant and cheaper to use. While solar energy is everywhere, the actual means to convert the sun's rays into energy is not. Conversely, coal-fired power plants and gasoline-powered engines, older technologies used during the industrial revolution, remain quite common throughout the world. Reliance on nonrenewable resources continues to grow due to availability and existing infrastructure, but use of renewable energy is also increasing as it becomes more economically competitive with nonrenewable resources.

In addition to sources of energy, nonrenewable resources also include any materials that can be exhausted, such as precious metals, precious stones, and freshwater underground aquifers. Although abundant, most nonrenewable sources of energy are not sustainable because their creation takes so long. While renewable resources are sustainable, their use must be properly overseen so that they remain renewable. For example, the beautiful African island of Madagascar is home to some of the most amazing rainforest trees in the world. Logging companies cut, milled, and sold thousands of them in order to make quick profits without planning how to ensure the continued health of the forests. In this way, renewable resources were mismanaged and thus essentially became nonrenewable due to the length of time it takes for replacement trees to grow. In contrast, many United States paper companies that harvest pine trees must utilize planning techniques to ensure that mature pine trees will always be available. In this manner, these resources remain renewable for human use in a sustainable fashion.

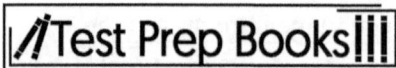

Geography, Culture, and the Behavioral and Social Sciences

Renewable sources of energy are relatively new in the modern economy. Even though electric cars, wind turbines, and solar panels are becoming more common, they still do not provide enough energy to power the world's economy. As a result, reliance on older forms of energy continues, which can have a devastating effect on the environment. Beijing, China, which has seen a massive boom in industrial jobs, is also one of the most polluted places on Earth. Furthermore, developing nations with very little modern infrastructure also rely heavily on fossil fuels due to the ease in which they are converted into usable energy. Even the United States, which has one of the most developed infrastructures in the world, still relies almost exclusively on fossil fuels, with only ten percent of the required energy coming from renewable sources.

Physical and Human Geographic Factors, Political Divisions, Relationships, and Policies

Conflict and cooperation have transformed societies throughout history. Conflict often results in power shifting between countries. Typically, after a conflict, some of the countries emerge with more territory and greater global influence, while others dissolve into fragmented or diminished entities. In addition, conflict can force countries into adopting internal reforms, such as a new system of government. Cooperation between countries generally strengthens their countries' economy and military. Examples of cooperation between countries include military alliances and trade agreements. Cooperation can also result in countries ceding some of their sovereignty to create more global forms of governance.

Examples of conflict exist from ancient societies through the modern day. As discussed above, armed rebellion led to the fall of the Roman Empire, arguably the strongest political entity in human empires. That conflict led to the Byzantine Empire consolidating power in the East, while the West became fragmented and power became localized. World War I was one of the most significant conflicts in modern history due to the unprecedented deaths and destruction. Approximately 14 million soldiers and civilians lost their lives during World War I, and the Great War cost the participants more than $300 billion. In addition, the conflict's political consequences cannot be overstated. The aftermath caused the collapse of four powerful monarchies—Russia, Austria-Hungary, Germany, and Turkey—and it led to the end of colonialism. The world would suffer an even more horrific and transformative conflict only a few decades later in World War II.

Examples of cooperation in recent history have roots in the aftermath of World War II. Immediately following the war, the United States created the Marshall Plan, which gave Western Europe more than $12 billion to rebuild the shattered region. In addition to financial aid, the United States and Western Europe formed NATO, a defensive pact formed in 1949 to counter the power of the Soviet Union and prevent the further spread of Communism. Signatory countries pledged to come to any member's defense in the event of an attack by a foreign power. Similarly, the Soviet Union created the Warsaw Pact to facilitate cooperation between territories held by the Soviets following World War II. These military alliances amplified the power of the two superpowers and provided protection against another global conflict by creating a powerful deterrent. Military alliances continue to be an important part of cooperation between nations.

In addition to military alliances, countries often cooperate with trade agreements. Not only does creating these economic ties benefit the participants' internal economies, but trade agreements also serve as a deterrent against conflict. The role of trade is discussed in greater detail in the section, "The Role of Trade and Other Forms of Economic Exchange Both Within Societies and in Contacts Between Societies."

Other examples of modern cooperation between countries are illustrated by the creation of supranational political entities, like the United Nation and European Union. The United Nations was established on October 24, 1945, for the primary purpose of preventing a third disastrous global conflict. It is the most inclusive political organization in the world, consisting of 193 member states. Currently, the United Nations primarily works to maintain global peace and security, promote human rights, facilitate economic development, and provide humanitarian aid during natural disasters and armed conflict. The modern European Union was later formally established in 1992. The European

Union's primary purpose is to establish a common internal market to ensure the free movement of goods, capital, and services.

Nation, state, and nation-state are terms with very similar meanings, but knowing the differences aids in a better understanding of geography. A nation is an area with similar cultural, linguistic, and historical experiences. A **state** is a political unit with sovereignty, or the ability to make its own decisions within defined borders. A **nation-state** is both a nation and a sovereignly governed state. For example, in the United States, the state of Texas is not an independent nation-state. Instead, it is part of the United States and thus, is subject to its laws. The United Kingdom encompasses four member states: England, Wales, Northern Ireland, and Scotland. Although citizens of those countries may consider themselves to be sovereign, or self-governing, the reality is that they cannot make decisions regarding international trade, declarations of war, or other important decisions regarding the rest of the world. Instead, they are semi-autonomous, meaning that they can make some decisions regarding how their own state is run but must yield more major powers to a centralized authority. In the United States, this sort of system is called Federalism, or the sharing of power among Local, State, and Federal entities, each of whom is assigned different roles in the overall system of government.

Nation-states and their boundaries are not always permanent. For example, after the fall of the Soviet Union in 1991, new nations emerged that had once been a part of the larger entity called the Union of Soviet Socialists Republics. These formerly sovereign nations were no longer forced to be a part of a unifying communist government, and as a result, they regained their autonomy and became newly independent nations that were no longer satellite nations of the Soviet Union. In a historical sense, the United States can be seen as a prime example of how national boundaries change. After the conclusion of the American Revolution in 1781, the Treaty of Paris defined the United States' western boundary as the Mississippi River; today, after a series of conflicts with Native American groups, the Mexican government, Hawaiian leadership, the Spanish, and the purchase of Alaska from the Russians, the boundaries of the United States have changed drastically. In a similar fashion, nations in Europe, Africa, and Asia have all shifted their boundaries due to warfare, cultural movements, and language barriers.

During the aftermath of World War II, a variety of regional, religious, and ethnic movements gained independence; however, many of these movements were frustrated by the former colonies' imperial boundaries. As a result, this led to some movements seeking to gain more autonomy. One such conflict was the 1948 **Arab-Israeli War**. Following Israel's declaration of independence in 1948, Palestinians revolted. Specifically, the Palestinians rejected Israel's claim of territories, which were based on the imperial boundaries set under the **United Nations Partition Plan for Palestine** in 1947.

Several Arab countries—Egypt, Jordan, Syria, and Iraq—invaded Israel to support the Palestinian movement. Israel defeated the Arab coalition in 1949 and captured more than half of the land granted to the Palestinians under the Partition Plan. From the end of the 1948 Arab-Israeli War through the present day, Palestinians have continued to seek more autonomy from Israel with limited success. Kurdish nationalists similarly sought to gain autonomy in Turkey, Iraq, Syria, and Iran. Those states formed as a result of the Ottoman Empire's dissolution and European decolonization, but the Kurds never received sovereignty. Instead, millions of Kurds were divided among those four states, so they were subject to Arab and Muslim rulers. The **Kurdish nationalist movement** was most successful in northern Iraq where they've enjoyed semi-autonomy since 1970.

Britain recognized India and Pakistan's independence in 1947. The Middle East also gained independence after Britain and France withdrew their forces in the late 1940s, and a series of countries gained independence, including Jordan, Iraq, Israel, Syria, and Lebanon. All European powers began withdrawing from Africa during the late 1950s, and the pace of decolonization rapidly increased throughout the 1960s. Between 1957 and 1975, the UN recognized the independence of more than forty African countries. Following Japan's defeat in World War II, China regained

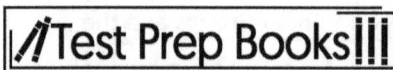

Manchuria and other territory located in present-day northern China, and the Korean peninsula was freed from Japanese imperial control.

In the modern world, boundaries continue to change. For example, the Kurds, an ethnic minority in the Middle East, are still fighting for the right to control their people's' right to self-determination, but have not yet been successful in establishing a nation for themselves. In contrast, the oil-rich region of South Sudan, which has significant cultural, ethnic, and religious differences from Northern Sudan, successfully won its independence in a bloody civil war, which established the nation's newest independent nation. In recent years, Russia has made the world nervous by aggressively annexing the Crimean Peninsula, which has been part of Ukraine since the end of the Cold War. Even the United Kingdom and Canada have seen their own people nearly vote for their own rights to self-determination. In 1995, Quebec narrowly voted against becoming a sovereign state through a tightly contested referendum. Similarly, Scotland voted to remain part of the Crown even though many Scots see themselves as inherently different from other regions within the UK.

Decolonization, or the removal of dependency on colonizers, has altered the political landscape of Africa, allowed more autonomy for the African people, and redefined the boundaries of the entire continent. Essentially, political geography across the globe is constantly changing.

Sociological, Anthropological, and Psychological Concepts and Processes

Role of Culture

Human behavior is influenced by culture and cultural changes, human adaptation, and diversity. Every person is different. People are born into different types of families, religions, geographic areas, and other circumstances. These differences affect how people act. Respecting differences is key to influencing human behavior.

<u>Culture and Culture Change</u>
Culture derives from the beliefs, values, and behaviors of people in a community. These beliefs, values, and behaviors tend to be passed from one generation to the next. Culture can change over time and from generation to generation.

All people are born into a certain culture, which can be embedded within families, schools, businesses, social classes, and religions. Within these cultural institutions, people learn positive and negative reinforcement, dialect and slang, diet, acceptable and unacceptable practices of society, and many more societal norms.

The social class that people are born into also influences their behavior. A social class is determined by someone's social and economic status and can change over time. Indicators of social class include wealth, education level, job perspectives, marital status, and standard of living. Some living in poverty may strive to attain a higher education level to find a better job and become upwardly mobile. However, others living in poverty may continue to support themselves day to day and use government assistance funds. The culture in which one was raised will influence how a person lives their life. As a person's social class changes, they will adapt their behavior to new situations.

<u>Human Adaptation and Diversity</u>
Over time, the environment in which a person lives changes. Humans adapt their behaviors to fit the needs of their new environment, as well as their own needs. Every person adapts to situations in a unique way simply because everyone is different. Diversity accounts for differences in race, gender, sexual orientation, economic status, and language. Culture creates a set of norms to compare what is considered different or diverse within a given culture.

In every culture, there is a minority and majority group. The majority of the culture typically sets the norm and then influences people's behaviors within the society.

Race and Gender Relations in the United States

Over the course of its history, the United States has experienced a multicentury democratization process that has reinforced diversity and promoted equality among the various racial, ethnic, religious, and gender groups within its citizenship. In terms of race and gender, the culture of the United States has not always been a beacon of equality. Slavery and patriarchy have dominated the social, political, and economic institutions of the country since its inception. Beginning with abolition in the 1860s and women's suffrage in the 1920s, the United States has gradually progressed from a staunchly racist and sexist republic to a more open-minded limited democratic-republic. The moral victories won by the nonviolent protests of the women's rights and civil rights movement have brought about positive democratic change. The nature of race and racism in the United States is a far cry from slavery, and the nature of gender roles is a far cry from Victorian values. Nevertheless, racism and gender-based forms of discrimination still exist in the United States in the form of segregation and economic ceilings. Although people of color and women are earning more, as respective groups, than they ever have in U.S. history, white men continue to earn more on average. The women's rights and civil rights movements in this country have, therefore, had to adapt to new challenges that have formed since the peak of the Cultural Revolution in the 1960s. Today, these movements live on in modern-day feminist movements and the Black Lives Matter movement.

How Cultures and Societies Both Change and Maintain Continuity

Modernization

Developing nations are nations that are struggling to modernize their economy, infrastructure, and government systems. Many of these nations may have difficulty providing basic services to their citizens like clean water, adequate roads, or even police protection. Furthermore, government corruption makes life even more difficult for these countries' citizens. In contrast, developed nations are those that have relatively high Gross Domestic Products (GDP), or the total value of all goods and services produced in the nation in a given year. The United States, one of the wealthiest nations on Earth, has a GDP of over twenty-one trillion dollars, while Haiti, one of the poorest nations in the Western Hemisphere, has a GDP of over fourteen billion dollars. This comparison is not intended to disparage Haiti or other developing nations, but rather to show that extreme inequities exist in very close proximity to one another, and it may be difficult for developing nations to meet the needs of their citizens and move their economic infrastructure forward toward modernization.

In the modern world, industrialization is the initial key to modernization and development. For developed nations, the process of industrialization took place centuries ago. England, where the Industrial Revolution began, actually began to utilize factories in the early 1700s. Later, the United States and some Western European nations followed suit, using raw materials brought in from their colonies abroad to make finished products. For example, elaborate weaving machines spun cotton into fabric, allowing for the mass production of textiles. As a result, nations that perfected the textile process were able to sell their products around the world, which produced enormous profits. Over time, those nations were able to accumulate wealth, improve their nation's infrastructure, and provide more services for their citizens. Nations throughout the world are undergoing a similar process in modern times. China exemplifies this concept. While agriculture is still a dominant sector of the Chinese economy, millions of citizens are flocking to major cities like Beijing, Shanghai, and Hangzhou due to the availability of factory jobs that allow workers a certain element of social mobility, or the ability to rise up to a better socioeconomic situation.

Theoretical Foundations of Sociology

A group consists of people who interact with one another on a consistent basis based on their shared and/or intersecting interests, values, or norms. Group membership is contingent upon a willingness to affirm the interests, values, and norms of a group for the sake of remaining in good standing. When a person subscribes as a member of a particular group, they yield to others the right to judge their behaviors.

Roles are the behaviors, obligations, and privileges assigned to a particular person at birth as a result of status. The difference between a status and a role is that people play roles, but occupy statuses in society. Roles are significant in sociology because they establish expectations for people. An entire matrix of roles form society at large.

Status refers to the position that someone occupies within society. There are ascribed statuses and achieved statuses. Ascribed statuses are inherited; achieved statuses are earned/accomplished. One may be born into a lower socioeconomic status but achieve wealth throughout their life.

Statuses, specifically socioeconomic statuses, usually create some sort of stratification in society. Socioeconomic stratification is part of types of governments and economic systems. In some societies, stratification may be based on religious caste, as in India.

Values are the glue that holds groups together. Values are the belief systems, world views, and ethical frameworks that inform a person's identity and group membership.

A variety of theories have been used to explain different aspects of sociology. Functionalism focuses on the structure of society and is based on the idea that the different sections of society work together to create a functioning whole. Each part of society, often represented by social institutions, serve different purposes to meet the needs of the larger group.

Conflict theory, as proposed by Karl Marx, suggests that society is based on a power struggle predicated by competition for a restricted supply of resources. Limited resources include food, housing, and education.

Symbolic interactionism is a theory that hinges on the communication and relationships among individuals in society. Words and symbols that individuals use to define and understand the world around them shape the larger society.

Social Institutions

Society refers to the community in which people live together. Human behavior is greatly influenced by society. People may feel pressure to live by certain standards or act in a specific way. Certain societal norms influence a person's behavior in both positive and negative ways.

Additionally, groups can influence how people behave. Peer pressure and the pressure to conform to certain group norms are present throughout life. Peer pressure is often greatest during adolescence, where young people seek the approval of those around them and are willing to do nearly whatever it takes to get their peers' approval. Opinions on any topic belonging within a social circle can change drastically with a few dominant personalities. Another concern is peer pressure involving substance abuse. Adolescents may drink alcohol or do drugs because their friends are doing it and they want to be part of the crowd.

Mass media also influences behaviors by providing access to information to society. It is also an institution that has undergone significant changes recently. When traditional media dominated the industry, citizens were passive consumers of news. The traditional media dictated what was covered and how it was covered, and there was a limited supply of alternative perspectives. Following the creation of the digital landscape, consumers can now follow current events in real time, particularly on social media. With changes in how media is presented, there are concerns with the mainstream media's ability to provide unbiased news coverage.

The field of science and its constant development affect people in society and their behaviors. Every person has the ability to formulate their own scientific worldview. Science is not only highly complex, but it is also tentative in nature—humans make educated guesses about the information and data they collect. This information and data change over time, and, as a result, new vocabulary, terms, and phrases are constantly shadowing new discoveries, data analysis, and findings. Scientific inquiry may begin with simple questions, or hypotheses, but it may end with new concepts and terminology. The more questions scientists ask, the more necessary it is to apply words to both the preconceived questions and logical answers. Scientific inquiry, in many ways, is a combination of logic and imagination, and scientific imagination is usually the force driving the creation of new specialized vocabulary, terms, and phrases. Scientific enterprise is a larger process of checks and balances, which allows scientific findings to be debated through intellectual dialogue.

While society and groups impact a person's behavior significantly, institutions also influence human behavior. Institutions have formal and informal rules, and an individual must choose whether they comply with the rules. There are five major types of social institutions that can influence human behavior: family, religion, government, education, and economics.

Family

- Regulates sexual behavior (monogamy)
- Creates and provides for new society members
- Socializes new society members

Religion

- Provides explanations for the unexplainable
- Supports societal norms and values
- Provides a means of coping with life situations

Government

- Institutionalizes norms (by creating laws)
- Enforces laws
- Protects members of society
- Provides a means of resolving conflict

Education

- Prepares society members to contribute to the society in specified roles
- Teaches skills necessary to function within the society

Economics

- Produces and distributes goods needed by society members
- Provides services necessary to the society

Roles of Men, Women, Children, and Families in Historical and Contemporary Cultures

Traditional family structure includes a man, a woman, and one or more children who are either biological or adopted. This is also referred to as a nuclear family. In most of human history, the extended family, which includes grandparents, aunts, uncles, and cousins, would live in the same area and work together. The idea of an extended

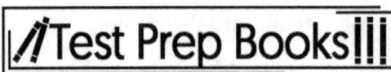

family living and working together broke with the rise of individualism and financial stability in the United States and Europe after World War II. In the modern-day West, the nuclear family is the most common family structure. In addition, the traditional family in the West has grown to include cohabitation families, single-parent families, and same-sex families.

In the Middle East, Africa, Asia, and India, it is still common to have multigenerational households and extended family networks living in close proximity. It is also common to pass down a trade or family business, like a restaurant or masonry business. The role of women is more domestic in these areas. In contrast, women in the United States and Europe more commonly participate in the workforce. In many societies, the wealthier classes educated woman in music and arts but did not encourage much education in mathematics and science. For the most part, the Middle East, Africa, Asia, and India have remained more constant in their family structure and gender roles, while Europe and the United States have seen the most changes in family structure. Examples include divorce and remarriage, evolution of the nuclear family, and change in traditional gender roles.

Until the modern age, girls of the higher classes were often taught housekeeping skills, music, drawing, needlework, and languages. These were often discouraged after marriage, apart from housekeeping, which became a woman's main duties along with childrearing. Boys in the wealthiest class were often educated at elite schools, and though some managed their estates or were members of government, most were expected to use and enjoy their wealth and status without laboring at a job.

Boys of the middle class would seek a profession such as a lawyer, teacher, or minister, often with some college training. Some would be apprenticed to a trade or learn the family business. Girls in the middle class were trained to manage a household, including preparing meals and balancing the family budget, while the higher-class girls focused more on how to entertain guests and manage servants.

Many of the lowest class and orphans, both boys and girls, were used in factory and coalmining work, where quick hands and nimble bodies were useful. For the lower classes, education was not common until the late 1800s. Previously, the wealthier classes suppressed literacy and education for the lower classes, finding it to be a good way of controlling the social and financial status quo. However, girls who received any form of education usually learned domestic skills, simple math, and needlework. Boys of the lower classes would follow the men of their family into whatever work they did, such as coalmining, farming, or factory work.

Nobility and landowners, until World War I, sought to preserve their lineage and wealth through a single male line. The wealth of this class and many of the male heirs were lost in World Wars I and II. Often primogeniture, or the inheritance of an intact estate with all the land, wealth, and titles, was legally passed to the firstborn son. A daughter would only inherit if no male heir was available.

Socialization, Cultural Values, and Norms

Socialization is the term used to refer to the lifelong social experience that develops the potential and cultural values/norms of a person or group of persons. Cultural values/norms therefore vary according to the context—historical time and space—of a person or group of persons. Socialization is varied according to context and the variables of nurture that exist within that context. This is especially evident when one keeps in mind the effects of complete social isolation as in the tragic cases of the abusive childhood deprivation of social experience. Social experience is crucial in forming behaviors and personality/identity, the main components of cultural values/norms. Although socialization is a complex, lifelong process, the early childhood years are the most crucial in personality and cultural development. Nevertheless, the process of socialization can, without a doubt, extend into adulthood as people and groups are exposed to more people, groups, ideas, and contexts. The cultural values/norms acquired through socialization influence the ways in which relationships are built, reinforced, and abandoned in a particular context or set of contexts. Relationships, much like identities, are therefore subjective constructs that are reinforced

Theoretical Foundations of Psychology

People have been studying the human thoughts, behavior, and the mind for thousands of years in a broad sense. The empirical basis of psychology has its roots in the work of philosophers in Ancient Greece. Socrates and Plato, two of the most well-known Ancient Greek philosophers shared the perspective of **dualism**, which posited that the body and mind were separate entities, and after death, only the mind survived. They also contended that ideas are innate, in that humans are born with them. On the other hand, thought Socrates and Plato were mentors for Aristotle, he disagreed with them and was a proponent of **monism**, which posited that the body and mind were united as one inseparable entity. Moreover, rather than believing ideas are innate or products of nature, Aristotle believe ideas were a product of nurture, in that they were brought about by experiences.

Records of interest in psychological thought are then sparse until the Renaissance. In the 1600s, Rene Descartes studied the body-mind connection by dissecting animals to visualize their brains and nervous systems. Like Socrates and Plato, Descartes was curious about how the physical body worked with the conceptual mind. John Locke was the father of **empiricism**, which contends that knowledge is derived from experiences. He believed that our minds are *tabula rasa* at birth, which means that they are blank slates. It is through lived experiences that the mind starts forming ideas and connections.

Locke, along with his contemporary Frances Bacon, started trying to investigate the mind in a scientific way, using the scientific method instead of just casual observations and anecdotes. The work of these early philosophers and physicians lay the groundwork for what would become the official discipline of psychology in 1879. Additionally, it can be seen that even thousands of years ago, the nature versus nurture debate was one of the most central questions pertaining to human behavior and thought.

The theoretical foundations of modern-day psychology are usually traced back to the social-scientific analyses of Sigmund Freud. Freud linked human development to biology. Trained as a physician, he believed that human instincts were biologically fixed. He believed certain personality types derived from two basic needs that drove humans from birth: *eros* (life instinct) and *thanatos* (death instinct). Freud believed that life instincts stemmed from biological drives for sex and emotional nurture, and death instincts stemmed from an aggressive, unconscious, animalistic drive in humans. Freud's theories laid the foundations of modern psychology, which tried to understand the biological nature of our behaviors. Freud believed that we internalize social norms and that developmental experiences have a lasting impact on our psyche. Freud's work opened the gateway to future psychological studies on cognitive development (Jean Piaget), moral development (Lawrence Kohlberg), and gender development (Carol Gilligan).

Human Identity, Development, and Learning

Learning is a process in which individuals gain skills or knowledge through experiences, studying, or instruction. Throughout people's lives, human beings are continuously learning and, therefore, the way in which they behave may be affected by new information that is learned. As people learn new things, their behaviors affect how they view their environment, culture, and society. This is also known as a behavioral theory.

Using new technology can affect how people interact with one another. For instance, a new technology allowing people to shop for groceries online and then merely pick up the goods or have them delivered will limit in-store impulse purchases, decrease or eliminate customer service communication, and potentially affect the quality of

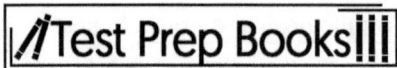

goods sold if individuals do not personally hand select their own products. Learning processes will constantly change and therefore human behaviors will constantly evolve.

Along with learning, people will continuously adjust their personal identity. Personal identity is a person's own perception of themself throughout their lifespan. Someone's personal identity can relate to where they grew up, race, religion, social class, and many other life experiences. Keep in mind, with new experiences, people learn and may change their viewpoints on topics. Although people may identify with one subgroup or culture now, it does not mean they will agree with that subgroup or culture in the future, or that they have in the past. Personal identity will continue to change an individual's behavior throughout life.

As a person's identity adjusts throughout life, they also develop new skills. Development and learning go hand-in-hand in affecting a person's behavior. Development stems from learning. A person's development progresses through life, and people's behaviors will change many times throughout their lives. New experiences or events, learning something new, identifying with a different group, or natural development in itself will all affect an individual's behaviors.

Behavioral psychology is known for its emphasis on different types of learning, which include insight learning, latent learning, and social learning. Insight learning involves how someone finds a solution to a problem through a sudden realization and without the need of continuous trials. An individual can draw upon their prior experiences while also using novel and logical ways of perceiving causality. However, insight isn't an unprompted occurrence, but actually requires a pre-solution period involving research into a particular domain, as well as some idle time before an idea or concept is spontaneously formulated. An example of this phenomenon includes a monkey in a cage unsuccessfully reaching for a nearby banana before finally poking it with a stick and devising a method of using the stick to successfully acquire the banana, and then doing the same thing the following day.

Latent learning involves an unconscious learning and retention of certain information without reinforcement or any particular type of motivation. An example of this type of learning includes a child observing proper table manners but not exhibiting any knowledge of them until a situation arises that prompts them to put those manners to use. Social learning proposes how new behavior can be attained by simply observing and imitating others performing that behavior, and then become motivated to recreate that learned behavior. According to social learning theory, learning is a cognitive process in social environments, whether through observation or direct instruction, even if there's an absence of any direct reinforcement. Along with observation, learning can take place in the presence of vicarious reinforcement, where reward and punishment are merely observed and thus experienced more indirectly.

One of the most famous experiments demonstrating social learning is psychologist Albert Bandura's Bobo Doll experiment. Children watched adults hit a blow-up doll that looked like a clown, and afterwards, results showed that the children modeled the adults by engaging in that same aggressive behavior with the doll. Social learning starts with paying attention in order to learn, followed by retaining the information that has been observed, reproduction of the learned behavior via its implementation, and being motivated to reproduce the behavior, or in some cases refraining from reproducing it. Principles of social learning have been applied in the fields of criminology and developmental psychology, and have been used to investigate the impact of media violence on aggression and how media can be used to encourage positive social change.

Psychological Principles and Processes

Early psychologists like Sigmund Freud believed that human motivation and personality stemmed from biological factors and unconscious tensions. For Freud, human motivation— the reasoning behind our behaviors—was almost always rooted in basic instincts, particularly sex. Freud also believed our personalities and perceptions—categorized into the id, ego, and superego—were also derived from basic needs and social experiences. Later psychologists believed Freud's theories were overly simplified and patriarchal, noting that motivation, personality, and perception stemmed from a greater variety of variables than sex and basic needs. Psychologists like Jean Piaget and Lawrence Kohlberg enhanced scholarship on such psychological principles as sensation (experiencing the world through senses) and cognition (experiencing the world through abstract ideas), noting different stages in sensorimotor and moral development. These psychologists departed from Freudian theory by making note of the complexity of biological maturation and social development. Still limited by their sociological models, these psychologists demonstrated that sensation and cognition often moved beyond pain and pleasure to include abstract visions of the senses and perception. Nevertheless, all these psychologists—from Freud to Kohlberg—enhanced scholarship in the social sciences by illustrating the ways in which biological processes and social experiences can come together to create unique behaviors, notions of self, and relationships with others.

Practice Quiz

1. A developing nation is more likely to have which of the following?
    a. Complex highway networks
    b. Higher rates of subsistence farmers
    c. Stable government systems
    d. Little economic instability

2. Which term is best defined as a group of people joined by a common culture, language, heritage, history, and religion?
    a. State
    b. Nation
    c. Regime
    d. Government

3. Deindustrialization from the 1960s through the 1980s in cities in the Industrial North (now called the *Rust Belt*) would be considered an example of which of the following?
    a. Political push factor
    b. Political pull factor
    c. Economic push factor
    d. Economic pull factor

4. Which of the following best describes how culture is transmitted across society?
    a. Culture is almost always transmitted through hierarchical relationships, and it has a trickle-down effect.
    b. Culture is primarily transmitted through religion, economic activities, and government policies.
    c. Cultural exchanges on the internet have given rise to a global popular culture in recent years.
    d. Culture can be transmitted through an endless variety of activities, and the transmission can either be intentional or spontaneous.

5. In international relations, which of the following is NOT a basic tenet of Realism?
    a. States are the central actors.
    b. States act rationally to advance their self-interest.
    c. States should seek to form international organizations to increase global cooperation and respond to international issues.
    d. All states are interested in maintaining or expanding their power as a means of self-preservation.

See answers on the next page.

Answer Explanations

1. B: Developing nations tend to have higher levels of impoverished citizens. As a result, many of their citizens must rely on subsistence farming, or producing enough food to feed their families, in order to survive. In contrast, developed nations tend to produce surpluses of food and very few, if any, of its citizens engage in subsistence farming. Developing nations are less likely to have complex highway systems, stable governments, and economic stability due to financial pressures.

2. B: A Nation is defined as a group of people who have common traits, such as heritage, history, language, culture, and religion. It has nothing to do with borders, sovereignty, power, people in office, or the rules by which a government operates (many of which are found in the other answer terms of state, government, and regime).

3. C: Deindustrialization led to a significant drop in jobs available in industrial hubs like Buffalo, Cleveland, Chicago, and Milwaukee, causing people to move elsewhere to find employment. Displacement as a result of an economic downturn is an example of an economic push factor.

4. D: For example, powerful institutions can sometimes unilaterally shift the culture to achieve a goal, but other times cultural change is a natural byproduct of social interactions that spiral in an unforeseen direction.

5. C: Choice C is correct. The two major theories of international relations are realism and liberalism. Realism analyzes international relations through the interactions of states under the assumption that states act rationally to maintain or expand power as a means of self-preservation, which inevitably leads to conflict in an anarchical system. The question asks for the choice that doesn't adhere to realism, and the other choices state three of the four basic tenets of realism. In contrast, Choice C states a principle of liberalism. Realists don't value international organizations or prioritize global cooperation.

Government and Citizenship

Democratic Principles and Government in the United States

US Constitution and Other Important Historical Documents

Constitutional Underpinnings
The role of government is to maintain a society and provide public services through its formal institutions, protect the citizens of the state, and regulate the economic system. To determine how a government should perform these functions and to protect the rights and liberties of the citizens, states enact a constitution, a written document that typically establishes the form of government and delegation of powers within the government, delineates limits on government, and defines protected rights, liberties, and privileges.

Constitution
The US Constitution was drafted in 1787 at the Constitutional Convention in Philadelphia. The goal was to create a government with checks and balances, and by dividing it into three branches, no single branch had ultimate governmental control. They designated the two legislative bodies—the House and Senate—as the Congress. This document is recognized as the world's first formal plan for a modern democracy and the oldest working constitution in existence.

Many people made significant contributions toward expanding the rights and freedoms of Americans by fighting in the Revolutionary War, signing the Declaration of Independence, and serving as delegates to the Constitutional Convention. The men who shaped the democracy of the United States are often referred to as America's Founding Fathers. This prestigious group includes:

- George Washington
- Alexander Hamilton
- James Madison
- John Adams
- Thomas Jefferson
- James Monroe
- Benjamin Franklin

Washington, Adams, Jefferson, Madison, and Monroe became U.S. Presidents, and Washington, Hamilton, and Madison were instrumental in leading the charge for discussion at the Constitutional Convention.

Checks and Balances
The branches of governments have a system of checks and balances between them. This is to ensure that no branch oversteps its authority. They include:

- Checks on the Legislative Branch:
    - The president can veto bills passed by Congress.
    - The president can call special sessions of Congress.
    - The judicial branch can rule legislation unconstitutional.

Government and Citizenship | Democratic Principles and Government in the United States

- Checks on the Executive Branch:
    - Congress has the power to override presidential vetoes by a two-thirds majority vote.
    - Congress can impeach or remove a president, and the chief justice of the Supreme Court presides over impeachment proceedings.
    - Congress can refuse to approve presidential appointments or ratify treaties.
- Checks on the Judicial Branch:
    - The president appoints justices to the Supreme Court, as well as district courts and courts of appeals.
    - The president can pardon federal prisoners.
    - The executive branch can refuse to enforce court decisions.
    - Congress can create federal courts below the Supreme Court.
    - Congress can determine the number of Supreme Court justices.
    - Congress can set the salaries of federal judges.
    - Congress can refuse to approve presidential appointments of judges.
    - Congress can impeach and convict federal judges.

The three branches of government operate separately, but they must rely on each other to create, enforce, and interpret the laws of the United States.

Checks and Balances

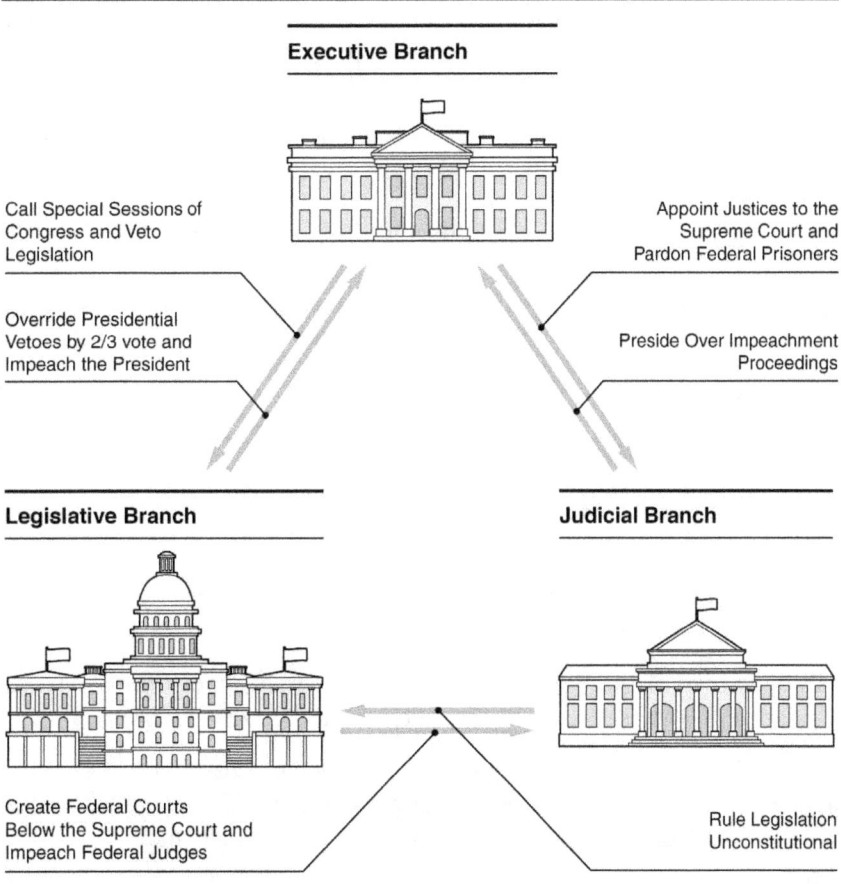

Federalism

To strengthen the central government, while still appeasing the individual states who preferred to remain sovereign over their territories, the framers of the Constitution based the new government upon the principle of Federalism—a compound government system that divides powers between a central government and various regional governments. The Constitution clearly defined the roles of both the state governments and the new federal government, specifying the limited power of the federal government and reserving all other powers not specifically granted by the Constitution to the federal government to the states in the Tenth Amendment to the Constitution, commonly referred to as the Reservation Clause.

The framers of the Constitution signed the Constitution on September 17, 1787, but the Articles of Confederation required nine of the thirteen states to ratify the document. Conventions were held in all thirteen states and sparked heated debates between those who supported and those who opposed the new system of government. The Federalists supported the expansion of the federal government, and the anti-Federalists feared that a stronger central government would weaken the states. The anti-Federalists also sought additional protection for civil liberties. The debates between these two parties continued for two years and inspired two series of essays known as the Federalist Papers and the Anti-Federalist Papers that debated various topics surrounding the ratification of the Constitution. The essays were authored anonymously by leaders of the respective parties. Scholars are fairly confident of the authorship of the *Federalist Papers*, but the authorship of many of the *Anti-Federalist* Papers is still uncertain.

Notable Federalists include:

- George Washington: commander-in-chief of the Continental Army and future first president of the United States (Washington never officially joined the Federalist party, but he was a strong supporter of ratifying the Constitution)

- Alexander Hamilton: founder of the Federalist Party, advocate for a centralized financial system, and author of 51 of the Federalist Papers

- James Madison: one of the primary drafters of the Constitution, the future fourth president of the United States, and author of 29 of the Federalist Papers

- John Jay: president of the Continental Congress, future first chief justice of the United States, and author of 5 of the Federalist Papers

- John Adams: future second president of the United States

Notable anti-Federalists include:

- Thomas Jefferson: primary author of the Declaration of Independence and future third president of the United States

- Patrick Henry: governor of Virginia (1776 – 1779, 1784 – 1786) and author of works frequently included in the Anti-Federalist Papers

- Samuel Adams: governor of Massachusetts (1794 – 1797), lieutenant governor of Massachusetts (1789 – 1794), and president of the Massachusetts Senate (1782 – 1785, 1787 – 1788)

- George Mason: one of only three delegates who did not sign the Constitution at the Constitutional Convention and author of Objections to This Constitution of Government (1787) and the Virginia Declaration of Rights of 1776, which served as the basis for the Bill of Rights

The first state to ratify the Constitution was Delaware in a unanimous vote on December 7, 1787. Pennsylvania, New Jersey, Georgia, Connecticut, Massachusetts, Maryland, and South Carolina followed and, after six months,

New Hampshire became the ninth state to ratify the Constitution in June 1788. However, some states still remained divided between Federalist and anti-Federalist sentiments and had yet to approve the document, including the two most populous states, Virginia and New York. To reconcile their differing views, the Federalists agreed to include a bill of rights if anti-Federalists supported the new Constitution. Federalist sentiment prevailed, and the remaining states approved the document. On May 29, 1790, the last holdout, Rhode Island, ratified the Constitution by two votes. As promised, the Bill of Rights—the first 10 amendments to the Constitution—was added in 1791, providing expanded civil liberty protection and due process of law.

Separation of Powers

The Constitution establishes the specific powers granted to the federal and state governments.

- Delegated powers: the specific powers granted to the federal government by the Constitution
- Implied powers: the unstated powers of the federal government that can be reasonably inferred from the Constitution
- Inherent powers: the reasonable powers required by the federal government to manage the nation's affairs and maintain sovereignty
- Reserved powers: the unspecified powers belonging to the states that are not expressly granted to the federal government or denied to the state governments by the Constitution
- Concurrent powers: the powers shared between the federal and state governments

The Constitution delegated the following expanded powers to the federal government:

- Coin money
- Declare war
- Establish federal courts
- Sign foreign treaties
- Expand the territories of the United States and admit new states into the union
- Regulate immigration
- Regulate interstate commerce

The following powers were reserved for the states:

- Establish local governments
- Hold elections
- Implement welfare and benefit programs
- Create public school systems
- Establish licensing standards and requirements
- Regulate state corporations
- Regulate commerce within the state

The *concurrent* powers granted to both the federal and state governments in the Constitution include:

- The power to levy taxes
- The power to borrow money
- The power to charter corporations

Declaration of Independence

The Second Continental Congress met on May 10, 1775 and appointed George Washington as chief of the Continental Army. Although skirmishes began to occur, the Continental Congress made one more attempt to

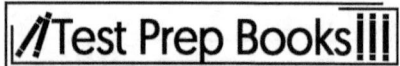

reconcile with the British by sending them the Olive Branch Petition. The petition was refused, and this rejection, combined with a pamphlet written by Thomas Paine in early 1776 called *Common Sense*, pushed the colonists to seek independence in earnest. A committee was chosen to draft a Declaration of Independence, which was written by Thomas Jefferson and approved on July 4, 1776. Another committee was appointed to create an organized government, which was adopted by Congress in November 1777 as the Articles of Confederation. However, this was not approved by all the states until March 1781; therefore, throughout much of the Revolutionary War, there was no official form of government.

Bill of Rights

Collectively referred to as the Bill of Rights, the first ten amendments to the Constitution were added to protect the individual rights of U.S. citizens and to keep the federal government from wielding too much control. These are rights such as freedom of speech, freedom of religion, freedom of the press, and right to a fair trial. The Constitution has been amended twenty-seven times in order to accommodate changes and updates. Some of these amendments were made to be more inclusive to the wide range of American citizens. For example, the 14th Amendment, adopted in 1868, abolished slavery and stated that all citizens must be treated equally under Constitutional law and allowed the same protection within each state.

Separation of Church and State

The First Amendment to the Constitution is widely considered the most important and easily the most memorable to most Americans. To more wholly understand pieces of the uber-important First Amendment, let's look at two key pieces. The first is the establishment clause. This states that "Congress shall make no law respecting the establishment of religion." This guarantees the separation of church and state. The other key clause of the First Amendment is the free exercise clause. This clause, also centered around religion, states that Congress may not pass a law "prohibiting the free exercise of religion."

Popular Sovereignty

Another key piece of limited government is popular sovereignty. The term refers to the people's consent to be governed. This concept was particularly important to early Americans after the rule of the British, and simply stated that a government draws its power from the people only. Put concisely, if a government loses the faith of its people, it is no longer a recognized government.

Structure and Functions of the Government Created by US Constitution

A political institution is an organization created by the government to enact and enforce laws, act as a mediator during conflict, create economic policy, establish social systems, and carry out some power. These institutions maintain a rigid structure of internal rules and oversight, especially if the power is delegated, like agencies under the executive branch.

Government and Citizenship | Democratic Principles and Government in the United States

The Constitution established a federal government divided into three branches: legislative, executive, and judicial.

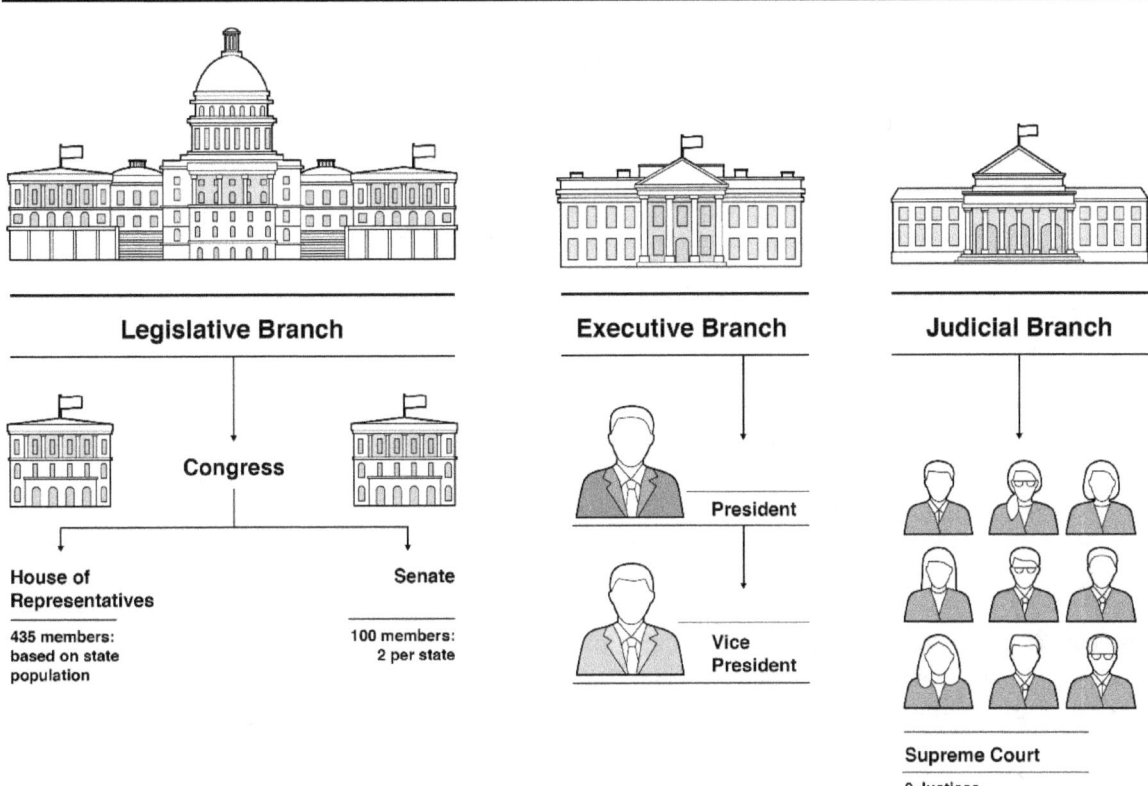

Executive Branch

The executive branch is responsible for enforcing the laws. The executive branch consists of the president, the vice president, the president's cabinet, and federal agencies created by Congress to execute some delegated task or authority.

The president of the United States:

- Serves a four-year term and is limited to two terms in office
- Is the chief executive officer of the United States and commander-in-chief of the armed forces
- Is elected by the Electoral College
- Appoints cabinet members, federal judges, and the heads of federal agencies
- Vetoes or signs bills into law
- Handles foreign affairs, including appointing diplomats and negotiating treaties
- Must be at least thirty-five years old, a natural-born U.S. citizen, and have lived in the United States for at least fourteen years

The vice president:

- Serves four-year terms alongside and at the will of the president
- Acts as president of the Senate

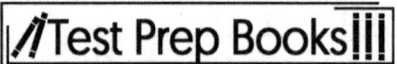

- Assumes the presidency if the president is incapacitated
- Assumes any additional duties assigned by the president

The cabinet members:

- Are appointed by the president
- Act as heads for the fifteen executive departments
- Advise the president in matters relating to their departments and carry out delegated power

Note that the president can only sign and veto laws and cannot initiate them himself. As head of the executive branch, it is the responsibility of the president to execute and enforce the laws passed by the legislative branch.

Although Congress delegates their legislative authority to agencies in an enabling statute, they are located in the executive branch because they are tasked with executing their delegated authority. The president enjoys the power of appointment and removal over all federal agency workers, except those tasked with quasi-legislative or quasi-judicial powers.

Legislative Branch

The legislative branch is responsible for enacting federal laws. This branch possesses the power to declare war, regulate interstate commerce, approve or reject presidential appointments, and investigate the other branches. The legislative branch is bicameral, meaning it consists of two houses: the lower house, called the House of Representatives, and the upper house, known as the Senate. Both houses are elected by popular vote.

Members of both houses are intended to represent the interests of the constituents in their home states and to bring their concerns to a national level while also being consistent with the interests of the nation as a whole. Drafts of laws, called bills, are proposed in one chamber and then are voted upon according to that chamber's rules; should the bill pass the vote in the first house of Congress, the other legislative chamber must approve it before it can be sent to the president.

The two houses (or chambers) are similar though they differ on some procedures such as how debates on bills take place.

House of Representatives

The House of Representatives is responsible for enacting bills relating to revenue; impeaching federal officers, including the president and Supreme Court justices; and electing the president in the case of no candidate reaching a majority in the Electoral College. College.

In the House of Representatives:

- Each state's representation in the House of Representatives is determined proportionally by population, with the total number of voting seats limited to 435.

- There are six nonvoting members in the House, one each from Washington, D.C.; Puerto Rico; American Samoa; Guam; the Northern Mariana Islands; and the U.S. Virgin Islands.

- The Speaker of the House is elected by the other representatives and is responsible for presiding over the House. In the event that the president and vice president are unable to fulfill their duties, the Speaker of the House will succeed to the presidency.

- The representatives of the House serve two-year terms.

Government and Citizenship | Democratic Principles and Government in the United States

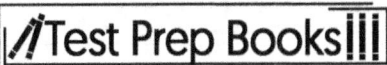

- The requirements for eligibility in the House include:
    - Must be twenty-five years of age
    - Must have been a U.S. citizen for at least seven years
    - Must be a resident of the state they are representing by the time of the election

Senate
The Senate has the exclusive powers to confirm or reject all presidential appointments, ratify treaties, and try impeachment cases initiated by the House of Representatives.

In the Senate:

- The number of representatives is one hundred, with two representatives from each state.
- The vice president presides over the Senate and breaks a tied vote, if necessary.
- The representatives serve six-year terms.
- The requirements for eligibility in the Senate include:
    - Must be thirty years of age
    - Must have been a U.S. citizen for the past nine years
    - Must be a resident of the state they are representing at the time of their election

Legislative Process
Although all members of the houses vote on whether or not bills should become laws, the senators and representatives also serve on committees and subcommittees dedicated to specific areas of policy. These committees are responsible for debating the merit of bills, revising bills, and passing or killing bills that are assigned to their committee. If it passes, they then present the bill to the entire Senate or House of Representatives (depending on which they are a part of). In most cases, a bill can be introduced in either the Senate or the House, but a majority vote of both houses is required to approve a new bill before the President may sign the bill into law.

Judicial Branch
The judicial branch, though it cannot pass laws itself, is tasked with interpreting the law and ensuring citizens receive due process under the law. The judicial branch consists of the Supreme Court, the highest court in the country, overseeing all federal and state courts. Lower federal courts are the district courts and the courts of appeals.

In the Supreme Court:

- Judges are appointed by the president and confirmed by the Senate.
- Judges serve until retirement, death, or impeachment.
- Judges possess sole power to judge the constitutionality of a law.
- Judges set precedents for lower courts based on their decisions.
- Judges try appeals that have proceeded from the lower courts.

Processes by which the US Constitution can be Changed

When the final details of the Constitution were being ironed out, many argued about the necessity for changes to the Constitution down the line. Worries over the aging of the document as the United States grew left many within the convention asking questions about how the Constitution would fare over time. With many factors to be considered—such as war, technology, and societal changes—the Framers felt the need to allow the people the option to change the Constitution if need be.

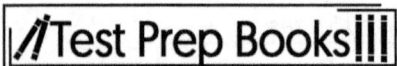

What came next was Article V. Article V set the parameters for the people to add amendments to the Constitution. The method the delegates provided was a difficult one, as they intended, so that the government could not work through amendments without the full and unconditional support of the people.

Within Article V, there were two avenues for an amendment to be added. The first was the congressional proposal method, which would originate with two-thirds of both chambers of Congress passing an amendment, followed by the state legislatures passing the amendment if three-fourths of the states voted to pass. The second avenue was the convention method. This method called for a national convention of the states obtaining two-thirds vote to propose an amendment. Then, three-fourths of special state conventions would need to approve for the amendment to be added. And the process succeeded in being difficult: since the founding, only twenty-seven amendments have been ratified.

Enacting Laws in the United States

To enact a new law:

- The bill is introduced to Congress.
- The bill is sent to the appropriate committee for review and revision.
- The approved bill is sent to the Speaker of the House and the majority party leader of the Senate, who places the bill on the calendar for review.
- The houses debate the merits of the bill and recommend amendments.
    - In the House of Representatives, those who wish to debate about a bill are allowed only a few minutes to speak, and amendments to the bill are limited.
    - In the Senate, debates and amendments are unlimited, and those who wish to postpone a vote may do so by filibuster, refusing to stop speaking.
- The approved bill is revised in both houses to ensure identical wording in both bills.
- The revised bill is returned to both houses for final approval.
- The bill is sent to the president, who may
    - Sign the bill into law
    - Veto the bill
    - Take no action, resulting in the bill becoming law if Congress remains in session for ten days or dying if Congress adjourns before ten days have passed

Changes in Role of the U.S. Government Over Time

New Deal Legislation and Wartime Politics

In 1932, in response to the looming global Great Depression of the 1930s, U.S. voters elected President Franklin D. Roosevelt (FDR) to office because his presidential campaign promised to pull the United States out of economic despair. Unlike his predecessor—President Herbert Hoover—FDR eventually accepted the fact that the federal government would have to play a role in reviving the tattered U.S. economy. On March 4, 1933, FDR pledged the *New Deal* to the American people, one that would regain the trust of down-and-out American workers. This promise of a New Deal was followed by a deluge of socialist-democratic legislation. The New Deal attempted to revive the American economy through public works projects carried out by organizations such as the U.S. Civilian Conservation Corps. These public works projects and government-backed organizations provided jobs to unemployed men and women across the country and helped stimulate economic recovery for the U.S.

By the end of the 1930s, the FDR administration had spent nearly $10 billion on the construction of hundreds of thousands of public buildings, roads, bridges, and airports. The New Deal also created new government agencies to help struggling businesses and farms and dispersed billions of dollars to welfare and relief programs for the poor. The New Deal, however, was just the beginning of socialist-democratic policies being infused into the economic fiber of the United States. Although the New Deal economy only improved slowly prior to the advent of World War II, the changes brought about by FDR's administration transformed the entire essence of the U.S. government's beliefs regarding the role of government in business and the economy. Some describe FDR's policies as the beginning of a New Deal Order that continued well into the Obama administration of the early 2000s. Others call his policies the beginning of the U.S. welfare state. Regardless of the terminology used to describe the New Deal programs, one cannot deny that the New Deal revolutionized the relationship between the federal government and the economy. The New Deal extended the reach of federal government, paving the way to expanded executive powers.

The New Deal, however, did not solely pull the United States out of the Great Depression—the U.S. involvement in World War II hastened economic recovery through wartime policies and production. During this time, the United States expanded its military-industrial complex, paving the way to the economic excesses of the Cold War and the Space Race with the Soviet Union. This expansion, however, often came at the cost of civil rights, as thousands of Japanese Americans, perceived as a threat to national security, were interned throughout the war via FDR's Executive Order 9066. Executive Order 9066 perhaps sheds light on the darker side of the expansion of executive powers during the Second World War. Regardless of ethical analysis or judgment, Executive Order 9066 illustrates the ways in which the FDR administration expanded the reach of federal government, both prior to and during World War II.

Civil Rights

Citizens living in a democracy have several rights and responsibilities to uphold. The first duty is that they uphold the established laws of the government. In a democracy, a system of nationwide laws is necessary to ensure that there is some degree of order. Therefore, citizens must obey the laws and also help enforce them because a law that is inadequately enforced is almost useless. Optimally, a democratic society's laws will be accepted and followed by the community as a whole.

However, conflict can occur when an unjust law is passed. For instance, much of the civil rights movement centered around Jim Crow laws in the South that supported segregation between black and whites. Yet these practices were encoded in state laws, which created a dilemma for African Americans who wanted equality but also wanted to respect the law. Fortunately, a democracy offers a system in which government leaders and policies are constantly open to change in accordance with the will of citizens. Citizens can influence the laws that are passed by voting for and electing members of the legislative and executive branches to represent them at the local, state, and national levels.

This, however, requires citizens to be especially vigilant in protecting their liberties because they cannot depend solely on the existing government to meet their needs. To assert their role in a democracy, citizens should be active voters and speak out on issues that concern them. Even with these safeguards, it is possible for systems to be implemented that inhibit active participation. For instance, many southern states had laws that prevented blacks from voting. Under such circumstances, civil rights leaders felt that they had no choice but to resist the laws in order to defend their personal rights. Once voting became possible, civil rights groups strove to ensure that their votes counted by changing state and national policy.

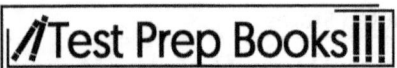

Changing Relationships Among the Three Branches of the Federal Government

War Powers Act

During his first administration, Franklin D. Roosevelt's New Deal political agenda met with a tremendous amount of hostility from the Supreme Court. The Supreme Court overturned many New Deal programs in just a few years because many justices believed Roosevelt's initiative was too radically socialist in nature. Despite these invalidations, Roosevelt won the 1936 election with a landslide victory. Roosevelt fought back against the Supreme Court by attempting to expand the number of appointed justices to a total of fifteen. On February 5, 1937—after initiating his efforts in an address to Congress and in a Fireside Chat—Roosevelt set forward the Judicial Procedures Reform Bill of 1937, which, among other things, attempted to add the six extra Supreme Court justices. The plan was eventually shot down by the checks and balances system of the U.S. government. Congress believed the bill was unconstitutional and placed too much power in the hands of the executive branch and that it would make the government into one of men rather than one of law. This power increased to the point that Congress eventually passed the War Powers Act of 1973 that officially tried to limit the president's power to declare an armed conflict. This act emerged in the years following the Korean and Vietnam armed conflicts that waged on for many years without an official declaration of war.

Judicial Review

The case of *Marbury vs. Madison* established the policy of judicial review, which declared that the Supreme Court could rule whether or not an act of Congress was constitutional. The case of *McCullough vs. Maryland* affirmed that Congress had the power to pass laws that were necessary and proper in order to carry out its other duties. The case also upheld the supremacy of federal laws over state laws when they came into conflict.

Constitutional Amendments

Thirteenth Amendment

The Thirteenth Amendment abolished slavery and involuntary servitude, except as punishment for a crime. The issue of slavery was no longer in the states' hands. Although the Emancipation Proclamation freed slaves in the Confederacy, the status of former slaves remained uncertain as the war neared its conclusion. Many Northerners did not hold strong views on slavery, but most wanted to punish the South and resolve the primary cause of the bloody Civil War. The Northern states all immediately ratified the amendment, and in December 1865 enough reconstructed Southern states ratified the amendment for it to be adopted into law.

Fourteenth Amendment

The Fourteenth Amendment (1868) granted citizenship to all persons born or naturalized in the United States; prohibited states from depriving any citizen of life, liberty, or property without due process of law; and prevented the states from violating equal protection based on race, color, or previous condition of servitude. Although revolutionary for the theoretical rights of all American citizens, newly freed or otherwise, the Fourteenth Amendment was not federally enforced until the Civil Rights Act of 1964.

Jim Crow Laws

Southern states circumvented the Fourteenth Amendment and imposed what were referred to as Jim Crow laws, which established racial segregation of public facilities. These separate but equal facilities included the military, workplaces, public schools, restaurants, restrooms, transportation, and recreational facilities. Despite the label of separate but equal, most facilities reserved for African Americans were considerably inferior.

In 1896, the Supreme Court handed down a decision in the case of *Plessy vs. Ferguson*, in which Homer Plessy, a Louisiana man of mixed race, attempted to board a railway car reserved for whites only and was charged for violating the separate car law. Plessy subsequently filed suit against the state, claiming they violated his Fourteenth

Government and Citizenship | Democratic Principles and Government in the United States

Amendment rights. The Supreme Court decided in favor of the state, ruling that the law was not unconstitutional. The Supreme Court upheld separate but equal laws until the 1954 case of Brown vs. the Board of Education of Topeka where the Supreme Court ruled that racial segregation of public schools violated the Fourteenth Amendment.

Fifteenth Amendment

The Fifteenth Amendment prohibits the government from denying a citizen the right to vote for reasons of race, color, or previous condition of servitude. Adopted in 1870, the last of the Reconstruction Amendments, the Fifteenth Amendment sought to protect newly freed slaves' right to vote. As discussed below, most states interpreted the amendment to only apply to male suffrage. In addition, Southern states passed a series of laws to systematically disenfranchise African Americans including poll taxes, literacy tests, and residency rules. The use of violence and intimidation for political purposes was also common. Meaningful change did not occur until the Civil Rights Movement, nearly one hundred years later. In 1964, the Twenty-Fourth Amendment prohibited the states and federal government from charging a poll tax or fee to vote. Later, the Voting Rights Act of 1965 empowered the federal government to enforce the Fifteenth Amendment in the states for the first time.

Seventeenth Amendment

The Seventeenth Amendment, which was passed in 1913, allows for the direct election of U.S. senators by the American people. This amendment is considered a victory for American liberal democracy and the multi-century efforts for democratization in U.S. society. By allowing the direct election of U.S. senators, the U.S. government continued its transition from a classical republic to a democratic-republic that allowed for limited spheres of popular democratic practices.

Nineteenth Amendment

The Women's Rights Movement in the U.S. ranged from 1848 to 1920. While the goals of the movement changed over time, at the beginning This movement called for a woman's right to vote (suffrage), the right to bodily autonomy, the right to divorce and custody of children, the right to work, the right to fair wages and equal pay, the right to own property, the right to obtain an education, and the right to equality in religion and moral freedom from sexual violence, the right to hold public office, the right to work, the right to fair wages and equal pay, and the right to own property and obtain an education. Famous early women's rights activists include Susan B. Anthony, Lucretia Mott, Lucy Stone, and Elizabeth Cady Stanton, who authored the Declaration of Rights and Sentiments, which demanded access to the civil liberties granted to all men.the right was removed in 1807. The fight for women's suffrage continued in the middle of the nineteenth century. Famous women's rights activists include Susan B. Anthony, Lucy Stone, and Elizabeth Cady Stanton, who authored the *Declaration of Rights and Sentiments*, which demanded access to the civil liberties granted to all men. Women gained the right to vote in 1869 in Wyoming and 1870 in Utah.

The Fourteenth Amendment specified equal treatment for all citizens; however, it did not establish a women's right to vote in elections. Although landowning women were allowed to vote in New Jersey in the late eighteenth century, the right was removed in 1807. The fight for women's suffrage continued in the middle of the nineteenth century and gained momentum in the early twentieth century due to the increased participation of women in the economy during World War I when much of the male workforce went overseas to fight. The National Women's Party picketed outside the White House and led a series of protests in Washington, resulting in the imprisonment of the party's leader, Alice Paul. In 1918, Woodrow Wilson declared his support for women's suffrage despite earlier opposition, and in 1920 Congress passed the Nineteenth Amendment, which made it illegal for states to withhold voting rights based on gender.

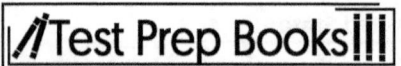

Twenty-Fourth Amendment

The Twenty-Fourth Amendment prohibited Congress and state governments from instituting poll taxes or any other types of taxes that limit voting rights. Prior to its ratification on January 23, 1964, several states—Virginia, Alabama, Texas, Arkansas, and Mississippi—maintained poll taxes that prohibited low-income voters, specifically black voters, from registering for elections. The passage of the Twenty-Fourth Amendment is considered a tremendous historical victory for the civil rights movement.

Twenty-Sixth Amendment

Signed into law by President Richard Nixon on March 10, 1971, the Twenty-Sixth Amendment to the US Constitution ruled in favor of a uniform national voting age for all local, state, and federal elections. Previously, the 1970 *Oregon v. Mitchell* Supreme Court decision decided that eighteen- to twenty-year-olds in the United States could only vote for the presidential elections, but not for state officials. This decision led to widespread protest, culminating in the Twenty-Sixth Amendment, which made eighteen the uniform national voting age for all elections.

Landmark Supreme Court Decisions

Regents of the University of California v. Bakke was a 1978 court case that witnessed Allan Bakke, a white applicant, sue the Medical School at the University of California at Davis when he was twice denied access to medical school even though his standardized test scores were significantly higher than some minority applicants who were admitted with lower MCAT scores. Bakke claimed that the admissions quotas for students of color violated the Fourteenth Amendment's Equal Protection Clause and Title IV Civil Rights Act of 1964. Although the California Supreme Court agreed that the quota system was discriminatory in nature, the Supreme Court, in a 5–4 decision, ruled that the quota system was constitutionally sound and did not violate the Equal Protection Clause of the US Constitution. Thus, race-based admissions continued in university systems across the United States.

Roe v. Wade was a 1973 court case that determined, in a 7–2 decision, written by Justice Harry Blackman, that a Texas statute that criminalized abortion was unconstitutional for its violation of Jane Roe's right to privacy. According to the Supreme Court decision, abortions occurring within the first trimester of pregnancy (and abortions related to maternal health carried out in the second and third trimesters) rested within a woman's zone of privacy. The Supreme Court legitimized this zone of privacy by citing the First, Fourth, Ninth, and Fourteenth Amendments. This landmark court case legitimized a woman's right to carry out an abortion in the first trimester.

Miranda v. Arizona was a landmark 1966 Supreme Court case that, in a 5–4 decision written by Chief Justice Earl Warren, ruled that police forces and other law enforcement agencies must inform criminal suspects of their constitutional rights, specifically of their right to an attorney and against self-incrimination. Ernesto Miranda, a criminal suspect who was eventually convicted of rape and murder, was detained, interrogated, and convicted without ever being read his rights. Miranda, who had a history of mental illness and low achievement levels in school, never had a counsel present during his interrogation, but he was still sentenced to twenty to thirty years in prison. After a failed appeal to the Arizona Supreme Court, Miranda and his attorney appealed to the U.S. Supreme Court. The court's decision to back Miranda's appeal helped protect individual rights by limiting police powers. Today, every suspected criminal must be read their Miranda Rights.

Prior to the 8–1 Supreme Court decision to *Engel v. Vitale* (1962), New York State law mandated that each school day begin with the Pledge of Allegiance and a nondenominational prayer to God. Although the law stated that students could abstain if they found the nondenominational prayer objectionable, Steven Engel, a Jewish parent, sued on behalf of his child, arguing that the New York State statute violated the First Amendment rights of his child. The 8–1 decision in favor of Engel's case was based on the belief that the purpose of the First Amendment was to prevent government meddling in religious affairs (and vice versa).

Brown v. Board of Education is a landmark unanimous civil rights decision in the Supreme Court in 1954 that made it unconstitutional to segregate public schooling based on race. This decision overturned *Plessy v. Ferguson* (1896), paving the way to the United States of America's first wave of lawful desegregation efforts. Citing the Equal Protection Clause of the Fourteenth Amendment, the Supreme Court, under the leadership of Chief Justice Earl Warren, unanimously decided that Oliver Brown, the parent of a child denied access to a white school in Topeka, Kansas, was justified in his battle against segregation in public schools. The case marked an important victory for the civil rights movement and paved the way to a revolution in race relations in the United States.

Schenck v. U.S. (1919) was a Supreme Court decision that witnessed the creation of a clear and present danger test in determining the limitations of free speech in the United States. The decision, which denied Schenck's suit, stated that a citizen's free speech could be limited if that speech presented a clear and present danger to the safety and security of the nation and its citizenry. Schenck, a socialist protester, was jailed for posing a clear threat to the United States. The decision reinforced the Espionage Act that placed limits on the First Amendment.

Plessy v. Ferguson (1896) set the stage for Jim Crow and legal segregation by claiming that separate but equal public facilities were constitutional. *Plessy v. Ferguson* was later overturned by *Brown v. Board of Education* (1954). Nevertheless, for nearly sixty years, it helped to legally separate U.S. citizens by the color of their skin.

Dred Scott v. Sanford was an infamous 1857 Supreme Court ruling that further decreased the rights of African Americans living in the United States by claiming that they were not citizens and therefore could not sue in federal courts. Additionally, the Supreme Court decision reinforced the belief that slavery could not be outlawed in western territories prior to statehood.

Cherokee Nation v. Georgia was a Supreme Court case in 1831 that solidified the unequal nature of U.S.-Indian relations by declaring that Indian nations, although marginalized and persecuted, were neither independent nor foreign in nature. They, therefore, did not possess constitutional protection, and the Supreme Court could not hear the Cherokee Nation's case against Georgia because they did not have the jurisdiction to resolve the case.

McCulloch v. Maryland (1819) declared that, by unanimous decision, the state of Maryland did not possess the right/power to tax the Bank of the United States. The Supreme Court decision made the Second Bank of the United States a constitutional institution and established the doctrine of *implied powers* that stated the state governments could not interfere with legal actions decided by the federal government.

Marbury v. Madison (1803) increased the power of the Supreme Court by making constitutional the principle of *judicial review* that allows the Supreme Court to strike down any act of Congress that runs counter to the laws of the Constitution.

Relationship Between the States and the National Government of the United States

Federalism is a set of principles that divides power between a central government and regional governments. Sovereign states often combine into a federation, and in doing so, they cede some degree of sovereignty to a functional central government that handles broad national policies. The United States and Canada are examples of governments with a Federalist structure.

While the federal government manages the nation as a whole, state governments address issues pertaining to their specific territory. In the past, states claimed the right, known as nullification, to refuse to enforce federal laws that they considered unconstitutional. However, conflicts between state and federal authority, particularly in the South in regard to first, slavery, and later, discrimination, have led to increased federal power, and states cannot defy federal laws. Even so, the Tenth Amendment limits federal power to those powers specifically granted in the

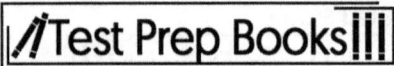

Government and Citizenship

Constitution, and the rest of the powers are retained by the states and citizens. Therefore, individual state governments are left in charge of decisions with immediate effects on their citizens, such as state laws and taxes.

In this way, the powers of government are separated both horizontally between the three branches of government (executive, legislative, and judicial) and vertically between the levels of government (federal, state, and local).

Like the federal government, state governments consist of executive, judicial, and legislative branches, but the exact configuration of those branches varies between states. For example, while most states follow the bicameral structure of Congress, Nebraska has only a single legislative chamber. Additionally, requirements to run for office, length of terms, and other details vary from state to state. State governments have considerable authority within their states, but they cannot impose their power on other states.

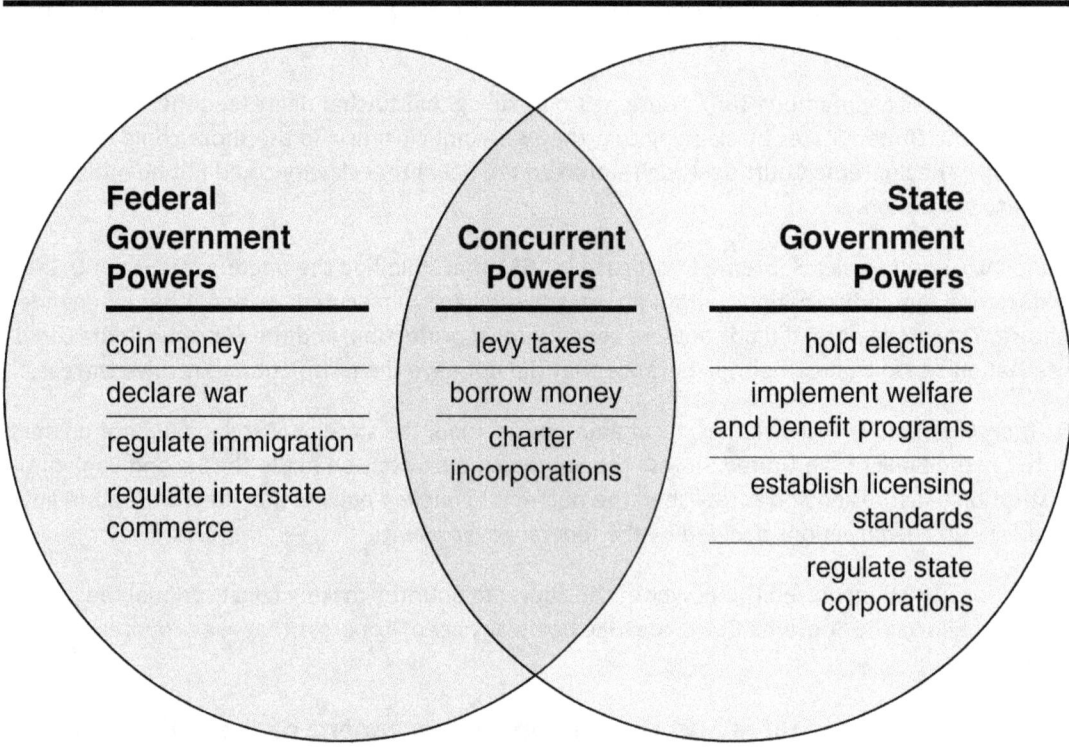

Texas State Government and Local Governments

The Texas state government is divided into three major branches: the legislative branch, the executive branch, and the judicial branch.

The legislative branch proposes and ratifies laws for the state. Like the U.S. federal legislative branch, the Texas state legislature is bicameral, which means it's divided into two houses. These are the House of Representatives and the Senate. Senators serve four-year terms; representatives serve two-year terms. In total, there are 31 members of the Texas Senate and 150 members of the Texas House of Representatives. Each senator and representative is responsible for a district that has roughly the same number of people as other districts. Both senators and representatives must be legal residents of their district for at least one year prior to campaigning for office. Representatives must be Texas citizens for 2 years, and they must be at least 21 years old. Senators must be Texas citizens for at least 5 years, and they must be at least 26 years old.

The legislative branch of Texas can create new laws and bring them to a vote at special periods called sessions. While the House and Senate share many legislative duties, only the House can propose and vote on laws that increase taxes or raise money for the state government. During these scheduled sessions, which can last up to 140 days, the legislature addresses bills and laws. At times, the governor can call special sessions, which last up to 30 days. It's also important to note that the legislature possesses the authority to impeach government officials. The most notorious impeachment in state history occurred in 1917, when Governor James Ferguson was removed for failing to properly enforce banking laws, among other violations.

There's a complex process to create new laws in the Texas state legislature. This process begins when legislators propose a bill. During sessions, clerks read the bill word for word to members of the House and/or Senate. Next, the Speaker of the House or Lieutenant Governor assigns a committee to each bill. Members of each committee—including the lead committee member, known as a chairperson—study the bill, rewrite sections, accept the bill, or reject the bill. The entire house votes and debates a bill once it receives approval by a committee. If the bill is rejected, it dies. In some cases, a conference committee is created, consisting of members from both houses of state Congress, so that the bill can be rehashed to satisfy more legislators. The governor then has the choice to sign the bill into law, ignore the bill until it becomes law in ten days, or veto the bill. If vetoed, a 2/3 vote by Congress could override the veto so that the bill becomes a law.

The most powerful and important official of the Texas executive branch is the governor. Governors serve four-year terms, with no limit on the amount of terms that a governor can serve. Candidates must be thirty years old to campaign for governor. As the head of the state executive branch, the governor often attempts to sway the motions of the legislature. Although a governor cannot create laws, s/he can urge the legislature to put new bills into motion. Governors can also veto bills. In addition, governors possess the right to use a line-item veto, which allows governors to delete portions of budget bills that they dislike. The governor also collaborates with the legislature by calling special sessions, and s/he can collaborate with the judicial branch by granting pardons for crimes or reprieves from the death penalty. Texas governors also work with the state military and National Guard in times of crisis. In extreme cases, governors can declare martial law or states of emergency.

Although there are thousands of elected executive officials that work with the governor, the most important secondary executive is the lieutenant governor. Lieutenant governors are essentially second in command; they work with the legislature and serve as active governor when the governor is out of state for business or travel. Hundreds of agencies fall under the umbrella of the executive branch in Texas. The largest is the Department of Criminal Justice, which focuses on crime prevention and public safety.

The Supreme Court heads the Texas judicial branch. All judges in the Supreme Court serve four to six year terms and must be U.S. citizens. Within the Texas Supreme Court, there is one Chief Justice and eight other justices. The justices examine cases for both criminal and civil law violations. The lower municipal, county, and district courses each hold trials for their own respective cases. Additionally, appellate courts oversee appeals. High courts in the Texas state judiciary system possess the right to label a law as unconstitutional through judicial review. Citizens also participate in the Texas judicial system as members of petit juries (civil and criminal trials) and grand juries (felony cases).

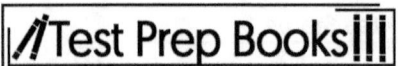

Citizenship and Political Processes in the United States

Political Parties, Interest Groups, and the Media in the U.S. Political System

Political Parties

A political party is an organized group of voters who share the same political values and support or oppose the same policies. Members of a political party vote for the candidates from their party who they believe share their values and will approve or reject the policies they support or oppose. Political parties often determine the positions party members take on issues of policy, such as the economy, taxation, and social services.

Slavery divided the nation and created unrest among the political parties, as members took opposing views and splintered into separate sects of the party or started new parties with members who shared their views. The Whig Party, so divided by the differing views of the members, collapsed.

Former Whigs joined or formed the following parties:

- Constitutional Union Party: Devoted itself to a single-issue platform of preserving the Union and recognizing the Constitution as the supreme rule of law. The party did not take a firm issue on slavery, but vigorously opposed secession.

- Democratic Party: Divided into northern and southern factions over slavery, but the Democrats sought to compromise and remain unified.

- Know-Nothing Party: Advocated for an anti-immigration single-issue platform, especially immigrants from Catholic countries.

- Republican Party: Formed in response to the Kansas-Nebraska Act, which threatened to extend slavery into new territories, called for the abolition of slavery and argued for a more modernized economy.

Modern Political Parties

Franklin D. Roosevelt, a Democrat, was elected president in 1933. Roosevelt instituted the New Deal, which included many social policies that built an expansive social welfare program to provide financial support to citizens during the Great Depression. The Republican Party opposed this interference by the government, and the two parties became more strongly divided. The political landscape again shifted during the Civil Rights Movement, as Southern Democrats fled to the Republican Party over their opposition to enforcing federal civil rights onto states. This strengthened the modern coalition between economic conservatives and social conservatives.

Today, the Democrats and Republicans are still the two major parties, though many third parties have emerged. The Republicans and Democrats hold opposing views on the degree of state intervention into private business, taxation, states' rights, and government assistance. The ideals of these parties include:

Republican (or the Grand Old Party [GOP])

- Founded by abolitionists
- Support capitalism, free enterprise, and a policy of noninterference by the government
- Support strong national defense
- Support deregulation and restrictions of labor unions
- Advocate for states' rights
- Oppose abortion
- Support traditional values, often based on Judeo-Christian foundations, including considerable opposition to same-sex marriage

Government and Citizenship | Citizenship and Political Processes in the United States

Democrat

- Founded by anti-Federalists and rooted in classical Liberalism
- Promote civil rights, equal opportunity and protection under the law, and social justice
- Support government-instituted social programs and safety nets
- Support environmental issues
- Support government intervention and regulation, and advocate for labor unions
- Support universal health care

Some prominent third parties include:

- Reform Party: support political reform of the two-party system
- Green Party: support environmental causes
- Libertarian Party: support a radical policy of nonintervention and small, localized government

Interest Groups

An interest group is an organization with members who share similar social concerns or political interests. Members of political interest groups work together to influence policy decisions that benefit a particular segment of society or cause. Interest groups might include:

- Activist groups, like the NAACP, American Civil Liberties Union (ACLU), or People for the Ethical Treatment of Animals (PETA)
- Corporations, like pharmaceutical companies or banks
- Small-business advocates
- Religious groups, like the Concerned Women PAC and the Muslim Public Affairs Council
- Unions, such as the Association of Teacher Educators and International Brotherhood of Electrical Workers

Lobbyists

To promote their causes and influence policy in their favor, many interest groups employ *lobbyists*, paid advocates who work to influence lawmakers. Lobbying is a controversial practice, but it is sanctioned and protected as free speech. Lobbying from interest groups has a powerful impact on many policy decisions made in the United States. Examples of lobbyist groups include American Israel Public Affairs Committee (AIPAC) and Pharmaceutical Research and Manufacturers of America.

Mass Media

Mass media refers to the various methods by which the majority of the general public receives news and information. Today mass media includes television, newspapers, radio, magazines, online news outlets, and social media networks. The general public relies on mass media for political knowledge and cultural socialization, as well as the majority of their knowledge of current events, social issues, and political news.

Evolution of Mass Media

- Until the end of the nineteenth century, print media such as newspapers and magazines was the only form of mass communication.
- In the 1890s, after the invention of the radio, broadcast media become a popular form of communication, particularly among illiterate people. By 1944, 32.5 million American households owned radios.
- In the 1940s, television superseded both print and broadcast media as the most popular form of mass media.
- In 1947, President Harry Truman gave the first political speech on television.

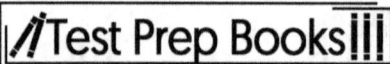

- In 1952, Dwight Eisenhower was the first political candidate to air campaign ads on television.
- Today, the internet is the most widespread mass media technology, and citizens have instant access to news and information, as well as interactive platforms on which they can communicate directly with political leaders or share their views through social media, blogs, and independent news sites.

Influence of Mass Media on Politics

Mass media has a powerful effect on public opinion and politics. Mass media:

- Shapes public interests
- Enables candidates to reach voters wherever they are
- Determines what is and is not considered important in society based on how it prioritizes events and issues
- Provides the context in which to report events
- Is paid for by advertisers who may pressure news outlets to suppress or report information in their own interests

Filling Elective and Appointive Public Offices

As members of a Constitutional Republic with certain aspects of a democracy, U.S. citizens are empowered to elect most government leaders, but the process varies between branch and level of government. Presidential elections at the national level use the Electoral College system. Rather than electing the president directly, citizens cast their ballots to select *electors* that represent each state in the college.

Legislative branches at the federal and state level are also determined by elections. In some areas, judges are elected, but in other states judges are appointed by elected officials. The U.S. has a two-party system, meaning that most government control is under two major parties: the Republican Party and the Democratic Party. It should be noted that the two-party system was not designed by the Constitution but gradually emerged over time.

Electoral Process

During the electoral process, the citizens of a state decide who will represent them at the local, state, and federal level. Different political officials that citizens elect through popular vote include but are not limited to:

- City mayor
- City council members
- State representative
- State governor
- State senator
- House member
- U.S. Senator
- President

The Constitution grants the states the power to hold their own elections, and the voting process often varies from city to city and state to state.

While a popular vote decides nearly all local and state elections, the president of the United States is elected by the Electoral College, rather than by popular vote. Presidential elections occur every four years on the first Tuesday after the first Monday in November.

Government and Citizenship | Citizenship and Political Processes in the United States

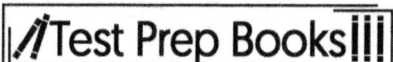

The electoral process for the president of the United States includes:

Primary Elections and Caucuses

In a presidential election, nominees from the two major parties, as well as some third parties, run against each other. To determine who will win the nomination from each party, the states hold primary elections or caucuses.

During the primary elections, the states vote for who they want to win their party's nomination. In some states, primary elections are closed, meaning voters may only vote for candidates from their registered party, but other states hold open primaries in which voters may vote in either party's primary.

Some states hold caucuses in which the members of a political party meet in small groups, and the decisions of those groups determine the party's candidate.

Each state holds a number of delegates proportional to its population, and the candidate with the most delegate votes receives the nomination. Some states give all of their delegates (winner-take-all) to the primary or caucus winner, while some others split the votes more proportionally.

Conventions

The two major parties hold national conventions to determine who will be the nominee to run for president from each party. The delegates each candidate won in the primary elections or caucuses are the voters who represent their states at the national conventions. The candidate who wins the most delegate votes is given the nomination. Political parties establish their own internal requirements and procedures for how a nominee is nominated.

Conventions are typically spread across several days, and leaders of the party give speeches, culminating with the candidate accepting the nomination at the end.

Campaigning

Once the nominees are selected from each party, they continue campaigning into the national election. Prior to the mid-1800s, candidates did not actively campaign for themselves, considering it dishonorable to the office, but campaigning is now rampant. Modern campaigning includes, but is not limited to:

- Raising money
- Meeting with citizens and public officials around the country
- Giving speeches
- Issuing policy proposals
- Running internal polls to determine strategy
- Organizing strategic voter outreach in important districts
- Participating in debates organized by a third-party private debate commission
- Advertising on television, through mail, or on the Internet

General Election

On the first Tuesday after the first Monday in November of an election year, every four years, the people cast their votes by secret ballot for president in a general election. Voters may vote for any candidate, regardless of their party affiliation. The outcome of the popular vote does not decide the election; instead, the winner is determined by the Electoral College.

Electoral College

When the people cast their votes for president in the general election, they are casting their votes for the electors from the Electoral College who will elect the president. In order to win the presidential election, a nominee must win 270 of the 538 electoral votes. The number of electors is equal to the total number of senators and representatives from each state plus three electoral votes for Washington D.C. which does not have any voting members in the legislative branch.

The electors typically vote based on the popular vote from their states. Although the Constitution does not require electors to vote for the popular vote winner, no elector voting against the popular vote has ever changed the outcome of an election. Due to the Electoral College, a nominee may win the popular vote and still lose the election.

For example, let's imagine that there are only two states — Wyoming and New Mexico — in a presidential election. Wyoming has three electoral votes and awards them all to the winner of the election by majority vote. New Mexico has five electoral votes and also awards them all to the winner of the election by majority vote. If 500,000 people in Wyoming vote and the Republican candidate wins by a vote of 300,000 to 200,000, the Republican candidate will win the three electoral votes for the state. If the same number of people vote in New Mexico, but the Republican candidate loses the state by a vote of 249,000 to 251,000, the Democratic candidate wins the five electoral votes from that state. This means the Republican candidate will have received 549,000 popular votes but only three electoral votes, while the Democratic candidate will have received 451,000 popular votes but will have won five electoral votes. Thus, the Republican won the popular vote by a considerable margin, but the Democratic candidate will have been awarded more electoral votes, which are the only ones that matter.

	Wyoming	New Mexico	Total # of Votes
Republican Votes	300,000	249,000	**549,000**
Democratic Votes	200,000	251,000	**451,000**
Republican Electoral Votes	3	0	3
Democratic Electoral Votes	0	5	5

If no one wins the majority of electoral votes in the presidential election, the House of Representatives decides the presidency, as required by the Twelfth Amendment. They may only vote for the top three candidates, and each state delegation votes as a single bloc. Twenty-six votes, a simple majority, are required to elect the president. The House has only elected the president twice, in 1801 and 1825.

Here how many electoral votes each state and the District of Columbia have:

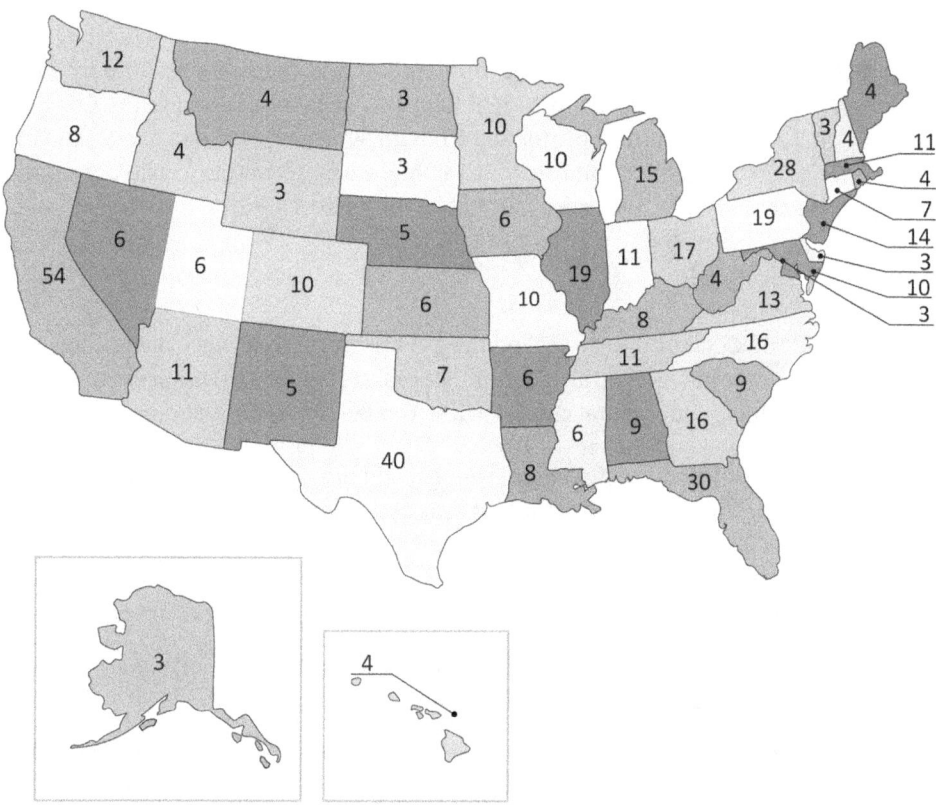

Processes for Making Policy in the United States

The legislative branch of the United States of America is the policy-making branch of the federal government. The legislative branch is made up of two houses: Congress and the House of Representatives. Together, these two branches make laws and amend the Constitution through a federal process of checks and balances. Policies can be enacted through petitions and lobbying efforts by common citizens. Protest is another highly visible way to call for legislative changes. Boycotts and strikes can grab the attention of lawmakers, forcing their hands to enact certain bills or amendments. Conventionally, common citizens change policy by electing officials at the local, state, and federal level via the U.S. voting process. Citizens can also enact change by taking office or joining local lobbying groups or nonprofits. Technology has recently changed the ways in which citizens try to enact change. The Internet and social media have paved the way to a new era of lobbying and protest. Millions of U.S. citizens now take to their smartphones, tablets, and computers to call for policy changes. This method of enacting policy change has actually been quite successful in the United States and abroad. The Arab Spring in the Middle East, for instance, was largely built upon the instant connection and revolutionary networking available via social media and the internet.

Rights Guaranteed by the US Constitution

Civil Liberties and Civil Rights

The protection of civil liberties is one of the most important political values upon which American society is based. Though the terms civil liberties and civil rights are commonly used interchangeably, they describe two very distinct types of protections. Civil liberties refer to the legal protections afforded to U.S. citizens against government action,

while civil rights refer to equal treatment under the law, especially in relation to minority groups, like women, African Americans, and Hispanics.

Civil Liberties

A civil liberty is a protection from legal action by the government. Civil liberties are granted by the Constitution in the first ten amendments, collectively known as the Bill of Rights, which were added to the Constitution in 1791. Civil liberties are conditional and do not afford protection from government action in every scenario. They can be restricted when they infringe on the rights of others; for example, with defamation, child pornography, or fighting words. They also may be suspended with just cause, such as in the case of limiting the freedom of press to protect national security.

The Bill of Rights

The first ten amendments of the Constitution are called the Bill of Rights. They were passed to win over anti-Federalists during the ratification of the Constitution. Anti-Federalists wanted assurances that the federal government would protect certain fundamental civil liberties. The Bill of Rights includes:

- Amendment I: Establishes freedom of religion, speech, and press; the right to assemble in peaceful protest; and the right to petition the government without fear of reprisal

- Amendment II: Establishes the right to bear arms

- Amendment III: Establishes the right to refuse to quarter, or house, soldiers in time of war

- Amendment IV: Establishes protection against unreasonable search and seizure and requires a warrant based on probable cause supported by specific information

- Amendment V: Protects against self-incrimination in criminal trials, except in cases of military court martial; protects against being tried more than once for the same crime, known as double jeopardy; and protects against seizure of private property for public use without compensation

- Amendment VI: Establishes extensive set of rights to protect defendants in a criminal trial—the right to a speedy and timely trial before a judge and impartial jury of peers, the right to be informed of criminal accusations, the right to present and compel witnesses in defense of the accused, the right to confront witnesses against the accused, and the right to assistance of counsel

- Amendment VII: Protects the right to a trial by jury in civil cases exceeding a dollar amount of $20

- Amendment VIII: Protects against cruel and unusual punishment and excessive fines

- Amendment IX: Establishes the existence of additional fundamental rights unnamed in the Constitution; protects those rights that are not enumerated

- Amendment X: Reserves all powers that are not specified to the federal government or prohibited to the states or the people, establishing the principles of separation of powers and Federalism

Civil Rights

Civil rights concern who is protected, while civil liberties concern what is protected. Civil rights refer to protection against unfair treatment based on characteristics such as gender, race, ethnicity, religion, sexual orientation, and disability. The struggle for civil rights has a long history in the United States. Following the Civil War, the ratification of three amendments—Thirteenth, Fourteenth, and Fifteenth, collectively known as the Reconstruction Amendments—expanded the constitutional protection of equal civil rights.

Government and Citizenship | Citizenship and Political Processes in the United States

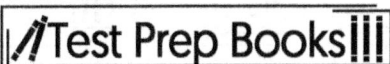

Democratic Process in the United States

Political Beliefs and Behaviors

Political beliefs are the beliefs held by the citizens of a nation about the government, leaders, policies, and the related political issues of their state. Political beliefs differ among individual citizens, but in America, a strong basis of democracy shapes the political beliefs, behaviors, and attitudes.

Democratic Values

The foundation of democratic values upon which the United States is based include:

- The people are sovereign, and they elect a representative government to exercise that sovereignty.
- The citizens of the nation are equal under the law.
- The peaceful transition of power is valued regardless of election results.
- The private property of individuals cannot be taken by force by the government without due process or fair compensation.
- The civil liberties of the citizens of the state cannot be abridged or violated by the government without due process.
- The government should be accountable to the citizenry.

Political Socialization

American citizens undergo a process of political socialization from early childhood to adulthood during which they develop their individual sense of political identity and civic pride. Children learn about politics in the home from an early age, whether from the views, opinions, and facts of family and friends, or through the media to which they are exposed.

In school, they learn about the nation's political history, basic politics, and democratic values, as well as the ideals of patriotism and the processes of government. As they grow older, they join interest groups, labor unions, religious groups, and political organizations that further influence their political beliefs. This socialization shapes not only the political beliefs and values of individual citizens and groups but the political ideals of the nation and public opinion.

Public Opinion

Public opinion is the shared political ideals, opinions, and attitudes of the people of a state regarding the politics, current events, and social issues that influence policy and shape the political atmosphere of a state. Public opinion is the result of political beliefs, socialization, and current events. Political scientists measure public opinion through:

- Distribution of opinion across demographics such as age, race, gender, and religion
- Strength of the opinion
- Stability of the opinion over time

Public opinion refers to the majority opinion in a democratic state. Citizens express public opinion through the interest groups they join, the media they consume and interact with, and the leaders they elect. To measure public opinion, scientists use polls to gather data. Accurate polling requires:

- Random sampling of representative populations
- Unbiased questions
- Clear instructions for how to answer questions
- Controlled procedures such as the use of telephone, mail, Internet, or in-person interviews with an unbiased pollster

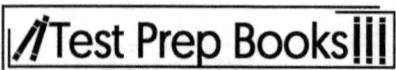

- Accurate reporting of the results, including information about methods, inconsistencies, respondents, and possible sources and degree of error

George Washington

George Washington, the first president of the United States of America, envisioned the creation of a classical republic rather than a democracy. Nevertheless, his leadership helped embed democratic values within the governmental fibers of the United States. Specifically, Washington set the precedent for limited terms as president, warning of the dangers of unchecked executive power. Although he also warned about the dangers of democracy, he is still heralded by Americans as a forefather of democracy because he believed in creating a nation that was governed by the people and for the people.

John Marshall

John Marshall served a lengthy tenure as chief justice during the presidencies of John Adams, Thomas Jefferson, James Madison, James Monroe, John Quincy Adams, and Andrew Jackson. He oversaw many crucial U.S. Supreme Court cases such as *McCulloch v. Maryland* (1819) and *Marbury v. Madison* (1803). Marshall is typically lauded for his push to expand the voting electorate to include more white men. As a delegate to the Virginia Constitutional Convention of 1829–1830, Marshall declared that any white man who served in the War of 1812 or promised military service should have the right to vote. His ideas were crucial for paving the way to an expanded white voting bloc during the Age of Jacksonian Democracy.

Frederick Douglass

Frederick Douglass was a former-slave-turned-statesman who vehemently fought for the rights of African Americans in both antebellum America and the era of Reconstruction. Douglass radically campaigned for the civil rights of African Americans, explicitly noting the obvious inequalities in society through his writings and oratory. Douglass, like other reformers at the time, also fought for women's suffrage as well as abolition.

Elizabeth Cady Stanton

Elizabeth Cady Stanton is famous for her *Declaration of Sentiments*, a women's suffrage document presented at the Seneca Falls Convention in 1848. Stanton was not only a leader in women's suffrage and the early women's rights movement, but she was also a dedicated abolitionist. As a social activist, she fought to extend civil and voting rights to African Americans and women fighting against the limitations of racism and patriarchy. Although she died before women's suffrage was fully realized, she paved the way to later democratic victories such as the Nineteenth Amendment.

Franklin D. Roosevelt

Franklin Delano Roosevelt was the president of the United States toward the tail end of the Great Depression and throughout World War II. During his multiterm presidency, FDR expanded the role of the federal government, instituting many famous public works and social welfare projects through his New Deal policies. FDR's policies and public works helped pave the way to an entire New Deal Order in American history that gradually socialized many of the United States' federal programs. His blend of democratic-socialism has traditionally been celebrated as a victory for democracy and social welfare.

Dr. Martin Luther King Jr.

Dr. Martin Luther King Jr. helped begin the peak of the civil rights movement in the United States in the 1950s and 1960s, paving the way to the infamous Civil Rights Act of 1964. This legislation helped protect African Americans from unequal voting laws and institutional discrimination. Dr. King is applauded for his willingness to peacefully protest injustice in the name of American democracy.

Major Reform Movements in the U.S. History

Abolitionist Movement

The abolitionist movement—which was driven by an antislavery sentiment—gained steam in the early to mid-1800s as the United States became increasingly sectionalized in character. The abolitionist movement was not a monolithic, static phenomenon, but rather changed over time as different groups created different visions for solving the United States' slave issue. The American Colonization Society (founded 1816), for instance, helped create the African colony of Liberia as a refuge for freed and enslaved blacks living in the United States. Even within this movement, reformers held different visions. Some simply wanted to send black residents back to Africa for the benefit of creating a less diverse and conflicted society; others saw Liberia as a way to help blacks regain their cultures overseas. Other movements included the American Anti-Slavery Society, the Philadelphia Female Anti-Slavery Society, the Anti-Slavery Convention of American Women, and the Female Vigilant Society. Led and motivated by women, these organizations brought the abolitionist and women's rights movements closer together, planting the seeds of a coalition that would once again join together in American history during the heart of the civil rights movement of the 1950s and 1960s. Abolition was achieved in part through President Lincoln's Emancipation Proclamation (1863), which freed slave in Confederate states during the Civil War, and fully through the Thirteenth Amendment to the Constitution (1865), thanks in part to the efforts of these reformers.

Public Education Reform Movement

The public education reform movement also gained steam during the early to mid-1800s, as reformers like Horace Mann of Massachusetts pushed for universal and compensatory free public education for all children in the United States of America. Mann and other public school reformers believed that free and compensatory public education would strengthen national unity and civic engagement and better prepare adolescents to enter the U.S. economy as laborers, inventors, and businessmen as adults. Mann and his followers wanted to create a more literate citizenry. By the end of the nineteenth century, Mann's dreams were becoming a reality, as public primary school was made compensatory and free for all citizens. Gradually, the movement expanded to fight for free and compensatory secondary education.

Temperance Movement

The temperance movement emerged out of the spiritual fervor of the Second Great Awakening and the urban decline associated with the Industrial Revolution and early Progressive Era. As early as 1874, concerned women had established the Women's Christian Temperance Union (WCTU). Concerned about rising rates of alcoholism in fathers and male laborers, these women fought for the prohibition of alcohol alongside urban religious leaders and organizations. The temperance movement culminated in the passage of the Eighteenth Amendment in 1917—the so-called Prohibition Amendment—that prohibited the sale and consumption of alcohol. Prohibition was one of the most profound victories for progressive citizens and legislators; however, the amendment was eventually repealed due to rising organized crime rates and immediate backlash from citizens.

Prison Reform Movement

Throughout the eighteenth century, religious leaders and legislators came together to establish the prison reform movement, which moved the United States of America away from public forms of execution and embarrassment and toward the construction of institutions dedicated to criminal reform and individual penitence. During this time, Quakers and other religious leaders helped create the first penitentiaries, or prisons. The most famous of these penitentiaries was Eastern State Penitentiary in Philadelphia, Pennsylvania. Nevertheless, despite their efforts to create a more human form of behavioral correction, these institutions were often characterized by inhumane facilities and cruel forms of punishment (at least by today's standards). This movement inaugurated the creation of the prison-industrial complex in the United States, creating later reform movements such as Angela Davis's prison abolition movement.

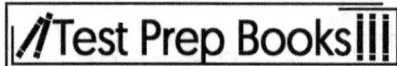

Women's Rights

Due to the Women's Liberation Movement and the creation of the National Organization for Women (NOW) in 1966, the 1960s and 1970s were an important time for women. Women gained the right to vote in 1920, but still were not on equal terms with men in many areas. Suffragist leader Alice Paul had introduced the Equal Rights Amendment (ERA) in 1923 to help bridge this gap. Congress finally passed the ERA in 1972 and sent it to the states for ratification. However, not all states ratified the amendment, and to date only a total of thirty-five have ratified it, which is three less than the thirty-eight required to pass. In the controversial 1973 court case *Roe vs. Wade*, the Supreme Court gave women the right to legally obtain abortions within the first three months of pregnancy.

Civil Rights Movement

Brown vs. the Board of Education prohibited segregation in 1954, but the Civil Rights Movement, led by the National Association for the Advancement of Colored People (NAACP) and such famous activists as Martin Luther King Jr. and Malcolm X, did not secure the enforcement of the Fourteenth Amendment until the passage of the Civil Rights Act of 1964, which outlawed discrimination based on gender, race, ethnicity, and religion. African American and Native American women, however, did not gain the right to vote until the Voting Rights Act of 1965, which enforced the voting rights articulated in the Fourteenth Amendment and Fifteenth Amendment. Section 5 of the Voting Rights Act prevented states with a history of discrimination from altering their voting laws without getting approval from the attorney general or a federal district court.

Civic Responsibilities

Civic responsibilities are the actions and values related to democratic government and participation. These actions serve people's communities and the government. Personal responsibilities are the ways people take care of themselves and their families. These responsibilities are part of their private lives.

Political Participation

Citizens express their political beliefs and public opinion through participation in politics. The conventional ways citizens can participate in politics in a democratic state include:

- Obeying laws
- Voting in elections
- Running for public office
- Staying interested in and informed of current events
- Learning U.S. history
- Attending public hearings to be informed and to express opinions on issues, especially on the local level
- Forming interest groups to promote common goals
- Forming political action committees (PACs) that raise money to influence policy decisions
- Petitioning government to create awareness of issues
- Campaigning for a candidate
- Contributing to campaigns
- Using mass media to express political ideas, opinions, and grievances
- Participating in jury duty

Voting

In a democratic state, the most common way to participate in politics is by voting for candidates in an election. Voting allows the citizens of a state to influence policy by selecting the candidates who share their views and make policy decisions that best suit their interests, or candidates who they believe are most capable of leading the country. In Canada, all citizens over 18—regardless of gender, race, or religion—are allowed to vote.

Government and Citizenship | Types of Political Systems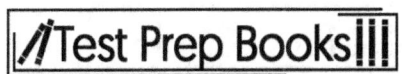

Since the Progressive movement and the increased social activism of the 1890s to the 1920s that sought to eliminate corruption in government, direct participation in politics through voting has increased. Citizens can participate by voting in the following types of elections:

- Direct primaries: Citizens can nominate candidates for public office.
- National, state, and municipal elections: Citizens elect their representatives in government.
- Recall elections: Citizens can petition the government to vote an official out of office before their term ends.
- Referendums: Citizens can vote directly on proposed laws or amendments to the state constitution.
- Voter initiatives: Citizens can petition their local or state government to propose laws that will be approved or rejected by voters.

Types of Political Systems

Major Political Ideas in History

Major Political Concepts

Politics is the process of governance, typically exercised through the enactment and enforcement of laws, over a community, most commonly a state. Political theory involves the study of politics, especially concerning the efficacy and legitimacy of those responsible for governance. The major concepts in political theory include power and authority. The concepts of power and authority are closely related but possess certain significant distinctions.

Power is the ability of a ruling body or political entity to influence the actions, behavior, and attitude of a person or group of people; in short, power implies a degree of control over a human community. In order to possess authority, the ruling body or political entity must be recognized as having the right and justification to exercise power. This is commonly referred to as legitimacy. In representative governments, authority is garnered from the citizens through democratic processes, but in more autocratic regimes, influential elites grant that authority. In some cases, a ruling body or political entity may possess authority recognized by its citizens or influential elites but lack the power to influence those citizens and political entities or effect change within the system of governance. When power and authority are not properly aligned, governments are extremely weak, often deadlocked, and at risk of collapse or revolution.

Government is the result of the decisions made by a society during the political process and is a physical manifestation of the political entity or ruling body. The government determines and enforces the power of the state. A government includes the formal institutions of a society with the power and authority to enact, enforce, and interpret laws. The many different forms of government are determined based on this delegation of power between those institutions. Government encompasses the functions of law, order, and justice and is responsible for maintaining the society.

Sovereignty refers to a political entity's right and power to self-govern, including enacting and enforcing its own taxes and laws without interference from external forces. A political entity may possess varying degrees of sovereignty, as some sovereign states may still be subject to influence by outside political entities. For example, the members of the European Union cede some sovereignty in order to enjoy membership. A state's sovereignty is legitimate when outside political entities recognize the right of the state to self-govern. Both sovereignty and legitimacy are requirements to form a state.

Governments provide different liberty and freedom, depending on the form of government that, in turn, is influenced by the states' shared history and culture. Philosophers started articulating defined rights and liberties

and arguing for their adoption and protection by the government during the Enlightenment. Liberalism advocates for increasing liberty and freedom in society and economics, while authoritarian regimes offer considerably less protection. The terms liberty and freedom both reference the same thing in society. Examples of liberty and freedom relate to speech, religion, press, economic pursuits, etc. The degrees and breadth of protections are context dependent, and they might be fluid and influenced by the political process. Many states delineate liberty and freedoms in their constitution. Rights and privileges are different because they involve something that is legal to do or possible according to the government sanctioning the action; thus, rights and privileges are typically more easily revoked from both specific individuals and larger communities.

A right is a freedom, protection, or entitlement afforded to a person. In political theory, a right or privilege specifically refers to that which is granted to the citizens of a political territory according to the legal system or the social conventions of the society. Rights and privileges typically cannot be removed without due process under the law, although this depends on the form of government. Like the distinction between liberty and freedom, the difference between rights and privileges is indistinguishable. They are often the concrete representations of liberty and freedom in a society; as rights and privileges grow in number and strength, the society enjoys more liberty and freedom. Rights are the privileges provided by the government; however, the term right is commonly used to refer to a privilege of higher status that receives more scrutiny and protection from the state, usually requiring more due process to revoke or alter.

Example of a right: the right to vote

Example of a privilege: the privilege to receive a driver's license

Governments must establish law, order, and justice through the government's political institutions. Protecting citizens' rights under the systems of laws, as well as effectively punishing the violators, is one of government's foundational responsibilities. Establishing law, order, and justice is an exercise in sovereignty—states that do not impose law and order under a reasonable standard of justice risk public unrest and challenges to the regime's legitimacy.

Law is the system of rules, policies, and regulations that govern behavior that is enacted by a political entity and enforced by the formal institutions created by the political entity. Order refers to each citizen, institution, and political entity acting as the law. Political entities secure order through the execution of laws through its enforcing institutions, like the police and justice system.

The term justice often refers to the fairness in the political entity's treatment of its citizens. When discussing its relation to law and order, justice refers to the necessary, agreed-upon consequences for failure to act according to the law. In political theory, justice is the social contract between the political entity and its citizens in which all parties involved have agreed upon what is considered fair in a society and what the consequences of acting contrary to the law should be.

Citizenship is the political term referring to the legal status of an individual recognized by the state or government as a protected member. Citizens are subject to the laws of their state and granted the rights and liberties afforded by that state, including the right to vote and be elected to office.

Citizenship does not necessarily denote nationality, which refers to the relationship between an individual and a nation, rather than a legal status. Nationality is a component of citizenship, but nationality does not afford an individual any of the rights associated with citizenship of a state without official sanction from the state.

Oftentimes, **absolute monarchies** legitimized their right to supreme authority by **divine right**. For example, King Louis XIV claimed a divine right to rule based on God's mandate, meaning he rejected any earthly power attempting to restrict or overthrow his rule. The primary effect of centralized state power was the elimination of feudalism.

Absolute monarchs replaced feudal lords with large centralized bureaucracies and militaries under their hierarchical control. The consolidation of political and economic power facilitated colonization because absolute monarchs had the military strength and financial resources to sponsor expeditions. Additionally, absolute monarchies contributed to the growth of international trade because they were able to fund navies that could protect merchants and establish trading posts.

Social contract, an idea drawn from the teachings of Thomas Hobbes, was an integral part in the creation of the government. This theory is parallel to popular sovereignty in that it places importance on the consent of the governed. The social contract expresses the basic expectations of the people for their government. The people give up certain rights and they consent to be governed in exchange for the government protection of their other rights. This again draws on the idea of the people choosing to have their government, instead of a government being forced upon them.

Thomas Jefferson included the phrase, "Laws of nature and nature's God," in the Declaration of Independence to justify American independence. The phrase, "laws of nature," refers to the natural state of the world, and Enlightenment philosophers, such as John Locke and Thomas Hobbes, believed that humans were inherently free beings under the laws of nature. Locke and Hobbes believed people entered into a social contract in which they surrendered freedom in exchange for forming a state to protect them. Likewise, "nature's God," means that a divine being created the order of nature, and this order in turn endowed people with reason and freedom to decide how they will be governed.

The right to resist illegitimate governments, explicitly and frequently cited in the Declaration of Independence, was likewise based on Enlightenment philosophy. Under contract theory, if the government violates the rights it has guaranteed, then the people have the right to resist and overthrow the government. All representative governments implicitly acknowledge this right to resistance because political representation is based on popular sovereignty, meaning that citizens are the ultimate source of political legitimacy. However, the act of withdrawing sovereignty is inherently contentious and has historically led to sectarian armed conflicts.

Philosophies of Individuals in World History

Major Political Theorists
Hammurabi's Code of Laws, around 1750 BC
The Babylonian king Hammurabi established a complex set of laws, known as the Code of Hammurabi, which would set a precedent for future legal systems. This code was based on the idea of retributive justice; the punishment must match the crime. The collection of 282 laws covered economic, criminal, and civil issues.

Aristotle, 384 BC to 322 BC
A student of Plato, Aristotle was a Greek philosopher best known for his theories of rationality and ethics. In *Politics*, Aristotle asserted that man is a political animal and that man must actively participate in politics to further the political well-being of the city-state. He believed that man could only attain the happy life that nature intended through noble acts that bettered the community in which they lived. To this end, he envisioned an ideal society in which the most virtuous and knowledgeable men ruled and the citizens lived virtuous lives in the service of their city-state. Aristotle is one of the leading contributors to Western philosophy and, later, Liberalism. The Roman Republic applied much of his theories on ethics and civics to their government.

Justinian's Code of Laws, 529 A.D. to 534 A.D.
The Code of Justinian, also known as the *Corpus Juris Civilis*, is a fundamental collection of jurisprudence. It was intended to be the complete collection of laws governing the Byzantine Empire. The Code of Justinian is one of the

most influential pieces of legislation in world history, serving as the basis for future civil law jurisdictions and canon law of the Roman Catholic Church.

Magna Carta, 1215

The Magna Carta was originally written as a peace treaty to resolve issues between King John of England and his barons. The document consisted of sixty-three clauses that addressed specific complaints of the barons who were rebelling against the king's rule. However, many of the underlying principles, including the idea that all people, even the king, are bound by laws, became important values used in many political documents since its writing.

Niccolo Machiavelli, 1469 – 1527

Machiavelli was an Italian diplomat, politician, and historian during the Italian Renaissance. He is most known for his infamous political treatise, *The Prince,* which inspired the political philosophy known as Machiavellianism. In *The Prince,* Machiavelli instructed rulers that it is better to be feared than to be loved and asserted that a ruler must be willing to commit any acts necessary to maintain power and establish the stability of their society. He advocated violence, deceit, and immoral acts and advised rulers to seek out and eliminate any potential political rivals within the community. Machiavellianism prioritizes maintaining and consolidating power over all else.

Thomas Hobbes, 1588 – 1679

Thomas Hobbes was an English philosopher most notable as being the founder of social contract theory. In his 1651 book, *Leviathan,* Hobbes stated that without a strong central authority, the people would live in constant fear; they would go without industry, knowledge, or commodities if there was no system for enforcing good behavior As such, he asserted that the people enacted social contracts with ruling bodies, in which the people agreed to submit to the laws and limitations imposed by the ruling body in exchange for the protection and quality of life afforded to them. Hobbes was responsible for founding many of the fundamentals of liberal thought, stating that all men are naturally equal and that a ruling body may only gain legitimacy through the consent of the people.

John Locke, 1632 – 1704

John Locke was an English philosopher influenced by Thomas Hobbes' social contract theory. Though he agreed with the theory on some points, he argued against Hobbes' assertion that man requires protection from a ruling body in order to maintain a civilized society, Instead, Locke believed that men are rational and tolerant beings by nature. Locke is considered the *Father of Liberalism*. His works on political theory include the famous *Two Treatises on Government*, which contributed significantly to modern ideals of liberal theory, including espousing the need to protect the right to life, liberty, health, and possessions. Locke's philosophy on rights and self-government influenced the writers of the Declaration of Independence.

Jean-Jacques Rousseau, 1712 – 1778

Jean-Jacques Rousseau was a philosopher, writer, and composer during the Enlightenment in France whose political writings, *Discourse on Equality* and *The Social Contract,* influenced aspects of the French Revolutionary War and many modern political theories. Rousseau thought man was free in the more primitive stage, and this freedom could only be maintained in a state if the people remained sovereign through representative government. He advocated for religious equality and argued that the people are sovereign, rather than a divinely empowered monarch, and that the people should have the right to rule themselves. His work was banned in France, but his ideals influenced the people and inspired many of the political reforms that led to the Revolutionary War.

Immanuel Kant, 1724 – 1804

A German philosopher, Kant is best known for the set of ideas known as Kantianism, which states that individuals possess dignity and deserve respect. Although more famous for his philosophy, Kant discussed political theory in his essay, *Perpetual Peace: A Philosophical Sketch,* where he argued that world peace may be achieved through universal democracy and international cooperation. In this work, he explained that, in order to end all wars and create lasting peace, all states must form constitutional republics in which elected officials adhere to the rule of the constitutional law to govern the state.

John Stuart Mills, 1806 – 1873

John Stuart Mills, an English philosopher and political economist, was considered the most influential English-speaking philosopher of the nineteenth century and was best known for being the first member of Parliament to advocate women's suffrage. His book *On Liberty* promoted utilitarianism, which advocates that people should always make decisions based on what would achieve the greatest utility, or well-being. In his work, Mills sought to limit the power exercised upon the individual by any ruling body and stated that moral actions are those that promote utility and increase individuals' and society's well-being. He called for limited constraints upon individual behavior that only restrict those actions that cause harm to others.

Karl Marx, 1818 – 1883

Karl Marx, a philosopher, social scientist, historian, and revolutionary, is considered one of the most influential Socialist thinkers of the nineteenth century. His ideas became known as Marxism, and Marx heavily influenced powerful Socialist and Communist leaders, such as Vladimir Lenin, with his 1848 pamphlet *The Communist Manifesto*. In this pamphlet, he explained that in a capitalist society, perpetual class struggle exists in which a ruling class (bourgeois) controls the means of production and exploits the working class (proletariat), who are forced to sell labor for wages. He advocated for the working class to rebel against the ruling class and establish a classless society with collective ownership of the means of production. He envisioned world history as a series of stages in which capitalism eventually collapses into Communism.

Vladimir Lenin, 1870 – 1924

As a leading figure in the Russian Revolution and eventual founding of the Soviet Union, Lenin was one of the most controversial and influential political figures in the international Communist movement. Strongly influenced by Karl Marx, Lenin established the one-party system of government, which advocates pure Communism: a classless, egalitarian society in which the people abide by one rule—"From each according to his ability, to each according to his needs," a slogan coined by Marx. Lenin led the Bolsheviks into power after the Russian Revolution, and his Communist Party dominated the centralized one-party system. Lenin redistributed land among the peasants and nationalized most private industries, and he suppressed all political opposition with aggression, most notably during the Red Terror. Lenin advocated for Communist revolution across the world. Joseph Stalin, who further consolidated power of the increasingly authoritarian centralized government, succeeded Lenin as head of the Soviet Union.

How Governments have Affected Cultural Values and Provided for Social Control

Throughout history, governments have reflected the cultural values of nation-states because they are typically run by political leaders who in some way represent the people they govern, or have risen up from the populace they serve. In rare cases, such as colonial governments, politics do not always reflect the cultural values of the populace. Nevertheless, in most modern instances, the government remains a reflection of the sociohistorical values of a particular group or set of groups.

In some historical cases, governments can suppress the cultural values of the populace through aggressive means of social control. Authoritarian or oligarchical governments, for instance, usually serve a particular class or group of people over the masses. Some dictatorial regimes in Central and South America, for example, have maintained social control through fear and violence. Nazi Germany is another example of an authoritarian regime that controlled its citizens through violence and propaganda. Liberal democracy attempts to dismantle global authoritarianism by reflecting the voices and values of the populace. In some cases, however, even democratic institutions can verge on social control and coercion; some democratic countries tamper with voting practices to maintain hegemony over certain marginalized groups.

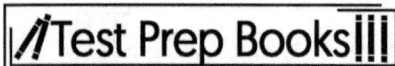

US Constitutional Republic and Other Contemporary Forms of Government

Forms of Government and Types of Regimes

Government is the physical manifestation of the political entity or ruling body of a state. It includes the formal institutions that manage and maintain a society. The form of government does not determine the state's economic system, though these concepts are often closely tied. Many forms of government are based on a society's economic system. However, while the form of government refers to the methods by which a society is managed, the term economy refers to the management of resources in a society. Many forms of government exist, often as hybrids of two or more forms of government or economic systems. Forms of government can be distinguished based on protection of civil liberties, protection of rights, distribution of power, power of government, and principles of Federalism.

Regime is the term used to describe the ruling body and corresponding political conditions under which citizens live. A regime is defined by the amount of power the government possesses and the number of people who comprise the ruling body. It is closely related to the form of government because the form of government largely creates the political conditions. Regimes are governmental bodies that control both the form and the limit of term of their office. For example, authoritarianism is an example of a form of government and type of regime. A regime is considered to be ongoing until the culture, priorities, and values of the government are altered, either through a peaceful transition of power or a violent overthrow of the current regime.

The forms of government operated by regimes include:

Aristocracy

An aristocracy is a form of government composed of a small group of wealthy rulers, either holding hereditary titles of nobility or membership in a higher class. Variations of aristocratic governments include:

- *Oligarchy*: form of government where political power is consolidated in the hands of a small group of people
- *Plutocracy*: type of oligarchy where a wealthy, elite class dominates the state and society

Though no aristocratic governments exist today, it was the dominant form of government during ancient times, including the:

- Vassals and lords during the Middle Ages, especially in relation to feudalism
- City-state of Sparta in ancient Greece

Communism

Communism is a radical political ideology that seeks to establish common ownership over production and abolish social status and money. Communists believe that the world is split between two social classes—capitalists and the working class (often referred to as the proletariat). Communist politics assert that conflict arises from the inequality between the ruling class and the working class; thus, communism favors a classless society. Political philosophers Karl Marx and Friedrich Engels argued that Communism is society's destiny since capitalism would ultimately collapse. The collapse of the Soviet Union weakened Communism across the world.

Republican Form of Government

America's Founding Fathers wanted to break away from the monarchy style of rule they had fled from in England. There, equality and freedoms were suppressed or non-existent. They decided to form a democratic style of government and preserving liberties was the core ideal. They realized that this style of government must have checks and balances in order to run smoothly and ensure the rights and freedoms of its citizens. Therefore, they devised a system of three separate branches—legislative, judicial, and executive. Although each has different responsibilities, the three branches work together to ensure that no one section of the government exerts too much power, and the rights of U.S. citizens are not overlooked or disregarded. Realizing the U.S. was such a huge landmass with many citizens spread out over a large area, they decided on a type of democracy referred to as a democratic republic—governed by the people in the form of elected representatives.

Democracy

Democracy is a form of government in which the people act as the ruling body by electing representatives to voice their views. Forms of democratic governments include:

- Direct democracy: democratic government in which the people make direct decisions on specific policies by majority vote of all eligible voters, like in ancient Athens

- Representative democracy: democratic government in which the people elect representatives to vote in a legislative body. This form of government is also known as a representative republic or indirect democracy. Representative democracy is currently the most popular form of government in the world.

The presidential and parliamentary systems are the most common forms of representative democracy. In the presidential system, the executive operates in its own branch distinct from the legislature. In addition, the people directly elect the president, and the president is typically both the head of state and head of government. Examples of presidential systems include Brazil, Nigeria, and the United States.

In the parliamentary system, the prime minister serves as the head of government. The legislative branch, typically a parliament, elects the prime minister and also has the authority to replace the prime minister with a vote of no confidence. This practically means that the parliament has considerable influence over the office of prime minister. Parliamentary systems often include a president as the head of state, but the office is mostly ceremonial, functioning like a figurehead. Examples of parliamentary systems include Germany, Australia, and Pakistan.

The presidential system is better designed to distribute power between separate branches of government, which theoretically provides more stability. Presidents serve for a limited number of years, while prime ministers serve until death, resignation, or dismissal. In the parliamentary system, the interconnectedness between parliament and the prime minister facilitates efficient governance, capable of adjusting to developing situations. In contrast, the presidential system is more prone to political gridlock because there is no direct connection between the legislative and executive branches. The legislature in a presidential system cannot replace the executive, like in the parliamentary system. The separation of powers in a presidential system can lead to disagreement between the executive and legislature, causing gridlock and other delays in governance.

Major Forms of Government in History

Monarchy

Monarchy is a form of government in which the state is ruled by a sovereign leader. This leader is called a monarch and is typically a hereditary ruler. Monarchs have often justified their power due to some divine right to rule, like the ancient Chinese Mandate of Heaven. Types of monarchies include:

- Absolute monarchy: a monarchy in which the monarch has complete power over the people and the state

- Constitutional monarchy: a type of monarchy in which the citizens of the state are protected by a constitution, and a separate branch, typically a parliament, makes legislative decisions. The monarch and legislature would share power, like in England during the Enlightenment.

- Crowned republic: a type of monarchy in which the monarch holds only a ceremonial position and the people hold sovereignty over the state. It is defined by the monarch's lack of executive power.

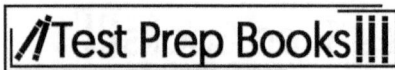

Examples of monarchies:

- Kingdom of Saudi Arabia is an absolute monarchy.
- Australia is a crowned republic.

Authoritarian

An authoritarian state is one in which a single party rules indefinitely. The ruling body operates with unrivaled control and complete power to make policy decisions, including the restriction of denying civil liberties such as freedom of speech, press, religion, and protest. Forms of authoritarian governments include autocracy, dictatorship, and totalitarianism.

- The Soviet Union, Nazi Germany, and modern-day North Korea are all examples of states with authoritarian governments.

Classical Republicanism

Classical republicanism developed from Renaissance Era reflections on the governmental practices of the Roman Empire in classical antiquity. According to classical republic theory, the Roman Empire created a government based on the principles of popular sovereignty, natural rights, and devotion to citizens for the common good. These principles were some of the major driving forces for the American Revolution and the founding of the United States of America. Both the Articles of Confederation and the US Constitution employ classical republican principles, pointing to the popular sovereignty of each state and the civic virtue of its leaders and citizens. The United States of America is still, in many ways, a republican nation, though it has democratized rapidly since its inception.

Liberal Democracy

Liberal democracy has its roots in Greek civilization and American history. Ancient Greece is often referred to as the cradle of Western civilization because its governmental institutions continue to influence modern-day nation-states. The Athenian form of democratic leadership has influenced the democratization process in the United States of America. Initially founded as a republic, the United States has adopted the Greek tradition of democracy, though it has limited democracy through its republic electorate system. Liberal democracy today is, therefore, manifested in the limited democratic systems of the United States. The United States is a beacon of electorate-based democracy, and since World War I, has become a leader in global democratization processes. Nevertheless, the United States limited liberal democracy does not necessarily promulgate popular democratic systems, because many leaders in the United States continue to believe that pure popular democracy is chaos. Still, citizenship in a liberal democracy bestows upon U.S. citizens voting responsibilities and individual human rights. Citizens in this type of democratic system are eligible to run for office.

Totalitarianism

Democracy runs counter to totalitarian forms of government; democracy and totalitarianism rest on different poles on the political spectrum. Totalitarian governments believe that no single sector of society can exist outside the direct/total control of the state. Both fascist and communist governments can fall under the broader umbrella of totalitarianism. All totalitarian governments—fascist or communist in nature—believe they are acting in the best interest of the citizenship by enforcing complete conformity to state ideals.

Democratic-Republican Government

As a result of both revolutionary and industrial pressures in Europe and the New World, many nations began to democratize in the early nineteenth century, which means they began to quickly gravitate toward traditional notions of popular sovereignty, which were first established by Greek philosophers. The democratic fervor of the era helped expand voting rights—first to working-class men, and eventually to all men (black and white) and women. Since **democracy** is based on popular suffrage, or voting, it makes sense that the logical progression globally throughout the nineteenth and early twentieth centuries was a gradual march toward universal suffrage in the Western world. Democracy, often labeled as chaos by its challengers, became the dominant political ideology of the United States and Latin America. In the United States, democracy took on a more limited form because of the Electoral College, which placed important voting rights in the hands of appointed officials. But in Latin America, many governments adopted popular forms of democracy that elected officials through direct votes.

Classical **liberalism** was not in direct conflict with democracy, but it did not promote popular sovereignty in the same manner. While classical liberalism, which arose from Enlightenment thinking and capitalist enterprises, was largely a political philosophy, much of its philosophical ponderings focused on the role of government in the political economy. Championed by such political thinkers as **John Locke**, author of *Second Treatise of Government* (1689) and **Adam Smith**, author of *The Wealth of Nations* (1776), classical liberalism promoted the free market, noting that freedom was contingent upon the economic self-interests of individuals. Liberalism, therefore, became very critical of extensive government intervention and the **welfare states** (i.e., a government that always watches out for the welfare of its people). Classical liberals championed a minimal state that protected the rights of individuals but did not interfere with the free market.

Enlightenment values inevitably found their way into some of the most fundamental, paradigm-shifting governance documents of the era. These documents include the American Declaration of Independence, the French *Declaration of the Rights of Man and Citizen*, and Bolivar's *Letter from Jamaica*. They helped fundamentally alter the governance structures of existing political authorities by disseminating revolutionary and democratic ideals.

Originally, during the American Revolution and the Age of the Early Republic, leaders of the United States of America envisioned the creation of a virtuous civic republic modeled after the governmental practices of the Roman Empire. Civic representation was a key component to this early republican system. Equality and popular sovereignty were embedded into the fiber of the Early Republic. These values, over time, gradually incorporated principles of Athenian democracy, paving the way to a mixed democratic-republican system. Gradually, the voting base of the United States expanded from only including white landowners to also including working-class whites, blacks, Native Americans, and finally women. This democratizing process was fueled by both popular uprisings and religious sentiments. American populism slowly chipped away at the parameters of the classical republican model, incorporating more popular practices. Nevertheless, the United States remains a democratic-republic rather than a popular democracy despite its historical populist undercurrents.

Practice Quiz

1. The presidential and parliamentary systems differ in which of the following ways?
    a. The presidential system establishes a separation of powers.
    b. The legislature elects the chief executive in a presidential system.
    c. Voters directly elect the prime minister in a parliamentary system.
    d. The parliamentary system never includes a president.

2. In the American election system, where do the candidates ultimately receive the nomination from their party?
    a. At the primary
    b. At the caucus
    c. At the debates
    d. At the party convention

3. Which one of the following most accurately describes a consequence of social contract theory?
    a. Social contract theory incentivized imperial conquests and colonization.
    b. Social contract theory contributed to an intense period of revolutions.
    c. Social contract theory incentivized an expansion of international trade networks.
    d. Social contract theory led to the growth of state power.

4. What are the two main parts of the federal legislative branch?
    a. President and vice president
    b. Federal and state
    c. District court and court of appeals
    d. Senate and House of Representatives

5. What is NOT a responsibility for citizens of democracy?
    a. To stay aware of current issues and history
    b. To avoid political action
    c. To actively vote in elections
    d. To understand and obey laws

See answers on the next page.

Answer Explanations

1. A: The presidential system establishes a separation of powers. In the presidential system, voters directly elect the chief executive, and the presidential system establishes a separation of powers between different branches of government. In contrast, the parliament elects the chief executive, and the increased collaboration and dependency creates a more responsive government. Choices *B* and *C* confuse how the executive is elected in each system. Choice *D* is incorrect because many parliamentary systems include a president, though the status of head of state is often purely ceremonial.

2. D: The two major political parties hold conventions to nominate their presidential candidate. The delegates are awarded based on candidates' performance in the primary elections or caucuses vote at the party convention to select the nominee. Primaries and caucuses are the democratic contests held by each state to award their delegates. The candidates participate in debates on the campaign issues, but they do not receive the nomination at debates.

3. B: According to social contract theory, if the state fails to fulfill its obligations, then the contract is broken. Because the contract is broken, people are released and free to form a new state. For example, French revolutionaries claimed the monarchy had broken the social contract by denying citizens basic liberties and legal protections. Social contract theory didn't incentivize imperialism or colonization; if anything, it did the opposite. International trade isn't directly related to social contract theory. Although a firm social contract would theoretically strengthen the state, social contract theory didn't directly lead to the growth of state power.

4. D: The president and vice president are part of the executive branch, not the legislative branch. The question focuses specifically on the federal level, so state government should be excluded from consideration. As for the district court and the court of appeals, they are part of the judicial branch. The legislative branch is made up of Congress, which consists of the House of Representatives and the Senate.

5. B: To avoid involvement in political processes such as voting is antithetical to the principles of a democracy. Therefore, the principal responsibility of citizens is the opposite, and they should be steadily engaged in the political processes that determine the course of government.

Economics and Science, Technology, and Society

Economic Concepts and Types of Economic Systems

Scarcity and Opportunity Costs

Economics is the study of human behavior in response to the production, consumption, and distribution of assets or wealth. Economics can help individuals or societies make decisions for themselves dependent upon their needs, wants, and resources. Economics is divided into two subgroups: microeconomics and macroeconomics.

Microeconomics is the study of individual or small group behaviors and patterns related to markets of goods and services. It specifically looks at single factors that could affect these behaviors and decisions. For example, the use of coupons in a grocery store could affect an individual's product choice, quantity purchased, and overall savings that could be directed to a different purchase. **Microeconomics** encompasses the study of many things, including scarcity, choice, opportunity costs, economics systems, factors of production, supply and demand, market efficiency, the role of government, distribution of income, and product markets.

Macroeconomics examines a much larger scale of the economy. It focuses on how aggregate factors such as demand, output, and spending habits affect the people in a society or nation. For example, if a national company moves its production overseas to save on costs, how will production, labor, and capital be affected? Macroeconomics explores any and all criterion and microeconomic elements that have an effect on the economy. Since macroeconomics concerns large-scale economic elements, it is used by governments and businesses to create economic policies and procedures.

Microeconomics

Scarcity

People have different needs and wants, and the question arises, are the resources available to supply those needs and wants? Limited resources and high demand create scarcity. When a product is scarce, there is a short supply of it. For example, when the newest version of a cellphone is released, people line up to buy the phone or put their name on a wait list if the phone is not immediately available. The new cellphone may become a scarce commodity. In turn, the phone company may raise their prices, knowing that people may be willing to pay more for an item in such high demand. If a competing company lowers the cost of the phone but has contingencies, such as extended contracts or hidden fees, the buyer will still have the opportunity to purchase the scarce product. Limited resources and extremely high demand create scarcity and, in turn, cause companies to acquire opportunity costs.

Choice and Opportunity Costs

On a large scale, governments and communities have to assess different opportunity costs when it comes to using taxpayers' money. Should the government build a new school, repair roads, or allocate funds to local hospitals? Each choice has a tradeoff, and decision makers must choose which option they think is best.

Economic Systems

Economic systems determine what is being produced, who is producing it, who receives the product, and the money generated by the sale of the product. There are two basic types of economic systems: market economies (including free and competitive markets), and planned or command economies.

- Market Economies are characterized by:
    - Privately owned businesses, groups, or individuals providing goods or services based on demand.
    - Demand determines the types of goods and services produced (supply).
    - Two types: competitive market and free market.

Competitive Market	Free Market
Due to the large number of both buyers and sellers, there is no way any one seller or buyer can control the market or price.	Voluntary private trades between buyers and sellers determine markets and prices without government intervention or monopolies.

- Planned or Command Economies:
    - Government or central authority determines market prices of goods and services.
    - Government or central authority determines what is being produced and the quantity of production.
    - Advantage: large number of shared goods such as public services (transportation, schools, or hospitals).
    - Disadvantages of command economies include wastefulness of resources.

Factors of Production

There are four factors of production:

1. Land: both renewable and nonrenewable resources
2. Labor: effort put forth by people to produce goods and services
3. Capital: the tools used to create goods and services
4. Entrepreneurs: persons who combine land, labor, and capital to create new goods and services

The four factors of production are used to create goods and services to make economic profit. All four factors strongly impact one another.

Distribution of Income

Distribution of income refers to how wages are spread across a society or segments of a society. If everyone made the same amount of money, the distribution of income would be equal. That is not the case in most societies. Wealth varies among people and companies. Income inequality gaps are present in America and many other nations. Taxes provide an option to redistribute income or wealth because they provide revenue to build new infrastructure and provide cash benefits to some of the poorest members in society.

Product Markets

Product markets are where goods and services are bought and sold. Product markets provide a place for sellers to offer goods and services and for consumers to purchase them. The annual value of goods and services exchanged throughout the year is measured by the Gross Domestic Product (GDP), a monetary measure of goods and services

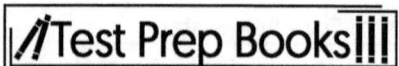

made either quarterly or annually. Department stores, gas stations, grocery stores, and other retail stores are all examples of product markets. However, product markets do not include any raw or unfinished materials.

Theory of the Firm

The behavior of firms is composed of several theories varying between short- and long-term goals. There are four basic firm behaviors: perfect competition, profit maximization, short run, and long run. Each firm follows a pattern, depending on its desired outcome. Theory of the Firm posits that firms, after conducting market research, make decisions that will maximize their profits.

- Perfect competition:
    - In perfect competition, several businesses are selling the same product simultaneously.
    - There are so many businesses and consumers that none will directly impact the market.
    - Each business and consumer is aware of the competing businesses and markets.
- Profit maximization:
    - Firms decide the quantity of a product that needs to be produced in order to receive maximum profit gains. Profit is the total amount of revenue made after subtracting costs.
- Short run:
    - A short amount of time where fixed prices cannot be adjusted
    - The quantity of the product depends on the varying amount of labor. Less labor means less product.
- Long run:
    - An amount of time where fixed prices can be adjusted
    - Firms try to maximize production while minimizing labor costs.

Overall, microeconomics operates on a small scale, focusing on how individuals or small groups use and assign resources.

Macroeconomics

Macroeconomics analyzes the economy as a whole. It studies unemployment, interest rates, price levels, and national income, which are all factors that can affect the nation as a whole, and not just individual households. Macroeconomics studies all large factors to determine how, or if, they will affect future trend patterns of production, consumption, and economic growth.

Measures of Economic Performance

Measurements of economic performance determine if an economy is growing, stagnant, or deteriorating. To measure the growth and sustainability of an economy, several indicators can be used. Economic indicators provide data that economists can use to determine if there are faulty processes or if some form of intervention is needed.

One of the main indicators of a country's economic performance is the Gross Domestic Product (GDP). GDP growth provides important information that can be used to determine fiscal or financial policies. The GDP does not measure income distribution, quality of life, or losses due to natural disasters. For example, if a community lost everything to a hurricane, it would take a long time to rebuild the community and stabilize its economy. That is why there is a need to take into account more balanced performance measures when factoring overall economic performance.

Other indicators used to measure economic performance are unemployment or employment rates, inflation, savings, investments, surpluses and deficits, debt, labor, trade terms, the HDI (Human Development Index), and the HPI (Human Poverty Index).

Unemployment

Unemployment occurs when an individual does not have a job, is actively trying to find employment, and is not getting paid. Official unemployment rates do not factor in the number of people who have stopped looking for work, but true unemployment rates do.

There are three types of unemployment: cyclical, frictional, and structural.

Cyclical
Comes as a result of the regular economic cycle and variations in supply and demand; This usually occurs during a recession
Frictional
When workers voluntarily leave their jobs; An example would be a person changing careers.
Structural
When companies' needs change and a person no longer possesses the skills needed.

Given the nature of a market economy and the fluctuations of the labor market, a 100% employment rate is impossible to reach.

Inflation

Inflation is when the value of money decreases and the cost of goods and services increases over time. Supply, demand, and money reserves all affect inflation. Generally, inflation is measured by the **Consumer Price Index (CPI)**, a tool that tracks price changes of goods and services. The CPI measures goods and services such as gasoline, cars, clothing, and food. When the cost of goods and services increase, manufacturers may reduce the quantity they produce due to lower demand. This decreases the purchasing power of the consumer. Basically, as more money is printed, it holds less and less value in purchasing power. When inflation occurs, consumers spend and save less because their currency is worth less. However, if inflation occurs steadily over time, the people can better plan and prepare for future necessities.

Inflation can vary from year to year, usually never fluctuating more than 2%. Central banks try to prevent drastic increases or decreases of inflation to prohibit prices from rising or falling too far. Inflation can also vary based on different monetary currencies. Although rare, any country's economy may experience hyperinflation (when inflation rates increase to over 50%), while other economies may experience deflation (when the cost of goods and services decrease over time). Deflation occurs when the inflation rate drops below zero percent.

Business Cycle

A business cycle is when the Gross Domestic Product (GDP) moves downward and upward over a long-term growth trend. These cycles help determine where the economy currently stands, as well as where it could be heading. Business cycles usually occur almost every six years and have four phases: expansion, peak, contraction, and trough. Here are some characteristics of each phase:

- Expansion:
    - Increased employment rates and economic growth
    - Production and sales increase
    - On a graph, expansion is where the lines climb.
- Peak:
    - Employment rates are at or above full employment and the economy is at maximum productivity.
    - On a graph, the peak is the top of the hill, where expansion has reached its maximum.

- Contraction:
  - When growth starts slowing
  - Unemployment is on the rise.
  - On a graph, contraction is where the graph begins to slide back down or contract.
- Trough:
  - The cycle has hit bottom and is waiting for the next cycle to start again.
  - On a graph, the trough is the bottom of the contraction prior to when it starts to climb back up.

When the economy is expanding or booming, the business cycle is going from a trough to a peak. When the economy is headed down and toward a recession, the business cycle is going from a peak to a trough.

Four phases of a business cycle:

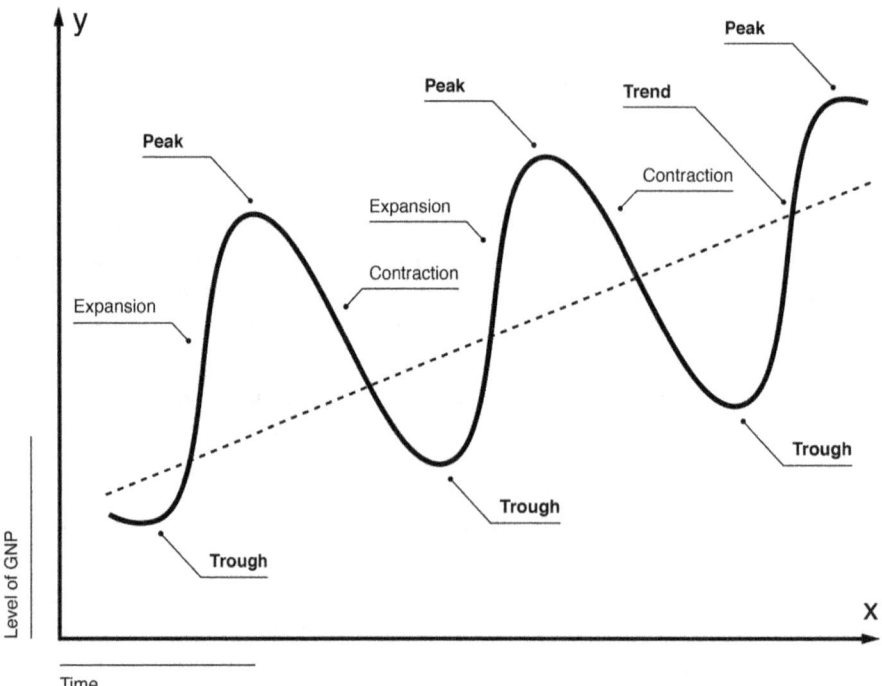

Circular-Flow Model of the Economy

The circular-flow model of the economy (depicted below) illustrates the interdependence between households and businesses. In both the resource market (households sell; businesses buy) and product market (businesses sell; households buy), inputs and outputs are exchanged based on the model of the market. Businesses (buy resources; sell products) accrue costs from the resource market, but gain resources from these costs. Households (sell resources; buy products) provide the resource market with labor, land, capital, and entrepreneurial ability, receiving money income (wages, rents, interest, profits) from the resource market. Households interact with the product market by providing consumptive expenditures in return for goods and services. Likewise, businesses provide goods and services to the product market in return for the incoming revenue from the households.

Circular Flow Model

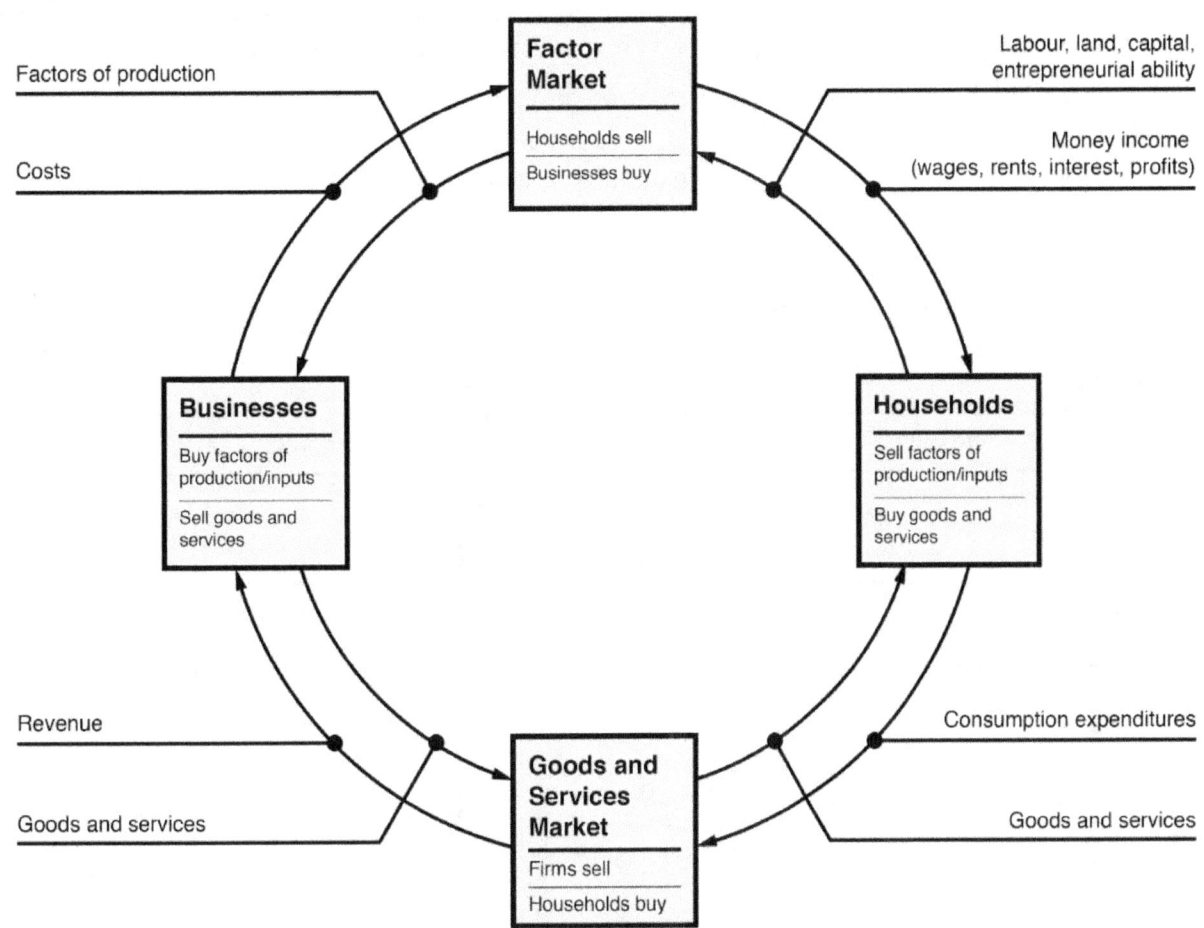

Supply and Demand

Shifts in supply and demand inevitably affect the prices of goods and services while also affecting the relationship of supply and demand to one another. Take the graphs below as evidence of the changes initiated by shifts in supply and demand. An increase in demand moves the demand curve to the right (D1 to D2) on Panel (a). The equilibrium price rises in this case. The actual supply curve (S1) does not shift on the graph in this instance; rather, the intersection between supply and demand experiences a slight movement. A decrease in demand shifts the demand curve to the left rather than the right (D1 to D2 on Panel (b). The equilibrium price falls in this case. The supply curve does not shift; rather, there is movement along the supply curve. An increase in supply will shift the supply curve to the right (S1 to S2) on Panel (c). The equilibrium price will fall with this shift. In this case, the demand curve (D1) does not move; rather, the intersection between supply and demand experiences a slight movement. An increase in supply shifts the supply curve to the left (S1 to S2) on Panel (d). The equilibrium price rises in this instance, and the quantity demanded increases. In this case, the demand curve (D1) does not move; rather, the intersection between supply and demand experiences a slight movement.

Factors for an increase in demand can include a shift in preferences that lead to greater consumption, a lower price for a complementary good/service, a higher price for a substitute good/service, an increase in income, or an increase in population.

Factors for a decrease in demand can include a shift in preferences that lead to a decrease in consumption, an increase in the price of a complementary good/service, a reduction in a substitute good/service, a reduction in income, or a reduction in population.

Factors leading to an increase in supply can include a reduction in the price of input/labor, a decline in returns for alternative uses of the inputs, an improvement in manufacturing or technology, or an increase in the number of firms.

Factors leading to a decrease in supply can include an increase in the price of input/labor, an increase in returns for alternative uses of the inputs, manufacturing or technology problems, or a reduction in the number of firms.

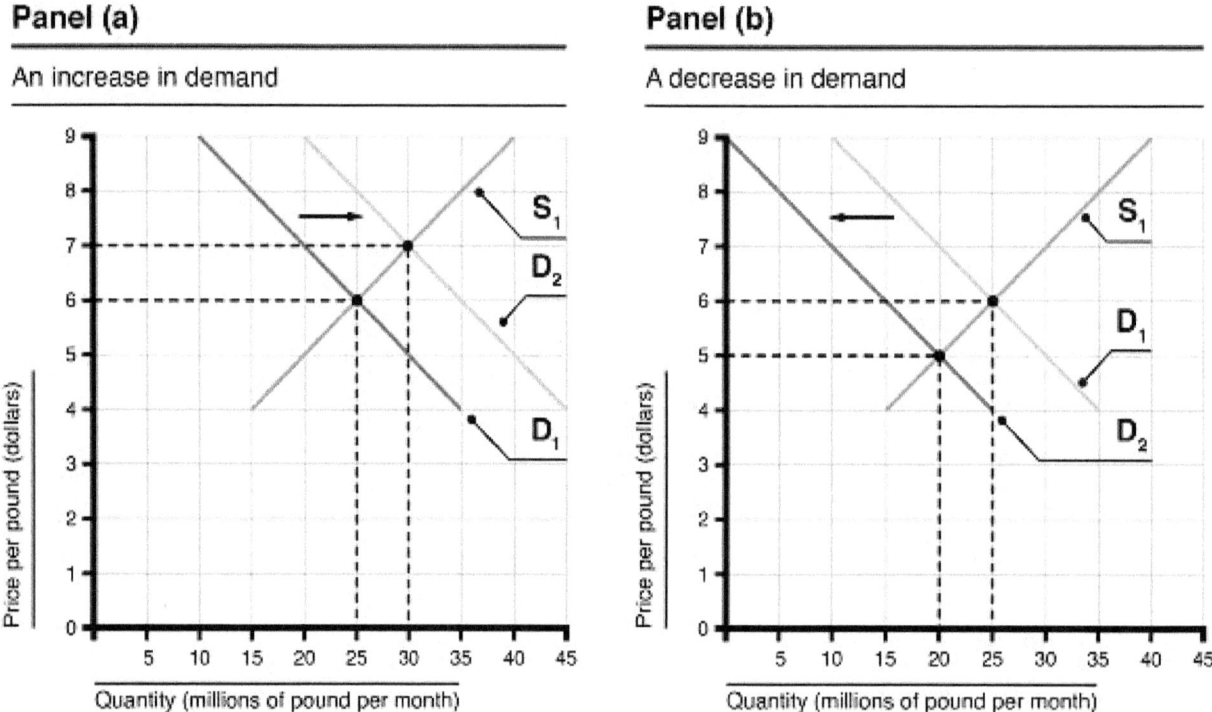

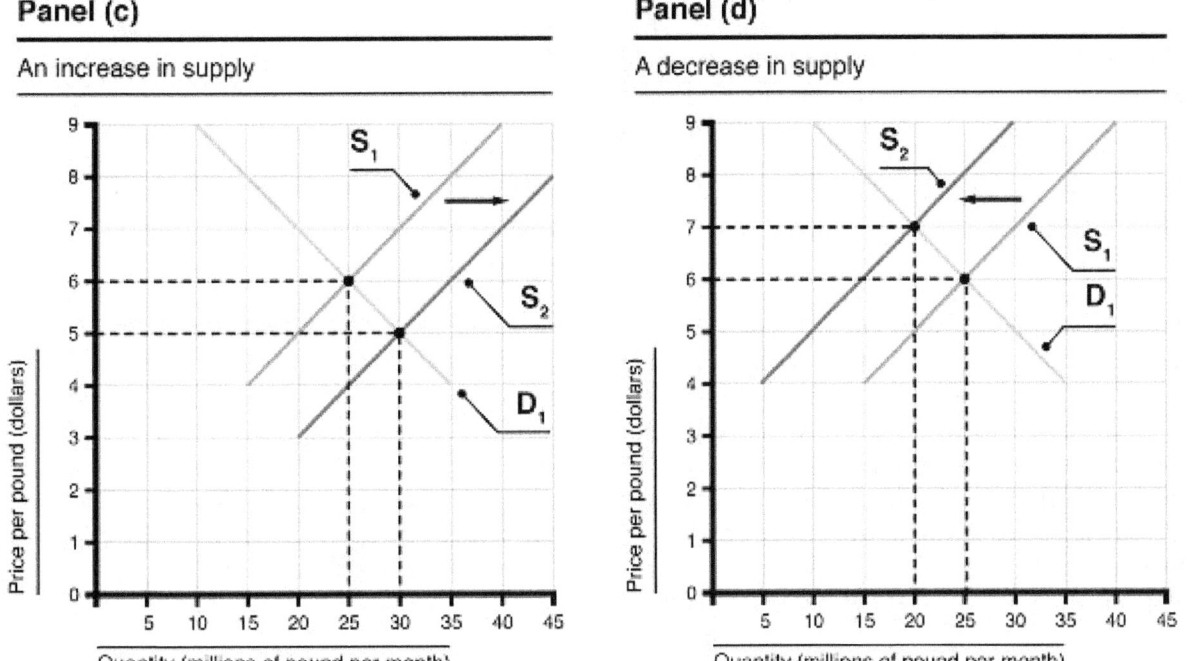

Contemporary Economic Systems

Communism is a political system and ideology characterized by a classless social system and communally controlled property. Communism encourages state control of the production and distribution of goods. It is an extreme branch of Marxist theory that blends Karl Marx's revolutionary theories with visions of a one-party government.

Socialism is a more moderate offshoot of Marxism. In a socialist nation, the state does not own the means of production, but exercises some influence over them. This political system takes a guiding role in the economy, but usually promotes democracy over dictatorship.

Capitalism is the free enterprise economic system that stemmed from the philosophies of Adam Smith and John Maynard Keynes. Capitalism promotes competition by denying government influence over the economy.

Economic Systems in Different Places and Eras

The world industrialized at different rates and at different times. Industrialization occurs when countries develop from a primarily agricultural society to an industrial economy. Beginning in Great Britain around 1760, the first Industrial Revolution spread throughout Europe until 1840. With the improvement of technologies discovered during this time period, the second Industrial Revolution took place from 1840 to 1870. Important technological innovations occurred in textiles, steam power, and iron making. The Industrial Revolution reached the United States shortly after the Civil War. During industrialization, the standard of living rose significantly, as did the discovery of new medicines, causing life expectancy to increase. Sanitation, improved living conditions, electricity, and education were all expanded as urbanization occurred. Over time, other areas of the world became industrialized, including East Asia during the late 1800s and early 1900s.

During the nineteenth century, Europe experienced what is known as the Great Divergence—a time of great economic growth in Europe. It was significant because Europe moved rapidly from a primitive economy to wealth surpassing the much larger, more established, and more sophisticated economies in East Asia, the Middle East, and

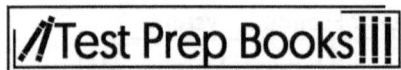

the Indian subcontinent. The timing coincided with the establishment of colonies and the solidification of trade routes. Europe maintained its economic dominance by embracing technology and transportation, like railroads and steamboats. In addition, mining technology brought greater wealth to European countries, and advances in agriculture allowed countries to support larger populations, even in new urban areas. Countries used their wealth to improve roads and sanitation and to fund education and medical advancement.

Types of market economies, or economies based on supply and demand, are capitalistic in nature and include laissez-faire, free market, and welfare capitalism. Laissez-faire is a set of economic principles that promote private interaction free from any government interference on the economy, like regulations, tariffs, subsidies, and taxes. Laissez-faire is more theoretical than an actual economic system. A free market economy curtails government intervention, allowing the forces of supply and demand to move the market. The free market economy promotes many laissez-faire principles, like individualism, freedom, and competition. Welfare capitalism is a type of free market in which the government places taxes on goods and services to pay for social services. Welfare capitalism is also referred to as a mixed economy. Welfare capitalism is common in Europe, especially in Scandinavia; however, all modern-day economies incorporate some form of welfare, such as social security and disability. The basic principles of market economies have been the most successful in history due to their superior production. The primacy of the market economy became entrenched after the collapse of the Soviet Union, the leading Communist economic system. Currently, China remains the only powerful Communist country, but the Chinese government has adopted numerous free market reforms in recent years.

Types of Market Structures

Competition in a capitalist economy like the U.S. economy is determined by market structure. Throughout U.S. and world history, there have been various forms of market structures, such as pure competition, monopolistic competition, oligopoly, and monopoly.

Pure Competition
A pure competition market system is the most competitive; it is dictated by the pure knowledge of all its buyers and sellers. In a pure competition market system, there are a large number of firms that create standardized products; the products become so homogenous in nature that consumers become indifferent about their company choices. This pure competition system has low barriers for entering and exiting a particular industry. Thus, firms are more likely to come and go as they please. In this pure competition market system, prices are determined by consumer demand, and no supplier maintains any significant influence over prices. In this system, suppliers are often called price takers.

Monopolistic Competition
Monopolistic competition is much like pure competition in terms of the number of suppliers and barriers. Monopolistic competition structures also have low barriers to entering and exiting the industry, so there are many suppliers. In a monopolistic competition market, suppliers often try to attain price advantages through product differentiation. Suppliers justify higher prices as a result of this differentiation of similar products. Monopolistic competition is only successful when suppliers actually convince consumers of the higher quality of their standard products. Beauty supplies and other retail vanity goods are great examples of products that may achieve higher sales through monopolistic competition.

Oligopoly
Oligopolies are markets that establish a few large firms as the major sellers/distributors. A good example of an oligopoly is the American automobile industry. Each automobile firm tries to maximize profit by producing marginal costs that equal marginal revenues. High barriers to entry limit the number of firms that can enter an oligopoly. These firms, therefore, maintain a great deal of influence over the market prices of their products. In the case of the

American automobile oligarchy, auto manufacturers tend to limit entry into the industry by maintaining high costs for manufacturing.

Monopoly

Pure monopoly is very different from pure competition. Pure monopolies seek to create barriers for entry into the industry. In this system, there is only one seller of a particular product or commodity, and the sole seller attempts to restrict firms from exiting and entering the industry at will.

International Trade

International trade is when countries import and export goods and services. Countries often want to deal in terms of their own currency. Therefore, when importing or exporting goods or services, consumers and businesses need to enter the market using the same form of currency. For example, if the United States would like to trade with China, the U.S. may have to trade in China's form of currency, the *Yuan*, versus the dollar, depending on the business.

The exchange rate is what one country's currency will exchange for another. The government and the market (supply and demand) determine the exchange rate. There are two forms of exchange rates: fixed and floating. Fixed exchange rates involve government interventions (like central banks) to help keep the exchange rates stable. Floating, or flexible, exchange rates constantly change because they rely on supply and demand needs. While each type of exchange rate has advantages and disadvantages, the rate truly depends on the current state of each country's economy. Therefore, each exchange rate may differ from country to country.

Advantages and Disadvantages of Fixed Versus Floating Exchange Rates			
Fixed Exchange Rate: government intervention to help keep exchange rates stable		Floating or Flexible Exchange Rate: Supply and demand determines the exchange rate	
Advantages	*Disadvantages*	*Advantages*	*Disadvantages*
-Stable prices -Stable foreign exchange rates -Exports are more competitive and in turn more profitable	-Requires a large amount of reserve funds -Possibly mispricing currency values Inflation increases	-Central bank involvement is not needed. -Facilitates free trade	-Currency speculation -Exchange rate risks -Inflation increases

Countries may have differing economic statuses and exchange rates, but they rely on one another for goods and services. Prices of imports and exports are affected by the strength of another country's currency. For example, if the United States dollar is at a higher value than another country's currency, imports will be less expensive because the dollar will have more value than that of the country selling its good or service. On the other hand, if the dollar is at a low value compared to the currency of another country, importers will tend to avoid buying international items from that country. However, U.S. exporters to that country could benefit from the low value of the dollar.

When an individual or group can produce a larger quantity of a good or service in the same amount of time relative to their competitors, this is called *absolute advantage*. Adam Smith first described the concept of absolute advantage in *The Wealth of Nations* (1776) to explain why mercantilism is less productive than a free trade system in which the participants specialize in producing goods and services according to their absolute advantage.

When an individual or group can produce a good or service at relatively lower opportunity costs than their competitors, this is called *comparative advantage*. David Ricardo first proposed the theory of comparative advantage in 1817 to describe how a country would still benefit from international trade even if it held an absolute advantage in every good and service. According to Ricardo, economic productivity is maximized when countries export goods and services according to their comparative advantage.

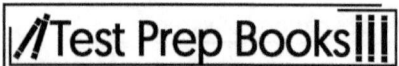

Today, countries primarily trade within the parameters of mutually agreed-upon trade agreements. These trade agreements theoretically increase the performance of every trade partner's economy by allowing countries to specialize in their strengths and trade for what they do not produce. However, people in developed countries often fear that manufacturing and other traditionally blue collar work will be lost to less developed countries. Similarly, people in less developed countries often criticize the agreements for mandating investment in lower-paying jobs. Thus, even as greater wealth is accumulated, free trade agreements can cause conflict within society. Modern trade commonly involves questions concerning who is the true beneficiary of trade.

Structure and Operation in the U.S. Free Enterprise System

Free Enterprise System in the United States

In a free enterprise, or capitalist, economic system, business can be conducted without interference from government. Without government interference, business owners, entrepreneurs, and corporations can decide how they want to run their companies with limited direction from local, state, and federal legislators. The free enterprise market system in the United States of America is heavily tied to the laws of supply and demand rather than government regulations. Supply is the term used to describe the quantities of goods and/or services that sellers are willing and able to sell at varied prices over an established period of time. Demand is the term that refers to how much of the goods/services buyers are willing to purchase from sellers. Along with competition, supply and demand affect pricing in a free enterprise system. Prior to the Industrial Revolution of the eighteenth and nineteenth centuries, many towns and cities in the United States were centered on a single economic activity. Mill towns produced and processed grains. Members of farming communities devoted their whole lives to agriculture and animal husbandry. Mining towns and logging towns focused all their energies on resource extraction and refinement. The economic activities of these towns and cities were limited by the lack of modern communication and transportation.

All this changed with the Industrial Revolution of the eighteenth and nineteenth centuries. Towns and cities began to realize that an overreliance on one economic activity could result in financial catastrophe. The Industrial Revolution brought about changes to human civilization by increasing and diversifying productivity through technological advancement, improving the reach and efficiency of transportation and communication, and standardizing parts and services for mass production. As a result, many business conglomerates, oligopolies, and monopolies emerged, and these companies extended the reach of the economy while also limiting access to entry in the industry. The Industrial Revolution is responsible for embedding the free enterprise market system into the American economy; nevertheless, it also planted the seeds of discontent, paving the way to a socialist and anarchist backlash against big business. Although the government began to regulate business, especially during the trust-busting years of the Progressive Era, free enterprise remained at the heart of the American economic system, leading to a multicentury debate over the role of government in business.

Free-market economic principles related to the profit incentive and competition have been increasingly adopted across the global marketplace in the late twentieth century and twenty-first century. Multinational corporations have prioritized maximizing profits and shareholders' wealth above all else. In addition, multinational corporations compete for a global workforce and customer base, and the pursuit of profits is not bound by national borders. Free trade agreements have facilitated this development by removing barriers to the movement of labor, capital, goods, and services. Oftentimes, governments' public economic institutions explicitly negotiate free trade agreements to benefit specific multinational corporations. Free trade agreements also commonly fail to protect against environmental degradation, which serves to maximize the profitability of multinational corporations. Labor unions were one of the most powerful economic institutions in the twentieth century, but their power has markedly declined since the end of the Cold War. Organized labor increases businesses' costs, so many governments have enacted pro-business policies to attract investment.

U.S. Economic Growth from the 1870s to the Present

The American economy has changed dramatically since the 1700s, a century where agriculture was the main economic activity. The First Industrial Revolution began in the early 1800s when steam-powered machines were used to increase productivity, especially in the textile industry. The invention of steamboats and railroads made it much cheaper and faster to ship goods across the country in the mid-1800s as well. After the Civil War, the Second Industrial Revolution led to increased productivity and efficiency in the many industries, including metallurgy, chemicals, telecommunications, and energy. This led to significant social changes as immigration and urbanization increased. Workers began to form labor unions in order to demand better wages and working conditions, which led to strikes and conflict with law enforcement officials.

The **Progressive ethos of reform** emerged as a political platform between the 1870s and 1920s. Progressivism was directed by the belief that progress in technologies must also be balanced by progress of social welfare and justice. Progressive reformers in the United States and Great Britain, largely driven by a Christian sense of social welfare and justice, attempted to eradicate the social ills associated with urban life through philanthropic, political, and legal measures. The Progressive mindset gripped all levels of society; it influenced government, business, and the common masses.

Progressivism also gripped the minds of the Western world's greatest businessmen. **Philanthropy** emerged as the foremost method for alleviating poverty and creating opportunity for the common citizen. Businessmen like Andrew Carnegie, Cornelius Vanderbilt, and John D. Rockefeller tried to impact society in a positive manner through philanthropic donations. These tycoons of industry established libraries, universities, parks, and other public institutions in hopes of making the world a better place.

Carnegie, in particular, adhered to what was known as the **Gospel of Wealth**, or the **Social Gospel**, which combined the forces of Protestant Christianity and capitalism in order to enhance the common good. Carnegie's Gospel of Wealth was applauded by some and protested by others. Some believed it to reflect the limitless capacities of Christian industry; others believed it was a hypocritical platform that shrouded the steel tycoon's evident exploitation of the working classes. Regardless of this debate, Carnegie's philanthropic measures, without a doubt, helped establish institutions that served public interest. His philanthropy and Gospel of Wealth was not only a symbol of prosperity, but also of Progressivism.

While tycoons like Carnegie, Vanderbilt, and Rockefeller were spreading philanthropy, they were also securing their business **monopolies**. These industrialists tried to consolidate—or monopolize—production within the scope of one business enterprise. This allowed them to control mining, production, shipping, and wholesale processes, which, in turn, limited the amount of corporate competition. While some applauded these monopolies as the emblems of American capitalism, others derided such enterprises as a social evil. Progressive politicians, in particular, targeted monopolies as exploitative entities. They feared that the unregulated reach of business, symbolized by Gilded Age corruption in politics, would poison Western democracy.

Progressivism began as an urban outgrowth of Populism, but quickly ascended to the American presidency. Presidents Roosevelt, Taft, and Wilson became trust-busting Progressive beacons who attempted to rein in the excesses of laissez-faire capitalism by fracturing monopolies like Rockefeller's Standard Oil. Legislation, such as the **Sherman Anti-Trust Act,** had already set the precedent for these political reforms in the 1890s. Presidents Roosevelt, Taft, and Wilson leaned on these legislative precedents in order to continue busting monopolies and trusts that threatened U.S. trade. Roosevelt, in particular, had a sympathetic Supreme Court that allowed him to attack powerful industrialists like J. P. Morgan, earning him the moniker *The Trust Buster*.

European governments seized total control over their economies during World War I to implement a total war military strategy. In the immediate aftermath of the war, economic control reverted back to private industries in most European countries with the Soviet Union being a notable exception. The Soviet Union was communist, so the government dictated economic affairs through central planning. In contrast, American and Western European governments mostly eliminated rations and reduced regulations.

While these deregulated economies produced considerable economic growth during the roaring twenties, it also led to the creation of unmanageable consumer debt and economic bubbles in the financial sector. Rampant financial speculation, diminishing economic productivity, and unsustainable levels of debt caused the New York Stock Exchange to collapse on October 20, 1929. This collapse directly triggered a global economic crisis known as the **Great Depression**. From 1929 to 1932, a series of bank panics destabilized global credit and currency markets, and European unemployment rates skyrocketed from five percent to thirty percent. Overall, the Great Depression reduced global economic production by nearly fifteen percent.

American and Western European governments attempted to improve economic conditions by adopting Keynesian economic principles during the Great Depression. As originally proposed by British economist **John Maynard Keynes**, Keynesianism generally involves the government playing a more active role in the economy. More specifically, **Keynesian economic policies** aim to increase government spending to stimulate demand for products and services. Government expenditures were increased by expanding social services, hiring more government employees, and investing in public infrastructure projects. Furthermore, governments created central banks to increase the money supply, lower interest rates, and incentivize private investments. Keynesian policies successfully increased employment and improved economic conditions, but the Great Depression didn't officially end until the start of World War II.

International trade dramatically increased after countries entered into more expansive free trade agreements, including the **General Agreement on Tariffs and Trade** (1947). Greater global integration heavily contributed to the post-war economic boom, which resulted in global economic production increasing by more than five times. Second, decolonization led to the creation of more independent countries, and major world powers were no longer able to unilaterally dictate economic policies in foreign lands for their own benefit.

In the early 20th century, Henry Ford introduced the moving assembly line to the automobile manufacturing industry, which made it easier for middle- and working-class families to buy cars. Other industries adopted Ford's methods, which led to lower prices for many consumer goods. The stock market crash in 1929 helped trigger the Great Depression, which resulted in a vicious downward economic spiral. Franklin D. Roosevelt introduced the New Deal to try and boost the economy, but only the outbreak of World War II led to full employment. The United States emerged from World War II as the world's largest economy and pent-up consumer demand fueled prosperity during the post-war era.

World War II was followed by one of the most productive economic booms in human history. During the 1950s and 1960s, the Allies enjoyed four to five percent annual economic growth and achieved nearly full employment. Most economists attribute the boom to the continuation of Keynesian economic policies, particularly in large infrastructure investments that built housing, bridges, and large-scale highway systems. The United States assisted the recovery effort in Europe through the **Marshall Plan**. After Congress passed the Marshall Plan in 1948, European governments received more than $12 billion, which amounts to $100 billion in present-day dollars. American economic investment in Europe was partially motivated to halt communism's spread into Europe. So, the European recovery impacted the global balance of power by solidifying the alliance between the United States and Western Europe.

World War II radically transformed the global political order. With the rest of the world still recovering from the conflict's widespread destruction, the United States and Soviet Union emerged as undisputed global superpowers. The World War II alliance between the United States and the Soviet Union, forged when both fought on the side of the Allies, was not to be permanent. The United States championed democratic values and emphasized individual liberties, such as freedom of expression, freedom of the press, and religious freedom. In contrast, the Soviet Union was authoritarian, and the leader of the Communist Party exercised unilateral control over all political matters.

In addition, the countries had opposing economic systems. The United States was capitalist, while the Soviet Union was communist. **Capitalism** protects private property rights, allows the free market to set prices through supply and demand, and promotes economic competition based on the incentive to maximize profits. **Communism** rejects the concept of private property, empowers a central government to set prices through controlling the supply, and shares the resulting profits among the public. Both the United States and Soviet Union attempted to spread their ideologies across the globe during the post-World War II era, resulting in the **Cold War**.

The development of computers in the latter part of the 20th century improved communications and led to greater economic efficiency. However, it also marked the beginning of the post-industrial economy in the United States. Traditional manufacturing jobs began to disappear as robots replaced unskilled workers.

As the knowledge economy supplanted the industrial economy in the early twenty-first century, Europe and the United States relocated much of its industrial production to Asia and Latin America. This transition was facilitated through free trade agreements. Free trade agreements remove tariffs, provide access to labor markets, and incentivize greater foreign investment in the developing world. In effect, companies can reduce costs by moving manufacturing production to Asia and Latin America where there is cheaper labor and less environmental protection. Because free trade agreements remove tariffs, the resulting products can then be shipped back to the home country with minimal economic cost. In return for opening their labor markets, Asian and Latin American countries benefit from foreign companies building commercial infrastructure that boosts employment. However, the relocation of manufacturing has proven controversial. The loss of manufacturing jobs has decimated blue-collar communities in the United States and Europe, and labor conditions in Asian and Latin American countries have been criticized for failing to protect workers from abusive practices and dangerous working conditions.

Types of Business Ownership

Within the United States' free enterprise system, there are four major types of business ownership: sole proprietorships, partnerships, limited liability companies, and corporations. Sole proprietorships are unincorporated companies that have one owner who pays all the income taxes on profits made from the business. Partnerships bring together two or more individuals to establish and maintain business at large. In a partnership, both owners share responsibilities and are equally liable for debts. Limited liability companies reduce the risk of investing in a business by making investors responsible only for investments and not debts. Corporations are legal entities that enjoy most of the responsibilities of individuals (i.e., the right to enter into contracts, sue and be sued, loan and borrow money, etc.), but the shareholders of the corporation maintain limited liability despite their right to profit from dividends.

Saving, Investing, and Borrowing

All economic markets strive for an efficient allocation of resources. The supply of loanable money comes from institutional or personal savings. Savings are dollars of postponed spending. In terms of investing, many financial institutions offer interest rates on savings to compensate households for postponing their spending in the name of saving money. Higher interest rates typically lead to higher saving rates. The supply of loanable funds increases as savings' interest rates increase. Loans are a form of financial borrowing. People who receive loans are willing to pay an interest price on the funds they borrow. Loans are preferred at lower interest rates; higher interest rates mean more money lost. Much like market prices, market interest rates perform locative functions. Some companies or individuals take loans out to invest in such things as construction or education. Financial institutions, such as banks and credit unions, typically dictate interest rates for both saving and borrowing.

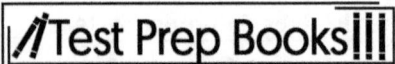

Role of Government in the U.S. Free Enterprise System

Market Efficiency and the Role of Government (Taxes, Subsidies, and Price Controls)

Market efficiency is directly affected by supply and demand. The government can help the market stay efficient by either stepping in when the market is inefficient and/or providing the means necessary for markets to run properly. For example, society needs two types of infrastructure: physical (bridges, roads, etc.) and institutional (courts, laws, etc.). The government may impose taxes, subsidies, and price controls to increase revenue, lower prices of goods and services, ensure product availability for the government, and maintain fair prices for goods and services.

The Purpose of Taxes, Subsidies, and Price Controls

Taxes	Subsidies	Price Controls
-Generate government revenue -Discourage purchase or use of bad products such as alcohol or cigarettes	-Lower the price of goods and services -Reassure the supply of goods and services -Allow opportunities to compete with overseas vendors	-Act as emergency measures when government intervention is necessary -Set a minimum or maximum price for goods and services

Fiscal Policy

Fiscal policy refers to how the government adjusts spending and tax rates to influence the functions of the economy. Fiscal policies can either increase or decrease tax rates and spending. These policies represent a tricky balancing act, because if the government increases taxes too much, consumer spending and monetary value will decrease. Conversely, if the government lowers taxes, consumers will have more money in their pockets to buy more goods and services, which increases demand and the need for companies to supply those goods and services. Due to the higher demand, suppliers can add jobs to fulfill that demand. While increases in supply, demand, and jobs are positive for the overall economy, they may result in a devaluation of the dollar and less purchasing power.

Money and Banking

Money is a means of exchange that provides a convenient way for sellers and consumers to understand the value of their goods and services. As opposed to bartering (when sellers and consumers exchange goods or services as equal trades), money is convenient for both buyers and sellers.

There are three main forms of money: commodity, fiat, and bank. Here are characteristics of each form:

- Commodity money: a valuable good, such as precious metals or tobacco, used as money
- Fiat money: currency that has no intrinsic value but is recognized by the government as valuable for trade, such as paper money
- Bank money: Money that is credited by a bank to those who deposit it into bank accounts, such as checking and savings accounts or credit

While price levels within the economy set the demand for money, most countries have central banks that supply the actual money. Essentially, banks buy and sell money. Borrowers can take loans and pay back the bank, with interest, providing the bank with extra capital.

A central bank has control over the printing and distribution of money. Central banks serve three main purposes: manage monetary growth to help steer the direction of the economy, be a backup to commercial banks that are suffering, and provide options and alternatives to government taxation.

The Federal Reserve is the central bank of the United States. The Federal Reserve controls banking systems and determines the value of money in the United States. Basically, the Federal Reserve is the bank for banks.

All Western economies have to keep a minimum amount of protected cash called required reserve. Once banks meet those minimums, they can then lend or loan the excess to consumers. The required reserves are used within a fractional reserve banking system (fractional because a small portion is kept separate and safe). Not only do banks reserve, manage, and loan money, but they also help form monetary policies.

Monetary Policy

The central bank and other government committees control the amount of money that is made and distributed. The money supply determines monetary policy. Three main features sustain monetary policy:

1. Assuring the minimum amount held within banks (bank reserves): when banks are required to hold more money in reserve funds, they are less willing to lend money to help control inflation.

2. Adjusting interest rates: raising interest rates makes borrowing more costly, which can slow down unsustainable growth and lower inflation. Lowering interest rates encourages borrowing and can stimulate struggling economies.

3. Purchasing and selling bonds (open market operations): Controlling the money supply by buying bonds to increase it and selling bonds to reduce it.

In the United States, the Federal Reserve maintains monetary policy. There are two main types of monetary policy: expansionary and contractionary.

- Expansionary monetary policy:
    - Increases the money supply
    - Lowers unemployment
    - Increases consumer spending
    - Increases private sector borrowing
    - Possibly decreases interest rates to very low levels, even near zero
    - Decreases reserve requirements and federal funds
- Contractionary monetary policy:
    - Decreases the money supply
    - Helps control inflation
    - Possibly increases unemployment due to slowdowns in economic growth
    - Decreases consumer spending
    - Decreases loans and/or borrowing

The Federal Reserve uses monetary policy to try to achieve maximum employment and secure inflation rates. Because the Federal Reserve is the bank of banks, it truly strives to be the last-resort option for distressed banks. This is because once these kinds of institutions begin to rely on the Federal Reserve for help, all parts of the banking industry—such as those dealing with loans, bonds, interest rates, and mortgages—are affected.

Government Policies and International Trade

Governments' involvement in their domestic economies varied throughout the Cold War, depending on the countries' history and ideology. European countries were capitalist, meaning that considerable economic freedom was granted to private corporations and individuals. However, European countries continued Keynesian style economic policies, so the government continued to play a role in regulating economic activity as well as heavily investing in social programs and infrastructure. In contrast, the Soviet Union and China continued to exercise centralized control over the economy through Five-Year plans that directed economic activity and controlled the supply of goods. Many African, Middle Eastern, South American, and Southeast Asian countries had considerable government involvement in their domestic economies. Land reform, nationalization of industries, and robust social

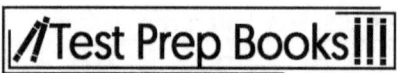

service programs were common in those regions as countries sought to spur development. However, these developing countries often lacked capital to fund development projects, forcing them to cede some economic control to multinational corporations or the **International Monetary Fund (IMF).**

Along with the World Bank, the IMF was a global association that developed after World War II. These global associations provided loans to governments for the purpose of development. The loans often had extensive conditions that reduced the recipient state's control over the economy. For example, loans from the IMF regularly forced states to privatize state-owned companies, cut social programs, and reduce government subsidies. In addition to global financial associations, some countries entered into free trade agreements. These agreements successfully increased trade, but they also reduced the countries' flexibility in economic policy. For example, free trade agreements limited the signatories' ability to impose tariffs on foreign goods or provide subsidies to certain domestic industries. Examples of twentieth century free trade agreements include the: **General Agreement on Tariffs and Trade** (1947), **European Coal and Steel Community** (1951), **North American Free Trade Agreement** (1994), and the **World Trade Organization** (1995).

Economic Growth, Stability, Full Employment, Freedom, Security, Equity, and Efficiency

In the U.S. free enterprise system, the main reason for the government regulation of private business is to control prices. Since investment and economic growth are important for increasing and stabilizing the U.S. gross domestic product (GDP), the government often works with the financial market to create growth or equilibrium. In certain cases, antitrust laws may be enacted, such as the Sherman Antitrust Act, to deter or bust monopolistic mergers or predatory practices that restrict competition. Throughout history, government regulation has increased and decreased based on the political context of the time. On both sides of the debate over regulation and deregulation, legislators have full employment, freedom, security, equity, and efficiency in mind. The ways each side of the debate define these terms differ based on political disposition. During the 1980s, under the leadership of President Ronald Reagan, for example, the U.S. government entered an era of considerable deregulation in business. Reagan believed lessening regulation would promote freedom, security, equity, and efficiency in business so that the United States could push forward toward full employment for its citizenry. Proponents of increased regulation point to the growing socioeconomic gap between the rich and the poor that is created by rampant deregulation in free enterprise. These proponents of increased regulation see pure free enterprise as a threat to the freedom, security, equity, and efficiency of the American citizenry.

Economic Growth

The most common tool for measuring economic growth is the **Gross Domestic Product (GDP)**. The increase of goods and services over time indicates positive movement in economic growth. The quantity of goods and services produced is not always an indicator of economic growth, however; the value of the goods and services produced matters more than the quantity.

There are many causes of economic growth, which can be short- or long-term. In the short term, if aggregate demand (the total demand for goods and services produced at a given time) increases, then the overall GDP increases as well. As the GDP increases, interest rates may decrease, which may encourage greater spending and investing. Real estate prices may also rise, and there may be lower income taxes. All of these short-term factors can stimulate economic growth.

In the long term, if aggregate supply (the total supply of goods or services in a given time period) increases, then there is potential for an increase in capital as well. With more working capital, more infrastructure and jobs can be created. With more jobs, there is an increased employment rate, and education and training for jobs will improve. New technologies will be developed, and new raw materials may be discovered. All of these long-term factors can also stimulate economic growth.

Other causes of economic growth include low inflation and stability. Lower inflation rates encourage more investing as opposed to higher inflation rates that cause market instability. Stability encourages businesses to continue investing. If the market is unstable, investors may question the volatility of the market.

Potential Costs of Economic Growth:

- Inflation: When economic growth occurs, inflation tends to be high. If supply cannot keep up with demand, then the inflation rate may be unmanageable.
- Economic booms and recessions: The economy goes through cycles of booms and recessions. This causes inflation to fluctuate over time, which puts the economy into a continuous cycle of rising and falling.
- Account inefficiencies: When the economy grows, consumers and businesses increase their import spending. The increase of import spending affects the current account and causes a shortage.
- Environmental costs: When the economy is growing, there is an abundance of output, which may result in more pollutants and a reduction in quality of life.
- Inequalities: Growth occurs differently among members of society. While the wealthy may be getting richer, those living in poverty may just be getting on their feet. So while economic growth is happening, it may happen at very different rates.

While these potential costs could affect economic growth, if the growth is consistent and stable, then it can occur without severe inflation swings. As technology improves, new ways of production can reduce negative environmental factors as well.

Consumers, Labor, and Business in the U.S. Free Enterprise System

In a free enterprise system, labor is provided to the resource market—and, in turn, business—from the household. In this system, laborers not only extract/provide goods and services for business, but they also double as consumers in the market economy. Labor and consumption are both tied to business. As laborers, they produce the goods/services that give themselves and others satisfaction or utility in everyday life. As consumers, they buy the goods/services for satisfaction or utility. As laborers and consumers, citizens in the U.S. free enterprise system can affect business efficiency and profits. They can choose to strike as laborers or boycott goods/services as consumers. On the flip side, businesses can affect the lives of consumers/laborers by decreasing or increasing wages, cutting or creating jobs, or controlling the prices of goods and services. The rights and responsibilities of consumers and laborers are to offer—or deny—work and expenditures to business. The rights and responsibilities of businesses are to protect the rights of workers and provide adequate goods/services to consumers. At times throughout history, these rights and responsibilities have been denied or disrupted, leading to labor unrest and/or business collapse.

Personal Financial Literacy and Consumer Economics

Consumer economics is a term used to describe the ways in which consumers make decisions about their roles in a capitalist economy. The factors that consumers consider when buying goods and services include satisfaction and utility. Most consumers want to obtain as much satisfaction and/or utility from their purchase as possible; in colloquial terms, they want the biggest bang for the buck. Consumers also have to consider the quantity of goods and services they are able to purchase at any given time, in accordance with the current price. This phenomenon is known as demand. When individual demand combines with aggregate demand, it is called market demand. Individual demands and market demands are also factors that consumers must consider when making decisions. These demands—individual and aggregate—drive consumer tastes. Most consumers do not demand goods that do not provide them with utility or satisfaction.

Consumers must also consider supply and scarcity. Consumers do not always have enough time or money to make their purchases, and this is known as scarcity. Scarcity basically means that consumers have to make choices: they cannot always have all the goods they want and participate in all their preferred activities. Likewise, all consumers—individuals, households, businesses, and governments—are bound to the supply chains of goods. At times, the actual goods or services might become scarce, meaning there are not enough products or services to meet consumer demand. As a result, consumers might have to consider alternative options for utility or satisfaction.

When an individual decides between possibilities, that individual is making a choice. Choices allow people to compare opportunity costs. **Opportunity cost**s are benefits that a person could have received, but gave up, in choosing another course of action. What is an individual willing to trade or give up for a different choice? For example, if an individual pays someone to mow the lawn because he or she would rather spend that time doing something else, then the opportunity cost of paying someone to mow the lawn is worth the time gained from not doing the job himself or herself.

Individuals earn an income by trading their labor—both mental and physical—for pay. They then budget their money through spending or saving it. As consumers, every choice has an opportunity cost since they must choose which goods and services they want to buy with a limited income. By purchasing one good or service, they give up the chance to purchase another.

Additionally, consumers have the choice to save money when they don't have enough money to purchase what they want, or when they want to utilize a savings account to use during emergencies or periods of economic difficulty. People also choose to save for retirement, a time when they will no longer be working and drawing a salary. Saving money by putting it in a bank is considered low-risk—the bank will pay the saver a low interest rate to keep it safe, but it will not increase much in value. A riskier path is investing money through the purchase of valuable items (or assets) in the hopes that they will increase in worth over time and yield returns (or profits). Assets can include shares in companies, real estate or land investments, or capital such as money, equipment, and structures used to create wealth.

Science, Technology, and Society

Major Scientific and Mathematical Discoveries and Technological Innovations

The following section looks at the ways the three major agricultural revolutions in history—the First Agricultural Revolution, the Second Agricultural Revolution, and the Green Revolution—affected technological innovations throughout history.

First Agricultural Revolution

For several millennia after Cro-Magnon human beings first developed their modern physical appearances some forty thousand years ago, the men and women of the Old Stone Age survived by wandering from place to place in search of animals and plant life. These early nomads roved in bands of no more than forty people, living off the land and hunting game for survival. The Paleolithic hunter-gatherers of this era separated their bands into gendered, skill-based categories: The majority of men developed wood, bone, and stone toolkits to slay prehistoric beasts, while the majority of women fashioned digging sticks and storage containers to unearth, uproot, gather, and store the land's available roots, fruits, grains, grasses, plants, and berries. By inventing these basic tools, Paleolithic hunter-gatherers managed to increase their food supplies. Cro-Magnon humans sharpened stones into knives to kill and butcher wild animals. Wooden spears helped roving nomadic tribes kill game at greater distances. Lion claws and mammoth tusks transformed into hooks and harpoons for fishing. Bone needles helped Cro-Magnons sew the animal-hide gear they needed to hunt for long periods of time in the cold and stampede wild animals off icy cliffs. Together, these Stone Age innovations laid the paradigmatic foundations for later technological shifts such as the Neolithic Revolution, also known as the First Agricultural Revolution.

The First Agricultural Revolution began around ten thousand-plus years ago when early nomadic men and women began scattering seed near regular campsites. As early human beings witnessed crops growing from these seed disposal locations, they recognized that they had some relative power over ecological conditions. This seemingly insignificant (and likely accidental) realization inaugurated a shift from food gathering to food producing methods at early human campsites, and the subsequent ideas and ideals that stemmed from these new tactics sowed the seeds for a broader agricultural revolution that, to this day, represents one of the greatest breakthroughs in human history. The revolutionary Neolithic transformation from hunting-gathering bands to farming-based societies had far-reaching effects on technological innovation, population, and human culture at large. For the first time in history, humans across the globe developed innovative food production methods effective enough for sustaining highly populated, complex city-states and civilizations.

Scientists and historians have not come to a consensus as to why the agricultural revolution occurred around ten thousand years ago. However, most theories tend to highlight the broader impact climate change had on the First Agricultural Revolution in some capacity. Around ten thousand years ago, the end of the last Ice Age in human history set the stage for rising worldwide temperatures and longer growing seasons. Specifically, favorable Neolithic temperatures and drier landscapes made grasses and grains more readily available for immediate nourishment and future cultivation. Warmer climates also eliminated many weather- and starvation-induced deaths, which contributed to a small population boom of sorts. The coinciding climate and population changes of the Neolithic Age created a global context that demanded a more sustainable food source. Farming, in particular, became an attractive alternative to hunting and gathering because it placed more control in the hands of burgeoning human populations. Farming, unlike hunting and gathering, offered human beings a rich supply of grains, roots, fruits, and vegetables that could be planted and harvested on a systematic basis.

In fact, human communities became more systematic as a whole during the First Agricultural Revolution. Independently, Neolithic villages across the globe evolved into sophisticated city-states and civilizations sourced from the same central, revolutionary milieu. The favorable climate changes and population booms of the Neolithic Age coalesced into a collection of unique, independent global culture hearths. These culture hearths took root in such divergent places as Egypt, Iraq, Pakistan, China, Mexico, Central America, and Peru. Known as hearths of domestication to some scholars, the globe's earliest Neolithic villages eventually evolved into complex, fertile centers of systematic social advancement, allowing many of the unconscious participants of the First Agricultural Revolution to cling closely to the new, institutionalized processes of permanent human settlement.

The microcosmic processes of war, trade, migration, drought, famine, personal contact, and mass communication catalyzed this larger process of cultural diffusion, forcing each civilization into a sort of cultural symbiosis with the other. Each burgeoning city-state relied on other city-states for obtaining new objects, ideas, and customs. The transformation from village to city-state—and the accompanying cultural diffusions that followed—spanned several generations, making it difficult for scholars to pinpoint the origins of many specific agricultural-based practices. The cultural diffusion spawned by the First Agricultural Revolution created a web of interrelated objects, ideas, and practices that multilaterally affected the social institutions and geographic dispositions of many of the world's first civilizations.

Second Agricultural Revolution

Prior to the eighteenth century, most village farms in England and its colonies remained family owned and operated; these small farms, fashioned by pastoral notions of freedom and virtue, emphasized family values and familial subsistence over mass production and financial gain. All this changed, however, as the English Empire turned into a colonial powerhouse in the early to mid-1700s, marking a transition from family farming to early agribusiness. At this time, an expanding English economic catalyzed the broader transformative processes of the Industrial Revolution and the coinciding Second Agricultural Revolution. The English Crown (and its vassal colonies) reaped the benefits of imperial resources and cheap labor forces, paving the way to simultaneous paradigm shifts in industry and agriculture.

The economic strength and political stability of England in the early to mid-1700s made its burgeoning empire the perfect candidate for the growing global demand for new technologies and greater food production. Industrialization—the process by which mechanized technologies produce both natural and synthetic products for human beings—required a tremendous amount of resources and human labor. By the mid-eighteenth century, England could readily industrialize because it had:

- Enough water power and coal to fuel new technologies
- An extensive slave system, indentured servant system, and tenant farm system that offered free/cheap labor
- Established iron ore mines for new machines and buildings
- Extensive river systems and canals for intranational trade
- Extensive colonial structures for international trade
- A powerful navy to protect trade
- Elaborate harbor systems to welcome trade
- A complex and highly developed banking system to back industrial growth

In all, England had the three major factors necessary for fruitful industrialization: land, labor, and capital. And, to make matters even better, although England suffered its fair share of wars during the eighteenth century, none of these international military crises occurred on English soil. Consequently, eighteenth-century England became the home of some of the most unique inventors, inventions, businessmen, and businesses in world history. Moreover, the broader processes of English industrialization created beneficial, symbiotic relationships with the budding processes of the English agricultural revolution that eventually witnessed a massive increase in the output of machine-made goods and textiles.

The Second Agricultural Revolution shadowed the Industrial Revolution as it spread from England to Continental Europe and North America (and later to South America, Africa, and Asia). Much like the First Agricultural Revolution, the Second Agricultural Revolution spawned an increase in technological innovation and food production. During the Second Agricultural Revolution, wealthy capitalist landowners began buying out family-owned farms and creating tenant farm systems that forced former village farmers into essential waged servitude. Similarly, the worldwide system of slavery continued to grip the globe in the eighteenth century: Slavery and capitalism joined hand in hand on plantations, as wealthy landowners forced African slaves into perpetual submission for the sake of mass production. Slavery existed long before the Second Agricultural Revolution, but persisted during this era, even with technological advancements and calls for abolition. This excess in free/cheap labor, coupled with near-perfect economic conditions, encouraged wealthy landowners and businessmen to experiment with new machinery and new farming methods. The resulting agricultural revolution sowed the seeds of technological and scientific advances.

The coinciding Industrial and Second Agricultural Revolutions impacted society at a time when the Enlightenment had also reached its full fruition. Thus, it makes sense that science, scientific inquiry, scientific research, and scientific advancement—all crux characteristics of the Enlightenment Era—inevitably impacted the paradigmatic shifts of the Industrial and Second Agricultural Revolutions. Prior to the Enlightenment, many agriculturalists in Europe and North America relied heavily upon Christian theology and dogma to influence their decision-making processes: Most pre-Enlightenment farmers spoke of the floods of God rather than the minds of men when analyzing ways to till, plant, and harvest the soil. In other words, these early farmers placed a greater emphasis on the mysteries of God than on the capabilities of science. While a belief in God did not totally perish with Enlightenment advances, scientific practice began to slowly take precedence over prayer, especially when it came to strategic farming. As a result, the Second Agricultural Revolution witnessed an intense wave of new technology and new agricultural practices that relied heavily on scientific objectivity.

The Second Agricultural Revolution helped create an entirely new class of scientific farmers. This new class of farmers criticized and abandoned outdated farming tools and techniques in favor of scientific approaches and mechanized practices. Perhaps one of the most recognizable scientific farmers in history was Jethro Toll of Berkshire, England. Toll was an agriculturalist who believed scattering seed across the ground by hand was wasteful and inefficient. Recognizing that much of the seed failed to take root once scattered, Toll decided to bank on new industrial advances to create a complex agricultural machine called the seed drill. Invented in 1701, Toll's seed drill capitalized on the advancements of the Industrial Revolution: It employed a grooved, artisan-made rotating cylinder that methodically sowed well-spaced rows of seed into channels dug at specified depths by a cutting-edge, front-end steel plough. A rear-end, mechanized harrow provided closure to the entire process by immediately covering the sewn seeds with soil. The seed drill boosted crop yields by mechanically designating the necessary depths and spaces needed for seeds to germinate at a more efficient rate. The invention also cut farmers' costs by conserving seed for future crops.

The Second Agricultural Revolution also witnessed the rise of various textile industries in England and its Anglo-American colonies. During this time period, the English Empire became a world leader in wool, linen, and cotton manufacturing and exports, thanks to new technological advancements in the textile industries. Colonial merchants unified smaller mills and spinneries under the umbrella of big business and a burgeoning global capitalist system in England and North America. Similarly, businessmen and landowners formed partnerships with the expanding plantation system in agriculture so that these mills and factories could be supplied with an excess of textile materials. These merchants, businessmen, landowners, and plantation farmers boosted their overall profits by mechanizing the formerly arduous spinning and weaving processes. Inventors not only transformed planting and harvesting processes by introducing new technologies, but they also revolutionized merchant machinery in the first-ever textile factories. These large warehouses of industry depended on the efficient production capabilities of new machineries such as John Kay's flying shuttle, James Hargreaves's spinning jenny, and Eli Whitney's cotton gin. Each of these new machines assisted early capitalists in their efforts to enhance wool, linen, and cotton production.

Green Revolution

The beginnings of the Green Revolution have traditionally been traced to the agricultural theories and practices developed by Norman Borlaug—often referred to as the *Father of the Green Revolution*—in Mexico in the 1940s. In 1944, the Mexican Ministry of Agriculture recruited Borlaug, an American biologist who received his PhD in plant pathology and genetics from the University of Minnesota in 1942, to conduct research on wheat production. In a joint venture with the world-famous Rockefeller Foundation, Borlaug and several other American scientists founded a new scientifically driven movement to increase agricultural production and catalyze economic growth in developing nations all over the world.

Traditional histories of the Green Revolution place Norman Borlaug and the high-yielding variety of seeds he developed at the praxis of a global paradigm shift in agricultural techniques and technologies. As the story goes, it is Borlaug and his team of scientists who inaugurated a paradigmatic revolution that helped stave off world hunger by ensuring disease resistance through techniques such as dwarfing, which, in turn, led to high crop yields and agricultural production.

According to this narrative, Borlaug, who later received a Nobel Peace Prize for his scientific advances in the 1970s, set forth a revolutionary wave of agronomic activity that placed chemical engineering, mechanized farming, and scientifically enhanced, disease-resistant cultivars at the forefront of global agro-capitalist interests and enterprises. The positive results of his efforts, according to this narrative, were:

- A newfound reliance on high-yield varieties (HYV) of seed

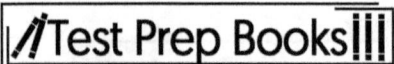

- Highly efficient methods of chemical and mechanized farming
- Increased food production
- Reduction in hunger on a global scale
- Economic stimulation, thanks to an increase in crop production and a higher demand for chemicals and mechanized farming equipment
- Increased income
- Sustained population growth

This master narrative, however, places too much emphasis on the positive impact of one man and, consequently, fails to shed light on the broader, highly complicated historical picture.

In many ways, Borlaug was the inheritor of a Green Revolution that has its roots in the arid soil of the Dust Bowl and Great Depression of the 1930s. Borlaug, who came of age during an era of widespread American poverty and famine, inherited the technological shifts and scientific efforts of the Dust Bowl and Depression that sought to refertilize the American agricultural landscape with new ideas and economic opportunities. Borlaug's work in the 1940s was a direct cultural correlate of the agricultural failures of America in the 1930s and the transformative efforts to retake the soil of the Republic. During the tumultuous thirties, the United States came to terms with the fact that poor decisions and a lack of agricultural and cultural foresight had ravaged the banks and breadbaskets of America, bringing both Wall Street and the Heartland to their knees. Borlaug, who had a brief stint in the Civilian Conservation Corps in the 1930s, was well aware of federal and global efforts to bring labor and agriculture closer together for the sake of economic stimulation.

The Green Revolution, in this sense, can be interpreted as a direct cultural response to the Dust Bowl and the Depression rather than a revolution inaugurated by one man. Borlaug is, without a doubt, a crucial character in this broader narrative, but he is by no means the only revolutionary. Borlaug inherited a cultural context ripe for agricultural advances and a marriage between science and the economy.

The Green Revolution responded to an increased need for global food production during the Great Depression, World War II, and the post–World War II baby boom era. The scientific and technological advances of the Green Revolution, without a doubt, helped combat global hunger and poverty. Nevertheless, as is the case with any revolution, the effects of the Green Revolution were not only positive. The economic excesses of the Green Revolution, which were often tied to capitalist interests, also fed global inequality. The Revolution was not spread evenly around the world; it did not always take hold in the so-called Third World countries of Africa and Southeast Asia. The Green Revolution tended to impact the United States and the West more positively than nations residing outside these global alliances. Nevertheless, the Green Revolution also took its toll on the United States and the West.

Some of the negative consequences of the Green Revolution include:

- Ecological damage from over-irrigation
- Ecological damage from a dependency on harmful chemicals and pesticides
- Indiscriminate use of toxic fertilizers
- Pollution from an overreliance on gas-powered agricultural machines
- Overproduction and an increased amount of food waste
- An inflation in the cost of agricultural technology and high-yield seeds
- Economic disparity; greater disparities between the rich and poor
- Uneven development (even in the United States, especially in poorer rural areas such as Appalachia)
- Increased ground water extraction
- Water table depletion
- Overpopulation

In all, the Green Revolution, like any other revolution in history, had both its positive and negative effects. Today, historians and scholars of human geography continue to debate the historical legacy of the Green Revolution and its impact on the globe.

Origin and Diffusion of Mathematics, Science, and Technology Ideas

Under the leadership of the infamous Alexander the Great, during the Hellenistic period of the Greek civilization, Ancient Greece entered an era of intercultural exchange with Egypt, Persia, India, the Near East, and the Mediterranean world. During this time, Alexander created military trading posts all over his empire, establishing Greek as the dominant language of communication. Throughout this era, the center of scholarship shifted away from Athens and toward Alexandria. Alexandria became the center of mathematical and scientific discoveries; it became a hub of technological innovation. Hellenistic astronomers, such as Ptolemy, flocked to Alexandria's world-renowned observatory. Scholars such as Eratosthenes skillfully computed the earth's circumference in Alexandria's library. Mathematicians such as Eratosthenes and Aristarchus previewed geometry texts written by Euclid; these texts, housed in Alexandria's library, stirred the intellect of these mathematicians, helping them to make advances in geometry and physics.

Alexandria became the West's greatest beacon of intercultural exchange; hundreds of Indian, Egyptian, and Persian scholars flocked to the center of Hellenistic culture, which unified and synthesized the ideas and technologies that had been amassed over time in the earliest hearths of civilization: the River Valley Civilizations, Classical India, Ancient Egypt and Persia, and Classical Greece. By the time the Roman Empire came to power, Alexandria had already endured centuries of scholarly advancement. The Roman Empire inherited Alexandria as an academic center, and it remained the capital of Roman and Byzantine Egypt for almost a thousand years.

Following the Muslim conquests of the seventh century, Alexandria shifted into the hands of Arab caliphates until 1200. During this period, Alexandria remained a center for intercultural exchange as famous Arab mathematicians, such as al-Khwarizmi of Baghdad, disseminated new ideas, such as Arab numerals, across the Arab world. These Arab numerals were actually based off his study of Indian math, illustrating the dramatic ways in which the Arab world interacted with other cultures during the era of the Muslim caliphates. Thousands of miles away, China was also entering a golden age in mathematics as the Chinese developed concepts such as zero and negative numbers throughout the Tang and Song Dynasties. The vast expansion of the Mongol Empire brought many Chinese ideas and technologies to the Middle East and Europe, furthering cultural exchange. Thus, by the time of the Ming Dynasty, China was beginning to create stronger ties with the West through the Silk Road. This exchange paved the way to the Age of Exploration and a new era of scientific exchange and advancement.

Contributions of Significant Scientists and Inventors

Emboldened by the theories of the Enlightenment and backed by the new tools and techniques of the Scientific Revolution, many astronomers began challenging the authority of ancient and medieval philosophers. Above all, the greatest challenge to traditional knowledge was the notion that the cosmos was heliocentric rather than geocentric. This concept was validated by the theories set forth by pathbreaking scientists such as Copernicus, Galileo, and Newton.

Later, scientific breakthroughs by Thomas Edison, Albert Einstein, and Marie Curie continued to revolutionize the scientific world.

Nicolaus Copernicus
The notion of a heliocentric universe was not new by the time **Nicolaus Copernicus** began toying with it in the 1500s. In fact, some ancient Greek scientists and philosophers had believed that the sun—rather than the earth—was at the center of the universe. Copernicus validated this ancient Greek belief by studying the earth, the stars,

and other celestial bodies for over twenty-five years. There was only one major problem with this Copernican theory—it went completely against the canonical laws and beliefs of the Roman Catholic Church. The Roman Catholic Church had long assumed that the universe revolved around the earth, and, more specifically, around humanity (God's creation). Copernicus believed the Roman Catholic Church was wrong quite some time before he published *On the Revolutions of the Heavenly Bodies*, which was not published until 1543, the last year of his life. He had not published the treatise earlier, fearing retaliation by the Roman Catholic Church. Copernicus was right about his fears; those who championed his heliocentric theory after his death faced ridicule by the Roman Catholic Church, and, in some cases, inquisition and exile.

Galileo Galilei

It was the Italian scholar **Galileo Galilei** who ultimately thrust Copernican theory into full-blown heresy. First, at only seventeen years old, Galileo used scientific observation to disprove Aristotle's theory that claimed a pendulum swung at a slower rhythm before approaching its resting place. Galileo uncovered the true law of the pendulum by carefully timing the back-and-forth swings of a chandelier. He used math and science to disprove archaic theories. His discoveries proved to be influential for the young Galileo, who spent most of his life disproving other theories. Next, he went on to disprove Aristotle's theory that claimed that heavy objects fall to earth faster than lighter objects.

These findings set the stage for future gravitational theory. Lastly, after building his own telescope (a new invention for the time), Galileo published his telescopic observations in a study entitled *Starry Messenger*. This study undermined canonical law more than any other scientific study to that point. It proved that celestial bodies (such as the Moon) were not perfect (that is, not completely smooth). It argued that Jupiter had its own set of moons and the Sun had its own set of dark spots. Lastly, it supported Copernican theory by providing observations that backed Kepler's laws of motion.

The Catholic Church warned Galileo to stop publishing his findings in support of Copernican theory. Galileo ignored these warnings, publishing a pro-Copernican tract entitled *Concerning the Two Chief World Systems* in 1632. Galileo was called to the Roman Catholic court to stand trial for his findings. Under the threat of inquisition and exile, Galileo had to deny his alleged heresy. He knelt before the cardinals of the Roman Catholic Church and denied his findings, a move that saved him from punishment or exile but somewhat tarnished his scientific contributions.

Sir Isaac Newton

Sir Isaac Newton spent a great deal of time studying objects, forces, and how an object's motion responds to forces. He went on to publicize his Theory of Universal Gravitation that proposed the idea that gravity is a force that acts on all objects on earth. Newton also made great advancements by using mathematics to describe the motion of objects and to predict future motions of objects by applying his mathematical models to situations. Through his extensive research, Newton is credited with summarizing the basic laws of motion for objects here on Earth.

Marie Curie

Marie Curie (1867–1934) was a physicist and chemist who achieved major breakthroughs in radioactivity, and she remains the only person to win multiple Nobel Prizes in different scientific fields. Curie coined the term radioactivity and developed a theory to describe how atoms become radioactive when unstable nuclei lose energy. Curie's experiments yielded groundbreaking results, such as the isolation of radioactive isotopes and the discovery of two new elements (polonium and radium). Additionally, Curie pioneered the use of radioactive isotopes in medical treatment, and her mobile X-ray units treated more than a million soldiers during World War I.

Thomas Edison

Thomas Edison (1847–1931) is widely regarded as the most influential American inventor. The prolific and trailblazing Edison held 1,093 United States patents, and he constructed one of the world's first modern research laboratory facilities, in Menlo Park, New Jersey. Edison's first major invention was the phonograph, which recorded and reproduced sound. He further revolutionized mass communication through the invention of a carbon telephone transmitter and the motion picture camera. In addition, Edison invented a more effective incandescent light bulb, more efficient rechargeable batteries, and new methods of directing electric currents and distributing electric power.

Albert Einstein
During the 1920s and 1930s, the discovery of **quantum mechanics** overturned some aspects of Newtonian physics and enabled the harnessing of nuclear power, resulting in changes to other scientific fields, military strategy, economics, and society. Albert Einstein, Werner Heisenberg, Erwin Schrödinger, Enrico Fermi, and Niels Bohr all won Nobel Prizes for their contributions to this revolutionary breakthrough in physics. Einstein was also responsible for challenging and expanding upon Newtonian theories and developed a theory of special and general relativity.

Scientific and Mathematical Discoveries and Technological Innovations

From 1750 onward, the world experienced dramatic cultural, political, social, and economic shifts brought about by the processes of industrialization, modernization, and urbanization. Throughout this vast period, human beings were able to produce steam-powered mechanics, coal-and-gas-powered forms of transportation, and electric-powered urban infrastructure and communications. The discoveries of coal, oil, and electricity revolutionized technology. As mathematicians and scientists mastered subjects such as trigonometry, calculus, nuclear physics, and quantum theory, the world became both a more interesting and dangerous place for global citizens. Nikola Tesla and Thomas Edison helped create and domesticate the power of electricity. Edward Jenner and other medical professionals helped lessen the severity of such diseases as smallpox through vaccination discoveries. Albert Einstein and other physicists helped the United States and other countries obtain nuclear capabilities. Watson and Crick discovered DNA, paving the way to a better understanding of the human genome. President Kennedy and NASA helped fund a voyage to the Moon that only could take place because of advances in rocket engineering.

Inventors and entrepreneurs such as Bill Gates and Steve Jobs revolutionized the computer industry. All these scientific advances have helped the United States of America evolve from an agricultural new nation to a technological world leader. These changes have affected society in a positive way, but also in a negative manner. Industrialization has led to environmental pollution. Computer technologies have spawned drone attacks. Nuclear energy has led to the threat of nuclear war and the reality of nuclear meltdowns. Genetic advances have created so-called Frankenfoods that can sometimes cause more environmental harm than help.

Developments in Science, Technology, and the Free Enterprise System

Advances in science and technology have waxed and waned with the economy of the United States throughout the nineteenth and twentieth centuries. Since the advent of the Industrial Revolution in the nineteenth century, the U.S. economy has changed dramatically. Shifts in the free enterprise system of the United States have led to a fair share of economic panics and depressions. The most notable of these economic downturns was the Great Depression of the 1930s. Prior to this time, technological advances in consumer culture encouraged an era of excess and inflation. The consumer practices of the Roaring Twenties, therefore, gave way to the economic collapse of the 1930s. Ironically, it was also advances in science and technology that helped resuscitate the U.S. free enterprise system during World War II. The expansion of the military-industrial complex helped lead the United States out of the Great Depression and into the Golden Age of the 1950s. Consumer capitalism and military spending, therefore, can be a double-edged sword: On the one hand, in excess, it can create economic panic; on the other hand, within reason, it can induce economic stimulation.

Agricultural productivity improved as a result of the mechanization of farm labor. New machines, such as the seed drill, allowed agricultural productivity to increase in a variety of farming activities. For instance, the cotton gin,

invented by **Eli Whitney**, helps efficiently separate cotton fibers from seeds, which normally consumes a lot of time when carried out by hand. The cotton gin streamlined agricultural productivity so much that the total export of cotton in 1793 (the same year of Whitney's patent) was less than ten thousand bales, even with the rise of slave labor in the American South. By 1860, thanks to the invention of the cotton gin, the total export of cotton reached four million bales. Ironically, however, as cotton became king of the American South, slavery increased as well. The rise of the Industrial Revolution in the agricultural sector became synonymous with the cries for and against slavery and abolition. Slave labor shifted from a purely manual process to one that focused on specialization. Much like the textile factories in the North, the cotton plantations of the South trended toward specialized labor roles.

The discovery and consequential development of oil wells in the United States around 1860 gave the world exactly the fuel source that it needed to launch a second wave of industrialization, one that would witness the emergence of gas lamps, electricity, and automobiles. Crude petroleum further revolutionized the Industrial Revolution. It served as not only a source for machine power, but also for light. By 1873, a United States citizen by the name of G. H. Brayton had developed a more efficient petroleum engine that mixed the vapor of petroleum with air constituted by the fuel.

The Bessemer process, named after Henry Bessemer who patented the process in 1856, made it much easier to produce high quality steel by removing impurities during the smelting process. This allowed for stronger and higher-quality steel that revolutionized the industry.

The application of petroleum engines to households, factories, and new modes of transportation paved the way to new furnace heating systems, gas lamps, and automotive transportation. In particular, the discovery of oil wells by George Bissell and Edwin L. Drake in Titusville, Pennsylvania in 1859 revolutionized the ways in which cities were illuminated. New gas lamps, in which the wicks were not discarded, were installed across cities in Europe and the United States. Eventually electric light bulbs replaced these gas lamps, but the gas lamps became the first great source of illumination for urbanization.

The **Second Industrial Revolution** refers to the technological innovations of the 1860s–1920s. This wave of industrialization witnessed the emergence of the steel, chemical, and oil industries. This era, sometimes referred to as **The Gilded Age**, witnessed the completion of transcontinental railroads in the United States and Russia. It also witnessed the invention of the light bulb and electricity, which helped quicken the pace of industrialization. The early telephone gave businesses and governments new ways to connect across countries and networks, making business and management much easier. Gasoline-fueled engines and automobiles eventually replaced steam-powered engines and trains in this era. Chemical production helped strengthen both the manufacturing and agricultural industries by creating new materials and pesticides. Precision machinery aided the production of highly-intricate mechanisms and consumer goods. This is the era that launched the United States into the position of an industrial-imperial world leader.

Computing power rapidly increased in the 1950s and 1960s. Computers had been used during World War II primarily to crack enemy codes, but by the 1950s, they were capable of launching satellites. The Soviet Union launched **Sputnik 1** in 1951, and it was the first satellite to successfully orbit the Earth. This initial success triggered a **Space Race** between the United States and Soviet Union. On July 20, 1969, the United States achieved the first Moon landing in human history during the **Apollo 11** mission. Due to American and Soviet public investment in computers during the Space Race, personal computers were developed in the 1970s.

Moral and Ethical Issues Related to Science and Technology

The impact of science and technology reaches well beyond the realm of free enterprise upswings and downturns and into the very heart of morality/ethics as well as into standards of living in the United States. Excesses in consumer science and technology can spawn economic depressions, which, in turn, may lower the overall standard of living. In the case of the Great Depression, the standard of living in the United States dropped to an all-time low. This, in turn, also affected people's morality in both a positive and negative manner. In a positive way, the Great Depression brought people together through economic struggle, encouraging many to cling to the ethics of their faith. In a negative way, the Great Depression also brought many doubts to the moral consciences of the nation; some citizens began to question whether God was on America's side during this time. Technological advances are also often accompanied by power and hegemony. In the case of the expansion of the military-industrial complex in the Cold War era, financial excess led to economic stimulation and a higher standard of living on average. Nevertheless, the global hegemony and moral weight spawned by this expansion also created a tremendous amount of fear, calling into question the ethics of nuclear capabilities.

Human population growth, economic developments, and developments in science and technology have caused considerable environmental harm since the start of the twentieth century. More than half of the world's tropical forests have been lost to **deforestation**, meaning the forest is cleared for economic purposes. Deforestation is driven by global demand for paper and lumber, and forests are regularly converted to farmland, grazing pastures, and housing. The overexploitation of land has also caused a phenomenon known as **desertification**, which results in soil being unable to support vegetation. Common causes of desertification include deforestation, overgrazing, unsustainable water usage, and modern agricultural practices, including the use of pesticides and fertilizers.

Deforestation and desertification have caused a steep decline in the amount of arable land. As such, conflicts often arise between corporations, governments, and/or local farmers when a government sells its land to a foreign corporation without obtaining the consent of local farmers or conducting sufficient oversight. Given the continually diminishing supply of land, competition over land will likely increase for the foreseeable future unless there is a major change in the global demand for food.

Pollution has also led to a decline in air quality and the freshwater supply. The primary causes of air pollution are the burning of fossil fuels for power, industrial emissions, and exhaust from motor vehicles. Europe and the United States introduced clean air legislation in the 1960s and 1970s, and they largely succeeded by regulating industrial polluters and overseeing the transition to higher quality sources of fuel. However, air pollution continues to be a major problem in the developing world, especially in countries undergoing rapid industrialization, like China and India. The World Health Organization estimates that outside air pollution contributes to more than three million deaths per year in the twenty-first century. Similarly, more than half of the world's freshwater supply has been polluted by agricultural runoff, industrial pollutants, and/or inadequate treatment of wastewater.

Additionally, climate change, inefficient water management practices, and increased agricultural demands have placed further strains on the supply of freshwater. Consequently, corporations and countries have been drawn into conflict over freshwater. Several bottled water producers have come under scrutiny for diverting millions of gallons of water from drought-stricken areas. There is also a possibility that water scarcity could lead to armed conflict, especially in the Middle East, Africa, and Central Asia. For example, in the twenty-first century, there has been considerable tension over the management of the Euphrates-Tigris river system, Jordan River, Nile River, and Aral Sea.

Global temperatures increased approximately two degrees Fahrenheit during the twentieth century due to the **greenhouse effect**. Greenhouse gases absorb heat, preventing it from being released into the upper atmosphere. Carbon dioxide and methane are greenhouse gases, and human activity has increased the concentration of both gases in the lower atmosphere. Carbon dioxide is primarily created through the burning of fossil changes, and methane has a variety of sources, including livestock and landfills. Rising temperatures have resulted in the melting of Arctic sea ice, rising sea levels, more frequent extreme weather events, more rapid desertification, greater ocean acidity, and changes to global precipitation patterns. These changes exacerbate issues related to water scarcity, threaten global food production, and could potentially trigger a climate refugee crisis. Climate scientists estimate that global temperatures could increase between one degree Fahrenheit and nine degrees Fahrenheit in the twenty-first century, depending on climate feedback loops, greenhouse gas emissions, and policymaking.

Climate change has led to several heated debates. Although the greenhouse effect's role on rising temperature was first noted in the 1950s, the issue didn't receive significant public attention until the late 1980s. During the late 1980s and 1990s, European and American conservatives began a debate with the scientific community over the existence of climate change. At first, conservatives denied the existence of climate change and/or claimed recent trends were part of a cyclical climate pattern. Some conservative think tanks and fossil fuel companies financed scientific studies to debunk climate change in its entirety.

By the late 1990s and 2000s, the debate had changed to what, if any, impact human activity had on the climate. However, in the 2010s, the scientific community reached a consensus that the greenhouse effect causes climate change, and that human activity heavily contributes to the greenhouse effect. Currently, the debate has shifted to what should be done about climate change. Many conservatives argue that some combination of human technological innovation, adaptive policymaking, and climate engineering will solve the crisis. On the other hand, the scientific community and liberals have argued for taxing carbon emissions and investing in renewable energies, like solar and wind. This would mark a dramatic departure from the global status quo, and it's uncertain whether enough countries will risk sacrificing economic growth to make the transition away from fossil fuels.

Standard of Living in the United States

Technological innovation in communication and transportation exponentially increased the rate of human exchange and affected the standard of living in the United States during the twentieth century. Developed in the early twentieth century, the radio transmitted sounds through radio waves, making it the first wireless form of communication. The radio allowed for near instantaneous dissemination of information to a mass audience. By the 1920s, radios had transformed commerce, entertainment, and military strategy. The development of cell phones marked a significant jump in communication technologies. Compared to the radio, cell phones were far more functional because they allowed people to directly communicate over even longer distances with significantly less interference.

The first cell phones were introduced to the public in the 1980s, and they became increasingly popular in the 1990s. The Internet further facilitated communication by allowing people to communicate through instantaneous electronic messages. American military scientists invented a forerunner of the Internet in the 1960s, and it was first widely adopted by the public in the 1990s. Unlike the radio and cell phones, the Internet constituted an interactive digital space where people could post and locate information about every imaginable topic. In addition, the Internet gained mobile functionality after it was incorporated into cellular devices.

Innovations in transportation technologies reduced the physical problem of traveling over long distances. Cars were first popularized after Henry Ford's mass production of the Model T in 1908. Mass production drove down cost to the point where families could purchase cars. The widespread adoption of cars led to the creation of suburbs because workers could more easily commute to urban centers. Commercial aviation developed after World War II, and air travel similarly changed daily life by reducing the time it took to carry cargo or people over long distances. The standardization of shipping containers in the 1950s similarly helped facilitate the relatively rapid exchange of goods between faraway lands. Standardization increased the amount of cargo a ship could carry, and it expedited the process of handling and moving cargo once it reached shore.

Global integration heavily influenced the development of arts, entertainment, and popular culture in the late twentieth century and twenty-first centuries. Increased cultural exchange was facilitated through technological innovation, especially television and the internet. Following the end of the Cold War, the United States was the lone remaining superpower, and it enjoyed an outsized role in global capitalism. As such, American popular and consumer culture played a dominant role in the newly globalized society. American fast food corporations, movies, television shows, sports, and musicians all achieved a global presence.

Medical innovations made during the twentieth century increased the average life expectancy by several decades. After its founding in 1948, the **World Health Organization (WHO)** worked with experts across the world to develop new and/or improved vaccines for smallpox measles, mumps, HPV, polio, and the flu. Hundreds of life-saving antibiotics were invented to fight bacterial infections, including penicillin. Surgery was also revolutionized in the twentieth century with the development of cardiac surgery in the 1940s, organ transplants in the 1960s, and laparoscopic surgery in the 1990s. Medical advancements and scientific developments in blood groups, vaccines, antibiotics, and surgery altered demographics by increasing life expectancy. In the 1950s, the average life expectancy was approximately sixty years in the developed world and thirty years in the developing world. By 2015, life expectancy had increased to approximately seventy-five years old in the developed world and sixty-five years old in the developing world.

Practice Quiz

1. What is NOT an effect of monopolies?
    a. Promote a diverse variety of independent businesses
    b. Inhibit developments that would be problematic for business
    c. Control the supply of resources
    d. Limit the degree of choice for consumers

2. Which method is NOT a way that governments manage economies in a market system?
    a. Laissez-faire
    b. Absolute monarchy
    c. Capitalism
    d. Self-interest

3. Which of the following is NOT a purpose of the central bank?
    a. Manage interest rates.
    b. Set the tax rate.
    c. Back up the commercial banks.
    d. Set reserve requirements.

4. What is the name for the movement, started in the 1970s, that began the conservative pushback against the increasing role the government was taking in the economy?
    a. Fiscal policy
    b. Keynesian economics
    c. Fiscal responsibility
    d. Supply-side economics

5. Which one of the following is an economic benefit of free trade agreements?
    a. Free trade agreements increase international trade by reducing barriers to trade.
    b. Free trade agreements reduce the cost of reparations.
    c. Free trade agreements allow countries to protect domestic iron and steel production.
    d. Free trade agreements facilitate imperialism and the creation of lucrative empires.

See answers on the next page.

Answer Explanations

1. A: Rather than competition, a monopoly prevents other businesses from offering a certain product or service to consumers.

2. B: Absolute monarchy, which is built on the vision of full government control over the economy, is a hallmark of command economies. Laissez-faire, capitalism, and self-interest, in contrast, are all fundamental concepts behind the market system.

3. B: The central bank is responsible for all of these except for setting the tax rate. This is done by the government.

4. D: Fiscal policy is the term for what the government decides to do when it comes to its impact on the economy. Keynesian economics is the liberal economic belief that says that the government should have a role in the economy. Fiscal responsibility refers to taxation and government spending. Supply-side economics is the correct answer, as it refers to the pushback against government in the economy.

5. A: Free trade agreements seek to increase international trade by limiting or eliminating tariffs and subsidies for domestic industries. Reparations aren't directly related to free trade agreements, so Choice *B* is incorrect. Choice *C* is incorrect because free trade agreements generally prohibit countries from subsidizing or protecting domestic industries. Free trade agreements don't facilitate imperialism, so Choice *D* is incorrect.

Social Studies Foundation, Skills, Research, and Instruction

Social Studies Foundations and Skills

Philosophical Foundations of Social Science Inquiry

Social science inquiry involves the study of societies, particularly the relationships between individuals, groups, governments, and socioeconomic power structures. The breadth of this inquiry presents an incredible challenge given the multidisciplinary nature of the social sciences, which include anthropology, economics, history, human geography, linguistics, political science, psychology, and sociology. Thus, the social studies teacher must understand the philosophical foundation of the social sciences to effectively instruct and guide students, who have limited experience with such inquiry.

The philosophical foundations of social science inquiry can be broadly classified as positivist and humanist approaches. Positivism tends to emphasize scientific analysis of social science inquiries. In contrast, humanism is more concerned with investigating and analyzing people's lived experiences, including the societal consequences of those experiences. These approaches are not mutually exclusive, and there is no universal agreement as to which approach is more effective for social science inquiry.

Positivism developed as a philosophical foundation for social science inquiry during the Enlightenment (1600–1800) and the Romantic period (1800–1890). Although hardline positivism somewhat fell out of favor during the twentieth century, its focus on reliability and validity continue to influence social science inquiry through the present day. In general, positivism seeks to apply the principles of natural science inquiry to the social sciences. So the positivist approach emphasizes objectivity and methodology in the analysis of social science inquiry through qualitative and quantitative studies. Quantitative research involves empirical observations using statistical and mathematical models, while qualitative research is characterized by less structure and more descriptive observations. Regardless of the type of research, the positivist approach relies on maintaining a consistent methodology.

The positivist approach to social science inquiry closely resembles the scientific method. For the sake of simplicity, this approach can be broken down into five steps. First, the researcher identifies a problem, issue, or question to be answered. Second, the researcher develops a hypothesis, meaning an initial proposal to explain the problem at hand. Third, the researcher assembles all the relevant data, including but not limited to facts, patterns, theories, and statistics. Fourth, the researcher analyzes the data, using a clearly defined and logical methodology, to test the hypothesis. Fifth, the researcher draws a conclusion based on their analysis. This approach isn't universally applicable to every social science inquiry, but the methodology is inarguably valuable.

Humanism has a rich intellectual history with roots in the ancient world, the Italian Renaissance (1400–1600), and the Enlightenment (1600–1800). Humanism has been a part of secondary school education since at least the mid-nineteenth century. Compared to the positivist approach, the humanist approach is less concerned with data; instead, humanism prioritizes how people interact with the world around them. Consequently, humanists generally favor qualitative studies over quantitative studies. Humanist approaches to social science inquiry also tend to place more value on historical figures' emotions, ethics, and evolution.

Humanism is generally more amenable to incorporating aspects of multiple social science disciplines when making inquiries. The combination of disciplines provides additional context in order to pursue a more holistic understanding of historical figures and events. Furthermore, humanists often explicitly view progress as a universally beneficial societal good, which has proven controversial. Critics have characterized such progressivism as anti-scientific, and they have leveled accusations of bias, saying that humanists introduce subjective value judgments into historical narratives. While humanist approaches to social science inquiry can undoubtedly distort facts, the same can be said for nearly every theoretical framework. This is why teachers must be aware of authors' philosophical foundations and points of view to ensure that lessons maintain the type of balance that is essential to teaching social studies.

Social Studies Terminology

There is no denying that social studies classrooms are some of the most demanding for students when it comes to literacy and language acquisition. In social studies, students will not only have to comprehend basic verbs, nouns, and adjectives, but they will also have to understand complex social studies terms for particular contexts, places, eras, persons, movements, and groups. Social studies standards across different states typically demand that students obtain a relative amount of terminological specificity. In other words, literacy in a social studies classroom can be hyperspecific, which poses problems with students of all learning types and grade levels. In particular, social studies terminology can pose problems for Section 504 students, special education (SPED) students, and English language learners (ELLs). It is important that social studies teachers introduce students to best practices such as 1) using study cards, cognitive maps, and organizational charts for understanding social studies terms, 2) finding individualized structures and styles for note-taking, 3) employing memory games and mnemonic devices for recalling important information, and 4) using timelines and charts for understanding the importance of context, time, and sequence when it comes to social studies terms. Understanding and using social studies terminology correctly is almost always contingent on properly understanding the notion of time and context in history.

Although general literacy is usually enough to understand social studies texts, some authors use specialized vocabulary for the field of social studies. Traditionally, these specialized vocabulary terms can be separated into eight major categories: people, places, events, groups, movements, eras, documents, and analytical trends. The field of social studies centers on those who have shaped history on both the microcosmic and macrocosmic levels. Much of the social studies vocabulary terms test takers encounter is focused on famous leaders or historical agents. An **agent** is someone who does something; historical agents do something historically significant.

Social studies concepts also include geography and are linked with geography in general, so it is important that test takers have a good understanding of place and its influences on history. Additionally, it is important for test takers to understand historical events: wars, assassinations, political victories, resignations, marches, parades, and celebrations. Groups are also important to understanding social studies. In particular, some groups form social movements, factions of people devoted to some larger changes. At times, these movements succeed in changing history; at other times, they fail. Historians tend to also categorize history in segments of time known as eras. Eras can be as strict as decades (for example, the Roaring Twenties) or as fluid as ideas (for example, the Progressive Era).

Sometimes social studies texts also refer to the titles of primary and secondary texts, which have their own unique vocabulary terms. An example of an important primary text is the Declaration of Independence, while a secondary text might be a textbook discussing the Declaration of Independence. All these concepts—from people to documents—influence historical analyses, which are usually secondary texts. Historians and scholars may create their own analytical paradigms, which carry their own specialized vocabulary. For instance, some historians refer to themselves as quantitative historians because their analytical lenses are influenced heavily by quantitative data. Quantitative historians have their own specialized vocabulary for analytical trends.

Knowledge Generated by the Social Science Disciplines

Teachers must first assist students with understanding their own identities before they try to expose them to diverse identities and communities within the social sciences. Implementing social and emotional learning (SEL) activities can help students understand themselves as well as their peers. SEL activities, such as personal reflections or class diaries, can help students in the social sciences prepare for interacting within the broader world. SEL activities help students understand the idea of community while also helping them build community in the classroom. Student growth and development in the social sciences should begin with identity and gradually branch out to classroom community, family, and personal community. Once students understand themselves better and the ways in which their ideas and emotions operate, then they will be more ready to comprehend the similarities and differences they have with their teachers and peers. As the complex components of the in-class community are more readily understood, students should be ready to deconstruct their relationships to their individual families and communities.

Teachers should prompt students to understand the *why* of their beliefs and emotions as well as the source. This is crucial in a social sciences classroom because students are consistently analyzing identity, culture, society, and social relations. Without this basic foundation, it is difficult for students to respect their own cultures. Moreover, it may be difficult for them to share about their own cultures and collaborate with people who may reside outside of their cultures. The routines and expectations of every social sciences classroom should therefore be mandated by some sort of community agreement or constitution. To design and implement effective learning experiences, the entire community must buy into a particular social contract. Teachers should create nonnegotiable aspects of class culture, but they should also call upon students as experts and engineers of their own context. Social science classes with poor management typically fail to implement student voice and choice when it comes to routines and expectations, especially for working cooperatively within the community.

How Social Science Disciplines Relate to Each Other

As mentioned earlier, teachers must extend interdisciplinary study to include fields and content areas that exist outside the traditional social sciences (i.e., history, political science, social studies, geography, psychology, government, ethics, economics, environmental studies, and sociology). The future of the social sciences depends heavily on communication with fields that traditionally fall under the STEM (Science, Technology, Engineering, and Math) or STEAM (Science, Technology, Engineering, Art, and Math) categories. Disassociating the social sciences from these other fields is not beneficial for young students. In an increasingly technological world, students must be prepared to incorporate skills, ideas, concepts, and practices from STEM and STEAM courses into their social science classrooms. It is difficult to imagine future historians, political scientists, social studies teachers, geographers, psychologists, government officials, ethicists, economists, environmentalists, and sociologists functioning without science, technology, engineering, art, and mathematics. Future historians, for example, will likely have to be forensic computer scientists who sift through old files and data to better understand history and historical agents. Whenever possible, teachers should explicitly expose students to the ways in which these fields perpetually affect each other within the global economy and popular culture.

Sources of Social Studies Information; Interpreting and Communicating Social Studies Information

Primary and Secondary Sources

Traditionally, historical documents have been separated into two major categories: primary sources and secondary sources. Understanding the features of each is crucial for building foundational historical inquiry skills in the K-6 classroom. Students must learn to deconstruct primary and secondary sources to gain a better understanding of historical context and personal perspective.

Primary sources contain firsthand documentation of a historical event or era. Primary sources are provided by people who have experienced an historical era or event. Primary sources capture a specific moment, context, or era in history. They are valued as eyewitness accounts and personal perspectives. Examples include diaries, memoirs, journals, letters, interviews, photographs, context-specific artwork, government documents, constitutions,

Social Studies Foundation, Skills, Research, and Instruction | Sources of Social Studies Information; Interpreting and Communicating Social Studies Information

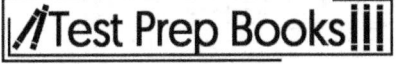

newspapers, personal items, libraries, and archives. Another example of a primary source is the Declaration of Independence. This historical document captures the revolutionary sentiment of an era in American history.

Authors of secondary sources write about events, contexts, and eras in history with a relative amount of experiential, geographic, or temporal distance. Normally, secondary source authors aren't firsthand witnesses. In some cases, they may have experienced an event, but they are offering secondhand, retrospective accounts of their experience. All scholars and historians produce secondary sources—they gather primary source information and synthesize it for a new generation of students. Monographs, biographies, magazine articles, scholarly journals, theses, dissertations, textbooks, and encyclopedias are all secondary sources. In some rare instances, secondary sources become so enmeshed in their era of inquiry that they later become primary sources for future scholars and analysts.

Teachers and students alike must spend a great deal of time analyzing the relationships between primary sources, secondary sources, and their historical scopes. Juxtaposing primary sources with secondary sources helps teachers and students attain a deeper understanding of the material they are studying.

Validity of Social Studies Information

Relevant information is that which is pertinent to the topic at hand. Particularly when doing research online, it is easy for students to get overwhelmed with the wealth of information available to them. Before conducting research, then, students need to begin with a clear idea of the question they want to answer.

For example, a student may be interested in learning more about marriage practices in Jane Austen's England. If that student types "marriage" into a search engine, he or she will have to sift through thousands of unrelated sites before finding anything related to that topic. Narrowing down search parameters, then, can aid in locating relevant information.

When using a book, students can consult the table of contents, glossary, or index to discover whether the book contains relevant information before using it as a resource. If the student finds a hefty volume on Jane Austen, he or she can flip to the index in the back, look for the word *marriage* and find out how many page references are listed in the book. If there are few or no references to the subject, it is probably not a relevant or useful source.

In evaluating research articles, students may also consult the title, abstract, and keywords before reading the article in its entirety. Referring to the date of publication will also determine whether the research contains up-to-date discoveries, theories, and ideas about the subject or is outdated.

There are several additional criteria that need to be examined before using a source for a research topic.

The following questions will help determine whether a source is credible:

Author

- Who is he or she?
- Does he or she have the appropriate credentials—e.g., M.D, PhD?
- Is this person authorized to write on the matter through their job or personal experiences?
- Is he or she affiliated with any known credible individuals or organizations?
- Has he or she written anything else?

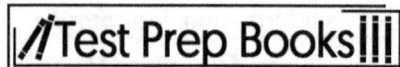

Publisher

- Who published/produced the work? Is it a well-known journal, like National Geographic, or a tabloid, like The National Enquirer?
- Is the publisher from a scholarly, commercial, or government association?
- Do they publish works related to specific fields?
- Have they published other works?
- If a digital source, what kind of website hosts the text? Does it end in .edu, .org, or .com?

Bias

- Is the writing objective? Does it contain any loaded or emotional language?
- Does the publisher/producer have a known bias, such as Fox News or CNN?
- Does the work include diverse opinions or perspectives?
- Does the author have any known bias—e.g., Michael Moore, Bill O'Reilly, or the Pope? Is he or she affiliated with any organizations or individuals that may have a known bias—e.g., Citizens United or the National Rifle Association?
- Does the magazine, book, journal, or website contain any advertising?

References

- Are there any references?
- Are the references credible? Do they follow the same criteria as stated above?
- Are the references from a related field?

Accuracy/Reliability

- Has the article, book, or digital source been peer reviewed?
- Are all of the conclusions, supporting details, or ideas backed with published evidence?
- If a digital source, is it free of grammatical errors, poor spelling, and improper English?
- Do other published individuals have similar findings?

Coverage

- Are the topic and related material both successfully addressed?
- Does the work add new information or theories to those of their sources?
- Is the target audience appropriate for the intended purpose?

Multiple Points of View and Frames of Reference

Many people want to rise above their historical contexts, but it is an impossibility. Whether one likes it or not, the ideas of humanity are always influenced by the forces of history. The individual and collective consciousness of humanity is often dictated by historical events and situations. A Jew writing in Germany during World War II would inevitably be affected in some capacity by the anti-Semitic tendencies of Nazism. A Texas-based Mexican national writing during the Mexican-American War of the 1840s would inevitably be influenced by American expansionism. A college student writing and liking posts on Facebook during the Great Recession of 2008 would inevitably be exposed to the effects of the stock market's decline. Even if the author does not comment on these events, they still shape the author's point of view. When analyzing a history text or a historical cartoon, test takers should first ask key questions: When, where, and why was this documented created? Often the answers to these questions provide test takers with the evidence they need to properly analyze the documents and answer multiple choice questions.

In some cases, the author of a document explicitly comments on history. The author may refer to historical persons, events, or dates. Test takers should take note of these persons, events, and dates because they offer evidence for answering questions or prompts. For instance, a primary source such as Anne Frank's diary directly refers to the events of World War II and the aggressions of Germans. In other cases, it is up to the test taker to decode the implicit messages embedded in a text in order to gain a better understanding of historical influences. A good place to start with this decoding process is the date the document was created. If test takers know the date of a document, they can begin to illuminate historical correlations. For instance, a historian writing in the 1960s might not explicitly discuss the historical opinions of the New Left (a political movement of the 1960s), but a test taker may be able to decode the implicit messages embedded in the text and infer that the historian may have been influenced by that era of political thought.

Evaluating Whether the Author's Evidence is Factual, Relevant, and Sufficient

It's important to read any piece of writing critically. The goal is to discover the point and purpose of what the author is writing about through analysis. It's also crucial to establish the point or stance the author has taken on the topic of the piece. After determining the author's perspective, readers can then more effectively develop their own viewpoints on the subject.

If the argument is that wind energy is the best solution, the author will use facts that support this idea. That same author may leave out relevant facts on solar energy. The way the author uses facts can influence the reader, so it's important to consider the facts being used, how those facts are being presented, and what information might be left out.

Making Judgments About How Different Ideas Impact the Author's Argument

To reach supportable judgments and conclusions in social studies, teachers and students must be prepared to categorize and synthesize a variety of primary and secondary sources, paying close attention to which sources are legitimate sources of fact or opinion. Students must also be able to justifiably quote information from these sources to establish historical generalizations, or general statements that identify themes that unite or separate source materials. Often, a generalization identifies key features, relationships, or differences found throughout multiple sources.

Identifying Bias

Bias exists in all forms of written and visual documentation. In social studies, it is especially important to look out for bias, in both primary and secondary sources. Bias can stem from various sources, including: historical context, cultural background, personal beliefs, political affiliation, and religious values. All these things shape the way an individual sees and writes about history and society. For example, a conservative author writing in the late 1980s may have been likely to support the political initiative known as the War on Drugs. This likelihood is due to political affiliation and historical context. The 1980s was a conservative era in American politics, thanks to the rise of President Ronald Reagan. It was also a historical era that responded accordingly to the crack epidemic and gained conservative support for expanded police enforcement. Additionally, a communist political cartoonist in the Soviet Union during the Cold War may be likely to paint a picture of the United States as an aggressor. That era of history pitted the Soviet Union against the United States on a global level. Biases even emerge in secondary sources; people analyzing history are influenced by their own cultural-historical contexts.

Outlines, Reports, Databases, Narratives, Literature, and Visuals

Students should not only be able to analyze maps and other infographics, but they should also be able to create graphs, charts, tables, documents, maps, timelines, and other visual materials to represent geographic, political, historical, economic, and cultural features. Students should be made aware of the different options they have to present data. They should understand that maps visually display geographic features, and they can be used to

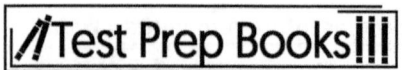

Social Studies Foundation, Skills, Research, and Instruction

illustrate key relationships in human geography and natural geography. Maps can indicate themes in history, politics, economics, culture, social relationships, demographic distributions, and climate change. Students can also choose to display data or information in a variety of graphs: Bar graphs compare two or more things with parallel bars; line graphs show change over time with strategic points placed carefully between vertical and horizontal axes; and pie graphs divide wholes into percentages or parts. Likewise, students can choose to use timelines or tables to present data/information. Timelines arrange events or ideas into chronological order, and tables arrange words or numbers into columns or rows. Outlines can be used by students to organize data into topics and subtopics. Narratives and reports can be used to present findings and thoughts in a cohesive written format. These are just some of the visual tools teachers and students can use to help visually convey their historical questions or ideas.

Maps and Other Graphics

Geographers utilize a variety of maps in their study of the spatial world. Projections are maps that represent the spherical globe on a flat surface. Conformal projections attempt to preserve shape but distort size and area. For example, the most well-known projection, the Mercator projection, drastically distorts the size of land areas at the poles. In this particular map, Antarctica, one of the smallest continents, appears massive, while the areas closer to the equator are depicted more accurately. Other projections attempt to lessen the amount of distortion; the equal-area projection, for example, attempts to accurately represent the size of landforms. However, equal-area projections alter the shapes and angles of landforms regardless of their positioning on the map. Other projections are hybrids of the two primary models. For example, the Robinson projection tries to balance form and area in order to create a more visually accurate representation of the spatial world. Despite the efforts to maintain consistency with shapes, projections cannot provide accurate representations of the Earth's surface due to their flat, two-dimensional nature. In this sense, projections are useful symbols of space, but they do not always provide the most accurate portrayal of reality.

Unlike projections, topographic maps display contour lines, which represent the relative elevation of a particular place and are very useful for surveyors, engineers, and/or travelers. For example, hikers may refer to topographic maps to calculate their daily climbs.

Similar to topographic maps, **isoline maps** are also useful for calculating data and differentiating between the characteristics of two places. These maps use symbols to represent values and lines to connect points with the same value. For example, an isoline map could display average temperatures of a given area. The sections which share the same average temperature would be grouped together by lines. Additionally, isoline maps can help geographers study the world by generating questions. For example, is elevation the only reason for differences in temperature? If not, what other factors could cause the disparity between the values?

Thematic maps are also quite useful because they display the geographical distribution of complex political, physical, social, cultural, economic, or historical themes. For example, a thematic map could indicate an area's election results using a different color for each candidate. There are several different kinds of thematic maps, including dot-density maps and flow-line maps. A *dot-density map* uses dots to illustrate volume and density; these dots could represent a certain population, or the number of specific events that have taken place in an area. Flow-line maps utilize lines of varying thicknesses to illustrate the movement of goods, people, or even animals between two places. Thicker lines represent a greater number of moving elements, and thinner lines represent a smaller number.

Social Studies Foundation, Skills, Research, and Instruction | Sources of Social Studies Information; Interpreting and Communicating Social Studies Information

Mediums for Communicating Social Studies Information

<u>Using Graphs with Appropriate Labeling, and Using the Data to Predict Trends</u>
Being literate in social studies means that teachers and students must be ready to interpret a variety of forms of data. In social studies, data is usually numerical or statistical information offered in the form of a graph, chart, table, document, map, or timeline.

In social studies, teachers and students will encounter many types of graphs. The two most common graphs used in social studies classes are bar graphs and line graphs. Bar graphs are made of parallel bars of varying lengths. Bar graphs help teachers and students compare two or more things. Line graphs are composed of a series of strategically placed points that are connected by one or more lines. Line graphs, much like timelines, help teachers and students of social studies gain a better understanding of change over time. Remember that all graphs need to have appropriate labels on the axes with units.

Sometimes valuable data can also be embedded in documents, maps, or timelines. Thus, it is important that every student is also exposed to these data-based tools in a social studies classroom. Much like all sources, students should be challenged to determine the validity of the data presented in graphs, charts, tables, documents, maps, and timelines.

Economic Indicators

Economists use a number of tools to analyze the market and determine what business cycle or phase the market is in. The leading indicators of the market based on certain signals (e.g., a high number of homes under construction or recent stock market activity) help to predict where the economy is headed.

Coincident indicators reflect the state of the economy at any given time and are tied directly to economic shifts. Lagging indicators are signals that the economy is either improving or declining. These might include higher or lower than normal profit reports of Fortune 500 companies, significant increases or reductions in wages, or a change in debt-to-income ratios among consumers.

Understanding business cycle stages helps understand levels of economic activity. There are four key phases of the business cycle:

- Phase 1 – Expansion: Business conditions are good and economic indicators remain strong. During this phase, stock prices, house prices, and wages are high, and job opportunities are plentiful.
- Phase 2 – Peak: The high point of the expansion phase when economic indicators tend to be on the downswing. During this stage, there's less investing and spending activity.
- Phase 3 – Contraction: Commonly identified as a recession or, in extreme cases, a depression.
- Phase 4 – Trough: Downtrends begin to level off and then stop, which sets the stage for a new cycle of expansion.

Economic Models

Teachers must incorporate economic models in lessons related to economic theories, concepts, and issues. Some of the most important economic models include supply-and-demand graphs, circular-flow charts, and production-possibility curves (production-possibility frontiers).

Supply-and-demand graphs analyze how the economic concepts of supply and demand impact the price of a good or service. Supply is the quantity of a good or services that is available for consumers to purchase in a marketplace, while demand refers to the quantity of a good or service that consumers can afford and want to buy. Supply-and-demand graphs contain the supply curve and demand curves for a given product, and the intersection of the curves determines the unit price for the good when demand and supply reach an economic equilibrium when assuming perfect competition.

The following diagram is an example of a supply-and-demand graph.

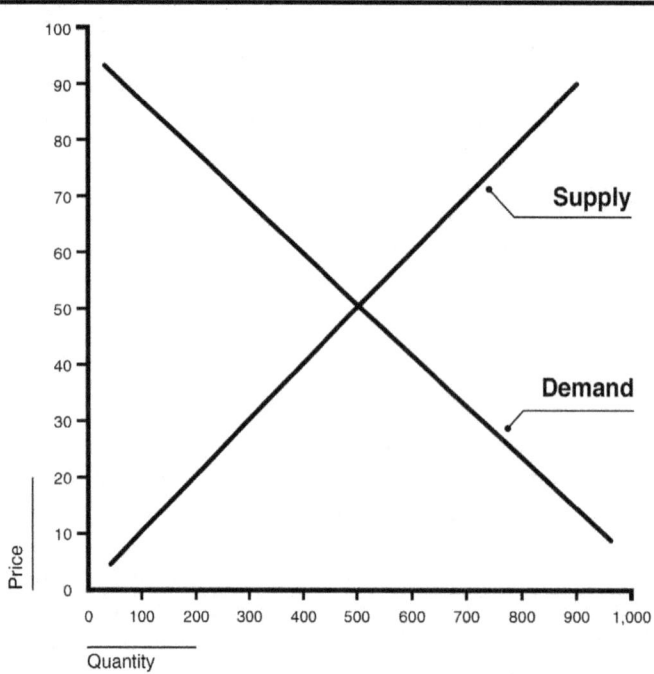

According to the supply-and-demand graph, supply and demand for widgets in New York City will reach an economic equilibrium at $50, which can be determined based on where the curves intersect.

Circular-flow charts represent how resources flow between different parts of the economy. These visual representations are most commonly used to illustrate the relationship between households, firms, and markets. Variables depicted on circular-flow charts are typically goods, services, capital, costs, revenue, profits, wages, and/or labor. Circular-flow charts are more useful for identifying broad patterns than evaluating specific factors.

The diagram below is an example of a circular-flow chart.

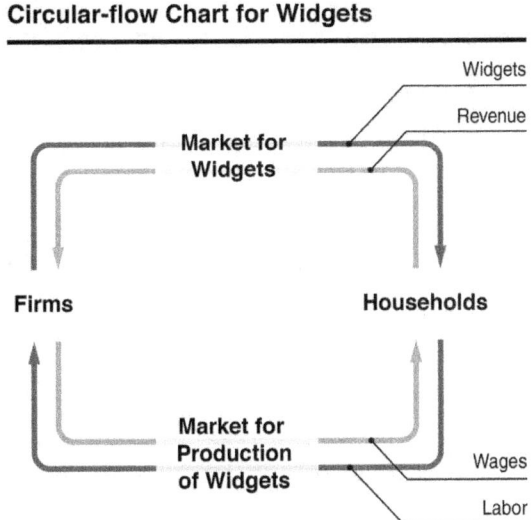

The circular-flow chart illustrates the interdependence between firms and households in regard to the production and sale of widgets. Accordingly, firms rely on households for labor to produce the widgets as well as revenue from the sale of widgets to households. In turn, households receive wages in exchange for their labor and the opportunity to purchase widgets.

Production-possibility curves illustrate the economic tradeoffs involved in the production of two different goods. This type of graph assumes that the same resources will be used in production and that the production will be perfectly efficient. Economists primarily use production-possibility curves to measure opportunity costs, efficiency, and scarcity.

The following diagram illustrates the utility of a production-possibility curve as an economic model.

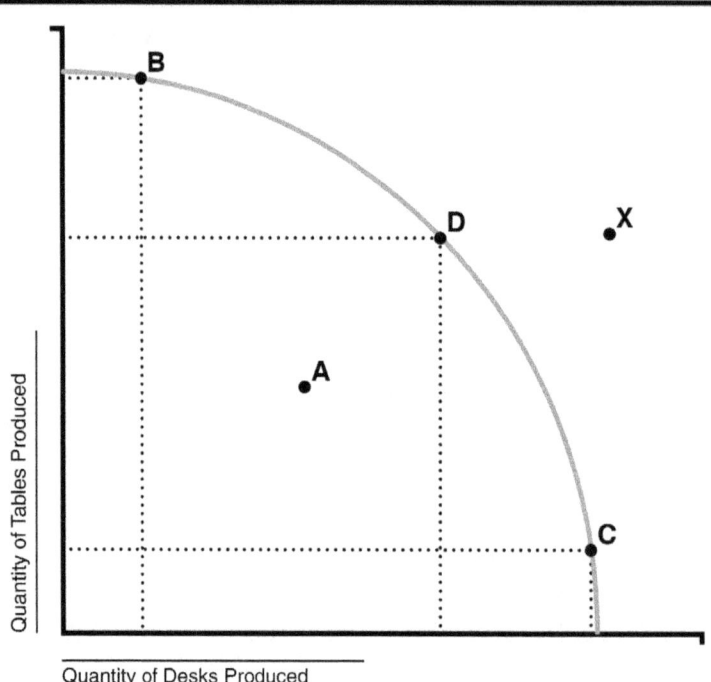

According to the production-possibility curves, points B, D, and C represent levels of maximum production for both desks and tables. Since point A falls within the curve, it represents an inefficient production. Point X represents an impossible level of production because it is located outside of the curve.

Social Studies Research

Research Questions

The purpose of all research is to provide an answer to an unknown question. Therefore, all good research papers pose the topic in the form of a question, which they will then seek to answer with clear ideas, arguments, and supporting evidence.

A research question is the primary focus of the research piece, and it should be formulated on a unique topic. To formulate a research question, writers begin by choosing a general topic of interest and then research the literature to determine what sort of research has already been done—the literature review. This helps them narrow the topic into something original and determine what still needs to be asked and researched about the topic. A solid question is very specific and avoids generalizations. The following question is offered for evaluation:

What is most people's favorite kind of animal?

This research question is extremely broad without giving the paper any particular focus—it could go any direction and is not an exceptionally unique focus. To narrow it down, the question could consider a specific population:

What is the favorite animal of people in Ecuador?

While this question is better, it does not address exactly why this research is being conducted or why anyone would care about the answer. Here's another possibility:

What does the animal considered as the most favorite of people in different regions throughout Ecuador reveal about their socioeconomic status?

This question is extremely specific and gives a very clear direction of where the paper or project is going to go. However, sometimes the question can be too limited, where very little research has been conducted to create a solid paper, and the researcher most likely does not have the means to travel to Ecuador and travel door-to-door conducting a census on people's favorite animals. In this case, the research question would need to be broadened. Broadening a topic can mean introducing a wider range of criteria. Instead of people in Ecuador, the topic could be opened to include the population of South America or expanded to include more issues or considerations.

Acting as amateur social scientists and historians, students should formulate research questions and reconstruct the past by locating sources in libraries, online sites, and physical and digital archives. Once students gather a diversity of sources, they should organize, analyze, synthesize, and interpret these sources by determining the meanings, points of view, frames of reference, biases, main ideas, and validity of each source. Once this is accomplished, students will be able to create new historical research questions. Throughout the process, students should keep an eye out for both qualitative and quantitative data to gain a greater understanding of a particular historical context or question.

Supportable Judgments and Conclusions in Social Studies

To reach supportable judgments and conclusions in social studies, teachers and students must be prepared to categorize and synthesize a variety of primary and secondary sources, paying close attention to which sources are legitimate sources of fact or opinion. Students must also be able to justifiably quote information from these sources to establish historical generalizations, or general statements that identify themes that unite or separate source materials. Often, a generalization identifies key features, relationships, or differences found throughout multiple sources.

Once the thesis or main idea of a work has been determined, the textual evidence that supports interpretation of that thesis or main idea should be examined. Supporting details should back up the author's assertions and expand the thesis. The additional information and related details should be examined for credibility, the author's use of outside sources, and whether the direct evidence supports the author's claims. Some details provide strong support and others only additional information that is nice to know but not necessary. Being able to make this differentiation will help to determine whether an argument is supportable, and a valid conclusion has been reached.

Research Methodologies

Social studies research attempts to answer novel questions or challenge existing theories. Since social studies is an incredibly broad subject, social studies research is often multidisciplinary and interdisciplinary. Multidisciplinary research involves the combined efforts of people from multiple disciplines, while an interdisciplinary researcher directly integrates and synthesizes multiple disciplines.

Two of the most important aspects of social studies research are evidence and methodology. Social scientists and historians gather evidence in different ways. Social scientists are more likely than historians to research contemporary topics; therefore, social scientists have more opportunities to gather information by interviewing witnesses, observing ongoing events, conducting surveys, and collecting fresh data. Historians sometimes collect evidence using these methods, but they generally research events that have already occurred. Therefore, historians primarily gather evidence by finding relevant passages from secondary sources, primary sources, and historical data

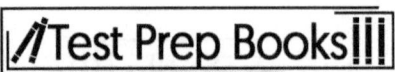

Social Studies Foundation, Skills, Research, and Instruction

and statistics. This process has been greatly expedited in recent decades due to the digitization of historical sources. Social scientists are more likely to rely on secondary sources to incorporate context or if they're primarily focusing on past events.

Once the evidence is gathered, social scientists and historians typically organize it before conducting an analysis. The organization of evidence allows the researcher to recognize patterns, optimize statistical analysis, and develop a working hypothesis, which is the first step in most research methodologies. Researchers almost always adhere to a well-established research methodology because it is the most efficient way of safeguarding reliability and validity.

Most well-established research methodologies closely resemble the scientific method, particularly when the research involves conducting experiments, surveys, and statistical analyses. The scientific method consists of identifying an issue, proposing a hypothesis, gathering evidence, conducting an analysis, and drawing a conclusion. Historians are less likely to conduct experiments and surveys, but they take a similarly methodological approach to assessing the relative authority of sources, integrating competing sources, and constructing a strongly supported argument.

Surveys and statistical analysis have additional methodological requirements. Survey requirements mostly involve the selection of a representative sample, prevention of statistical interference, and construction of questions. These requirements are also influenced by how the data is collected, such as by telephone, mail, email, or online forms. Statistical analyses help researchers interpret raw data, and methodological requirements include using an appropriate sample size, limiting the introduction of biases, and differentiating between correlation and causation.

Once a social scientist or historian completes their research, they typically seek to report their conclusions. Publication is a critical aspect of social studies research because it subjects the researcher's findings to peer review. Peers are impartial people from the same academic discipline with similar competencies as the researcher, and the process of peer review enhances the credibility of the research. If peers disagree with the findings, then the researcher has an opportunity to reinvestigate the issue and reexamine their research methodology. The successful completion of peer review is usually a requirement for publication in scholarly journals, which is the primary way that social studies research is disseminated.

Analyzing Social Studies Information

Social studies students must understand how to determine the timeline/chronology of events through a process called sequencing. Sequencing allows student to gain a better understanding of change over time in history. Social studies classrooms often employ test questions that force students to recall the correct chronology, or time order, of important historical events.

Along with sequencing, social studies students should be able to carry out a process known as categorizing. Categorizing is the process by which historical themes, events, agents, persons, movements, or ideas are placed in designated categories that help students understand their historical significance. Categorization is usually most effective when certain words or phrases are organized by themes or concepts. For instance, the categorical concept of economic depression could help students better understand such historical events as the Panic of 1819, the Great Depression, and the Great Recession. Categorization allows students to link unrelated events in history.

Identifying associations and cause-and-effect relationships strengthens a student's ability to sequence events in history. All U.S. history is a series of associated events leading to still other events. A cause is what made something happen. An effect is what happens because of something. Understanding cause-and-effect helps students to understand the proverbial *why* of history; it helps them breathe more meaning into history.

Comparing and contrasting is another strategy that will make students more historically informed. In history, we often compare two or more things to understand their similarities and differences better. Part of the historical process is understanding what historical characteristics are unique or utterly common. Students might, for instance, compare and contrast the American Revolution to the Texas Revolution to gain a better understanding of the ways in which such variables as time, geographic location, and contributing persons affect history.

Summarizing is a strategy that is also used often throughout the historical process in a social studies classroom. Students will not only have to summarize the meaning of historical events or eras, but they will also need to know how to summarize the important points of primary and secondary sources. Summaries allow students to convey their knowledge in a short, concise, digestible fashion. Part of summarizing requires that students find the main idea of a particular article, source, or paragraph. Main ideas help students make their summaries even more concise and effective. Summarizing sometimes requires students to make generalizations or draw inferences/conclusions. Often there are gaps of information in the sources provided to students. Students will have to use background knowledge and critical-thinking skills to fill in these gaps with generalizations (broad, sweeping statements) or inferences/conclusions (educated guesses, predictions, or assumptions).

Analyzing Social Studies Data

Being literate in social studies means that teachers and students must be ready to interpret a variety of forms of data. In social studies, data is usually numerical or statistical information offered in the form of a graph, chart, table, document, map, or timeline.

A set of data can be described in terms of its center, spread, shape and any unusual features. The center of a data set can be measured by its mean, median, or mode. The spread, or variability, of a data set refers to how far the data points are from the center (mean or median). The spread can be measured by the range or by the quartiles and interquartile range. A data set with all its data points clustered around the center will have a small spread. A data set covering a wide range of values will have a large spread.

When a data set is displayed as a histogram or frequency distribution plot, the shape indicates if a sample is normally distributed, symmetrical, or has measures of skewness or kurtosis.

When graphed, a data set with a normal distribution will resemble a bell curve.

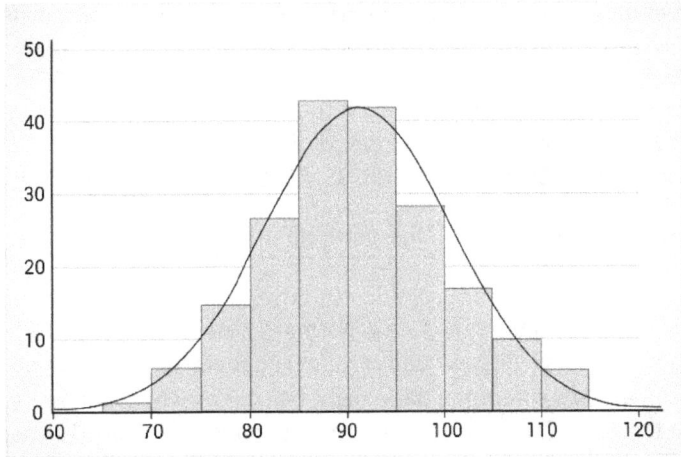

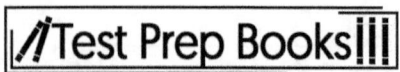

If the data set is symmetrical, each half of the graph when divided at the center is a mirror image of the other. If the graph has fewer data points to the right, the data is skewed right. If it has fewer data points to the left, the data is skewed left.

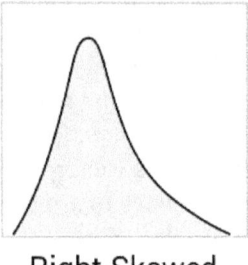
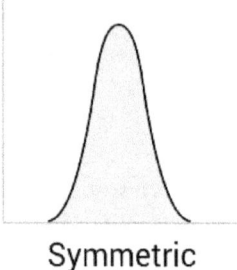
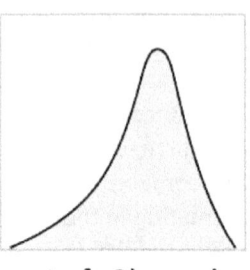

Right-Skewed   Symmetric   Left-Skewed

Kurtosis is a measure of whether the data is heavy-tailed with a high number of outliers, or light-tailed with a low number of outliers.

A description of a data set should include any unusual features such as gaps or outliers. A gap is a span within the range of the data set containing no data points. An outlier is a data point with a value either extremely large or extremely small when compared to the other values in the set.

The range of a data set is the difference between the highest and the lowest values in the set. The range can be considered to be the span of the data set. To determine the range, the smallest value in the set is subtracted from the largest value. The ranges for the data sets A, B, and C above are calculated as follows: A: $14 - 7 = 7$; B: $51 - 33 = 18$; C: $173 - 151 = 22$.

The center of a set of data (statistical values) can be represented by its mean, median, or mode. These are sometimes referred to as measures of central tendency.

Mean

Suppose that you have a set of data points and some description of the general properties of this data need to be found.

The first property that can be defined for this set of data is the mean. This is the same as average. To find the mean, add up all the data points, then divide by the total number of data points. For example, suppose that in a class of 10 students, the scores on a test were 50, 60, 65, 65, 75, 80, 85, 85, 90, 100. Therefore, the average test score will be:

$$\frac{50 + 60 + 65 + 65 + 75 + 80 + 85 + 85 + 90 + 100}{10} = 75.5$$

The mean is a useful number if the distribution of data is normal (more on this later), which roughly means that the frequency of different outcomes has a single peak and is roughly equally distributed on both sides of that peak. However, it is less useful in some cases where the data might be split or where there are some outliers. Outliers are data points that are far from the rest of the data. For example, suppose there are 10 executives and 90 employees at a company. The executives make $1000 per hour, and the employees make $10 per hour.

Therefore, the average pay rate will be:

$$\frac{\$1000 \cdot 10 + \$10 \cdot 90}{100} = \$109 \; per \; hour$$

Social Studies Foundation, Skills, Research, and Instruction | Social Studies Research

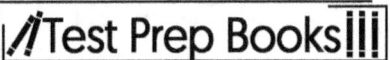

In this case, this average is not very descriptive since it's not close to the actual pay of the executives *or* the employees.

Median

Another useful measurement is the median. In a data set, the median is the point in the middle. The middle refers to the point where half the data comes before it and half comes after, when the data is recorded in numerical order. For instance, these are the speeds of the fastball of a pitcher during the last inning that he pitched (in order from least to greatest):

$$90, 92, 93, 93, 95, 96, 97, 97, 97$$

There are nine total numbers, so the middle or median number is the 5th one, which is 95.

In cases where the number of data points is an even number, then the average of the two middle points is taken. In the previous example of test scores, the two middle points are 75 and 80. Since there is no single point, the average of these two scores needs to be found. The average is:

$$\frac{75 + 80}{2} = 77.5$$

The median is generally a good value to use if there are a few outliers in the data. It prevents those outliers from affecting the middle value as much as when using the mean.

Since an outlier is a data point that is far from most of the other data points in a data set, this means an outlier also is any point that is far from the median of the data set. The outliers can have a substantial effect on the mean of a data set, but usually do not change the median or mode, or do not change them by a large quantity. For example, consider the data set (3, 5, 6, 6, 6, 8). This has a median of 6 and a mode of 6, with a mean of $\frac{34}{6} \approx 5.67$. Now, suppose a new data point of 1000 is added so that the data set is now (3, 5, 6, 6, 6, 8, 1000). This does not change the median or mode, which are both still 6. However, the average is now $\frac{1034}{7}$, which is approximately 147.7. In this case, the median and mode will be better descriptions for most of the data points.

Outliers in a given data set are sometimes the result of an error by the experimenter, but oftentimes, they are perfectly valid data points that must be taken into consideration.

Mode

One additional measure to define for *X* is the mode. This is the data point that appears most frequently. If two or more data points all tie for the most frequent appearance, then each of them is considered a mode. In the case of the test scores, where the numbers were 50, 60, 65, 65, 75, 80, 85, 85, 90, 100, there are two modes: 65 and 85.

A data set may have a single mode, multiple modes, or no mode. If different values repeat equally as often, multiple modes exist. If no value repeats, no mode exists. Consider the following data sets:

- A: 7, 9, 10, 13, 14, 14
- B: 37, 44, 33, 37, 49, 44, 51, 34, 37, 33, 44
- C: 173, 154, 151, 168, 155

Set A has a mode of 14. Set B has modes of 37 and 44. Set C has no mode.

The range of a data set is the difference between the highest and the lowest values in the set. The range can be considered the span of the data set. To determine the range, the smallest value in the set is subtracted from the

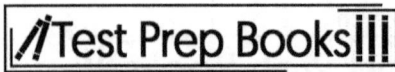

largest value. The ranges for the data sets A, B, and C above are calculated as follows: A: 14 − 7 = 7; B: 51 − 33 = 18; C: 173 − 151 = 22.

Social Studies Instruction and Assessment

Promote Students' Use of Social Science Skills

In social studies, vocabulary terms typically focus on particular people, places, groups, or features that happened or existed in the past (or present). Social studies vocabulary terms can be particularly challenging because there is a certain specificity that goes along with complex identities, groups, and events. To promote student understanding of these complex vocabulary terms, it is important that teachers connect the terms to larger concepts (i.e., words or phrases that refer to categories of information). Concepts allow social studies students to organize large amounts of information using historical context and change over time. When analyzing concepts, students should pay close attention to the definition of the concept and examples of the concept. For instance, one concept that can be bequeathed to students is the concept of war in American history. Under the umbrella of this concept, students can chronologically or thematically organize such disparate vocabulary terms as *French and Indian War, American Revolution, War of 1812, Mexican-American War, Civil War, Spanish-American War, World War I,* and *World War II*. Students may even broaden this concept to include such terms as *Cold War* and *War on Drugs*.

To promote study skills in the classroom, teachers can introduce students to such strategies as using study cards. This is particularly helpful for visual learners who need to see a certain term or concept to make an impression in their minds. Additionally, teachers can introduce students to the art of note-taking, which will help them succeed in both K–12 and higher-education classrooms. Students should be explicitly taught how to underline, highlight, color-code, and take notes in the margins. Test-taking skills should also be explicitly taught to students—students should know the E.R.A. approach to standardized tests that encourages them to examine the question, recall what they know, and apply what they know. Lastly, students should be exposed to research tools such as libraries, databases, archives, citation styles, and public museums. To be prepared for the twenty-first century, students should also be exposed to digital versions of these tools. It is quite possible that students can even go on digital tours of museum collections, thanks to the Internet and computer technologies.

Instructional Practices

Teachers should strive to move beyond textbooks in the classroom, introducing students to a variety of primary and secondary sources. Written secondary sources can include professional monographs, popular histories, historical fiction, magazines, newspapers, and scholarly journals and articles. Written primary sources can include journals, diaries, newspaper clippings, government documents, context-specific literature, letters, biographies and autobiographies, folklore, and cultural mythology. Students should also be exposed to visual sources such as political cartoons, artwork, ads, signs, graphs, charts, tables, photographs, and videos. Students can also be introduced to relevant musical works. As digital archives and histories are becoming more relevant in 21st century classroom, it's important that students are exposed to computer-based resources.

Social science students should not solely be focused on history and the past. Students should be exposed to disciplines such as political science, social studies, geography, psychology, government, ethics, economics, environmental studies, and sociology. These disciplines all emphasize present-day issues and trends in society; students should use these disciplines to determine the essence of their own historical context. Students must be able to not only understand social science concepts, but also apply the problem-solving and decision-making skills of the social sciences to the real world. Even history can help students better understand the present and have enough foresight to protect the future. The social sciences, in this sense, are as much about civic engagement as they are about content acquisition.

Teachers must adopt developmentally appropriate instructional practices and activities to optimize the instruction of social studies. Setting clear and consistent expectations for students is one of most important instructional practices; the other is providing universal rules to ensure that the classroom remains a safe and positive learning environment. Additionally, instructional practices for tasks should be clear, and students should be allowed to request clarification. The appropriateness of some instructional practices will differ based on age and level of development. For example, long lectures would be inappropriate for younger students, who would have difficulty maintaining attention.

Technologies and materials play a critical role in teaching, but they must be accessible and developmentally appropriate for students. Technology is a valuable learning tool, but teachers should ensure that such technology is universally available and accessible to students. For example, if a student doesn't have reasonable access to the Internet at home, the teacher must either avoid digital homework assignments or make reasonable accommodations for the student, such as reserving school resources for the student. All activities should be appropriately difficult with clear instructions, an appropriate pace, and smooth transitions between tasks. Developmental appropriateness will greatly impact the selection of activities.

Teachers should prioritize enhancing students' knowledge, improving skills, and achieving progress. All lessons, activities, and assessments must be tailored toward these goals. Lessons and activities primarily relate to knowledge of the subjects contained in the social curriculum studies and practicing relevant skills. Assessments function as an opportunity to gauge students' retention of knowledge and skills, which allows teachers to track students' progress more accurately. When students are struggling to progress, teachers must identify and remove obstacles to learning.

Current Technology as a Tool for Teaching

Computer technology—especially with regard to the Internet, smartphones, tablets, and social media—is progressing at a rate that is often difficult for teachers to keep up with what is pertinent, effective, and relevant for their students. With the world becoming increasingly connected (and separated) by technology, it is important for every student in the social sciences to be exposed to contemporary techniques and practices for incorporating technology into the classroom. Students must know how to use the Internet, smartphones, tablets, and social media in their social sciences classroom to adequately prepare for the next era of college learning and professional research. Teachers must acquaint themselves with up-to-date, research-based practices for incorporating technology in the classroom. Specifically, in a social studies classroom, students must be prepared to access sources online and differentiate whether they are primary or secondary sources. More importantly, students must be able to assess whether the sources are legitimate enough to incorporate into research or presentations. Teachers should explicitly teach students how to research on technological devices while also teaching them how to assess the validity of sources and databases. In an increasingly digitized world, it is important to expose students to digital museums and databases. It is also important to use technology—specifically social media and smartphone apps—to hook students onto a particular topic or area of inquiry.

Different technological tools serve different functions. To function in the developing world, students need to learn and understand digital literacy—the knowledge, dexterity, and critical thinking skills involved in using technology to create, evaluate, and present information. The best techniques for instructing students on choosing and using technological tools involve educating them on the advantages and disadvantages of each, demonstrating how to use them, breaking down their different aspects, assigning students homework or projects in which they will utilize different technological resources, and instructing them on when it is appropriate to use each kind. The most common types of tools used for communication are as follows:

- Smartphones/apps
- Email

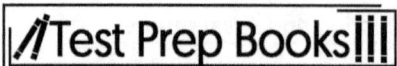

Social Studies Foundation, Skills, Research, and Instruction

- Microsoft Office
- iMovie
- Skype
- Twitter
- Facebook
- Instagram
- Google Drive
- Various blogging websites
- Online bulletin boards
- Wikis

A good way to introduce students to varying technological tools is by using them in the classroom. It would be helpful to teach students how to use a PowerPoint presentation, for example, by giving a PowerPoint presentation. If a student asks a question to which the teacher does not know the answer, they can discover the answer together by using a reliable source on the Internet, projecting the process on the board, so that they can see exactly how it's done. Students can also receive homework and updates on school and classroom events through a personal blog or class bulletin board the teacher has designed so that they may become familiar with using online communication. Students can also be assigned to use personal blogs to practice and improve their writing skills.

The most effective method for learning new skills is a hands-on approach. Students can be educated on the pros and cons of each technological tool, but the best way for them to learn is to allow them to find out for themselves by assigning projects and asking them to give the reasoning behind choosing a specific tool.

Instructional Strategies to Ensure Reading Comprehension

A potential educator needs to be aware that teaching reading comprehension involves developing skills beyond mere word recognition. It involves being able to teach critical thinking skills and being able to teach students how to process unfamiliar material based on prior knowledge. It involves getting students involved in what they read, based on their interests, and their ability to relate to the material. It involves encouraging students to ask questions and explore.

Activating students' prior knowledge—sometimes referred to as schemas—means being able to get students to ascertain what they already know, so they can apply it to their reading. A common strategy to use prior to reading is a K-W-L chart, a graphic organizer which has students determine what they already know about a topic, what they want to know, and what they learned after reading. Having students complete the K section before reading is a tangible way to activate their schemas.

It is important students make connections and relate reading passages to their own experiences—referred to as text to self, to their world knowledge— referred to as text to world, and to other texts— referred to as text to text. The ability to make these connections helps students better understand what they have read.

Potential teachers should be able to model asking questions during the reading experience and model the finding of those answers, based on prior knowledge. Having students read, then write about the connections they make to the text will increase reading comprehension skills. Of course, teaching students to activate and use their schema as it applies to their reading is a skill that should be taught over time. Encourage students to ask how text passages relate to what they already know within their own lives, how those passages relate to what they already know about the world, and how those passages relate to other things they've read. Doing so will result in more critical thinkers and, in turn, more critical readers.

Metacognitive strategies ask the student to decode text passages. In part, they require the student to preview text, be able to recognize unfamiliar words, then use context clues to define them for greater understanding. In addition, meta-cognitive strategies in the classroom employ skills such as being able to decode imagery, being able to predict, and being able to summarize. If a student can define unfamiliar vocabulary, make sense of an author's use of imagery, preview text prior to reading predict outcomes during reading, and summarize the material, he or she is achieving effective reading comprehension. When approaching reading instruction, the teacher who encourages students to use phrases such as *I'm noticing*, *I'm thinking*, and *I'm wondering* is teaching a meta-cognitive type strategy.

It has been shown that the teacher who employs multiple reading strategies in a variety of reading situations has the most success in fostering critical thinkers. Teachers should strive to make reading an active, observable process. Active reading involves reading with a purpose and determination to not only understand, but evaluate text using critical reading skills. Critical reading skills need to be fostered in a way that allows students to read and retain information and then gain interactive feedback experience with peers and with an instructor. Employing multiple reading strategies, either through assigned, independent reading with follow up or through a shared experience, aids in active reading.

The following are some of the reading strategies that should be utilized:

- Modeling prediction
- Modeling inference
- Asking students to connect text to self, the world, and to other text
- Asking students to visualize what they read (playing the video in their head)
- Asking students to partner in their reading experiences
- Helping students determine the importance of ideas in what they read
- Modeling the critical thinking process
- Modeling analyzation
- Modeling summarization

Meaning and Pronunciations of Unfamiliar Words

Reference materials are indispensable tools for beginners and experts alike. Educators should introduce students to different types of reference materials as well as when and how to use them. One of the main reasons to utilize these types of resources is to locate the meaning and pronunciation of unfamiliar words.

Dictionaries provide an explanation of a word's meanings as a single word can have multiple definitions. A dictionary organizes these definitions based on their parts of speech and then arranges them from most to least commonly used meanings or from oldest to most modern usage. A pronunciation guide is included so that the pronunciation of each word can be decoded. Many dictionaries also offer information about a word's etymology and usage. With all these functions, then, a dictionary is a basic, essential tool in many situations. Students can turn to a dictionary when they encounter an unfamiliar word or when they see a familiar word used in a new way.

Whereas a dictionary entry lists a word's definitions, a thesaurus entry lists a word's synonyms and antonyms—i.e., words with similar and opposite meanings, respectively. A dictionary can be used to find out what a word means and where it came from, and a thesaurus can be used to understand a word's relationship to other words. A **thesaurus** can be a powerful vocabulary building tool. By becoming familiar with synonyms and antonyms, students will be more equipped to use a broad range of vocabulary in their speech and writing. Of course, one thing to be aware of when using a thesaurus is that most words do not have exact synonyms. Rather, there are slight nuances of meaning that can make one word more appropriate than another in a given context. In this case, it is often to the

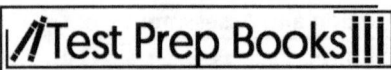

Social Studies Foundation, Skills, Research, and Instruction

user's advantage to consult a thesaurus side-by-side with a dictionary to confirm any differences in usage between two synonyms.

Like dictionaries, **glossaries** also offer explanations of terms. However, while a dictionary attempts to cover every word in a language, a glossary only focuses on terms relevant to a specific field. Also, a glossary entry is more likely to offer a longer explanation of a term and its relevance within that field. Glossaries are often found at the back of textbooks or other nonfiction publications in order to explain new or unfamiliar terms to readers. A glossary may also be an entire book on its own that covers all of the essential terms and concepts within a particular profession, field, or other specialized area of knowledge.

An atlas can be used when researching unfamiliar social studies terminology. Atlases are comprised of maps of different regions, countries, or even the world. These collections of maps can be organized in a variety of ways depending on what type of atlas it is. They can also include diagrams, statistics, and vocabulary specific to that particular atlas.

Making Connections Between Methods in Social Studies and Other Content Areas

Over the course of the last twenty-five years, the K–12 and higher-education systems in the United States have been gradually adopting interdisciplinary practices that encourage teachers and students to integrate skills, concepts, and ideas across a variety of different disciplines. This has become especially true in the social sciences at the K–12 level, where teachers and students must continually combine theories and practices from such disparate fields as history, political science, social studies, geography, psychology, government, ethics, economics, environmental studies, and sociology. Additionally, twenty-first-century teachers and students will be expected to make connections between the social sciences, sciences, arts, and mathematics. While teachers should strive to enrich their knowledge of content in their particular field of inquiry, they should also strive to make connections between fields.

This means they should employ instructional practices in the classroom that explicitly and implicitly expose students to the interconnected nature of all learning. One way this could be accomplished is through collaboration with colleagues who are experts in other fields. Another way is by introducing textbooks, articles, and materials from other fields into content-specific social science classrooms. Lastly, teachers can help students to relate skills, concepts, and ideas across different social science disciplines by incorporating project-based learning (PBL) activities into the classroom that require students to analyze/approach/solve real-world problems through collaboration with peers, professionals, and public agencies with unique, discipline-specific experiences. PBL activities ensure that students not only grasp interdisciplinary content, but also *apply* this content to real-life problems, projects, and scenarios.

Promoting Various Points of View

Teaching point of view is a critical aspect of social studies. Point of view is multifaceted, encompassing interrelated subconscious biases, cultural background, and value judgments. Often people with different points of view can disagree about certain events, or they draw conflicting conclusions about a common fact pattern. In general, teachers must be aware of three different points of view: their personal point of view, their students' point of view, and the points of view in the study materials.

Teachers approach social studies from a specific point of view that can influence which topics they cover in class, the amount of time devoted to each topic, and the characterization of historical actors and events. Given the power of point of view to alter historical narratives, teachers must be careful to craft well-rounded and balanced lessons. For example, lessons on the Texas Revolution should incorporate the perspectives from multiple groups, including American Indians, Mexicans, Americans, and Anglo-American settlers in Texas.

Likewise, students arrive in the classroom with a preexisting point of view, and teachers must be aware of how these differences can influence the learning process. Students' points of view can prove especially challenging when they conflict with a teacher's point of view. For example, a teacher who characterizes the arrival of Europeans in Texas as a positive event might have difficulty reaching Mexican-American or American Indian students. The most effective way to handle the conflicting point of views of students is to directly address how different groups perceived the same events.

All study materials contain a point of view. Primary sources inherently express the author's point of view. For example, an Anglo-American witness to the Council House Fight might emphasize how the American Indians didn't attend the peace conference in good faith, while an American Indian survivor might focus on how the Texans indiscriminately fired upon the peace delegation. To avoid portraying an author's point of view as an incontrovertible truth, teachers should provide relevant information about the author's background, purpose of the writing, and the intended audience.

Secondary sources present a similar set of challenges. As with primary sources, teachers should provide necessary and appropriate context to elucidate the source's point of view. Some secondary sources are opinion-based arguments, which typically have a clear point of view. Other secondary sources, such as textbooks, strike a neutral tone and attempt to maintain objectivity by sticking to facts. However, neutrality and objectivity don't necessarily remove the author's point of view.

Given the vast amounts of available information, writing a social studies textbook necessarily requires some consolidation and omission. In addition, American textbook authors have historically approached social studies from a Eurocentrism point of view that prioritizes the accomplishments of Europeans and Americans over those of other cultural groups. Therefore, teachers should incorporate supplemental materials with alternative and valuable points of view. Furthermore, class discussions on point of view can help students better understand how authors can influence historical narratives.

Forms of Assessment

Differentiated assessments are crucial for tailoring the educational environment for individual learning types. Teachers must be aware and sensitive to the neurodiversity in their classrooms. When designing social science assessments, teachers should keep in mind the unique learning types and cognitive skills. Whenever possible, social science teachers should make their materials and assessments personally and culturally relevant.

Also try to vary assessments by incorporating design-thinking, inquiry-based learning, project-based learning, and student voice and choice. Inevitably, a good teacher will respond to student needs and concerns and offer alternative assessments without diminishing the crucial nature of the standards.

Types of Assessments

Formal assessments are partially based on observation, but are planned and implemented with the design to see how students respond to specific stimuli. They give a clearer indication of students' strengths and weaknesses regarding the material. There are two primary methods for conducting formal assessments. The most conventional is a simple pencil-and-paper test in which students read prewritten questions and respond to them in writing. These physical answers provide a direct window into what the students know and how their reading comprehension is progressing.

Informal assessments are not planned and lack a typical format or timeline. They can be as simple as watching and listening to how the students respond to answers in class or perform classwork. Observation is key. The instructor should perceive how students respond to reading and language concepts as well as how they interpret them. If a student isn't understanding something such as a cultural reading concept, it may indicate that a more in-depth explanation is required. This will help the teacher adapt the instruction to enable the student to self-correct their own performance.

Performance assessments are a little less concrete but can provide a lot of insight into the student's mind-set and reactions that are more three-dimensional than a written assessment. This method does not use written responses, but instead analyzes students' performance in response to reading questions or activities. When giving performance assessments, it's important to bear in mind key questions: Does the student understand what they just read? Did they seem uncomfortable when presenting their answer? How accurate was their response? From here, new teaching strategies can be implemented, or the instructor can identify ways to provide specialized assistance to boost students' skills.

Formal assessments, such as selected-response questions, are a useful and quick way to grade students as opposed to free response assessments. However, informal assessments are an even quicker and more frequently used method of assessing students. Informal assessments can be conducted after a modeled lesson and before independent practice. The use of individual whiteboards and a few quick selected response questions prepared before the lesson is a helpful tactic for teachers to quickly survey which students grasped the concepts and which students need additional reinforcement. Those who still need to master the skill can then be efficiently identified and grouped together for a small reteach.

Demonstrating Ability to Interpret Results

When using the results from formal assessments addressing multiple skills, it is important to group students according to ability for the particular skill of interest from the assessment and not just on the overall score. However, the overall score may be beneficial for grouping with regards to pacing and complexity of questions.

Results of Assessments

Lessons and groups should be adjusted to the needs of the students; therefore, student groupings may need to change on a daily or weekly basis. Each student's needs change from concept to concept. Assessments must be ongoing and frequent. Results from these ongoing assessments should be the driving force behind the grouping of students.

Planning Social Studies Instruction

Besides traditional lectures, textbook work, PowerPoints, and direct instruction, teachers can diversify pedagogical methods in their classrooms by incorporating inquiry-based practices, project-based learning, field work, role plays, sociodramas, skits, simulations, field trips, student-specific academic interventions, debates, and identity-based social-emotional learning activities into social science courses. The goal is to differentiate sources, instruction, and assessments so all students have access to social science content.

Besides direct classroom instruction, teachers can take students on field trips to different communities, historical sites, and museums. Teachers should introduce students to the notion that history exists in all settings, finding opportunities for students to carry out research projects, project-based learning, and experiential learning in surrounding communities. Students should recognize that all materials—buildings, streets, schools, antiques, common objects—possess some semblance of historical agency. Each material item has a unique biography. By taking to the streets, students will be more prepared for interdisciplinary scholarship and field research in higher education. Students can also be encouraged to explore their own communities to collect formal and oral histories for the classroom. Special events such as Freedom Week, which focuses on celebrating the values and ideals of the founding of our country, can provide opportunities for additional student learning in a variety of ways.

Teachers and students must also engage parents/caregivers, colleagues/peers, and the community to convey the overall importance of a social studies education. When challenged about the importance of a social studies education, teachers and students can illustrate the ways in which a social studies education can help people become better writers, researchers, and presenters. Moreover, a quality social studies education will also make teachers and students better problem solvers, decision makers, and civic engagers. A knowledge of social studies can help teachers and students understand many problems faced in present-day global society. Politicians, businessmen, and common citizens all could benefit from enriching their historical consciousness so that they can effectively diagnose and implement positive changes for their government, customers, families, or fellow citizens. Social studies can help rebuild communities and prevent international conflicts; it can help teachers and students become better citizens in an often-conflicted global society.

Practice Quiz

1. Firsthand accounts of an event, subject matter, time period, or individual are referred to as what type of sources?
    a. Primary
    b. Secondary
    c. Direct
    d. Indirect

2. A student encounters the word *aficionado* and wants to learn more about it. It doesn't sound like other English words he knows, so the student is curious to identify the word's origin. What resource should he consult?
    a. A thesaurus
    b. A dictionary
    c. A style guide
    d. A grammar book

3. A student is starting a research assignment on Japanese American internment camps during World War II, but she is unsure of how to gather relevant resources. Which of the following would be the most helpful advice for the student?
    a. Conduct a broad internet search to get a wide view of the subject.
    b. Consult an American history textbook.
    c. Find websites about Japanese culture such as fashion and politics.
    d. Locate texts in the library related to World War II in America and look for references to internment camps in the index.

4. Which of the following should be considered before utilizing a technological device in the classroom?
    a. The age of the students
    b. Whether it is user friendly
    c. If it will be used in the real world
    d. All of the above

5. When a student looks back at a previous reading section for information, he or she is using which of the following?
    a. Self-monitoring comprehension
    b. KWL charts
    c. Metacognitive skills
    d. Directed reading-thinking activities

See answers on the next page.

Answer Explanations

1. A: Firsthand accounts are given by primary sources—individuals who provide personal or expert accounts of an event, subject matter, time period, or individual. They are viewed more as objective accounts than subjective. Secondary sources are accounts given by an individual or group of individuals who were not physically present at the event or who did not have firsthand knowledge of an individual or time period. Secondary sources are sources that have used research in order to create a written work. *Direct sources* and *indirect sources* are not standard terms.

2. B: A word's origin is also known as its *etymology*. In addition to offering a detailed list of a word's various meanings, a dictionary also provides information about a word's history, such as when it first came into use, what language it originated from, and how its meaning may have changed over time. A thesaurus is for identifying synonyms and antonyms, so Choice A is incorrect. A style guide provides formatting, punctuation, and syntactical advice for a specific field, and a grammar book is related to the appropriate placement of words and punctuation, which does not provide any insight into a word's origin. Therefore, Choices C and D are incorrect.

3. D: Relevant information refers to information that is closely related to the subject being researched. Students might get overwhelmed by information when they first begin researching, so they should learn how to narrow down search terms for their field of study. Both Choices A and B are incorrect because they start with a range that is far too wide; the student will spend too much time sifting through unrelated information to gather only a few related facts. Choice C introduces a more limited range, but it is not closely related to the topic that is being researched. Finally, Choice D is correct because the student is choosing books that are more closely related to the topic and is using the index or table of contents to evaluate whether the source contains the necessary information.

4. D: The age of the students is an important aspect to consider when using technology because many devices have basic requirements for motor and comprehension skills. User friendliness is important as not all students have the same amount of technological literacy. Teaching students to use a device that they will never use again is futile, so it's more practical to use technology that they will use in the real world. Choice D is the correct answer because it includes all of these aspects; Choices A, B, and C are incorrect because they only include one of the above aspects.

5. C: Asking oneself a comprehension question is a metacognition skill. Readers with metacognitive skills have learned to think about thinking. It gives students control over their learning while they read. KWL charts help students to identify what they already know about a given topic.

Practice Test

World History

1. Which of the following civilizations developed the first democratic form of government?
    a. Roman Empire
    b. Ancient Greece
    c. Achaemenid Empire
    d. Zhou Dynasty

2. Which of the following statements most accurately describes the Achaemenid Empire in Persia until the fourth century BC?
    a. Islam was the official religion.
    b. Achaemenid emperors constructed the entire Silk Road network.
    c. The Achaemenid Empire successfully conquered Greece.
    d. None of the above

3. The Silk Roads caused which of the following?
    a. Spread of Buddhism from India to China
    b. The devastation of European economies
    c. Introduction of the Bubonic Plague to the New World
    d. The Great War

4. What caused the end of the Western Roman Empire in 476 A.D.?
    a. Invasions by Germanic tribes
    b. The Mongol invasion
    c. The assassination of Julius Caesar
    d. Introduction of Taoism in Rome

5. Which of the following statements most accurately describes the Mongol Empire?
    a. The Mongol army was largely a cavalry force.
    b. Mongol rulers did not tolerate other religions.
    c. Mongol rulers neglected foreign trade.
    d. The Mongol Empire is known for its discouragement of literacy and the arts.

6. What social consequence did the Black Death have in Europe?
    a. It gave birth to the concept of absolute monarchy.
    b. It ignited the Protestant Reformation.
    c. The Black Death eroded serfdom in Europe.
    d. It gave rise to child labor laws in England.

Practice Test | Social Studies Instruction and Assessment

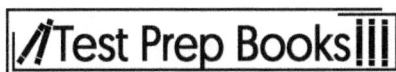

7. Renaissance scholars and artists were inspired by which classical civilization?
   a. Ancient Greece
   b. Ancient Egypt
   c. The Zhou Dynasty
   c. The Ottoman Empire

8. Nicolaus Copernicus was a key figure in which cultural phenomena?
   a. The Scientific Revolution
   b. The Age of Enlightenment
   c. The Renaissance
   d. The Protestant Reformation

9. Which of the following statements best describes King Louis XIV of France?
   a. He abdicated his throne during the French Revolution.
   b. He supported the American Revolution.
   c. He was the ultimate example of an absolute monarch.
   d. He created the concept of the Mandate of Heaven.

10. Which of the following resulted from the Age of Enlightenment?
    a. The discovery of the heliocentric theory
    b. The birth of Lutheranism
    c. The American Revolution
    d. The Renaissance

11. Which of the following consequences did NOT result from the discovery of the New World in 1492 A.D.?
    a. Proof that the world was round instead of flat
    b. The deaths of millions of Native Americans
    c. Biological exchange between Europe and the New World
    d. The creation of new syncretic religions

12. Which of the following statements best describes the relationship, if any, between the revolutions in America and France?
    a. The French Revolution inspired the American Revolution.
    b. The American Revolution inspired the French Revolution.
    c. They both occurred simultaneously.
    d. There was no connection between the French and American revolutions.

13. Which of the following was NOT a consequence of industrialization in Europe during the 1800s?
    a. The birth of the working class
    b. The expansion of European empires in Africa and Asia
    c. Improved transportation and economic efficiency
    d. All of the above

14. Which of the following was a consequence of increasing nationalism in Europe in the 1800s?
    a. The unification of Spain
    b. The unification of France
    c. Increasing competition and tension between European powers
    d. More efficient trade between nations

235

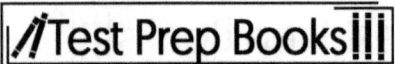

15. Which of the following military technologies did NOT play a role in World War I from 1914 to 1918?
    a. The atomic bomb
    b. Poison gas
    c. Armored tanks
    d. Aircraft

16. Which of the following statements best describes international affairs between World War I and World War II?
    a. A lenient World War I peace treaty for Germany delayed the start of World War II.
    b. The policy of appeasement only encouraged further aggression by Hitler.
    c. A powerful League of Nations fostered increased cooperation and negotiation.
    d. Tensions grew between Germany and Japan.

17. Which of the following was a consequence of World War II?
    a. The collapse of British and French empires in Asia and Africa
    b. A communist revolution in Russia
    c. The end of the Cold War
    d. The death of Franz Ferdinand, the Archduke of Austria

18. Which of the following trends did NOT occur after the end of the Cold War in 1991?
    a. A decrease in nationalistic tension
    b. An increase in cultural and economic globalization
    c. An increase in religious fundamentalism
    d. An increase in environmentalism

19. What impact, if any, did the introduction of the movable type printing press have in Europe?
    a. It increased the cost of books because the process was labor intensive.
    b. It led to an increase in literacy.
    c. The Catholic Church used it to effectively suppress the Protestant Reformation.
    d. It led to the Dark Ages.

20. In which phase(s) of the Space Race did the United States achieve victory over the USSR?
    a. Putting the first satellite into orbit
    b. Putting the first man into space
    c. Putting the first man on the Moon
    d. All of the above

21. Which of the following is NOT a sect of Islam?
    a. Shinto
    b. Sunni
    c. Shi'a
    d. Sufi

22. Which form of economic exchange allowed the Chinese to maintain political control over their empire?
    a. Potlatches
    b. Tribute
    c. Bartering
    d. All of the above

U.S. History

23. Which of the following documents outlawed slavery throughout the United States?
    a. US Constitution
    b. Compromise of 1850
    c. Emancipation Proclamation
    d. 13th Amendment

24. What were the consequences of the Spanish-American War?
    a. The US acquired colonies in the Caribbean and Pacific oceans.
    b. The US acquired large swaths of territory in the Southwestern United States.
    c. It led to the formation of the League of Nations.
    d. It ended the Great Depression.

25. Which constitutional amendment gave women the right to vote in the United States?
    a. 15th
    b. 18th
    c. 19th
    d. 21st

26. What consequences did the Great Migration have?
    a. It led to conflict with Native Americans in the West in the 1800s.
    b. It led to increased racial tension in the North in the early 1900s.
    c. It led to increased conflict with Mexican immigrants in the 1900s.
    d. It led to increased conflict with Irish and German immigrants in the 1800s.

27. Which Supreme Court decision struck down the separate but equal doctrine?
    a. *Roe v. Wade*
    b. *Brown v. Board of Education*
    c. *Plessy v. Ferguson*
    d. *Marbury v. Madison*

28. Which of the following led to the American Revolutionary War?
    a. The Stamp Act
    b. The Boston Massacre
    c. The Boston Tea Party
    d. All of the above

29. Which event contributed to increasing sectional tension before the Civil War?
    a. Malcolm X's death
    b. The Bleeding Kansas conflict
    c. The 13th Amendment
    d. Shay's Rebellion

30. Which of the following caused America to join World War I in 1917?
    a. Germany's unrestricted submarine warfare
    b. The destruction of the USS *Maine*
    c. The Japanese attack on Pearl Harbor
    d. Franz Ferdinand's death in 1914

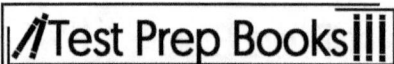

31. What consequences did World War II have?
    a. It led to the creation of the League of Nations.
    b. It led to a communist revolution in Russia.
    c. It made the US the only superpower in the world.
    d. None of the above.

32. Which event was the last major armed conflict between US forces and Native Americans?
    a. Trail of Tears
    b. Tecumseh's War
    c. Wounded Knee Massacre
    d. Battle of the Little Bighorn

33. What consequences did the Neolithic Revolution have?
    a. Native Americans domesticated cattle and horses.
    b. Native Americans began to grow crops.
    c. Native Americans developed steel weapons and tools.
    d. Native Americans began to emigrate to Canada.

34. Which document established the first system of government in the United States?
    a. Declaration of Independence
    b. Constitution
    c. Articles of Confederation
    d. Bill of Rights

35. What consequences did the New Deal have?
    a. It established a number of federal agencies and programs that continue to function in the 21st century.
    b. It led to a third political party.
    c. It established a two-term limit in the White House.
    d. It led to the Great Depression.

36. What advantage did the North have over the South during the Civil War?
    a. The North was defending their homes from damage.
    b. The North had free labor at home.
    c. The North had a larger population.
    d. The North had more experienced military leaders.

37. In which of the following areas did the United State achieve victory during the Cold War?
    a. The Korean War
    b. The Space Race
    c. The Vietnam War
    d. The Battle of Gettysburg

38. The presidential cabinet has which of the following duties?
    a. Advise the president
    b. Act as spokesperson for the US government administration.
    c. Solicit donations for the president's reelection campaign.
    d. Preside over the Senate

39. Which organization helped Ronald Reagan win the White House in 1980?
    a. Great Awakening
    b. Moral Majority
    c. Know-Nothings
    d. Anti-Defamation League

40. Since 1965, most immigrants to the United States have come from what region(s)?
    a. Central and South America and Asia
    b. Australia
    c. Europe
    d. Antarctica

41. Which event helped sparked the gay and lesbian rights movement in 1969?
    a. The Stonewall riots
    b. The murder of Matthew Shepard
    c. The murder of Vincent Chin
    d. The emergence of AIDS

42. Which of the following were characteristics of the Gilded Age?
    a. Social inequality
    b. Increasing urbanization
    c. Expanding industrialization
    d. All of the above

43. Which of the following were characteristics of the American political environment in the early 1900s?
    a. The Federalists and the Democratic Republicans
    b. The Populist Party and Progressive Reformers
    c. The Whig Party and the Democrat Party
    d. National Union Party and the Democrat Party

44. Which of the following motivated Christopher Columbus to sail across the Atlantic Ocean?
    a. A desire to establish a direct trade route to Asia
    b. A desire to confirm the existence of America
    c. A desire to prove the world was round
    d. A desire to spread Judaism

45. Which battle of the Revolutionary War was a key turning point in 1777 because it brought France into the war?
    a. The Battle of Lexington and Concord
    b. The Battle of Saratoga
    c. The Battle of Trenton
    d. The Battle of Bunker Hill

46. What did Radical Republicans hope to accomplish during Reconstruction?
    a. Equal rights for freed slaves
    b. Leniency for former Confederates
    c. Acquittal of President Johnson during impeachment
    d. Effective segregation laws

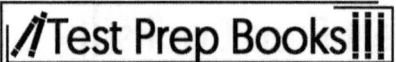

47. Which of the following were characteristics of the American economy after World War II?
    a. A return to depression
    b. An increased use of computers
    c. The decline of the Sun Belt
    d. The fall of the stock market

48. Which of the following agreements allowed territories to vote on whether they would become free or slave states?
    a. The Connecticut Compromise
    b. The Missouri Compromise
    c. The Compromise of 1850
    d. The Three-Fifths Compromise

49. Which of the following sets includes a primary cause and effect of the American Revolution?
    a. A cause was the taxation of the colonies, and an effect was the civil rights movement.
    b. A cause was the Declaration of Independence, and an effect was the Constitution.
    c. A cause was the French and Indian War, and an effect was the Bill of Rights.
    d. A cause was the debate over slavery, and an effect was the Seven Years' War.

50. Which of the following statements about the US Constitution is true?
    a. It was signed on July 4, 1776.
    b. It was enacted at the end of the Revolutionary War.
    c. New York failed to ratify it, but it still passed by majority.
    d. It replaced the Articles of Confederation.

Texas History

51. Which of the following American Indian groups consolidated control over the Texas Plains during the eighteenth century?
    a. Apache
    b. Comanche
    c. Karankawa
    d. Puebloans

52. The _____ is regarded as the final battle of the American Civil War, though it occurred after the Confederacy officially dissolved.
    a. Battle of Chickamauga
    b. Battle of Galveston
    c. Battle of Gonzales
    d. Battle of Palmito Ranch

53. Which statement correctly describes the relationship between the Fredonian Rebellion and the Texas Revolution?
    a. The Fredonian Rebellion marked the first official stage of the Texas Revolution.
    b. The Fredonian Rebellion was the first major land dispute between Anglo-American settlers, Mexicans, and American Indians.
    c. The Mexican government's response to the Fredonian Rebellion exacerbated its conflict with Anglo-American settlers in Texas.
    d. The leaders of the Fredonian Rebellion gained political and military experience that later proved invaluable during the Texas Revolution.

Practice Test | Social Studies Instruction and Assessment

54. Which politician participated in the drafting of both the Mexican Constitution of 1824 and the Constitution of the Republic of Texas?
    a. Antonio López de Santa Anna
    b. Lorenzo de Zavala
    c. Moses Austin
    d. Stephen F. Austin

Read the passage and answer questions 55 and 56.

And I promise you that you shall have a full cup of vengeance. For every man that fell fighting at the Alamo, for every one treacherously slaughtered at Goliad, you shall be satisfied. If I seem to be flying before the enemy now, it is for his destruction. Three Mexican armies united, we cannot fight. We can fight them singly. And every mile we make them follow us weakens them, separates them, confuses them. The low lands of the Brazos, the unfordable streams, the morasses, the pathless woods, are in league with us. And we must place our women and children in safety. Even if we have to carry them to General Gaines and the United States troops, we must protect them, first of all. I believe that we shall win our freedom with our own hands; but if the worst come, and we have to fall back to the Sabine, we shall find friends and backers there. I know President Jackson, my old general, the unconquered Christian Mars! Do you think he will desert his countrymen? Never! If we should need help, he has provided it. And the freedom of Texas is sure and certain. It is at hand. Prepare to achieve it. We shall take up our march eastward in three hours.

—Excerpt of a speech from *Remember the Alamo* by Amelia E. Barr, published in 1888.

55. Which historical figure most likely delivered this speech?
    a. John Bell Hood
    b. Moses Austin
    c. Sam Houston
    d. William B.   Travis

56. Which statement best explains why the Alamo and Goliad are mentioned in the speech?
    a. The Alamo and Goliad combined to form a powerful rallying cry for independence.
    b. The Alamo and Goliad demonstrated the ability of Texans to effectively resist the Mexican government.
    c. The Alamo and Goliad divided the Mexican military, allowing the Texans to pursue a divide-and-conquer strategy.
    d. The Alamo and Goliad convinced the United States to intervene and annex Texas.

57. Which of the following Texas politicians was NOT a leader of the Civil Rights Movement?
    a. Barbara Jordan
    b. Henry B. Gonzalez
    c. Lyndon B. Johnson
    d. Kay Bailey Hutchison

58. Vicente Córdova began his uprising against the Republic of Texas by recruiting Hispanic settlers and _____ allies.
    a. Atakapa
    b. Caddo
    c. Cherokee
    d. Comanche

59. _____ is widely credited as the author of the Texas Declaration of Independence.
   a. George Childress
   b. Haden Edwards
   c. Sam Houston
   d. Stephen F. Austin

60. Which statement best summarizes the legacy of Spindletop?
   a. Spindletop marked the first time a drilling rig successfully produced oil in the United States.
   b. Spindletop triggered an oil boom in Texas, exponentially increasing American oil production.
   c. Spindletop resulted in the formation of several new oil and gas companies.
   d. Spindletop produced the first and largest gusher of oil in American history.

Read the passage and answer questions 61 & 62.

But in a new and thinly settled country, the laws, however wise and good, cannot always be enforced. Magistrates and executive officers are few, and courts often at a distance. The new settlers, therefore, sometimes take the law into their own hands; and although they may not inflict the same punishment the law enjoins, I believe they generally do substantial justice. As an instance of the kind, I will state a case that happened on the bank of the Colorado river. A man settled there, who proved to be a notorious thief. He stole cattle, horses, hogs, or any thing he could lay his hands on. His neighbors resolved to endure his depredations no longer, and gave him notice to depart from that section of the country, or abide the consequences. After waiting awhile, and learning that he intended to remain, some half dozen of his neighbors went to his house in the evening, took him to a tree, and gave him thirty-nine lashes, well laid on. They then told him that the punishment should be repeated every week, as long as he remained in the neighborhood. Before a week came round, he left that section of the country, and has not been heard of since.

—Excerpt from *Trip to the West and Texas* by A.A. Parker, published in 1836

61. The neighbors in the passage acted most similarly to which group?
   a. Buffalo Soldiers
   b. Comanche band
   c. Confederate soldiers
   d. Texas Rangers

62. The scenario described in the passage illustrates which of the following factors that contributed to the Texas Revolution?
   a. The ineffectiveness of Mexican law enforcement led to Anglo-American settlers asserting sovereign claims over their land.
   b. The Mexican government sanctioned the Texas Rangers as an official law enforcement agency.
   c. The use of corporal punishment outraged the Mexican government and diminished support for self-government in Texas.
   d. Vigilante justice played an influential role in the historical development of Texas.

63. Which statement most accurately describes American Indians' land-use practices?
   a. American Indians' land-use practices had no impact on Texas's geographical features and ecological systems.
   b. American Indians' land-use practices led to the unsustainable consumption of natural resources.
   c. American Indians' land-use practices varied greatly based on local geographical and ecological circumstances.
   d. American Indians' land-use practices caused minimal environmental harm due to tribes' nomadic lifestyles.

Practice Test | Social Studies Instruction and Assessment

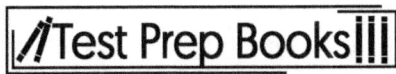

64. The Franciscan missionary _____ convinced Spain to devote more resources to the colonization of Texas.
   a. Álvar Núñez Cabeza de Vaca
   b. Francisco Hidalgo
   c. Fray Damián Massanet
   d. Moses Austin

65. The overwhelming majority of citrus production in Texas occurs in the _____.
   a. Gulf Coast
   b. Northern Plains
   c. Red River watershed
   d. Rio Grande Valley

66. What did Álvar Núñez Cabeza de Vaca contribute to the history of Texas?
   a. He provided detailed accounts of American Indian tribes in Texas.
   b. He was the first European to create a map of Texas.
   c. He received the first land grant from Spain to establish a colony in Texas.
   d. He authorized the construction of the Mission San Francisco de los Tejas.

Read the passage and answer questions 67 and 68.

The Indians, artfully feigning the treacherous semblance of friendship, pretented that they were looking for a suitable camping place, and enquired as to the exact locality of a water-hole in the vicinity, at the same time asking for a beef to appease their hungry—a want always felt by an Indian, when the promise of fresh meat loomed up in the distant perspective; and he would make such pleas with all the servile sicophancy of a slave, like the Italian who embraces his victim ere plunging the poniard into his heart.

Not daring to resent so formidable a body of savages, or refuse to comply with their requests, Mr. Benjamin F. Parker went out to them, had a talk and returned, expressing the opinion that the Indians were hostile and intented to fight, but added that he would go back and try to avert it. His brother Silas remonstrated, but he persisted in going, and was immediately surrounded and killed, whereupon the whole force—their savage instincts aroused by the sight of blood—charged upon the works, uttering the most terrific and unearthly yells that ever greeted the ears of mortals. Cries and confusion reigned.

—Excerpt from *Cynthia Ann Parker: The Story of Her Capture* by James T. DeShields, published in 1886

67. Which statement best describes the author's point of view?
   a. The author is highly antagonistic toward American Indians, creating a significant potential for bias in his historical account.
   b. The author is hostile to the specific American Indians described in the passage, but he otherwise considers American Indians to be allies.
   c. The author resents American Indians' dependence on Anglo-American settlements for survival.
   d. The author views American Indians as an existential threat to Anglo-American settlements, rivaling the danger posed by Italian colonization efforts.

68. Which statement most accurately summarizes the root of the conflict between American Indians and Anglo-American settlers in Texas?
   a. Anglo-American settlers and American Indians developed a codependent relationship, resulting in a vicious cycle of hostilities.
   b. Anglo-American settlers and American Indians were competing over the same resources, particularly land.
   c. Compared to Anglo-American settlers, American Indians were less committed to civil discourse and the peaceful resolution of conflicts.
   d. Anglo-American settlers viewed the American Indians as unproductive and irresponsible, especially their agricultural practices or lack of them.

Geography, Culture, and the Behavioral and Social Sciences

69. Which of the following is the primary problem with map projections?
   a. They are not detailed
   b. They do not include physical features
   c. They distort areas near the poles
   d. They only focus on the Northern Hemisphere

70. Which type of map illustrates the world's climatological regions?
   a. Topographic map
   b. Conformal projection
   c. Isoline map
   d. Thematic map

71. In which manner is absolute location expressed?
   a. The cardinal directions (north, south, east, and west)
   b. Through latitudinal and longitudinal coordinates
   c. Location nearest to a more well-known location
   d. Hemispherical position on the globe

72. Latitudinal lines are used to measure distance in which direction?
   a. East to west
   b. North to south
   c. Between two sets of coordinates
   d. In an inexact manner

73. Literacy rates are more likely to be higher in which area?
   a. Developing nations
   b. Northern Hemispherical nations
   c. Developed nations
   d. Near centers of trade

74. All EXCEPT which of the following are true of an area with an extremely high population density?
   a. Competition for resources is intense.
   b. Greater strain on public services exists.
   c. More people live in rural areas.
   d. More people live in urban areas.

Practice Test | Social Studies Instruction and Assessment

75. All of the following are negative demographic indicators EXCEPT which of the following?
    a. High infant mortality rates
    b. Low literacy rates
    c. High population density
    d. Low life expectancy

76. Which of the following characteristics best defines a formal region?
    a. Homogeneity
    b. Diversity
    c. Multilingualism
    d. Social mobility

77. Which statement is NOT true about a person's behavior?
    a. Behaviors change over time.
    b. Behaviors are influenced by a person's environment.
    c. It is untrue that a person will always have the same personal identity.
    d. Cultural changes influence a person's behavior.

78. Which group is most likely to succumb to or be influenced by peer pressure?
    a. Adolescents
    b. Senior women
    c. Middle-aged men
    d. Small children

79. Which of these is NOT a factor in which education can influence behavior?
    a. A school's rules and regulations
    b. Bullying establishing a system of social ranking
    c. School regulated social situations
    d. Grading

80. Which of these is NOT a true statement about culture?
    a. Culture derives from the beliefs, values, and behaviors of people in a community.
    b. All people are born into a certain culture.
    c. Cultures are stagnant and cannot be changed.
    d. Culture can be embedded within families, schools, businesses, social classes, and religions.

81. Differences in race, gender, sexual orientation, economic status, and language can be denoted as what?
    a. Behaviorism
    b. Peer pressure
    c. Adaptation
    d. Diversity

82. Which of the following are indicators of social class?
    a. Wealth
    b. Education level
    c. Standard of living
    d. All of the above

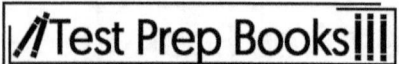

83. Which is NOT true of nonrenewable resources?
    a. They tend to be used more frequently than renewables.
    b. They are thought to be responsible for climate change.
    c. They are relied upon heavily in developing economies.
    d. They have slowed industrial growth.

84. Which of the following could be considered a pull factor for a particular area?
    a. High rates of unemployment
    b. Low GDP
    c. Educational opportunity
    d. High population density

85. In recent years, agricultural production has been affected by which of the following?
    a. The prevalence of biotechnology and GMOs
    b. Weaker crop yields due to poor soil
    c. Plagues of pests, which have limited food production
    d. Revolutions in irrigation, which utilize salinated water

86. The process of globalization can best be described as what?
    a. The integration of the world's economic systems into a singular entity
    b. The emergence of powerful nations seeking world dominance
    c. The absence of nation-states who seek to control certain areas
    d. Efforts to establish a singular world government for the world's citizens

Government and Citizenship

87. Which political concept describes a ruling body's ability to influence the actions, behaviors, or attitudes of a person or community?
    a. Authority
    b. Sovereignty
    c. Power
    d. Legitimacy

88. Which feature differentiates a state from a nation?
    a. Shared history
    b. Common language
    c. Population
    d. Sovereignty

89. Which political theorist considered violence necessary in order for a ruler to maintain political power and stability?
    a. John Locke
    b. Jean-Jacques Rousseau
    c. Karl Marx
    d. Niccolo Machiavelli

Practice Test | Social Studies Instruction and Assessment

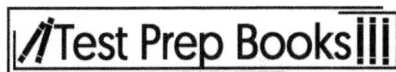

90. Which political theorist is considered the father of the social contract theory?
    a. John Stuart Mills
    b. Thomas Hobbes
    c. Aristotle
    d. Immanuel Kant

91. Which political orientation emphasizes maintaining traditions and stability over progress and change?
    a. Socialism
    b. Liberalism
    c. Conservatism
    d. Libertarianism

92. Which political orientation supports cooperation between states as a means to improve the quality of life for all states, nations, and people?
    a. Fascism
    b. Conservatism
    c. Anarchism
    d. Internationalism

93. Which political orientation emphasizes a strong central government and promotes violence as a means of suppressing dissent?
    a. Communism
    b. Socialism
    c. Nationalism
    d. Fascism

94. After the ratification of the Constitution, which power held by the states under the Articles of Confederation was ceded to the federal government?
    a. Power to levy taxes
    b. Power to establish courts
    c. Power to coin money
    d. Power to regulate trade

95. Under Federalism, which is considered a concurrent power held by both the states and the federal government?
    a. Hold elections
    b. Regulate immigration
    c. Expand the territories of a state
    d. Pass and enforce laws

96. Which check does the legislative branch possess over the judicial branch?
    a. Appoint judges.
    b. Call special sessions of Congress.
    c. Rule legislation unconstitutional.
    d. Determine the number of Supreme Court judges.

97. Which part of the legislative process differs in the House and the Senate?
    a. Who may introduce the bill
    b. How debates about a bill are conducted
    c. Who may veto the bill
    d. What wording the bill contains

247

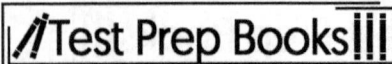

98. Which of the following is NOT included in the Bill of Rights?
    a. Freedom to assemble
    b. Freedom against unlawful search
    c. Freedom to vote
    d. Reservation of non-enumerated powers to the states or the people

99. Which political party was founded to advocate for the abolition of slavery?
    a. Constitutional Union
    b. Southern Democrat
    c. Republican
    d. Libertarian

100. What is NOT a common characteristic of an interest group?
    a. Seeks to influence public policy
    b. Employs lobbyists
    c. Regulates trade
    d. Benefits a specific segment of society

101. Which of the following is NOT a power of the mass media?
    a. Ability to shape public opinion
    b. Ability to regulate communications
    c. Ability to influence the importance of events in society
    d. Ability to determine the context in which to report events

102. Which form of government divides power between a regional and central government?
    a. Democracy
    b. Constitutional monarchy
    c. Federalism
    d. Feudalism

103. Which form of government most limits the civil liberties of the people?
    a. Authoritarianism
    b. Communism
    c. Socialism
    d. Federal monarchy

104. Which type of electoral system is considered the most proportionate?
    a. Majority
    b. Electoral College
    c. Plurality
    d. Single transferable vote

Economics and Science, Technology, and Society

105. Which of the following is the subgroup of economics that studies large-scale economic issues such as unemployment, interest rates, price levels, and national income?
    a. Microeconomics
    b. Macroeconomics
    c. Scarcity
    d. Supply and demand

106. A homeowner hires a landscaping company to mow the grass because they would like to use that time to do something else. The trade-off of paying someone to do a job to make more valuable use of time is an example of what?
   a. Economic systems
   b. Supply and demand
   c. Opportunity cost
   d. Inflation

107. Which kind of market does NOT involve government interventions or monopolies while trades are made between suppliers and buyers?
   a. Free
   b. Command
   c. Gross
   d. Exchange

108. Which is NOT an indicator of economic growth?
   a. GDP (gross domestic product)
   b. Unemployment
   c. Inflation
   d. Theory of the firm

109. In a business cycle, a recession occurs between which cycles?
   a. Expansion, peak
   b. Peak, contraction
   c. Contraction, trough
   d. Trough, expansion

110. What is the name of the central bank that controls the value of money in the United States?
   a. Commodity Reserve
   b. Central Reserve
   c. Federal Reserve
   d. Bank Reserve

111. Which option does NOT sustain monetary policies?
   a. Closed market operations
   b. Open market operations
   c. Assuring bank reserves
   d. Adjusting interest rates

112. What determines the exchange rate in a floating or flexible exchange?
   a. The government
   b. Taxes
   c. The Federal Reserve
   d. The market

113. Which statement is true about inflation and purchasing power?
   a. As inflation decreases, purchasing power increases.
   b. As inflation increases, purchasing power decreases.
   c. As inflation increases, purchasing power increases.
   d. As inflation decreases, purchasing power decreases.

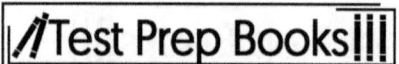

Practice Test

114. Which statement is true about goods and services?
    a. The quantity of goods and services matters more than their value.
    b. The value of goods and services matters more than their quantity.
    c. The quality of goods and services matters more than their production.
    d. The production of goods and services matters more than their quality.

115. Which of the following refers to the value of a good set by supply and demand rather than the actual value it represents?
    a. Commodity money
    b. Fiat money
    c. Bank money
    d. Reserve money

116. Which of the following is not a characteristic of contractionary monetary policy?
    a. Increases the money supply
    b. Possibly increases unemployment due to slowdowns in economic growth
    c. Decreases consumer spending
    d. Decreases loans and/or borrowing

117. Which of the following lists all four phases of the business cycle?
    a. Expansion, crest, peak, trough
    b. Expansion, contraction, peak, trench
    c. Peak, trough, contraction, expansion
    d. Peak, rise, trough, decline

118. Frictional unemployment is best described by which of the following?
    a. When a person is no longer qualified for a job
    b. When a person voluntarily leaves one job to pursue another
    c. When a person is laid off because of the business cycle
    d. When a person is unemployed for longer than six months

119. How is economic growth measured?
    a. By the rise in the inflation of a country
    b. By the amount of reserves that a country holds
    c. By the amount of exports that a country has
    d. By the GDP of a country

120. If a store has a large supply of item *xyz* and they are not selling many of them, what should they do?
    a. Raise the price so that when they do sell one, they will make a large profit.
    b. Lower the price so that hopefully demand will go up and they can get rid of it.
    c. Raise the price so that people will think that it is a limited, high value product and buy it.
    d. Offer the product in a low price bundle with other unrelated products.

121. Who is in control in a command economy?
    a. The consumer
    b. Private businesses
    c. The government
    d. Manufacturers

Practice Test | Social Studies Instruction and Assessment

122. Which of the following correctly lists the factors of production?
    a. Land, labor, material, entrepreneurship
    b. Land, labor, capital, equity
    c. Land, a building, capital, labor
    d. Land, labor, capital, entrepreneurship

Social Studies Foundation, Skills, Research, and Instruction

123. What is the name of the wealthy Venezuelan creole who helped stir revolutions across South America in the nineteenth century?
    a. Simon Bolivar
    b. Nelson Mandela
    c. Dr. Martin Luther King Jr.
    d. Antonio Lopez de Santa Anna

124. What country did Nelson Mandela become president of in 1994?
    a. Liberia
    b. Vietnam
    c. South Africa
    d. Argentina

125. The era following the Civil War is known as what?
    a. Antebellum Era
    b. Reconstruction
    c. Progressive Era
    d. Civil rights movement

126. Who did the state of Texas side with during the Civil War?
    a. North
    b. Union
    c. Mexican Republic
    d. Confederacy

127. What became the scholarly capital of the Hellenistic world during the reign of Alexander the Great?
    a. Jerusalem
    b. Athens
    c. Alexandria
    d. Constantinople

128. Which of the following religions is not a monotheistic Abrahamic religion?
    a. Hinduism
    b. Christianity
    c. Islam
    d. Judaism

129. What is the name given to institutional segregation in South Africa?
    a. Jim Crow
    b. Atlantic Slave Trade
    c. Apartheid
    d. Black Codes

251

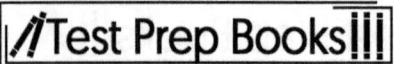

130. Who was a naval officer who pushed the United States of America toward oceanic imperialism in the late nineteenth century?
    a. Alfred Thayer Mahan
    b. Christopher Columbus
    c. Theodore Roosevelt
    d. Matthew Perry

131. The First Agricultural Revolution occurred how many years ago?
    a. 50
    b. 1000
    c. 200
    d. 10,000

132. What is the name of the policies developed by President Franklin Delano Roosevelt during the Great Depression?
    a. The Great Society
    b. The War Against Poverty
    c. Progressivism
    d. The New Deal

133. Which of the following fields falls under the umbrella of the social sciences?
    a. Biology
    b. English
    c. Psychology
    d. Geometry

134. Which of the following are markets that establish a few large firms as the major sellers or distributors?
    a. Free enterprise economies
    b. Pure monopolies
    c. Oligopolies
    d. Command economies

135. Which of the following is the best definition of a pure monopoly?
    a. When there is only one seller of a particular product or commodity and the sole seller attempts to restrict firms from entering the industry
    b. When prices are determined by consumer demand and no supplier maintains any significant influence over prices
    c. When people are completely free to buy the goods and services they want or need
    d. When a few large firms become the major sellers or distributors in an industry

136. The Third Agricultural Revolution is often referred to as what?
    a. Green Revolution
    b. Texas Revolution
    c. Industrial Revolution
    d. Computer Revolution

137. Which of the following is an example of a New Deal program?
    a. Head Start
    b. NASA
    c. Eisenhower Interstate System
    d. Civilian Conservation Corps

138. What does the following graph represent?

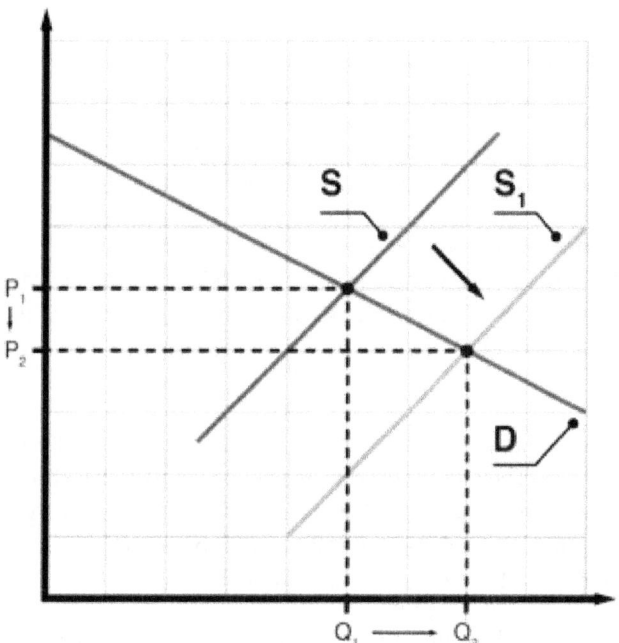

    a. Decrease in supply
    b. Increase in supply
    c. Decrease in demand
    d. Increase in demand

139. Who is considered the father of socialist theory?
    a. John Maynard Keynes
    b. Adam Smith
    c. Alfred Thayer Mahan
    d. Karl Marx

140. Communism is more attuned for which of the following?
    a. One-party system
    b. Liberal democracy
    c. Free enterprise economy
    d. Capitalist economy

Answer Explanations

World History

1. B: Ancient Greeks created many of the cultural and political institutions that form the basis of modern western civilization. Athens was an important Greek democracy, and all adult men could participate in politics after they had completed their military service. The Roman Empire, Choice A, evolved from the Roman Republic, but it was not democratic. The Achaemenid Empire and Zhou Dynasty, Choices C and D, were imperial monarchies that did not allow citizens to have much, if any, political voice.

2. D: During the Achaemenid Empire, Persians practiced the Zoroastrian faith and worshipped two gods. Islam only came about one thousand years later. The Achaemenids built a Royal Road that stretched across their empire, but the Silk Roads expanded throughout Asia. The Achaemenids twice tried to conquer Greece but failed both times.

3. A: The Silk Roads were a network of trade routes between Asia and the Mediterranean. Merchants and Pilgrims traveled along the Silk Roads and brought new ideas and technologies, as well as trade goods. For example, Buddhism spread from India to China. Chinese technologies also spread westward, including gunpowder and the printing press. The Silk Roads also spread the Bubonic Plague to Europe, but it did not arrive in the New World until Columbus landed there in 1492.

4. A: Invasions by Germanic tribes. Large numbers of Franks, Goths, Vandals, and other Germanic peoples began moving south in the fifth century A.D. They conquered Rome twice, and the Western Roman Empire finally disintegrated. The Mongol invasion, Choice B, pushed westward in the 13th century, long after the western Roman Empire was gone. The assassination of Julius Caesar, Choice C, led to the end of the Roman Republic and the birth of the Roman Empire. Taoism never spread to Rome, making Choice D incorrect.

5. A: The Mongols were a nomadic people who trained as horsemen from a young age. They used their highly mobile army to build a huge empire in Asia, the Middle East, and Eastern Europe. Mongol rulers were relatively tolerant of other religions because they wanted to reduce conflict within their empire, making Choice B incorrect. They also encouraged trade because they produced few of their own goods, making Choice C incorrect. The Mongol rulers also encouraged literacy and appreciated visual art, making Choice D incorrect.

6. C: Millions of people died during the Black Death, but those who survived found that their standard of living had improved, especially serfs. Before the Black Death, serfs had few rights and were expected to work without pay for their lord. Because labor was in such short supply after the Black Death, serfs found they were in a much better bargaining position. The Protestant Reformation was a cultural phenomenon, and the rise of absolutism was a political change. Neither had any connection to the Black Death, making Choices A and B incorrect. Choice D is also incorrect; although child labor laws came after the Black Death in the early 1800s, they weren't a direct result of the Black Death.

7. A: Renaissance scholars and artists sought to emulate classical Greek and Roman culture. They translated Greek and Roman political philosophers and literature. They also copied classical architecture. Europeans had little direct contact with China until the 13th century, which was long after the Zhou Dynasty collapsed, making Choice C incorrect. The Renaissance Era occurred within the continent of Europe and drew from other European styles, so nations of northern Africa and the Middle East, such as ancient Egypt and the Ottoman Empire, had little to no inspiration on Renaissance scholars and artists at that time. Therefore, Choices B and D are incorrect.

8. A: Copernicus exemplified the key techniques of the Scientific Revolution, including an emphasis on empirical data and the scientific method. He carefully observed the movement of the planets and found that his data did not

Answer Explanations | Social Studies Instruction and Assessment

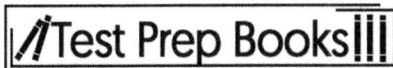

match the contemporary geocentric theory, which stated that the earth was the center of the universe. He found that his data indicated that the planets revolved around the sun instead.

9. C: Louis the XIV was an absolute monarch who ruled during the seventeenth and eighteenth centuries. He concentrated power on the throne by forcing nobles to spend most of their time at the royal court. The French Revolution occurred about 75 years after he died. Absolute monarchs like Louis the XIV bolstered their prestige by claiming they were appointed by God. The Mandate of Heaven was a similar concept, but it was developed by the Zhou Dynasty in China about two thousand years before Louis XIV was born.

10. C: The Age of Enlightenment in the eighteenth century focused on political and economic philosophy as opposed to scientific discoveries. English philosopher John Locke introduced the concept of a social contract between the ruler and his subjects. His ideas helped inspire revolutions in the British colonies in North America and later France. Choice A is incorrect; the discovery of the heliocentric theory happened in 1543. Luther began to criticize the Catholic Church about two hundred years before the Age of Enlightenment began, making Choice B incorrect. Choice D is also incorrect, as the Renaissance happened before the Age of Enlightenment from approximately 1300-1600.

11. A: Most scholars already knew the world was round by 1492. On the other hand, the arrival of Europeans in North and South America introduced deadly diseases that killed millions of native peoples. Europeans had developed immunity to diseases such as smallpox, while Native Americans had not. In addition, Europeans introduced a number of new plants and animals to the New World, but they also adopted many new foods as well, including potatoes, tomatoes, chocolate, and tobacco. Finally, Europeans tried to convert Native Americans to Christianity, but Native Americans did not completely give up their traditional beliefs. Instead, they blended Christianity with indigenous and African beliefs to create new syncretic religions.

12. B: The American Revolution occurred first in 1775, and a number of European soldiers fought for the patriots. The American Revolution, in part, inspired the French Revolution. The Marquis de Lafayette came to America in 1777 and was wounded during the Battle of Brandywine. He returned to France after the American Revolution and became a leader in the French Revolution in 1789.

13. D: The Industrial Revolution is probably one of the most important turning points in world history. The United States and Western Europe, especially Britain, were the first areas to industrialize. Steam engines were used to improve economic and transportation efficiency. They also gave western empires a military advantage over less developed countries in Asia and Africa. Finally, industrialization required large amounts of unskilled labor, which created the working class.

14. C: In the 1800s, nationalists in different parts of Europe encouraged their countrymen to take pride in their shared backgrounds. This led to tension between different nations, as each sought to increase its status and prestige. The French and British nearly came to blows in Africa, and nationalism ultimately led to World War I in 1914. France and Spain were unified several centuries before the 1800s.

15. A: The atomic bomb was created during World War II (1939-1945). Scientists and engineers did develop a number of other weapons in order to break through the heavily entrenched front lines during World War I. Poison gas killed or injured millions of men between 1914 and 1918. Aircraft were used to observe enemy positions and bombard enemy troops. Armored tanks were able to crush barbed wire fences and deflected machine gun bullets.

16. B: Eager to avoid another global conflict, European leaders tried to appease Hitler by letting him occupy Austria and Czechoslovakia. This policy failed because it only emboldened Hitler, and he invaded Poland in 1939. Rather than receiving leniency after World War I, Germany was forced to sign a humiliating peace treaty. Furthermore, the League of Nations failed to prevent conflict because it lacked any real power. This encouraged continued aggression from Italy, Germany, and Japan, which culminated in World War II.

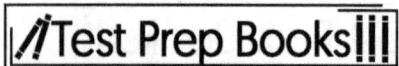

Answer Explanations

17. A: Devastated by World War II, Britain and France were unable to maintain their empires. Japan and Germany were also weak, which left only the United States and USSR as superpowers. The Russian Revolution had occurred during World War I, in 1917, making Choice *B* incorrect. Ideological and economic conflict between the US and the USSR led to the start of the Cold War shortly after World War II ended, making Choice *C* incorrect. Choice *D* is also incorrect; the death of Franz Ferdinand marked the beginning of World War I.

18. A: Nationalism remains a powerful force to this day. Nationalism drove conflict in Ireland, Spain, Yugoslavia, and elsewhere. However, the end of the Cold War removed many of the political barriers that had prevented interaction between the western and Communist blocs. In addition, religious fundamentalism became an increasingly common response to the rapid changes that occurred during the late twentieth and early twenty-first centuries. There was also a rise in cultural and economic globalization, as well as in environmentalism.

19. B: The printing press was much more efficient than previous methods, which required a single scribe to copy text by hand. This made books much more affordable and encouraged the growing middle class to read. No church or organization had a monopoly on the technology, so many different writers used it to spread the ideas of the Reformation, as well as the Renaissance, Scientific Revolution, and Age of Enlightenment.

20. C: The USSR put Sputnik, the first satellite into orbit, in 1951. They also claimed victory when the Soviet cosmonaut Yuri Gagarin went into space in 1961. The United States only surpassed the USSR by sending the Apollo 11 crew to the Moon in 1969.

21. A: The schism between Sunnis and Shi'as began shortly after the Islamic prophet Muhammad died in 632 A.D. Sunnis and Shi'a disagreed over who should have become Muhammad's successor. Sufism emerged about eighty years after Muhammad died, and they focused on perfecting their faith through meditation. Shintoism is a traditional polytheistic faith that is practiced mainly in Japan.

22. B: The Chinese required other countries to pay tribute in order to establish trade relations. Foreign emissaries also had to prostrate themselves before the Chinese emperor. Potlatches, Choice *A*, were a Native American form of gift giving. Bartering, Choice *C*, was a common form of economic exchange, but it had no political significance.

U.S. History

23. D: The US Constitution, Choice *A*, actually legalized slavery by counting slaves as three-fifths of a person. The Compromise of 1850, Choice *B*, banned the slave trade in Washington D.C. but also created a stronger fugitive slave law. The Emancipation Proclamation, Choice *C*, only banned slavery in the Confederacy. The 13th Amendment finally banned slavery throughout the country.

24. A: The Spanish-American War of 1898 made the US a colonial power because it acquired many former Spanish colonies. The Mexican-American War of 1846-48 led to the acquisition of California, Nevada, Utah, Arizona, and New Mexico, Choice *B*. World War I led to the formation of the League of Nations in 1919, Choice *C*. The Great Depression ended when Americans joined World War II in 1941, Choice *D*.

25. C: The 19th Amendment gave women the right to vote. The 15th Amendment, Choice *A*, gave all U.S. citizens, regardless of race or color, the right to vote. The 18th Amendment, Choice *B*, introduced alcohol prohibition. The 21st Amendment, Choice *D*, repealed prohibition.

26. B: More than one million African Americans in the South went north in search of jobs during and after World War I. The Great Migration led to increased racial tension as black and white Americans competed for housing and jobs in northern cities. The Great Migration also led to the Harlem Renaissance.

Answer Explanations | Social Studies Instruction and Assessment

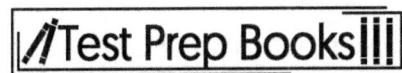

27. B: *Brown v. Board of Education* ruled that having separate schools for black and white students was inherently unequal and sparked demands for more civil rights. *Roe v. Wade* in 1973, Choice *A*, increased access to abortion. *Plessy v. Ferguson*, Choice *C*, established the "separate but equal" doctrine. *Marbury v. Madison* in 1803, Choice *D*, established the doctrine of judicial review.

28. D: All three events led to increasing tension and conflict between the colonists and the British government, which finally exploded at the Battle of Lexington and Concord in 1775. The Stamp Act of 1765 imposed a tax on documents. It was repealed after colonists organized protests. The Boston Massacre resulted in the death of five colonists in 1770. The Boston Tea Party was a protest in 1773 against a law that hurt colonial tea merchants. The British responded to the tea party by punishing the colony of Massachusetts, which created fear among the other colonies and united them against the British government.

29. B: The Bleeding Kansas conflict contributed to sectional tension before the Civil War. The application of popular sovereignty in Kansas led to conflict as free-soil and pro-slavery forces rushed into the territory. Malcolm X's death, Choice *A*, was in 1965, almost 100 years after the Civil War ended. The 13th Amendment, Choice *C*, was ratified in 1865 and was approved at the very end of the Civil War. Shay's Rebellion, Choice *D*, was an uprising during 1786 and 1787 in Massachusetts.

30. A: Because the British naval blockade during World War I was so effective, Germany retaliated by using submarines to attack any ship bound for Britain or France. This led to the sinking of the RMS *Lusitania* in 1915, which killed more than 100 Americans. The destruction of the USS *Maine*, Choice *B*, sparked the Spanish-American War in 1898. The Japanese attack on Pearl Harbor in 1941, Choice *C*, brought America into World War II, not World War I. Franz Ferdinand's death in 1914, Choice *D*, sparked the outbreak of World War I, but America did not join the war until 1917.

31. D: Choice *D*, none of the above, is correct because none of the answer choices describe consequences from World War II. World War I led to the League of Nations and the communist revolution in Russia, Choices *A* and *B*. The USSR and US both emerged as two rival superpowers after World War II. It was thus a bipolar, rather than unipolar, world. The tension and mistrust between the US and USSR eventually led to the Cold War, which ended in 1991.

32. C: The Wounded Knee Massacre in 1890 left at least 150 Native Americans dead, including many women and children, and was the last major engagement between Native Americans and American soldiers. The Trail of Tears involved the forced relocation of tribes from the American Southeast between 1830 and 1850. Although thousands of Native Americans died along the way, it was not a battle. Tecumseh launched his uprising in 1811, and conflict between Native Americans and US soldiers would continue for decades as the country expanded further west. The Battle of the Little Bighorn in 1876, also known as Custer's Last Stand, was a major Native American victory against the US army.

33. B: During the Neolithic Revolution, Native Americans began to cultivate beans, squash, chilies, and other vegetables. However, they did not domesticate many large animals (Choice *A*), only the dog in North America and the llama in Central America. Horses and cattle only arrived in North America as a result of European exploration. Native Americans also did not develop steel or iron, Choice *C*. Native Americans only obtained these items by trading with Europeans. Despite these limits, Native Americans did develop a semi-sedentary lifestyle, formed social hierarchies, and created new religious beliefs.

34. C: Issued in 1776, the Declaration of Independence explained why the colonists decided to break away from England but did not establish a government. That was left to the Articles of Confederation, which were ratified in 1781. The Articles of Confederation, Choice *C*, established a very weak central government and, in 1789, was

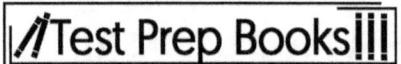

replaced by the Constitution, which established a stronger executive branch. In 1791, the Bill of Rights introduced 10 amendments the Constitution.

35. A: The New Deal introduced a number of programs designed to increase regulation and boost the economy. Many of them remain in effect today, such as the Social Security Administration and the Securities and Exchange Commission. The New Deal also led to the Republican and Democratic parties to reverse their ideological positions on government intervention. It did not lead to a third party, Choice *B*. President Franklin D. Roosevelt was actually elected to four terms in office, and the official two-term limit was not established until the 22nd Amendment was ratified in 1951. Until then, the two-term limit had been an informal custom established by President George Washington when he left office in 1797. Thus, Choice *C* is incorrect. Choice *D* is also incorrect. The Great Depression led to the New Deal, not the other way around.

36. C: The North had a population of about 18.5 million while the South had only 5.5 million citizens and 3.5 million slaves. This meant the Union could more easily replace men while the Confederacy could not. The South was defending their homes from damage, since most of the war happened in the South, so Choice *A* is incorrect. Choice *B* is incorrect—the South had free labor at home, so they didn't have to worry about leaving their farms to go to war. Finally, Choice *D* is incorrect; the South had more experienced military leaders due to their participation in the Mexican-American War.

37. B: Although the United States initially lagged behind the Soviets, the US successfully landed the first man on the Moon in 1969. However, the Korean War resulted in a stalemate in 1953, leaving Choice *A* incorrect. The Vietnam War, Choice *C*, was a defeat for US forces. Despite sending more than 500,000 troops to Vietnam, the Vietnam War became increasingly unpopular and the United States eventually withdrew in 1973. The communist North Vietnamese eventually captured the southern capital of Saigon in 1975. Choice *D*, Battle of Gettysburg, is part of the Civil War.

38. A: Although the Constitution makes no provisions for a presidential cabinet, President George Washington created one when he took office. Members of the cabinet advise the president on a wide variety of issues including, but not limited to, defense, transportation, and education. The White House press secretary acts as spokesperson for the US government administration. The cabinet members are not required to raise money for the president's reelection effort. The vice president, not the cabinet, presides over the Senate.

39. B: Conservative evangelicals formed the Moral Majority in 1979 in an effort to address issues like abortion. Their enthusiasm helped carry Reagan into the White House and bring the US Senate under Republican control for the first time in 28 years. The First and Second Great Awakenings were religious movements that took place in in the 1700s and 1800s. The Know-Nothings opposed Catholic immigration during the 1800s. The Anti-Defamation League focuses on combating anti-Semitism and Holocaust denial.

40. A: Congress passed immigration reform in 1965 that made it much easier for immigrants from Central and South America, as well as Asia, to enter the United States. During the Colonial Period, most immigrants came from Britain. During the mid-1800s, Irish and German immigrants became more numerous. That changed again around 1900 when an influx of immigrants from Southern and Eastern Europe began.

41. A: The riots began when patrons of the Stonewall Inn fought back against a police raid. The site became a national monument in 2016. Although he became an icon of the gay and lesbian rights movement, Matthew Shepard was murdered in 1998. Thus, Choice *B* is incorrect. The murder of Vincent Chin, Choice *C*, in 1982, became a rallying cry for Asian American activists. The gay and lesbian rights movement was well established when activists campaigned to raise awareness of AIDS during the 1980s and 1990s, making Choice *D* incorrect.

42. D: Mark Twain called the late 1800s the Gilded Age because the appearance of extreme wealth covered up massive social inequality. While many wealthy industrialists became very rich, many workers worked in poor

Answer Explanations | Social Studies Instruction and Assessment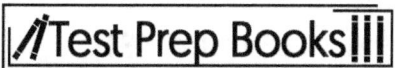

conditions for low wages. The onset of the Second Industrial Revolution led to an expansion of the chemical, telecommunications, and metallurgical industries. Urbanization also increased during this period as workers crowded into cities in search of work.

43. B: Progressive reformers sought to remedy some of the abuses that emerged during the Gilded Age. They wanted to break up monopolies that interfered with economic competition. Muckraking journalists, including Upton Sinclair and Jacob Riis, also exposed political corruption and social inequality. The Populist Party sought political reforms that would alleviate the plight of farmers and the working class, such as the abolition of national banks and government regulation of railroads.

44. A: King Ferdinand and Queen Isabella agreed to support Columbus' mission because he promised to establish a direct trade route to Asia that would allow European merchants to bypass Middle Eastern middlemen. Columbus had no idea that America existed, Choice *B*, and he believed he had landed in India when he arrived in the Caribbean. That's why he mistakenly called the natives *Indians*. It is a common myth that Columbus sought to prove experts wrong by showing them the world was round, not flat. Most European thinkers already knew the world was round, making Choice *C* incorrect. Choice *D* is also incorrect; Christopher Columbus practiced the Christian faith, not Judaism.

45. B: The Battles of Lexington and Concord marked the start of the American Revolution in 1775. The Battle of Bunker Hill in 1775 was a defeat for the Patriot cause but showed they could stand up to the British Army. The Battle of Trenton in 1776 bolstered morale in the Continental army but was not as significant as the Battle of Saratoga in 1777. In this engagement, the Continental Army captured thousands of British troops. This victory convinced the French King to support the Patriot cause, and his military aid was an important factor in the success of the American Revolution.

46. A: Radical Republicans wanted to ensure that recently freed slaves had the economic and political rights that would enable them to achieve self-sufficiency in the post-Civil War era. Democrats, such as Andrew Johnson, preferred leniency towards the South while Radical Republicans wanted a harsher punishment, making Choice *B* incorrect. This led to conflict between Johnson and Radical Republicans who almost succeeded in having him impeached in 1868.

47. B: World War II brought about an end to the Great Depression by switching over to wartime production. After the end of World War II, consumer demand remained high and unemployment was usually low. Computers began to become more powerful, efficient, and inexpensive in the latter part of the 20th century, and they became more common in business. The Sun Belt actually expanded after World War II as the traditional manufacturing base in the North and Midwest fell into decline. Land was cheaper in the South and West and wages were lower, so these regions were very attractive to businesses.

48. C: The Connecticut Compromise, Choice *A*, formed the basis for the Constitution by proposing a bicameral Congress. The Missouri Compromise, Choice *B*, banned slavery north of the 36°30′ parallel in the Louisiana Territory. The Compromise of 1850, Choice *C*, essentially undid the Missouri Compromise by introducing popular sovereignty, which allowed voters in territories to decide whether or not the state constitution would ban slavery. The Three-Fifths Compromise, Choice *D*, counted slaves as three-fifths of a human being when allocating representatives.

49. C: The Declaration of Independence occurred during the American Revolution, so it should therefore be considered an effect, not a cause. Similarly, slavery was a cause for the later Civil War, but it was not a primary instigator for the Revolutionary War. Although a single event can have many effects long into the future, it is also important to not overstate the influence of these individual causes; the civil rights movement was only tangentially connected to the War of Independence among many other factors, and therefore it should not be considered a primary effect of it. The French and Indian War (which was part of the Seven Years' War) and the Bill of Rights, on

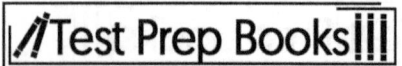

Answer Explanations

the other hand, were respectively a cause and effect from the American Revolution, making Choice *C* the correct answer.

50. D: The Constitution was signed in 1787; the Declaration of Independence was signed in 1776. It was successfully ratified by all the current states, including New York. Finally, the Articles of Confederation were established at the end of the American Revolution; the Constitution would replace the articles years later due to issues with the government's structure.

Texas History

51. B: During the late eighteenth century, the Comanche became a hegemonic power in the northern Texas Plains after achieving decisive military victories over the Puebloans, Apache, and Spanish settlers. The Comanche maintained a commanding presence in this region until the Red River War (1874–1875). Thus, Choice *B* is the correct answer. The Apache were one of the first American Indian tribes to adopt European horses, which helped the Apache dominate the northern Texas Plains during the seventeenth century. However, the Comanche drove out the Apache in the late eighteenth century, so Choice *A* is incorrect. Choice *C* is incorrect because the Karankawa lived in the Texas Gulf Coast and had minimal contact with the northern Texas Plains. Puebloans lived in the northern Texas Plains, but they weren't a regional power during the late eighteenth century; therefore, Choice *D* is incorrect.

52. D: The Battle of Palmito Ranch (May 12–13, 1865) occurred after the end of the American Civil War and the dissolution of the Confederacy. Historians continued to debate the Union commanders' decision to violate a longstanding local ceasefire agreement and launch a military strike despite their knowledge of Robert E. Lee's surrender at Appomattox Court House on April 9, 1865. Thus, Choice *D* is the correct answer. The Battle of Chickamauga (September 18–20, 1863) was fought in the middle of the Civil War, so Choice *A* is incorrect. The Battle of Galveston (January 1, 1863) broke a Union naval blockade, and it occurred more than two years before the Confederacy dissolved; therefore, Choice *B* is incorrect. Choice *C* is incorrect because the Battle of Gonzales (October 2, 1835) was the first skirmish in the Texas Revolution.

53. C: Haden Edwards launched the Fredonian Rebellion (1826–1827) to forcibly invalidate the territorial claims of Mexican and Spanish-speaking settlers in the area surrounding the city of Nacogdoches. The Mexican military swiftly shutdown this insurrection, and the Mexican government sought to increase the regulation of Anglo-American settlements and restrict immigration from the United States. These policies infuriated and united Anglo-American settlers, fueling their desire for independence. Thus, Choice *C* is the correct answer. Choice *A* is incorrect because the Fredonian Rebellion occurred nearly a decade before the beginning of the Texas Revolution. Land disputes between Anglo-American settlers, Mexicans, and American Indians predated the Fredonian Rebellion by several decades, so Choice *B* is incorrect. The primary leader of the Fredonian Rebellion, Haden Edwards, fled to the United States immediately after his defeat, which is partially why Mexican authorities accused the United States of interfering in Texas. Therefore, Choice *D* is incorrect.

54. B: Lorenzo de Zavala helped draft the Mexican Constitution of 1824, and, after Antonio López de Santa Anna seized dictatorial power, Zavala emigrated and participated in the Texas constitutional convention of 1836. Thus, Choice *B* is the correct answer. Antonio López de Santa Anna influenced the drafting of the Mexican Constitution of 1824, but he served as Mexico's top general to prevent Texas from achieving independence. So Choice *A* is incorrect. Choice *C* is incorrect because Moses Austin died before the drafting of both constitutions. Stephen F. Austin didn't participate in the drafting of the Mexican Constitution of 1824, and he didn't attend the Texas constitutional convention; therefore, Choice *D* is incorrect.

55. C: The speech was clearly delivered during the Texas Revolution; this interpretation is based on the references to the Battle of the Alamo and the Goliad massacre. Additionally, it can be inferred that the orator is a military

Answer Explanations | Social Studies Instruction and Assessment

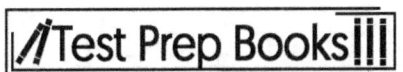

commander or revolutionary leader based on the overall tone and specific references to military strategy. Sam Houston served as the top commander of the revolutionary army, and he led the Texans to a decisive victory at the Battle of San Jacinto shortly after delivering this speech. Thus, Choice C is the correct answer. John Bell Hood was a Confederate officer in the American Civil War, and he was too young to fight in the Texas Revolution; therefore, Choice A is incorrect. Moses Austin died several decades before the Texas Revolution, so Choice B is incorrect. William B. Travis fought in the Texas Revolution, but he famously died at the Battle of the Alamo, which occurred prior to this speech. Therefore, Choice D is incorrect.

56. A: The speech refers to the Alamo and Goliad because they served as powerful rallying cries for independence. In both the Battle of the Alamo and the Goliad massacre, Mexican forces inflicted extreme levels of violence on outnumbered revolutionaries, and the widespread circulation of accounts of these events garnered enormous sympathy and fueled the outrage of Texans and Americans. Thus, Choice A is the correct answer. The Battle of the Alamo and the Goliad massacre were military disasters for the revolutionaries, so Choice B is incorrect. The speech mentions the strategy of dividing and confusing Mexican armies; however, the Battle of the Alamo and Goliad massacre didn't achieve this goal. Therefore, Choice C is incorrect. The United States never officially intervened in the Texas Revolution, and the annexation of Texas didn't occur until 1845. So, Choice D is incorrect.

57. D: Henry B. Gonzalez served in the House of Representatives and led the passage of the Civil Rights Act of 1964, the Voting Rights Act of 1965, and the Civil Rights Act of 1968. So Choice A is incorrect. James Farmer cofounded the Congress of Racial Equality (CORE), and this organization pioneered the strategy of nonviolent protests; therefore, Choice B is incorrect. President Lyndon B. Johnson played an essential role in securing the passage of numerous pieces of civil rights legislation, such as the Civil Rights Act of 1964 and the Voting Rights Act of 1965. Therefore, Choice C is incorrect. Kay Bailey Hutchison wasn't elected to public office until after the Civil Rights Movement, and even if she had been in Congress, it's unlikely, due to her politics, that she would have supported such a dramatic change to the status quo. Thus, Choice D is the correct answer.

58. C: The Córdova Rebellion (1838) sought to build grassroots support to overthrow the Republic of Texas, and Vicente Córdova worked to recruit Spanish-speaking settlers and Cherokee allies. The uprising collapsed in its early stages, and, in retaliation, President of the Republic of Texas Mirabeau B. Lamar seized the opportunity to expel the Cherokee from Texas. Thus, Choice C is the correct answer. The Atakapa collapsed in the late eighteenth century due to the unmitigated spread of infectious disease, so Choice A is incorrect. The Caddo were an American Indian tribe in eastern and southeastern Texas, and they weren't involved in the Córdova Rebellion; therefore, Choice B is incorrect. President Lamar leveraged public outrage over the Córdova Rebellion to build support for his anti-Comanche policies, but Córdova never offered to form an alliance with the Comanche. Therefore, Choice D is incorrect.

59. A: George Childress is widely credited with writing the most important draft of the Texas Declaration of Independence (1836), which he modeled after the American Declaration of Independence. Thus, Choice A is the correct answer. Haden Edwards organized the Fredonian Rebellion (1826–1827), and he fled to the United States before Texas declared independence. Therefore, Choice B is incorrect. Sam Houston spearheaded the revolutionary movement, but he didn't participate in the drafting of the Texas Declaration of Independence; therefore, Choice C is incorrect. Likewise, Stephen F. Austin was a revolutionary leader but didn't author the declaration, so Choice D is incorrect.

60. B: Spindletop is an oil field, and in 1901, drilling operations resulted in the largest gusher in world history. This discovery fueled the Texas oil boom, and the United States quickly became one of the top oil-producing countries in the world. Thus, Choice B is the correct answer. A drilling rig first struck oil in the United States in 1859, so Choice A is incorrect. Several new oil and gas companies, such as Gulf Oil and Texaco, formed as a result of the Spindletop discovery; however, the legacy of Spindletop is much broader. Therefore, Choice C is incorrect. Spindletop was the site of the largest gusher of oil in world, but it wasn't the first. Salt drillers accidentally triggered the first gusher in

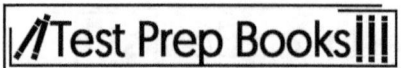

Answer Explanations

1815, and several drilling companies intentionally struck gushers prior to Spindletop. Therefore, Choice *D* is incorrect.

61. D: The passage describes how the inadequacies of local law enforcement led some neighbors to attack an alleged thief as an act of vigilante justice. The Texas Rangers were initially formed as an unofficial paramilitary group to protect Anglo-American settlements and carry out traditional law enforcement duties. The Mexican government never sanctioned the Texas Rangers, so they effectively functioned as vigilantes during the Mexican National Era. Thus, Choice *D* is the correct answer. Buffalo Soldiers were all-Black American military units, and the United States Army authorized and directed their activities in Texas. So Choice *A* is incorrect. Comanche bands are semi-autonomous kinship groups, and they weren't primarily involved in law enforcement or vigilantism; therefore, Choice *B* is incorrect. Confederate soldiers controlled much of Texas during the American Civil War, and the Confederacy sanctioned their activities. Therefore, Choice *C* is incorrect.

62. A: The passage describes how the Mexican government was unable to enforce its laws in Texas. Anglo-American settlements eventually filled this void by forming their own independent political institutions and law enforcement agencies. Law enforcement is closely related to the concept of sovereignty, meaning the supreme authority over territory. As Anglo-Americans began to increasingly exercise sovereignty over territory, the independence movement gained momentum and eventually reached a boiling point, resulting in the Texas Revolution. Thus, Choice *A* is the correct answer. The Mexican government never sanctioned or otherwise recognized the Texas Rangers as an official law enforcement agency, so Choice *B* is incorrect. The Mexican government limited self-government in Texas over more consequential concerns than extrajudicial corporal punishment, such as the refusal to pay taxes, illegal immigration, and the rampant violation of anti-slavery laws. Therefore, Choice *C* is incorrect. Vigilante justice has a long history in Texas, but it didn't directly contribute to the Texas Revolution aside from the relationship between vigilantism and sovereignty as expressed in Choice *A*. So, Choice *D* is incorrect.

63. C: American Indians adopted land-use practices based on local geographical and ecological circumstances. For example, the highly mobile American Indian tribes living on the northern Texas Plains hunted buffalo and gathered vegetation, while American Indians living in eastern Texas built permanent settlements and engaged in agriculture. Thus, Choice *C* is the correct answer. Land-use practices inherently alter geographical features and ecological systems, and American Indians were no exception; therefore, Choice *A* is incorrect. Although American Indians altered the natural environment, they generally adopted sustainable practices, especially in comparison to European settlers. Therefore, Choice *B* is incorrect. American Indian tribes weren't all nomadic, and some land-use practices radically transformed the environment, such as slash-and-burn agriculture; therefore, Choice *D* is incorrect.

64. B: Francisco Hidalgo was a Franciscan missionary, and after the Mission San Francisco de los Tejas failed, he lobbied the Spanish government to commit more resources to his missionary work in Texas. When Hidalgo was refused, he turned to the French colonial government of Louisiana for assistance, which prompted Spain to more fully invest in the colonization of Texas to bolster its defenses of New Spain. Thus, Choice *B* is the correct answer. Choice *A* is incorrect because Álvar Núñez Cabeza de Vaca explored the Gulf Coast more than a century before Spain seriously pursued the colonization of Texas. Fray Damián Massanet was a Franciscan missionary, but he stopped advocating for the colonization of Texas once his Mission San Francisco de los Tejas collapsed. So, Choice *C* is incorrect. Moses Austin pioneered the first major Anglo-American settlement in Texas, but Spain had already devoted more resources to the colonization of Texas by this time. Therefore, Choice *D* is incorrect.

65. D: The Rio Grande Valley is an extremely fertile floodplain at the southern tip of Texas, and it is responsible for an overwhelming amount of Texas's citrus production. Thus, Choice *D* is the correct answer. The Gulf Coast is more associated with fishing, shipping, and oil extraction than with citrus production, so Choice *A* is incorrect. The climate of the northern Plains cannot support large-scale citrus production because citrus trees are not frost hardy.

Therefore, Choice *B* is incorrect. Likewise, the Red River watershed cannot support citrus production due to the region's relatively warm winters as compared to southern Texas; therefore, Choice *C* is incorrect.

66. A: Álvar Núñez Cabeza de Vaca was the first European to provide a detailed account of American Indian tribes living in the present-day American Southwest, including the Texas Gulf Coast. Unlike the vast majority of his contemporaries, Cabeza de Vaca respected American Indians and forged strong ties with Texas tribes, which enhanced his understanding of their culture. Thus, Choice *A* is the correct answer. Choice *B* is incorrect because Alonso Álvarez de Pineda was the first European to create a map of Texas. Álvar Núñez Cabeza de Vaca never attempted to colonize Texas, so Choice *C* is incorrect. Choice *D* is incorrect because Fray Damián Massanet oversaw the construction of the Mission San Francisco de los Tejas in 1690.

67. A: The author offers an intensely negative portrayal of American Indians. Specifically, the author accuses American Indians of being inherently devious, hungry, and bloodthirsty. This overt hostility calls into question his description of the attack, making it seem likely he is exaggerating and mischaracterizing. Thus, Choice *A* is the correct answer. Based on his disparaging generalizations, the author definitely does not consider American Indians to be allies, so Choice *B* is incorrect. Although the author derides American Indians for allegedly asking for assistance, the author's point of view is much broader in its representation of the threat posed by American Indians; therefore, Choice *C* is incorrect. The author certainly views American Indians as an existential threat, but he only mentions the Italian as a way to negatively characterize American Indians; he does not discuss Italian colonization. Therefore, Choice *D* is incorrect.

68. B: The conflict between Anglo-American settlers and American Indians was largely the product of a competition over resources. American Indian tribes had lived in Texas for centuries prior to the arrival of Europeans. Once Anglo-American settlements gained a foothold in Texas, they aggressively and unilaterally expanded into American Indian tribes' historic territories, triggering a fierce competition over natural resources. Thus, Choice *B* is the correct answer. Although the relationship between Anglo-American settlers and American Indians featured a vicious cycle of hostilities, the relationship wasn't codependent because neither group enabled the problematic behavior of the other. Therefore, Choice *A* is incorrect. Anglo-American settlers weren't collectively committed to the peaceful resolution of conflicts. Whether intended or not, the settlement of American Indian territory was inherently an act of aggression. So, Choice *C* is incorrect. Like the author of the passage, many Anglo-American settlers viewed American Indians as unproductive and irresponsible; however, the conflict arose over resources and not alleged differences in lifestyle. Therefore, Choice *D* is incorrect.

Geography, Culture, and the Behavioral and Social Sciences

69. C: Map projections, such as the Mercator Projection, are useful for finding positions on the globe, but they attempt to represent a spherical object on a flat surface. As a result, they distort areas nearest the poles, which misrepresent the size of Antarctica, Greenland, and other high latitudinal locations. Map projects can include great detail; some illustrate the physical features in an area, and most include both the northern and southern hemispheres.

70. D: Thematic maps create certain themes in which they attempt to illustrate a certain phenomenon or pattern. The obvious theme of a climate map is the climates in the represented areas. Thematic maps are very extensive and can include thousands of different themes, which makes them quite useful for students of geography. Topographic maps, Choice *A*, are utilized to show physical features; conformal projections, Choice *B*, attempt to illustrate the globe in an undistorted fashion; and isoline maps, Choice *C*, illustrate differences in variables between two points on a map.

71. B: Latitudinal and longitudinal coordinates delineate absolute location. In contrast to relative location (Choice *C*), which describes a location as compared to another, better-known place, absolute location provides an exact place

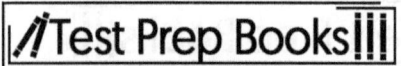

on the globe through the latitude and longitude system. Cardinal directions (north, south, east, west), Choice A, are used in absolute location, but coordinates must be added in order to have an absolute location. Absolute location is far more precise than simply finding the hemispherical position on the globe (Choice D).

72. B: Lines of latitude measure distance north and south. The equator is zero degrees, and the Tropic of Cancer is 23.5 degrees north of the equator. The distance between those two lines measures degrees north to south, as with any other two lines of latitude. Longitudinal lines, or meridians, measure distance east and west, even though they run north and south down the globe. Latitude is not inexact, in that there are set distances between the lines. Furthermore, coordinates can only exist with the use of longitude and latitude.

73. C: Developed nations have better infrastructural systems, which can include government, transportation, financial, and educational institutions. Consequently, its citizens tend to have higher rates of literacy, due to the sheer availability of educational resources and government-sanctioned educational systems. In contrast, developing nations, Choice A, struggle to provide educational resources to their citizens. Nations in the Northern Hemisphere, Choice B, have no greater availability to educational resources than those in the Southern Hemisphere, and centers of trade, Choice D, don't necessarily equate to higher levels of education, as many may exist in poorer nations with fewer resources.

74. C: Population density, which is the total number of people divided by the total land area, generally tends to be much higher in urban areas than rural ones. This is true due to high-rise apartment complexes, sewage and freshwater infrastructure, and complex transportation systems, allowing for easy movement of food from nearby farms. Consequently, competition among citizens for resources is certainly higher in high-density areas, as are greater strains on infrastructure within urban centers.

75. C: Although it can place a strain on some resources, population density is not a negative demographic indicator. For example, New York City, one of the most densely populated places on Earth, enjoys one of the highest standards of living in the world. Other world cities such as Tokyo, Los Angeles, and Sydney also have tremendously high population densities and high standards of living. High infant mortality rates, low literacy rates, and low life expectancies are all poor demographic indicators that suggest a low quality of life for the citizens living in those areas.

76. A: Homogeneity, or the condition of similarity, is the unifying factor in most formal regions. Regions have one or more unifying characteristics, such as language, religion, history, or economic similarities, which make the area a cohesive formal region. A good example is the Southern United States. In contrast, diversity and multilingualism, Choices B and C, are factors that may cause a region to lose homogeneity and be more difficult to classify as a region. Also, social mobility, Choice D, is a distractor that refers to one's ability to improve their economic standing in society and is not related to formal regions.

77. C: A person may identify with different subgroups or cultures at different times in his or her life. Personal identity will continue to change an individual's behavior throughout life.

78. A: Adolescents are most likely to be influenced by pressure from their peers in making life decisions.

79. B: While bullying may affect a person's life and often happens in schools, it does not establish ranking of any sort, and is not educational or part of the educational system. Choice A is correct because the rules established by the school help shape a sense of morals in students, or the lack thereof. Choice C is correct because the social situations foster sharing, patience, teamwork, and respect. Choice D is correct because grades establish a feeling of desire to meet expectations, as well as a fear of failing.

Answer Explanations | Social Studies Instruction and Assessment

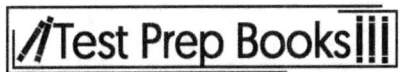

80. C: Each statement about culture is correct except for Choice C. Cultures often will adapt to the settings in which they are found. Improvements in technology, changes in social values, and interactions with other cultures all contribute to cultural change.

81. D: Diversity refers to how everything and everyone is uniquely different. Choice A (behaviorism) is the study of how behavior influences the way human beings interact with their environment. Choice B (peer pressure) is when a group uses the majority vote to try to persuade the minority into changing their minds. Finally, Choice C (adaptation) is also incorrect because adaptation refers to how a human being adjusts to their surroundings to create a desired outcome. Therefore, Choice D (diversity) is correct.

82. D: Each of these answers is an indicator of social class. Wealth and standard of living are often related as the amount of money you have helps determine your standard of living. Often times if the standard of living in an area is high, the education environment fosters a higher education level, which can cause a higher level of social class. The opposite is true if the standard of living is low.

83. D: Most nonrenewable resources are easier to harness and utilize than renewable sources. That may sound counterintuitive, but the reality is that it is harder to develop solar, wind, and geothermal infrastructure than it is to build a coal-fired power plant for the production of electricity. Consequently, developing nations tend to rely on these reliable sources in order to fuel their equally developing economy.

84. C: Pull factors are reasons people immigrate to a particular area. Obviously, educational opportunities attract thousands of people on a global level and on a local level. For example, generally areas with strong schools have higher property values, due to the relative demand for housing in those districts. The same is true for nations with better educational opportunities. Unemployment, low GDP, and incredibly high population densities may serve to deter people from moving to a certain place and can be considered push factors.

85. A: The use of biotechnology and GMOs has increased the total amount of food on Earth. Additionally, it has helped to sustain the earth's growing population; however, many activists assert that scientists are creating crops that, in the long run, will be destructive to human health, even though very little evidence exists to prove such an allegation. Agricultural production has not been affected by poorer soil, plagues of pests, or the use of saline for irrigation purposes.

86. A: Globalization has put students and workers in direct conflict with one another despite their relative level of physical separation. For example, students who excel in mathematics and engineering may be recruited by multinational firms who want the best talent for their business despite where they are educated. Furthermore, products produced in other nations are also in competition with global manufacturers to ensure quality craftsmanship at an affordable price. Globalization does not refer to world domination, an absence of nation-states, or a singular world government.

Government and Citizenship

87. C: Power is the ability of a ruling body or political entity to influence the actions, behavior, and attitude of a person or group of people. Authority, Choice A, is the right and justification of the government to exercise power as recognized by the citizens or influential elites. Similarly, legitimacy, Choice D, is another way of expressing the concept of authority. Sovereignty, Choice B, refers to the ability of a state to determine and control their territory without foreign interference.

88. D: Sovereignty is the feature that differentiates a state from a nation. Nations have no sovereignty, as they are unable to enact and enforce laws independently of their state. A state must possess sovereignty over the population of a territory in order to be legitimized as a state. Both a nation and a state must have a population, Choice C.

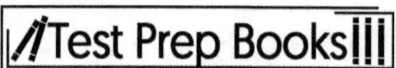

Answer Explanations

Although sometimes present, a shared history and common language are not requirements for a state, making Choices A and B incorrect.

89. D: In his book, *The Prince*, Niccolo Machiavelli advocated that a ruler should be prepared to do whatever is necessary to remain in power, including using violence and political deception as a means to coerce the people of a state or eliminate political rivals. John Locke, Choice A, contributed and advocated liberal principles, most prominently the right to life, liberty, and health. Jean-Jacques Rousseau, Choice B, heavily influenced the French Revolution and American Revolution by advocating individual equality, self-rule, and religious freedom. Karl Marx, Choice C, wrote that the struggle between the bourgeois (ruling class) and the proletariat (working class) would result in a classless society in which all citizens commonly owned the means of production.

90. B: Thomas Hobbes is considered the father of social contract theory. In his book *Leviathan,* Hobbes advocated for a strong central government and posited that the citizens of a state make a social contract with the government to allow it to rule them in exchange for protection and security. John Stuart Mills, Choice A, is most commonly associated with the political philosophy of utilitarianism. Aristotle, Choice C, believed that man could only achieve happiness by bettering their community through noble acts, while Immanuel Kant, Choice D, promoted democracy and asserted that states could only achieve lasting global peace through international cooperation.

91. C: Conservatism emphasizes maintaining traditions and believes political and social stability is more important than progress and reform. In general, Socialism, Choice A, seeks to establish a democratically elected government that owns the means of production, regulates the exchange of commodities, and distributes the wealth equally among citizens. Liberalism, Choice B, is based on individualism and equality, supporting the freedoms of speech, press, and religion, while Libertarian ideals, Choice D, emphasize individual liberties and freedom from government interference.

92. D: Internationalism promotes global cooperation and supports strong unity between the states in order to achieve world peace and improve quality of life for all global citizens. Fascism, Choice A, values the strength of a state over all foreign powers and emphasizes the state over individual liberties, and Fascists typically establish an authoritarian government and consider violence necessary to suppress dissent and revitalize a struggling nation. Conservatism, Choice B, is focused on maintaining the traditions and political institutions within a single country. Anarchism, Choice C, favors a completely free society ruled by a government composed of only voluntary institutions.

93. D: Fascism considers a strong central government, martial law, and violent coercion as necessary means to maintain political stability and strengthen the state. Neither the politics of Communism, a society in which the people own the means of production, nor Socialism, a society in which the government owns the means of production, promote violence but instead advocate a classless society that eliminates the class struggle. Thus, Choices A and B are incorrect. Nationalism, Choice C, emphasizes preserving a nation's culture, often to the exclusion of other cultures, but violence is not officially promoted as a means for suppressing dissent, as is the case with fascism.

94. C: Under the Constitution, the power to coin money is designated exclusively to the federal government, but both the states and the federal government maintain the power to collect taxes from the citizens under their jurisdictions and establish courts lower than the Supreme Court, though states may only establish regional courts within their states. The states reserve the right to regulate trade within their states (intrastate), while the federal government maintains the power to regulate trade between states (interstate).

95. D: Both the states and the federal government may propose, enact, and enforce laws. States pass legislation that concerns the states in their state legislative houses, while the federal government passes federal laws in Congress. Only states may hold elections and determine voting procedures, even for federal offices such as the

Answer Explanations | Social Studies Instruction and Assessment

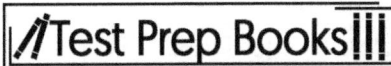

president of the United States, and only the federal government may expand any state territory, change state lines, admit new states into the nation, or regulate immigration and pass laws regarding naturalization of citizens.

96. D: The Constitution granted Congress the power to decide how many justices should be on the court, and Congress first decided on six judges in the Judiciary Act of 1789. The Constitution granted the power to appoint judges and to call special sessions of Congress to the president. Only the Supreme Court may interpret the laws enacted by Congress and rule a law unconstitutional and subsequently overturn the law.

97. B: The process by which the House and Senate may debate a bill differs. In the House, how long a speaker may debate a bill is limited, while in the Senate, speakers may debate the bill indefinitely and delay voting on the bill by filibuster—a practice in which a speaker refuses to stop speaking until a majority vote stops the filibuster or the time for the vote passes. In both the House and the Senate, anyone may introduce a bill. Only the president of the United States may veto the bill, so neither the House nor Senate holds that power. Before the bill may be presented to the president to be signed, the wording of the bill must be identical in both houses. Another procedural difference is that the number of amendments is limited in the House but not the Senate; however, this does not appear as an answer choice.

98. C: The first ten amendments to the Constitution are collectively referred to as the Bill of Rights. The Founding Fathers did not support universal suffrage, and as such, the Bill of Rights did not encompass the freedom to vote. The Fifteenth Amendment provided that the right to vote shall not be denied on the basis of race, color, or previous condition of servitude, and women did not receive the right to vote until passage of the Nineteenth Amendment. The other three answer choices are included in the Bill of Rights: the freedom to assembly is established in the First Amendment, the freedom against unlawful search is established in the Fourth Amendment, and the reservation of non-enumerated powers to the states or the people is established in the Tenth Amendment.

99. C: The Republican Party emerged as the abolitionist party during the Antebellum Period and succeeded in abolishing slavery after the North's victory in the Civil War. The Constitutional Union Party supported slavery but opposed Southern secession, while the Southern Democrats supported slavery and secession. The Whig Party splintered in the 1850s as a result of tension over slavery, leading to the creation of the Republican Party and Constitutional Union Party.

100. C: While interest groups attempt to influence the legislation and organizations that regulate trade, they do not possess the authority to enact or enforce laws necessary to regulate trade. However, they may influence policy through the use of petitions, civil suits against the government, and by the practice of lobbying, in which paid lobbyists put pressure on lawmaking bodies. Interest groups form due to a common connection between the members of a group attempting to bring about change that benefits a specific segment of society, such as teachers or pharmaceutical corporations.

101. B: The mass media does not have the ability to regulate communications. The mass media has the ability to shape public opinion, making Choice *A* incorrect. Mass media selects which events to report on and thereby influences the perceived importance of events in society and determines the context in which to report events, making Choices *C* and *D* incorrect. Only the federal government may regulate communications through agencies such as the Federal Communications Commission (FCC).

102. C: Federalism divides power between regional and federal governments, and it is the form of government upon which the United States is structured, according to the Tenth Amendment. While a constitutional monarchy, Choice *B*, is typically divided between a monarch, the head of state, and a legislative body, usually a parliament, power is not reserved to the regional government. A democratic government, Choice *A*, is a government ruled by the people and does not specify division of powers. Feudalism, Choice *D*, is an economic system popular in medieval Europe

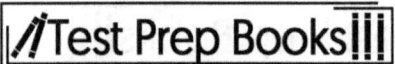

where the monarchy granted the nobility land in exchange for military service, and the nobility allowed serfs to live on their land in exchange for labor or percentage of crops.

103. A: An authoritarian government is ruled by a single party that holds complete control over the powerful central government. Authoritarian governments limit political freedom and civil liberties to diminish any opposition. Communism, Choice *B*, is one in which the class struggle between the ruling and working classes is eliminated because the means of production belongs to the people. Similarly, Socialism, Choice *C*, is classless, but in this type of government, the government owns the means of production and is often democratic. Unlike a regular monarchy, a federal monarchy, Choice *D*, is a federal government in which political power is divided between the monarch (head of state) and regional governments, resulting in checks and balances of power.

104. D: Proportional electoral systems reflect the divisions in an electorate proportionately in the elected body. In single transferable vote systems, voters rank individual candidates by their preference, and the top candidates' votes are transferred to the second-place candidate, and so on, once a candidate receives the minimum votes to win a seat in the election; thus, the single transferable vote system is the most proportionate electoral system. The Electoral College is the method of electing the President of the United States Although the Electoral College apportions a number of electors to each state according to the number of congressional seats in the state, it is not a proportional electoral system. To win a majority vote, a candidate must receive over 50% of the vote, so the minority's preferences are not proportionally reflected in the body. Similarly, a plurality only requires the highest percent of votes among any number of candidates, which often results in most voters voting *against* the winning candidate.

Economics and Science, Technology, and Society

105. B: Macroeconomics studies the economy on a large scale and focuses on issues such as unemployment, interest rates, price levels, and national income. Microeconomics, Choice *A*, studies more individual or small group behaviors such as scarcity or supply and demand. Scarcity, Choice *C*, is not correct because it refers to the availability of goods and services. Supply and demand, Choice *D*, is also incorrect because it refers to the quantity of goods and services that is produced and/or needed.

106. C: Opportunity cost refers to the value of what is lost when one alternative is chosen over another. Economic systems refer to methods of organizing the production and distribution of goods in society. Supply and demand is a economic model for how prices are determined. Finally, inflation, Choice *D*, refers to how the cost of goods and services increases over time.

107. A: A free market does not involve government interventions or monopolies while trading between buyers and suppliers. However, in a command market, the government determines the price of goods and services. Gross and exchange markets refer to situations where brokers and traders make exchanges in the financial realm.

108. D: The theory of the firm refers to the behavior that firms use to reach their desired outcome. GDP, unemployment, and inflation are all indicators that help determine economic growth.

109. C: Contraction and trough. A recession occurs between the contraction and trough phases of the business cycle. Between expansion and peak phases, employment and productivity are on the rise, causing a boom. Between the peak and contraction, unemployment rates are starting to fall, but have not yet hit an all-time low. Between trough and expansion phases, the economy is getting back on its feet and starting to increase employment again.

110. C: The Federal Reserve is the bank of banks. A commodity is the value of goods such as precious metals. While the Central Reserve and Bank Reserve may sound like good options, the term bank reserve refers to the amount of money a bank deposits into a central bank, and the Central Reserve is simply a fictitious name.

Answer Explanations | Social Studies Instruction and Assessment

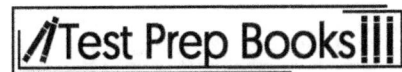

111. A: Closed market operations. Monetary policies are sustained by assuring bank reserves, adjusting interest rates, and open market operations. Closed market operations do NOT uphold monetary policies.

112. D: The market, through supply and demand, determines the exchange rate with a flexible or floating exchange rate. The government, Choice *A*, is not the correct answer because it is involved in fixed exchange rates to help keep exchange rates stable. Taxes, Choice *B*, is also incorrect because they create government revenue. The Federal Reserve, Choice *C*, is the bank of banks.

113. B: As inflation increases, purchasing power decreases. As more money is printed, the monetary value of the dollar drops and, in turn, decreases the purchasing power of goods and services. So, as inflation increases, consumers are not spending as much, and the value of the dollar is low.

114. B: The number of goods and services produced does not determine economic growth—the value of the goods and services does. For example, a real estate agent who sells 10 houses valued at $200,000 each would earn the same commission as an agent who sells one house valued at $2,000,000. Even though one sold more homes, the value of ten houses adds up to the same amount as the single home that the other realtor sold.

115. B: Fiat money. Commodity money, Choice *A*, refers to a good that has value, such as a precious metal. Bank money, Choice *C*, is money that is credited by a bank to those people who have their money deposited there. The term reserve money, Choice *D*, does not refer to anything.

116. A: In contractionary monetary policy, the money supply is decreased. All of the other choices are characteristics of contractionary monetary policy.

117. C: The four phases of the business cycle are peak, trough, expansion, contraction. The other answer choices include at least one wrong phase.

118. B: Frictional unemployment is considered a sign of a healthy, stable economy.

119. D: The GDP is used to measure an economy's growth. The inflation of a country doesn't tell us anything about their growth. A country may hold a lot of money in reserves, but this does not tell us if they are growing or not. The same can be said for having a lot of exports. It doesn't indicate that an economy is necessarily growing.

120. B: As the price of a product is lowered the demand should rise. Raising the price on an already hard to sell item would just make it harder to sell. If you offer it in a bundle of unrelated products, then people are unlikely to want to buy those products together.

121. C: In a command economy, the government controls the prices as well as what and how much of a product is produced.

122. D: The factors of production are land, labor, capital, and entrepreneurship. The other choices all include at least one option that is not a factor of production.

Social Studies Foundation, Skills, Research, and Instruction

123. A: Bolivar was a creole revolutionary who waged several revolutionary wars in South America. Nelson Mandela, Choice *B*, was the leader of South Africa at the end of apartheid. Dr. Martin Luther King Jr., Choice *C*, was the southern civil rights leader who helped end segregation in the United States. And Antonio Lopez de Santa Anna, Choice *D*, was the leader of the Mexican army at the Battle of the Alamo.

124. C: Nelson Mandela became the president of South Africa after the fall of apartheid. Liberia, Choice *A*, was the black colony established by Americans to send slaves and free blacks back to Africa. Vietnam, Choice *B*, was the

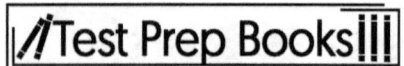

Answer Explanations

center of a U.S. military dispute over Communism in the 1960s and 1970s. Argentina, Choice *D*, is a South American country that drew support from both the right and the left under the leadership of Juan Peron.

125. B: Reconstruction was the Postbellum Era in which the United States tried to reinstate former Confederate states into the Union and rebuild the South through occupation. The Antebellum Era, Choice *A*, was the time frame that preceded the Civil War. The Progressive Era, Choice *C*, was the era of widespread reform in the late nineteenth and early twentieth century that set the stage for Prohibition. The civil rights movement, Choice *D*, is the era of US history that witnessed desegregation, reaching its culmination in the mid-1960s under the presidency of Lyndon B. Johnson.

126. D: Texas sided with the Confederate States of America during the Civil War, seceding from the Union, Choice *B*. Texas helped the South fight the North, Choice *A*. The Mexican Republic, Choice *D* is also not the right answer because it played only a limited role during the Civil War, and Texas most certainly did not side with the country it declared independence from decades earlier.

127. C: Alexandria became the capital. Jerusalem, Choice *A*, although the epicenter of Judaism and Christianity, did not host as many scholars as Alexandria during the Hellenistic period. Constantinople, Choice *D*, is incorrect because it was not yet created during the Hellenistic period. Athens, Choice *B*, the former capital of Greek scholarship, is not the answer because scholarly culture shifted from Athens to Alexandria during this period.

128. A: Hinduism is a polytheistic religion that originated in India and is not Abrahamic in character. Judaism, Choice *D*, Christianity, Choice *B*, and Islam, Choice *C*, are the so-called Abrahamic monotheistic religions.

129. C: Apartheid is the name given to institutional segregation and precolonial and postcolonial South Africa. Jim Crow, Choice *A*, refers to segregation in the southern United States in the early twentieth century. The Atlantic Slave Trade, Choice *B*, refers to the centuries of slavery that sparked trade across the Atlantic Ocean. Black Codes, Choice *D*, refer to the codes instituted to strip freed African Americans of their rights during Reconstruction.

130. A: Mahan wanted the United States to become an imperial power through naval prowess and seaward expansion. Christopher Columbus, Choice *B*, is the European explorer who discovered the New World during the Age of Exploration. Although Theodore Roosevelt, Choice *B*, was a strong proponent of both imperialism and the navy, he was a president and not a naval officer. Matthew Perry, Choice *D*, was a naval officer who opened Japan to the West in 1854.

131. D: The First Agricultural Revolution occurred 10,000 years ago. Choice *A* and Choice *C* respectively point to the Green Revolution (50 years) and the Second Agricultural Revolution (200 years). Choice *B*—1000 years—is just an erroneous number listed to trick the test takers.

132. D: Following his election during the Great Depression, Franklin Delano Roosevelt pledged a New Deal for the American people, inaugurating an era of social welfare and public works programs. The Great Society, Choice *A*, also set forth social welfare and public works programs, but under the presidency of Lyndon B. Johnson (LBJ). The War Against Poverty, Choice *B*, was a subcategory of LBJ's Great Society—it promised to declare war on poverty like any nation would declare war on a foreign threat. Progressivism, Choice *C*, brought about reforms much like the New Deal, but during the early twentieth century, prior to the Great Depression and FDR's administration.

133. C: Psychology is a social science that studies the ways in which the mind and cognition affect social relationships and identities. Biology, Choice *A*, is a hard science that studies life. English, Choice *B*, would be placed under the umbrella of the humanities. Geometry, Choice *D*, would fall under the category of mathematics.

134. C: Free market economies, Choice *A*, allow for more competition, while command economies, Choice *D*, allow for greater government control. Pure monopolies, Choice *B*, are dominated by one firm rather than a few.

135. A: A pure monopoly is when there is only one seller of a particular product or commodity, and the sole seller attempts to restrict firms from exiting and entering the industry at will. Choices *B* and *C* describe a free enterprise economy. Choice *D* describes an oligopoly.

136. A: The Green Revolution is often the name given to the Third Agricultural Revolution, which witnessed the rise of a scientifically driven movement in the early twentieth century to increase agricultural production and catalyze economic growth in developing nations all over the world. The Texas Revolution, Choice *B*, had nothing to do with agriculture and everything to do with politics and independence. The Industrial Revolution, Choice *C*, coincided with the Second Agricultural Revolution. The Computer Revolution, Choice *D*, took place in the 1980s and 1990s with the advent of personal computers, video games, and the internet.

137. D: The Civilian Conservation Corps was a New Deal program that assisted with the conservation of federal and state parks. Head Start, Choice *A*, was an early childhood education program of the Great Society. NASA, Choice *B*, was a Cold War aeronautics program that launched astronauts to the Moon during the Kennedy administration. The Eisenhower Interstate System, Choice *C*, was a highway system built in the United States well after the death of FDR.

138. B: The graph shows an increase in supply because an increase in supply will shift the supply curve to the right (S1 to S2). A decrease in supply, Choice *A*, will shift the supply curve to the left. A decrease in demand, Choice *C*, shifts the demand curve to the left rather than the right. An increase in demand, Choice *D*, will move the demand curve to the right.

139. D: Marxist economic theories helped pave the way to the rise of Socialism (as well as Communism). Alfred Thayer Mahan, Choice *C*, was an imperialist naval captain who did not contribute greatly to economic theory. John Maynard Keynes, Choice *A*, and Adam Smith, Choice *B*, were economists whose theories paved the way to free enterprise economics.

140. A: Communism advocates a one-party system. It does not mix well with the democratic policies of liberal democracy, Choice *B*, and competitive economic systems of free enterprise or capitalist economies, Choices *C* and *D*. Although Communism is not always separate from democracy, its more radical ideals separate it from the moderations of liberal democracy. Moreover, the communal economic frameworks of Communism run counter to the competitive practices of capitalism/free enterprise.

Dear TExES Social Studies 7 - 12 Test Taker,

Thank you for purchasing this study guide for your TExES Social Studies 7 - 12 exam. We hope that we exceeded your expectations.

Our goal in creating this study guide was to cover all of the topics that you will see on the test. We also strove to make our practice questions as similar as possible to what you will encounter on test day. With that being said, if you found something that you feel was not up to your standards, please send us an email and let us know.

We have study guides in a wide variety of fields. If you're interested in one, try searching for it on Amazon or send us an email.

Thanks Again and Happy Testing!
Product Development Team
info@studyguideteam.com

FREE Test Taking Tips Video/DVD Offer

To better serve you, we created videos covering test taking tips that we want to give you for FREE. **These videos cover world-class tips that will help you succeed on your test.**

We just ask that you send us feedback about this product. Please let us know what you thought about it—whether good, bad, or indifferent.

To get your **FREE videos**, you can use the QR code below or email freevideos@studyguideteam.com with "Free Videos" in the subject line and the following information in the body of the email:

   a. The title of your product

   b. Your product rating on a scale of 1-5, with 5 being the highest

   c. Your feedback about the product

If you have any questions or concerns, please don't hesitate to contact us at info@studyguideteam.com.

Thank you!